NIHONGI

VOLUME I - CHRONICLES OF JAPAN FROM THE EARLIEST TIMES TO A.D. 697

W.G. ASTON

COSIMOCLASSICS

NEW YORK

NIHONGI:
Volume I - Chronicles of Japan from the
Earliest Times to A.D. 697

Cover Copyright © 2008 by Cosimo, Inc.

NIHONGI was originally published in 1896.

For information, address:
P.O. Box 416, Old Chelsea Station
New York, NY 10011

or visit our website at:
www.cosimobooks.com

Ordering Information:
Cosimo publications are available at online bookstores. They may
also be purchased for educational, business or promotional use:
- *Bulk orders:* special discounts are available on bulk orders for reading
groups, organizations, businesses, and others. For details contact
Cosimo Special Sales at the address above or at info@cosimobooks.com.
- *Custom-label orders:* we can prepare selected books with your cover or
logo of choice. For more information, please contact Cosimo at
info@cosimobooks.com.

Cover Design by www.popshopstudio.com

ISBN:978-1-60520-144-3

The Emperor said:—"When Heaven establishes a Prince, it is for the sake of the people.... [T]he people's poverty is no other than Our poverty; the people's prosperity is none other than Our prosperity. There is no such thing as the people's being prosperous and yet the Prince in poverty."

—from "Nintoku"

PREFACE.

THE chief object of preparing this translation of the standard native history of Ancient Japan, known as the *Nihongi*, was to make accessible to European scholars the very considerable store of material for the study of mythology, folk-lore, early civilization, and manners and customs which it contains. It may also prove of interest to those numerous Japanese who are acquainted with the English language, and who may have the curiosity to learn in what light their ancient history and traditions are viewed by a Western student.

As only a limited sale of a work of this kind could be expected, the translator was fortunate in being relieved from all pecuniary responsibility for its publication by the Japan Society. His special acknowledgments are due to those members by whose liberality a guarantee fund for this purpose has been provided.

It remains for him to express his indebtedness to other workers, by whose labours in the field of Japanese and Chinese learning he has freely profited. The writings of Messrs. Chamberlain and Satow [1] have been placed under frequent contribution, and for the latter part of the work, the scholarly German translation of the *Nihongi*, by Dr. Florenz, has been of the greatest possible assistance. He should also mention the names of Williams, Giles, Parker, Mayers, Gubbins, Hepburn, Anderson, Legge, and Eitel, whose writings are the indis-

---

[1] Now Sir Ernest Satow, K.C.M.G., H.M.'s Minister Plenipotentiary to Japan.

pensable companions of all students of Far-Eastern subjects.
Other sources of information are acknowledged in the notes.
Amongst native Japanese writers the chief authorities have
been the famous scholars Motoöri and Hirata. Their religious
and patriotic prejudices often lead them to take views from
which a European reader is forced to dissent, but no Western
scholar can hope to rival or even to approach their vast eru-
dition, clothed as it is in an easy and graceful style, undisfigured
by pedantry. The translator gladly seizes this opportunity of
expressing the strong admiration which he has long entertained
for them. For the Notes, the *Shūkai* edition of the *Nihongi*
and the *Tsūshō* Commentary have been largely drawn upon.
The references to Chinese literature have been usually taken
from these last-named sources. It is unnecessary to enumerate
more particularly the other native works of reference which
have been utilized. A copious list of them will be found in
Dr. Florenz's Introduction.

The translator should not omit to express his thanks to Mr.
W. Gowland for the use of the drawings and photographs
relating to the Imperial Misasagi and sepulchral mounds, from
which a number of the illustrations have been reproduced.

The vital importance of a good Index is fully recognized.
No pains will be spared to make this part of the work as
complete and satisfactory as possible.

CONTENTS OF PART ONE

INTRODUCTION.

Writing.—The art of writing is one of the numerous elements of civilization for which Japan is indebted to China. The date of its first introduction is not definitely known. There are indications that some acquaintance with the Chinese written character was possessed by individuals in Japan during the early centuries of the Christian era, but the first positive information on the subject belongs to A.D. 405, for which an erroneous date corresponding to A.D. 285 is given in the *Nihongi*. In this year a Corean named Wani or Wangin was appointed tutor in Chinese to a Japanese Imperial Prince. He was the first of a succession of teachers from that country whose instructions paved the way for a revolution in Japanese institutions and manners, not less profound and far-reaching than that produced in our own time by the influence of European ideas.

From its geographical position, Corea was the natural intermediary by which China became known to Japan. In these early times there was no direct sea communication between the two last-named countries. Travellers crossed the Strait from Japan to Corea, and pursued the rest of their journey by the circuitous overland route. But the Corean national genius seems to have left no impress of its own on the civilization which it received from China and handed on to Japan. Medicine, Buddhism, painting, and the mechanic arts were transmitted, as far as we can see, without modification, and there is little trace of any special Corean character in the knowledge of Chinese literature and science which Coreans communicated to Japan. They had themselves taken up this study only thirty years before Wani's departure.[1]

[1] See a paper on "Writing, Printing, and the Alphabet in Corea," in the "J.R.A.S.," July, 1895.

The newly-acquired Chinese characters were soon put to practical use. Wani himself is said to have been employed to keep the accounts of the Treasury. In the reign of Nintoku we are told that Ki no Tsuno no Sukune committed to writing an account of the productions of the Corean kingdom of Pèkché. The date given for this in the *Nihongi* is A.D. 353, to which, as in the case of other events of this period, two cycles or 120 years should probably be added. In the following reign (Richiu's) " recorders were appointed in the provinces in order to note down words and events." But from the specimens of their reports which are preserved in the *Nihongi*, these officials do not seem to have contributed much of importance to historical knowledge. Fabulous stories and accounts of monstrosities and portents form the staple of their compositions. It may be inferred, however, that such functionaries were already in existence at the capital, and indeed we find mention at this time of hereditary corporations of fumi-bito or scribes, known as the Achiki Be and Wani Be, the successors of Atogi and Wani, the Corean scholars who first taught Chinese at the court of the Mikado.

History. The Kiujiki.—The first literary efforts of the Japanese took the direction of history. No doubt the Norito or rituals of the Shinto religion and some poetical compositions date from an earlier period. But they do not seem to have been committed to writing. The earliest book of which we find mention is the *Kiujiki* or *Kujiki* (Chronicle of old matters of former ages), which was compiled in A.D. 620 under high official auspices, as indeed were all the historical works which have come down to us from these ancient times. The writing of history was, and still is, regarded as pre-eminently a matter of State concern in all those Eastern countries where Chinese ideas are predominant. The *Kiujiki* was entrusted to the keeping of the Soga House, but on its downfall in 645, a large portion was destroyed by fire, a part only, described as Kokuki or national annals, having been saved from the flames. Whether this work is or is not identical with the *Kiujiki* of our own day, is a question on which I shall have more to say afterwards. At present it is sufficient to note that the latter work contains nothing which is not also to be found in the *Kojiki* or *Nihongi* except a few passages in the mythological portion and a list of local governors. The historical part is almost word for word the same as the *Nihongi*, which, however, is very much fuller, and is brought down to a much later period.

The Kojiki.—In A.D. 682 a number of Princes and High Officials were formally commissioned by the Emperor Temmu to prepare a " History of the Emperors and of matters of high antiquity." Nothing is known of the result of their labours, but this measure led eventually to the compilation of the *Kojiki*, as we learn from a passage in the Preface to that work.[1] It was not completed, however, until A.D. 712. The *Kojiki* has fortunately been preserved to us. If the *Kiujiki* is excepted, as of doubtful authenticity, it is the earliest product of the Japanese historical muse, and indeed the oldest monument of Japanese literature. It presents many features of the highest interest, but it is needless to dwell here on a subject which has been so thoroughly dealt with by Chamberlain in the Introduction to his admirable translation of this work.

In 714, or two years after the completion of the *Kojiki*, the Empress Gemmiō gave orders for the preparation of a national history. We hear nothing more of this project, which may or may not have served to provide materials for the *Nihongi*.

The Nihongi—Date and Authorship.—We now come to the *Nihongi* itself. It has no title-page or preface, and our information as to its date and authorship is derived from other sources. The Kōnin Shiki (commentary on the *Nihongi*, of the period 810-824) informs us that it was completed and laid before the Empress Gemmiō in A.D. 720 by Prince Toneri and Yasumaro Futo no Ason. In addition to the thirty books which have come down to us, there was originally a book of genealogies of the Emperors which is no longer extant. The term used by the Shiki in speaking of its preparation is " selected afresh," which points obviously to compilation rather than original composition. An examination of the work itself favours this view. It consists of detached passages linked together by chronological sequence, and some endeavour is visible to shape the materials into a consistent whole, but the result has a more or less patchwork appearance, and falls far short of the stan-

---

[1] See Ch. K., p. 9.

dard of uniformity of style and method which we are accustomed to look for in historical compositions.

Materials for the Nihongi.—The remains of the *Kiujiki* must have formed a very important element of the authors' material. Indeed I lean to the belief that whether the present *Kiujiki* is authentic or not, much of the earlier part of the *Nihongi* (except the first two books) is practically the composition of the illustrious Shōtoku Daishi, its reputed author. It is recorded that he was a profound student of Buddhism and of Chinese classical literature, and internal evidence shows that the writer of this part of the *Nihongi* was well versed in these subjects. The *Kojiki* is not directly referred to, and little use seems to have been made of it. But it was well known to the authors. Indeed one of them, Yasumaro, was the very person who took down the *Kojiki* from the lips of Hiyeda no Are, a man (or woman) who had a remarkable memory, well stored with the ancient traditions of the Japanese race. That no community of style can be traced between the two works is easily explained by the circumstance that Yasumaro was in the first case little more than an amanuensis, and in the second a compiler. It is possible, too, that his associate, Prince Toneri, was the guiding spirit of the undertaking, and that Yasumaro simply carried out his directions.

The *Nihongi* contains a few phrases which show that the *Norito* or Rituals of the Shinto cult were familiar to the authors, but nothing of importance is drawn from this source.

Another stock of information which was probably at their disposal is referred to in the History of the reign of Jitō Tennō (A.D. 694), where it is stated that orders were given to eighteen of the principal noble Houses to deliver to the Government their genealogical records. Other historical works, notably a certain *Kana Nihongi*, have been spoken of as in existence before the date of the *Nihongi*, and that there was a copious historical or legendary literature accessible to the authors cannot be doubted. The work itself, as we have it, contains ample evidence of this in the numerous quotations from other writings, added, as most Japanese critics think, by the authors themselves, or, as I prefer to believe, by subsequent scholars soon after its appearance. These extracts are always referred to in later times as if they formed part of the *Nihongi*, and there can be no harm in accepting them as of equal authority with it. Some are, no doubt, of still greater antiquity.

An institution which must have contributed substantially, though perhaps indirectly, to the collection and conservation of the materials for the more legendary part of the *Nihongi* was the Katari Be, or hereditary corporation of reciters. Unfortunately we know very little about it. Hirata, in his *Koshi-chō*, states, on what authority does not appear, that the Katari Be came forward and recited "ancient words" before the Emperor at the festival of Ohonihe when he inaugurated his reign by sacrifices to the Gods. It is not probable that their services were confined to this occasion.

Character and Contents of the Nihongi.—The *Nihongi* consists of very heterogeneous elements which by no means all answer to our ideas of history. The earlier part furnishes a very complete assortment of all the forms of the Untrue of which the human mind is capable, whether myth, legend, fable, romance, gossip, mere blundering, or downright fiction. The first two books are manifestly mythological. They are followed by an account of Jimmu's Conquest of Yamato, which has probably a basis of truth, though the legendary character obviously predominates.

Most of the meagre details given us of the reigns, of the next eight Emperors have a Chinese stamp, and must, I fear, be pronounced simply fictitious. Nor need this greatly surprise us. There are other countries where

> Mortal men are ever wont to lie,
> Whene'er they speak of sceptre-bearing kings.

A portrait gallery in Holyrood Palace illustrates the same principle, though in a different way.

Then we have a series of legendary stories full of miraculous incidents, but in which grains of truth may here and there be discerned. The value of this early part of the work is enhanced by the numerous poems of great antiquity which have been incorporated into it, and which have considerable antiquarian and philological interest.

The narrative becomes more and more real as it goes on, until about the 5th century we find ourselves in what, without too violent a departure from the truth, may be called genuine

B

history, while from the beginning of the 6th century until A.D. 697, when it is brought to a close, the *Nihongi* gives us what is to every appearance a trustworthy record of events. We must still, however, be on our guard against the Chinese diction and sentiments which are put into the mouths of the Mikados and their Ministers, and there are some strange stories of a kind not likely to impose on our credulity. This part of the *Nihongi* is of very great value, comprising as it does a period of the highest importance in the life of the Japanese nation. It was at this time that the Japanese adopted and assimilated the civilization of China, material, moral, and political, together with the Buddhist religion, thereby profoundly modifying the entire course of their future history.

The defects of the *Nihongi* are due partly to the uncritical spirit of the age when it was written, but mainly to the circumstance that the authors were accomplished scholars deeply imbued with ideas derived from the classical and historical literature of ancient China. With exceptions to be noticed presently, the work is composed in the Chinese language. This is in itself an obstacle to the faithful representation of things Japanese. But unfortunately it is not all. Chinese ideas and traits of Chinese manners and customs are frequently brought in where they have no business. In the very first paragraph we have an essay spiced with Chinese philosophical terms which reads strangely incongruous as a preface to the native cosmogonic myth. Battle axes are mentioned at a time when no such weapons were in use by the Japanese, stone mallets are converted into swords, and we hear continually of the Temples of the Earth and of Grain, a purely Chinese metaphor for the State. No inconsiderable part of the work consists of speeches and Imperial decrees interlarded with quotations from Chinese literature, and evidently composed for the occasion in imitation of Chinese models. In one case the authors have gone so far as to attribute to the Emperor Yūriaku a dying speech of several pages, which is taken with hardly any alteration from a history of the Chinese Sui dynasty, where it is assigned to an Emperor who died 125 years later.

But what is far more misleading than these naive inventions is the confirmed habit common to the writers both of the *Kojiki* and of the *Nihongi*, though the latter are the greater offenders, of throwing back, no doubt more or less unconsciously, to more ancient times the ideas of their own age, when the national thought and institutions had become deeply modified by Chinese influences. As Dr. Florenz very justly remarks, "The little which European inquiry has hitherto been able to teach us of the real condition of Japan in the most ancient times shows that the historical representation of this period in the *Kojiki* and *Nihongi* (upon which rest all the later statements of the Japanese) is most profoundly penetrated by false principles. The newer relations, partly developed from native material, partly influenced by Chinese culture, are reflected back upon the oldest without due distinction, and the result is a confused picture in which the critical inquirer can, it is true, frequently separate what is original from subsequent additions, but must often let fall his hands in despair." A conspicuous instance of this is the way in which the Imperial theory of the universal authority of the Mikados is extended backwards to a time when their sway was really restricted to the provinces round the capital and a few other places. It is also exemplified by the treatment of territorial and official designations in the older part of the history as if they were already family names, which they did not become until a later period.

Chronology.—The *Kojiki* wisely has no chronology. But the authors of the *Nihongi*, or more probably of some of the works on which it is based, thought it necessary, in imitation of their Chinese models, to provide a complete system of dates extending as far back as the middle of the 7th century B.C., and giving the exact years, months, and even days for events which are supposed to have happened in this remote period. When it is remembered that there was no official recognition of the art of writing in Japan until A.D. 405, and that the first mention of calendar-makers belongs to A.D. 553, the historical value of such chronology may be readily estimated. After the Christian epoch there may have been some blundering and unsuccessful endeavours to give the right years, but for several centuries longer the months and days must have been simply supplied from the writers' imagination. Even so late as the beginning of the 5th century the chronology can be shown to be wrong in several cases by no less an interval than 120 years. Abundant proofs of its inaccuracy are revealed by a comparison with the contemporary histories of Corea and China, and an examination of the *Nihongi* itself yields many more. The impossible lengths attributed to the Emperors' reigns are a well-known example, and some, but by no means all, of the other evidence to this effect is indicated in the notes to the present version.

The first date in the *Nihongi* which is corroborated by external evidence is A.D. 461, but the chronology is not a little vague for some time longer. Perhaps if we take A.D. 500 as the time when the correctness of the *Nihongi* dates begins to be trustworthy, we shall not be very far wrong.

In an essay contributed to a Japanese magazine called *Bun*, in 1888, Mr. Naka has brought together absolutely overwhelming evidence of the utter inaccuracy in matters of chronology of the early part of the *Nihongi*, and I may be allowed to refer the reader to a paper on " Early Japanese History " read before the J.A.S. in December, 1887, in which the same thesis is maintained. Such scholars as Satow, Chamberlain, Bramsen, Griffis and others have expressed themselves to a similar effect, and it may be hoped that we have now heard the last of the thoughtless echoes of old Kaempfer's audacious assertion that since the time of Jimmu Tennō, the Japanese have been " accurate and faithful in writing the history of their country and the lives and reigns of their monarchs."

But enough has been said of the defects of the *Nihongi*. The above strictures apply almost exclusively to the earlier half of the work, and they must not be allowed to blind us to the fact that it after all presents a very full and varied picture of the civilization, manners and customs, and political, moral, and religious ideas of the ancient Japanese. Even the large untrue element which it contains is not without its value. Bad history may be good mythology or folk-lore, and statements the most wildly at variance with fact often throw a useful light on the beliefs or institutions of the age when they became current.

Estimation in which the Nihongi was held.—The importance of the *Nihongi* was at once recognized by the somewhat narrow circle of courtiers and officials for whom it was intended. Subsequent history contains frequent mention of its being publicly read and expounded to the

Mikado's Court, one of these notices belonging to the very next year after its completion. It threw wholly into the shade its predecessor the *Kojiki* and superseded the recitations of the Katari Be and other similar customs. Another testimony to its value is the series of commentaries which began to be written upon it immediately after its appearance. Some of these notes, known as Shiki or "private notes," have been preserved to us in a work called *Shaku-nihongi*, written about the end of the 13th century. They are described as of the periods Yōrō, (714—724), Kōnin (810—824), and Yengi (901—923).

This high estimation for the *Nihongi* has lasted until our own day. Its pre-eminence as a source of knowledge of Japanese antiquity was never contested until quite recent times. Even Motoöri [1] acknowledges its value, although his religious and patriotic prejudices lead him to give a preference to the *Kojiki*, which is less profoundly tainted by an admixture of Chinese ideas.

The Kojiki and the Nihongi.—Both the *Kojiki* and the *Nihongi* present to the eye a series of Chinese characters. A closer examination, however, reveals a marked difference in the way in which they are used by the respective authors. In the *Kojiki*, which was taken down from the mouth of a Japanese by a man with some tincture of Chinese learning, the Chinese construction is every now and then interrupted or rather helped out by Japanese words written phonetically, the result being a very curious style wholly devoid of literary qualities. It is in fact possible to restore throughout the original Japanese words used by Hiyeda no Are with a fair degree of probability, and this has actually been done by Motoöri in his great edition of the work known as the *Kojikiden*. This feature gives the *Kojiki* a far greater philological interest than the *Nihongi*. The

---

[1] Motoöri has left a poem to the following effect :—

> In all their fulness
> How should we know
> The days of old,
> Did the august Yamato writing (the *Nihongi*)
> Not exist in the world ?

Hirata says (" Kodō Taii," I. 36), " If we put aside the ornaments of style of Chinese fashion, there is none among all the writings in the world so noble and important as this classic."

latter is composed almost wholly in the Chinese language, the chief exception being the poems, for which it was necessary to use the Chinese characters with a phonetic value so as to give the actual words and not simply the sense, as is the case when they are employed as ideographs. The proper names in both works are naturally Japanese.

As a repertory of ancient Japanese myth and legend, there is little to choose between the *Kojiki* and *Nihongi*. The *Kojiki* is on the whole the fuller of the two, and contains legends which the *Nihongi* passes over in silence, but the latter work, as we now have it, is enriched by variants of the early myths, the value of which for purposes of comparison will be recognized by scientific inquirers.

But there can be no comparison between the two works when viewed as history. Hiyeda no Are's memory, however well-stored, could not be expected to compete in fulness and accuracy with the abundant written literature accessible to the writers of the *Nihongi*, and an examination of the two works shows that, in respect to the record of actual events, the latter is far the more useful authority. It should be remembered, too, that the *Nihongi* is double the size of its predecessor, and that whereas the *Kojiki* practically comes to an end with the close of the 5th century, the *Nihongi* continues the narrative as far as the end of the 7th, thus embracing an additional space of two hundred years of the highest importance in the history of Japan.

Text and Editions.—The class of readers for whom the present work is intended would be little interested in an account of the text of the *Nihongi* and of its various manuscripts and printed editions. In any case this subject has been so exhaustively treated by Dr. Florenz in his Introduction as to render research by other inquirers a superfluous labour.

A few words, however, should be said respecting the *Shūkai* (or *Shūge*, i.e. collected interpretations) edition, which has been taken as the basis of the present version. There are a few departures from it, chiefly where the translator has restored passages of the " Original Commentary " which the *Shūkai* editor has struck out or relegated to his notes.

The *Shūkai* edition is on the whole the most useful one, being well printed, and provided with a copious Chinese commentary. To facilitate reference to it the book and page of this edition have been noted throughout in the margin of the present translation.

The large black type of the *Shūkai* is the text. The "Original Commentary" and the quotations from other books are printed in a smaller type. Both of these are usually assumed to be part of the *Nihongi*, and are quoted as such. They have been included in the present translation, but they are distinguished from the *Nihongi* proper by being indented, or in the case of some very short passages, enclosed in square brackets. Still smaller characters are used by the editor for his notes. In addition to these, small Katakana characters may be seen at the side of many of the characters of the original text and commentary. They are frequently referred to in the notes of the present version under the description of the "interlinear Kana" or the "traditional Kana rendering," and consist of translations into Japanese of the Chinese characters alongside of which they stand, or add particles which are necessary to complete the sense in a Japanese translation. These glosses are of considerable but unknown antiquity. They are sometimes useful, especially in giving obsolete words and the pronunciation of proper names, but they cannot be implicitly relied on. They are often wrong, and still more frequently inadequate.

Spelling.—In transliterating Japanese words, the method adopted by the Japan Society has been followed pretty closely. It is nearly identical with that which is recommended by the Royal Geographical Society, and which may be briefly described as—"the vowels as in Italian, the consonants as in English." There are no silent letters.

Some inconsistencies will doubtless be observed in the spelling of proper names, in regard to which the Japanese themselves are often very vague. There is a good deal of confusion between the hard and soft consonants *t* and *d*, *ch* or *sh* and *j*, *h* and *b*, and *k* and *g*, which it is difficult for a European scholar always to avoid.

The spelling in the case of words of Japanese derivation follows the Japanese written language in representing an older pronunciation than that now current.

Corean proper names are spelt after the system described by

Sir E. Satow in his "List of Corean Geographical Names." It is based on the principle of the Royal Geographical Society's method above-mentioned. But the true pronunciation of these names is involved in much obscurity, and the rendering adopted is in many cases merely provisional.

In spelling Chinese proper names, the ordinary authorities have been followed. They do not agree very well among themselves, but it is hoped that the inconsistencies which have resulted will not occasion any difficulty to the reader.

ABBREVIATIONS.

T.A.S.J.—Transactions of the Asiatic Society of Japan.

Ch. K.—The translation of the " Kojiki" by Basil Hall Chamberlain in " T.A.S.J.," Vol. X. Supplement.

J.R.A.S.—Journal of the Royal Asiatic Society.

N.B.—Attention is drawn to the Table of Errata and Addenda in the second volume

NIHONGI.[1]

BOOK I.[2]

THE AGE OF THE GODS.

PART I.

OF old, Heaven and Earth were not yet separated, and the In and Yō[3] not yet divided.   They formed a chaotic mass like an

---

[1] Nihon, otherwise Nippon, the Niphon of our older maps, where it is wrongly limited to the main island of Japan. Japan is merely a Chinese pronunciation of this word, modified in the mouths of Europeans. Nihon, in Chinese 日 本, means sun-origin, i.e. sunrise. The country received this name from its position to the east of the Asiatic continent. China being the Great Central Land, other countries were given names with reference to it. Corea, for example, is the Tong-Kuk or East-Country. These Chinese characters are sometimes used to represent Yamato, the true old Japanese name of the country, as in the name of the first Emperor, Kamu-yamato-ihare-biko-hoho-demi, better known as Jimmu Tennō. I have little doubt that Nihon, as a name for Japan, was first used by the Corean scholars who came over in numbers during the early part of the seventh century. Perhaps the earliest genuine use of this term occurs in the lament for the death of Shōtoku Daishi by a Corean Buddhist priest in A.D. 620.

In 670 it was formally notified to one of the Corean kingdoms that this would be the name of the country in future, and from about the same time the Chinese also began to use it officially.

There are several cases of its being used retrospectively in places where it has no business, as in a supposed letter from the King of Koryö to the Emperor of Japan quoted in the " Nihongi " under 297 A.D.

" Nihongi," or the Chronicles of Japan, is the proper and original name of this work. But later editors and writers have introduced the syllable sho, writing, styling it the Nihon-shoki, which is its most usual literary designation at the present time.   It is also spoken of as the " Shoki."

[2] The first two books of the " Nihongi " contain the myths which form the basis of the Shinto religion.   For the further study of this subject, Chamberlain's admirably faithful translation of the Kojiki, and Satow's contributions to the " J.A.S.T." will be found indispensable.   Griffis's " Religions of Japan " may also be consulted with advantage.

[3] The Yin and Yang, or female and male principles of Chinese philosophy See " Mayer's Chinese Manual," p. 293.

egg which was of obscurely defined limits and contained germs.

The purer and clearer part was thinly drawn out, and formed Heaven, while the heavier and grosser element settled down and became Earth.

The finer element easily became a united body, but the consolidation of the heavy and gross element was accomplished with difficulty.

Heaven was therefore formed first, and Earth was established subsequently.

Thereafter Divine Beings were produced between them.[1]

Hence[2] it is said that when the world began to be created, the soil of which lands were composed floated about in a manner which might be compared to the floating of a fish sporting on the surface of the water.

At this time a certain thing was produced between Heaven and Earth. It was in form like a reed-shoot. Now this

[1] These opening sentences of the " Nihongi " have been justly condemned by modern Shinto scholars such as Motowori and Hirata as an essay of the Chinese rationalistic type, which has been awkwardly prefixed to the genuine Japanese traditions. Hirata mentions two Chinese works named 淮 南 子 and 三 五 曆 記, as among the originals from which the author of the " Nihongi " borrowed these ideas. See Satow's " Revival of Pure Shinto," pp. 19 and 51 (reprint), " Japan Asiatic Society's Transactions," 1875, Appendix. I take this opportunity of referring the reader to this treatise, which is much the most instructive and accurate work that has yet appeared on the ancient Japanese religion and mythology. No serious student of this subject can afford to neglect it.

The corresponding passage of the " Kiujiki " (vide Index) is as follows :— " Of old, the original essence was a chaotic mass. Heaven and Earth had not yet been separated, but were like an egg, of ill-defined limits and containing germs. Thereafter, the pure essence, ascending by degrees, became thinly spread out, and formed Heaven. The floating grosser essence sank heavily, and, settling down, became Earth. What we call countries were produced by the opening, splitting up, and dividing of the earth as it floated along. It might be compared to the floating of a fish which sports on the surface of the water. Now Heaven was produced first, and Earth afterwards."

[2] Motowori points out that hence has no meaning here. It is inserted clumsily to make it appear as if there were some connection between the Chinese essay which precedes and the Japanese tradition which follows. The author is fond of this word and frequently brings it in without much meaning.

became transformed into a God, and was called Kuni-toko- I. 2.[1]
tachi no Mikoto.[2]

[*The character 尊 is used owing to the extreme dignity of this
Deity. For the others the character 命 is used. Both are read
Mikoto. This rule is followed below.*]

Next there was Kuni no sa-tsuchi no Mikoto,[4] and next
Toyo-kumu-nu no Mikoto,[5] in all three deities.[6]

[1] The marginal references are to the Shukai edition of the original.

[2] Land-eternal-stand-of-august-thing.

[3] This distinction is, of course, an invention of the persons who committed
the myths to writing, and it is by no means consistently adhered to even in
the " Nihongi."

The passage in italics is from what is called the " Original Commentary,"
for which see introduction.

[4] Land-of-right-soil-of-augustness, i.e. his augustness the true soil of th
land. Sa, which I have rendered " right," is a mere honorific. Tsuchi is
written with a Chinese character which means "mallet," but it must be taken
here as put phonetically for tsuchi, land or soil.

[5] Rich-form-plain-of augustness. The meaning of many of the names of
the gods is obscure, and these renderings must be accepted with caution.
Compare the notes to Chamberlain's " Kojiki," where much attention has
been given to this subject. It may be remarked that there is great and
inextricable confusion as to the early deities between the various ancient
authorities, the " Kojiki," the " Kiujiki," the " Kogojiui," the various documents quoted in the " Nihongi," and the " Nihongi " itself.

[6] The Chinese 三 神 means simply three deities. But the interlinear
Kana has mi-bashira no Kami, i.e. Deities, three pillars, hashira or
bashira being the usual auxiliary numeral (like our head of cattle, sail of
ships, etc.) for gods in the ancient literature. Historical Shinto has no idols,
but does not this use of the word hashira suggest a time when the gods of
Japan were wooden posts carved at the top into a rude semblance of the
human countenance, such as are seen at this day in many savage lands ? In
Corea, closely related to Japan, there are gods of this kind. The mile-posts
there have their upper part fashioned into the shape of an idol, to which some
pompous title is given, and at a village not far from Söul, on the Wönsan
road, I have seen a group of a dozen or more of these pillar-gods, set up,
I was told, as guardians to the inhabitants during an epidemic of small-pox.

The word Kami, deity, has a very wide application in Japanese. It
means primarily upper, and hence nobles, the sovereign, gods, and generally
any wonderful or mysterious thing. The leopard and wolf are Kami, the
peach with which Izanagi put to flight the thunders which pursued him in
the land of Yomi, etc. See Hirata's interesting remarks translated by
Satow in " Revival of Pure Shinto," " J.A.S.T.," p. 42 (reprint).

The Aino ideas regarding Kamui are very similar. See Batchelor in
" J.A.S.T.," XVI., Pt. I., p. 17.

These were pure males spontaneously developed by the operation of the principle of Heaven.[1]

In one writing it is said :[2]—" When Heaven and Earth began, a thing existed in the midst of the Void.[3] Its shape may not be described. Within it a Deity was spontaneously produced, whose name was Kuni-toko-tachi no Mikoto, also called Kuni-soko-tachi[4] no Mikoto. Next there was Kuni no sa-tsuchi no Mikoto, also called Kuni no sa tachi[5] no Mikoto. Next there was Toyo-kuni-nushi[6] no Mikoto, also called Toyo-kumu-nu[7] no Mikoto, Toyo-ka-fushi-no[8] no Mikoto, Uki-fu-no-toyo-kahi[9] no Mikoto, Toyo-kuni-no[10] no Mikoto, Toyo-kuhi-no[11] no Mikoto, Ha-ko-kuni-no[12] no Mikoto, or Mi-no[13] no Mikoto."

In one writing it is said :—" Of old, when the land was young and the earth young, it floated about, as it were floating oil. At this time a thing was produced within the land, in shape like a reed-shoot when it sprouts forth. From this there was a Deity developed, whose name was Umashi-ashi-kabi-hiko-ji[14] no Mikoto. Next there was Kuni no toko-tachi no Mikoto, and next Kuni no sa-tsuchi no Mikoto."

I. 3

---

[1] The principle of Heaven is the same thing as the Yō or male principle of Chinese philosophy. This again is no part of the old tradition.

[2] These quotations are usually referred to as part of the " Nihongi." They were, in my opinion, added at a somewhat (but not much) later date. They afford some indication of the mass of written literature which existed on this subject

[3] In Japanese *sora*, to be distinguished from *ame* or *ama*, the heaven or firmament, which was regarded as a plain, as in the expression takama no hara, the plain of high heaven.

[4] Soko means bottom.   [5] Tachi means stand

[6] Rich-country-master.   [7] Rich-form-moor.

[8] Rich-perfume-joint-plain.   [9] Float-pass-plain-rich-buy.

[10] Rich-land-plain.   [11] Rich-bite (?) plain.

[12] Leaf-tree-land-plain.

[13] Mino is written with characters which suggest the derivation see-plain. But mi is more probably a honorific, to be rendered " august."

[14] Sweet-reed-shoot-prince-elder. There is some doubt about the precise signification of the word ji here rendered elder. It is the same root which we have in chichi father ; wo-ji, uncle ; oro-chi, serpent, and tsutsu or tsuchi, which is found in many names of gods. It is probably little more than a mere honorific.

In one writing it is said :—" When Heaven and Earth were in a state of chaos, there was first of all a deity,[1] whose name was Umashi-ashi-kabi-hiko-ji no Mikoto. Next there was Kuni-soko-tachi no Mikoto."

In one writing it is said :—" When Heaven and Earth began, there were Deities produced together, whose names were, first. Kuni-no-toko-tachi no Mikoto, and next Kuni no sa-tsuchi no Mikoto." It is further stated :—" The names of the Gods which were produced in the Plain of High Heaven were Ama no mi-naka-nushi[2] no Mikoto, next Taka-mi-musubi[3] no Mikoto, next Kami-mi-musubi[4] no Mikoto."

In one writing it is said :—" Before Heaven and Earth were produced, there was something which might be compared to a cloud floating over the sea. It had no place of attachment for its root. In the midst of this a thing was generated which resembled a reed-shoot when it is first produced in the mud. This became straightway transformed into human[5] shape and was called Kuni no toko-tachi no Mikoto."

In one writing it is said :—" When Heaven and Earth began, a thing was produced in the midst of the Void, which resembled a reed-shoot. This became changed into a God, who was called Ama no toko-tachi[6] no Mikoto. There was next Umashi-ashi-kabi-hiko-ji no Mikoto." It is further stated :—" There was a thing produced in the midst of the Void like floating oil, from

---

[1] Lit. a Divine man.

[2] Heaven-of-august-centre-master. The Pole-star god, according to O'Neill. *Vide* " Night of the Gods," pp. 535, 536.

[3] High-august-growth. " Personifications of highly abstract ideas are not unknown in myths of savages. The South Sea islanders have personified ' the very beginning,' and ' space.' " Lang's " Myth, Religion, and Ritual," Vol. I., p. 196. It is not quite clear whether this is the same as the Musubi or Musubu no Kami, a god who unites lovers, and to whom the rags hung on trees by the roadside are offered.

[4] Divine-august-growth. This corresponds nearly with the Kojiki myth.

[5] The Chinese character is 人, which the interlinear Kana coolly renders by Kami, deity.

[6] Heaven-of-eternal-stand.

which a God was developed, called Kuni toko-tachi no Mikoto."

The next Deities who came into being were Uhiji-ni[1] no Mikoto and Suhiji-ni no Mikoto, also called Uhiji-ne no I. 4. Mikoto and Suhiji-ne no Mikoto.

The next Deities which came into being were Oho-to nochi no Mikoto and Oho-to mahe no Mikoto.

One authority says Oho-to no he no Mikoto, otherwise called Oho-to-ma-hiko no Mikoto and Oho-to-ma-hime no Mikoto. Another says Oho-tomu-chi no Mikoto and Oho-tomu-he no Mikoto.[2]

The next Gods which came into being were Omo-taru no Mikoto and Kashiko-ne no Mikoto, also called Aya-kashiko-ne no Mikoto, Imi kashiki no Mikoto, or Awo-kashiki-ne no Mikoto, or Aya-kashiki no Mikoto.[3]

The next Deities which came into being were Izanagi no Mikoto and Izanami no Mikoto.[4]

One writing says:—" These two Deities were the children of Awo-kashiki-ne no Mikoto."

One writing says:—" Kuni no toko-tachi no Mikoto produced Ame kagami no Mikoto, Ame kagami no Mikoto produced Ame yorodzu no Mikoto, Ame yorodzu

---

[1] The names of these two Deities are of doubtful meaning. According to the Chinese characters Uhiji should mean mud-earth, and Suhiji sand-earth. Ni or ne is a honorific particle. *Vide* Chamberlain's " Kojiki," p. 17.

[2] These names are somewhat obscure. Oho-to means great door or house ; nochi, after, and mahe, before. He, is place ; toma, a coarse kind of mat ; tomu, wealthy ; and chi, ground. The other elements of these names have occurred above.

[3] Omo-taru means face-pleasing, and Kashiko, awful. Ne is a honorific suffix ; aya, an interjection like our ah ! Imi means avoidance, religious abstinence, taboo. Kashiki is probably only another form of Kashiko, awful. Awo is green.

[4] Izana is the root of a verb izanafu, to invite ; gi, a masculine, and mi, a feminine termination. These two names may therefore be rendered male-who-invites and female-who-invites. But it may be suspected that this is, after all, merely a volks-etymologie, and that Iza or Isa is simply the name of a place, na being another form of no, the genitive particle. Isa is known to Japanese myth. We shall find an Isa well in Heaven spoken of below. There are two places called Isa in Hitachi, and an Isa no Jirja in Idzumo.

no Mikoto produced Aha-nagi no Mikoto, and Aha nagi no Mikoto produced Izanagi no Mikoto." [1]

These make eight Deities in all. Being formed by the mutual action of the Heavenly and Earthly principles, they were made male and female.[2] From Kuni no toko-tachi no Mikoto to Izanagi no Mikoto and Izanami no Mikoto are called the seven generations of the age of the Gods.[3]

[1] Ame-kagami, heaven-mirror ; Ame-yorodzu, heaven-myriad ; Aha-nagi, foam-calm.

[2] This sentence is obviously from the pen of a student of Chinese philosophy.

[3] The eight Gods specially worshipped by the Jingikwan, or Department of the Shinto Religion in the Yengi period—901-922—were Taka-mi-musubi no Kami, Kami-mi-musubi no Kami, Tama-tsume musubi no Kami, Iku musubi no Kami, Taru musubi no Kami, Oho-miya no me no Kami, Mi Ketsu Kami, and Koto-shiro-nushi no Kami.

For the sake of comparison the Kiujiki scheme of the generations of early Deities is herewith added. It will still further exemplify the confusion of these traditions.

" Therefore a God was developed in the Plain of High Heaven whose name was Ame - yudzuru - hi - ame no sa- giri kuni-yudzuru-tsuki kuni no

heaven   transfer   sun heaven right mist land transfer moon land of

sa- giri no Mikoto, who was produced alone. After him were born two

right mist

generations of companion Gods and five generations of mated Deities. These make up what is called the seven generations of the Gods.

GENEALOGY OF THE AGE OF THE GODS.

The Heavenly parent, Ame yudzuru hi ame no sa-giri kuni yudzuru tsuki kuni no sa-giri no Mikoto.

1ST GENERATION.

Companion-born heavenly Gods.

Ame no mi-naka-nushi no Mikoto.

heaven   middle master

Umashi - ashi-kabi   hikoji no Mikoto.

sweet   reed-shoot prince elder

2ND GENERATION.

Companion-born heavenly Gods.

Kuni no   toko tachi no Mikoto.

land   eternal stand

Toyo-kuni-nushi no Mikoto.

rich land master

C

In one writing it is said :—"The gods that were produced in pairs, male and female, were first of all Uhiji ni

A Branch.

Ame - ya - kudari no Mikoto.
heaven eight descend

3RD GENERATION.
Heavenly Gods born as mates.
Tsuno - gui   no Mikoto.
horn   stake (name of place ?)
Iku - gui no Mikoto, his younger sister of wife.
live stake

A Branch.
Ame   mi   kudari no Mikoto.
heaven   three descend

4TH GENERATION.
Heavenly Gods born as mates.
Uhiji - ni   no Mikoto.
mud   earth (honorific affix)
Suhiji - ni no Mikoto, his younger sister or wife.
sand earth

A Branch.
Ama - ahi no Mikoto.
heaven meet

5TH GENERATION.
Heavenly Gods born as mates.
Oho-toma-hiko no Mikoto.
great mat prince
Oho - toma - he no Mikoto, his younger sister or wife.
great mat place

A Branch.
Ame   ya - wo - hi no Mikoto.
heaven eight hundred days

6TH GENERATION.
Heavenly Gods born as mates.
Awo - kashiki ne no Mikoto.
green awful (honorific)
Aya-kashiki ne no Mikoto, his younger sister or wife.
... ! awful

A Branch.
Ame no ya-so-yorodzu-dama no Mikoto.
eighty myriads spirits

no Mikoto and Suhiji ni no Mikoto. Next there were
Tsuno-guhi no Mikoto and Iku-guhi no Mikoto, next

7TH GENERATION.

Heavenly Gods born as mates.

Izanagi no Mikoto.

Izanami no Mikoto, his younger sister or wife.

A Branch.

Taka mi - musubi no Mikoto.

high august growth

Children.

Ama no omohi-game¦ no Mikoto.

heaven thought-compriser

Ama no futo-dama no Mikoto.

big jewel

Ama no woshi - hi no Mikoto.

endure sun

Ama no kamu-dachi no Mikoto.

god stand

Next there was—

Kamu mi musubi no Mikoto.

above growth

Children.

Ame no mi ke mochi no Mikoto.

august food hold

Ame no michi ne no Mikoto.

road (honorific)

Ame no kami-dama no Mikoto.

god jewel

Iku-dama no Mikoto.

live jewel

Next there was—

Tsu-haya-dama no Mikoto.

port quick jewel

Children.

Ichi - chi - dama no Mikoto.

market thousand jewel

Kogoto-dama no Mikoto.

(?)

Omo-taru no Mikoto and Kashiko-ne no Mikoto, and next
Izanagi no Mikoto and Izanami no Mikoto.''

Izanagi and Izanami on the Floating Bridge of Heaven.

Izanagi no Mikoto and Izanami no Mikoto stood on the
l. 5 floating bridge of Heaven, and held counsel together, saying :
" Is there not a country beneath ? "

Ama no ko-yane no Mikoto.
child-roof
Takechi - nokori no Mikoto.
brave milk remnant

Next there was—

Furu-dama no Mikoto.
shake jewel

Children.
Saki-dama no Mikoto.
first jewel
Ama no woshi - dachi no Mikoto.
endure stand

Next there was—

Yorodzu-dama no Mikoto.
myriad jewel

Child.
Ama no koha-kaha no Mikoto."
hard river

A number of these Deities are stated to be the ancestors of noble
Japanese families. The explanation of the meaning of these names is often

Thereupon they thrust down the jewel-spear of Heaven,[1] and groping about therewith found the ocean. The brine which

very conjectural. Some are probably names of places. Possibly some of the obscurer names are Corean. The "Seishiroku" speaks of a Corean Sagiri no Mikoto, and other known Corean Deities were worshipped in Japan. The reader will do well to consult here Satow's "Japanese Rituals" in "J.A.S.T.," Vol. VI., Pt. II., p. 120, where he makes the pregnant suggestion that the sun was the earliest among the powers of nature to be deified, and that the long series of gods who precede her in the cosmogony of the "Kojiki" and "Nihongi," most of whom are shown by their names to have been mere abstractions, were invented to give her a genealogy.

[1] Hirata conjectures that the jewel-spear (nu-boko or tama-boko) of Heaven was in form like a wo-bashira. Wo-bashira means literally male-pillar.

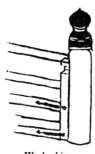

This word is usually applied to the end-posts or pillars of a railing or balustrade, no doubt on account of the shape of the top, which ends in a sort of a ball (the nu or tama), supposed to resemble the glans. That by wo-bashira Hirata means a phallus is clear from his quoting as its equivalent the Chinese expression 玉 莖, i.e. jewel-stalk, an ornate word for the penis. A Japanese word for this is wo-hashi, or wo-bashi, which contains nearly the same etymological elements as wo-bashira.

A writer quoted in the Tsū-shō commentary on the "Nihongi," says that the Tama-boko (or nu-boko) is the root of coition.

Wo-bashira.

The late Mr. J. O'Neill, in his "Night of the Gods" (pp. 31, 37, 67), proposed the theory that this spear and other spears of myth "are but symbols of the Earth-axis and its prolongation," an idea which is worked out with much ingenuity and learning in that remarkable work. At p. 88 he argues that this view is not inconsistent with the phallic interpretation.

There are other indications in the "Nihongi" and "Kojiki" of phallic worship in Ancient Japan, although, probably owing to the influence of Chinese ideas of literary propriety, there are fewer than might have been expected. *Vide* Index—Phallic worship.

All travellers in Japan, especially before the Revolution of 1868, must have observed numerous evidences of a phallic cult. The Government have of recent years done their best to suppress this very gross form of nature worship, but it still exists in out-of-the-way places, as has been shown in an interesting Essay by Dr. Edmund Buckley, of the University of Chicago, who has collected numerous facts relating to this subject. Dr. Griffis, in his "Religions of Japan," has also noticed several evidences of it.

Travelling from Utsunomiya to Nikko, in 1871, I found the road lined at intervals with groups of phalli, connected, no doubt, with the worship of the Sacred Mountain Nan-tai (male-form), which was visited every summer by

dripped from the point of the spear coagulated and became an island which received the name of Ono-goro-jima.[1]

The two Deities thereupon descended and dwelt in this island. Accordingly they wished to become husband and wife together, and to produce countries.

So they made Ono-goro-jima the pillar of the centre of the land.[2]

Now the male deity turning by the left, and the female [3]

hundreds of pilgrims of the male sex, access to females being at that time rigorously prohibited.

A cave at Kamakura formerly contained scores of phalli carved in stone.

I once witnessed a phallic procession in a town some miles north of Tokio. A phallus several feet high, and painted a bright vermilion colour, was being carried on a sort of a bier by a crowd of shouting, laughing coolies with flushed faces, who zig-zagged along with sudden rushes from one side of the street to another. It was a veritable Bacchic rout. The Dionysia, it will be remembered, had their phalli. A procession of this kind invaded the quiet thoroughfares of the Kobe foreign settlement in 1868, much to the amazement of the European residents.

That there are domestic shrines in the lupanars where these objects of worship are propitiated by having a small lamp kept constantly burning before them is, perhaps, not to be wondered at.

Is it a mere coincidence that wo-bashira, male pillar, should contain the element hashira which is used as a numeral for deities ? See above, p. 5.

Some of the Rai-tsui, or thunder-clubs, figured in Kanda's " Ancient Stone Implements," Plate VII., are probably phalli. Their size precludes the view that they were used as weapons.

It may be, however, that both the Earth-axis and the phallic interpretations of the nu-boko are too subtle. The Hoko may after all be a spear and nothing more, and the nu or jewel merely an ornate epithet, as indeed Hirata suggests.

[1] Spontaneously-congeal-island. Cf. Ch. " Kojiki," p. 19. Identified with a small island near Ahaji.

[2] The "Kiujiki" mentions a tradition according to which the two gods made the jewel-spear the central pillar of their house.

[3] The words for male and female are in the original Yō and In. It greatly excites the indignation of the Motowori and Hirata school to have these Chinese philosophical terms applied to Japanese deities. I cannot help thinking that some early marriage ceremony is adumbrated by this circumambulation. We have the ceremony of divorce further on. The erection of a house is not merely for practical reasons. It appears from several passages that a special building was a necessary preliminary to the consummation of a marriage in proper form.

deity by the right, they went round the pillar of the land separately. When they met together on one side, the female deity spoke first and said :—" How delightful ! I have met with a lovely youth." The male deity was displeased, and said :—" I am a man, and by right should have spoken first. How is it that on the contrary thou, a woman, shouldst have been the first to speak ? This was unlucky. Let us go round again." Upon this the two deities went back, and having met anew, this time the male deity spoke first, and said :—" How delightful ! I have met a lovely maiden."

I. 6.

Then he inquired of the female deity, saying :—" In thy body is there aught formed ? " She answered, and said :—" In my body there is a place which is the source of femineity." The male deity said :—" In my body again there is a place which is the source of masculinity. I wish to unite this source-place of my body to the source-place of thy body." Hereupon the male and female first became united as husband and wife.

Now when the time of birth arrived, first of all the island of Ahaji was reckoned as the placenta, and their minds took no pleasure in it. Therefore it received the name of Ahaji no Shima.[1]

Next there was produced the island of Oho-yamato no Toyo-aki-tsu-shima.[2]

Here and elsewhere 日 本 (*Nippon*) *is to be read Yama'o.*[3]

Next they produced the island of Iyo no futa-na,[4] and next the island of Tsukushi.[5]   Next the islands of Oki and Sado

I. 7.

---

[1] " The island which will not meet," i.e. is unsatisfactory. Ahaji may also be interpreted as " my shame." The characters with which this name is written in the text mean " foam-road." Perhaps the true derivation is " millet-land." Cf. Ch. " Kojiki," p. 21.

[2] Rich-harvest (or autumn)-of-island.

[3] Yamato means probably mountain-gate. It is the genuine ancient name for the province which contained Nara and many of the other capitals of Japan for centuries, and it was also used for the whole country. Several of Mikados called themselves Yamato-neko. It is mentioned by the historian of the Later Han dynasty of China (A.D. 25-220) as the seat of rule in Japan at that time. (See above, p. 1.)

[4] Now called Shikoku.

[5] Now called Kiushiu.

were born as twins. This is the prototype of the twin-births which sometimes take place among mankind.

Next was born the island of Koshi,[1] then the island of Oho-shima, then the island of Kibi no Ko.[2]

Hence first arose the designation of the Oho-ya-shima[3] country.

Then the islands of Tsushima and Iki, with the small islands in various parts, were produced by the coagulation of the foam of the salt-water.

It is also stated that they were produced by the coagulation of the foam of fresh water.

In one writing it is said :—" The Gods of Heaven addressed Izanagi no Mikoto and Izanami no Mikoto, saying : ' There is the country Toyo-ashi-hara-chi-i-wo-aki no midzu-ho.[4] Do ye proceed and bring it into order.' They then gave them the jewel-spear of Heaven. Hereupon the two Gods stood on the floating bridge of Heaven, and plunging down the spear, sought for land. Then upon stirring the ocean with it, and bringing it up again, the brine which dripped from the spear-point coagulated and became an island, which was called Ono-goro-jima. The two gods descended, dwelt in this island, and erected there an eight-fathom palace.[5] They also set up the pillar of Heaven."

I. 8.

Then the male Deity asked the female Deity, saying :—
" Is there anything formed in thy body ? " She answered and said :—" My body has a place completely formed, and called the source of femineity." The male god said :—
" My body again has a place completely formed, and called the source of masculinity. I desire to unite my source of

---

[1] Koshi is not an island. It comprises the present provinces of Ettchiu, Echigo, and Echizen.

[2] These two are not clear. Kibi is now Bingo, Bizen, and Bittchiu. Ko, " child or small," perhaps refers to the small islands of the Inland Sea.

[3] Great-eight-island.

[4] Abundant-reed-plain, thousand-five-hundred-harvest (or autumn) fair-ears.

[5] The " Kiujiki " makes the nu-boko or jewel-spear the central pillar of the house which they erected. Eight-fathom is simply a poetical expression for large. There is no special sacredness attached to the number eight.

masculinity to thy source of femineity." Having thus
spoken, they prepared to go round the pillar of Heaven,
and made a promise, saying :—" Do thou, my younger
sister, go round from the left, while I will go round from
the right." Having done so, they went round separately and
met, when the female Deity spoke first, and said :—" How
pretty ! a lovely youth ! " The male Deity then answered
and said :—" How pretty ! a lovely maiden ! " Finally
they became husband and wife. Their first child was the

The Leech Child as Yebisu.

leech, whom they straightway placed in a reed-boat and sent
adrift.[1] Their next was the Island of Ahaji. This also was
not included in the number of their children. Wherefore
they returned up again to Heaven, and fully reported the
circumstances. Then the Heavenly Gods divined this by
the greater divination. Upon which they instructed them.
saying :—" It was by reason of the woman's having spoken
first ; ye had best return thither again." Thereupon
having divined a time, they went down. The two deities

I. 9.

---

[1] The leech was identified in after times with the God Yebisu. See
Anderson's Catalogue of Paintings in the British Museum, p. 36. Hirata
attempts to show that he was the same as Sukuna-bikona, but is not con-
vincing. The reed boat recalls the Accadian legend of Sargon and his ark
of rushes, the Biblical story of Moses as an infant and many more, for which
the curious reader may consult the late John O'Neill's " Night of the Gods,'
p. 410.

accordingly went again round the pillar, the male Deity from the left,[1] and the female Deity from the right. When they met, the male Deity spoke first and said :— " How pretty ! a lovely maiden ! " The female Deity next answered and said :—" How pretty ! a lovely youth ! " Thereafter they dwelt together in the same palace and had children, whose names were Oho-yamato no Toyo-aki-tsu-shima, next the island of Ahaji, next the island of Iyo no futa-na, next the island of Tsukushi, next the triplet islands of Oki, next the island of Sado, next the island of Koshi, next the island of Kibi-no-ko. The country was accordingly called the " Great-Eight-Island Country."

In one writing it is said :—" The two Deities Izanagi no Mikoto and Izanami no Mikoto stood in the midst of the mist of Heaven, and said :—' We wish to find a country.' So they thrust down the jewel-spear of Heaven, and groped about till they found the island of Ono-goro. Then they drew back the spear and rejoiced, saying :— ' Good ! there is a country ! ' "

In one writing it is said :—" The two Deities Izanagi no Mikoto and Izanami no Mikoto sat in the Plain of High Heaven, and said :—' There must surely be a country.' So with the jewel spear of Heaven they scraped together the island of Ono-goro."

In one writing it is said :—" The two Deities Izanagi no Mikoto and Izanami no Mikoto spoke to one another, saying :—' There is something resembling floating oil. In the midst of this there is perhaps a country.' So they took the jewel-spear of Heaven and groping about formed with it an island which was called Ono-goro."

I. 10.

In one writing it is said :—" The female Deity spoke first and said :—' How pretty ! a handsome youth ! ' Now it was considered unlucky that the female Deity should have spoken first. Accordingly they went round again,

---

[1] Hirata says that as the left is superior to the right, and the man to the woman, it is proper that the man should go round from the left, and the woman from the right. He strongly condemns the Kojiki version of the story which reverses this order. The notion of the superiority of the left is really Chinese.

when the male Deity spoke first and said :—" How pretty! a lovely maiden!" Postemo cupiebant coire, sed artis nescii erant. Tum erat motacilla[1] quae advolavit, atque concussit suum caput et suam caudam. Quod cum vidissent duo Dei, imitati sunt eam, et in hoc modo artem coeundi potiti sunt.

In one writing it is said :—" The two Deities were united and became husband and wife. First of all, the islands of Ahaji and Aha being considered the placenta,[2] they produced the island of Oho-yamato no Toyo-aki-tsu-shima, next the island of Iyo, next the island of Tsukushi, next, as twins, the islands of Oki and Sado, next the island of Koshi, next Oho-shima, and next Kojima."

In one writing it is said :—" First there was born the island of Ahaji, next the island of Oho-yamato no Toyo-aki-tsu-shima, next the island of Iyo no futa-na, next the island of Oki, next the island of Sado, next the island of Tsukushi, next the island of Iki, and next the island of Tsushima."

In one writing it is said :—" The island of Ono-goro being considered the placenta, there was born the island of Ahaji, next the island of Oho-yamato no Toyo-aki-tsu, next the island of Iyo no futa-na, next the island of Tsu-kushi, next the island of Kibi no ko, next, as twins, the islands of Oki and Sado, and next the island of Koshi."

In one writing it is said :—" The island of Ahaji being considered the placenta, there was born the island of Oho-yamato Toyo-aki-tsu, next the island of Aha, next the island of Iyo no futana, next the triplet islands of Oki, next the island of Sado, next the island of Tsukushi, next the island of Kibi no ko, and next Oho-shima."

In one writing it is said :—" The female Deity spoke first and said :—' How pretty! a lovely youth!' She

---

[1] Anglice, wagtail.

[2] The Japanese word for placenta is *ye* or *yena*. *Ye* is also Japanese for elder brother. The Kiujiki has in the corresponding passage 兄 or elder brother.

forthwith took the hand of the male Deity, and they at length became husband and wife. There was born to them the island of Ahaji, and next the leech-child."

They next produced the sea, then the rivers, and then the mountains. Then they produced Ku-ku-no-chi, the ancestor of the trees, and next the ancestor of herbs, Kaya no hime.[1] *Also called Nudzuchi.*

After this Izanagi no Mikoto and Izanami no Mikoto consulted together, saying :—" We have now produced the Great-eight-island country, with the mountains, rivers, herbs, and trees. Why should we not produce someone who shall be lord of the universe?[2] They then together produced the Sun-Goddess, who was called Oho-hiru-me no muchi.[3]

Called in one writing Ama-terasu no Oho kami.[4]

In one writing she is called Ama-terasu-oho-hiru-me no Mikoto.[5]

The resplendent lustre of this child shone throughout all the six quarters.[6] Therefore the two Deities rejoiced, saying :—" We have had many children, but none of them have been equal to this wondrous infant. She ought not to be kept long in this land, but we ought of our own accord to send her at once to Heaven, and entrust to her the affairs of Heaven."

At this time Heaven and Earth were still not far separated,[7] and therefore they sent her up to Heaven by the ladder of Heaven.

They next produced the Moon-god.

---

[1] Ku-ku is evidently for ki-ki, trees. Chi is the same root which we have in the modern chichi, father, and kaya is the name of a kind of rush used for thatching. Nu-dzu-chi, moor-of-father.

[2] Universe. In the original, tenka, i.e. that which is under Heaven, subsequently the usual word for the Empire.

[3] Oho-hiru-me no muchi. Great-noon-female-of-possessor.

[4] Heaven-illumine-of-great-deity.

[5] Heaven-illumine-great-noon-female-of-augustness.

[6] North, South, East, West, Above, Below.

[7] "In the beginning the Heaven, Rangi, and the Earth, Papa, were the father and mother of all things. In those days the Heaven lay upon the Earth, and all was darkness. They had never been separated."
Maori myth, quoted by Lang, "Custom and Myth," p. 45.

Called in one writing Tsuki-yumi [1] no Mikoto, or Tsuki-
yomi no Mikoto.

His radiance was next to that of the Sun in splendour.
This God was to be the consort of the Sun-Goddess, and to
share in her government. They therefore sent him also to
Heaven.

Next they produced the leech-child, which even at the age
of three years could not stand upright. They therefore placed
it in the rock-camphor-wood boat of Heaven, and abandoned
it to the winds.

Their next child was Sosa no wo no Mikoto. [2]

Called in one writing Kami Sosa no wo no Mikoto or
Haya Sosa no wo no Mikoto. [3]

This God had a fierce temper and was given to cruel acts.
Moreover he made a practice of continually weeping and
wailing. So he brought many of the people of the land to an
untimely end. Again he caused green mountains to become
withered. Therefore the two Gods, his parents, addressed [4]

---

[1] Yumi means bow, yomi darkness. Neither is inappropriate as applied
to the moon.

[2] This name is written indifferently Sosa no wo and Susa no wo. The
accepted derivation refers *Susa* to *Susamu*, a verb which means "to be
impetuous." Hence the "Impetuous Male" of Chamberlain's and Satow's
translations. I am disposed to prefer a derivation suggested by the "Idzumo
Fudoki," a very old book, which states :—

"Village of Susa. Nineteen ri due west of the Town-house of the district.
Kamu Susa no wo no Mikoto said :—' This is only a small country, but it is
a Kuni-dokoro (local capital ?). Therefore my name shall not be affixed to
wood or stone.' This was accordingly the place where he allowed his
august spirit to repose. There were, therefore, established by him the
Greater Susa rice-lands and the Lesser Susa rice-lands."

Susa no wo is therefore simply the " male of Susa." It will be remembered
that by one Japanese tradition, Idzumo is the home of the Gods, and that
several of the legends respecting them relate to this locality. It is, however,
probable that the older derivation is really a volks-etymologie, which has
given colour to the stories told of this deity. Idzumo is a chief home of
the worship of Susa no wo at the present day. His wife's mother was called
Susa no Yatsu-mimi, but it has not occurred to anybody to make her an
"impetuous female." Hirata rejects the modern identification of this God
with Godzu Tennō.

[3] Kami, deity ; haya, quick.

[4] The character used is that appropriate to a sovereign addressing his
subjects.

Sosa no wo no Mikoto, saying :—" Thou art exceedingly wicked, and it is not meet that thou shouldst reign over the world. Certainly thou must depart far away to the Nether-Land." [1] So they at length expelled him.

In one writing it is said :—" Izanagi no Mikoto said : ' I wish to procreate the precious child who is to rule the world.' He therefore took in his left hand a white-copper mirror,[2] upon which a Deity was produced from it called Oho-hiru-me no Mikoto. In his right hand he took a white-copper mirror, and forthwith there was produced from it a God who was named Tsuki-yumi no Mikoto. Again, while turning his head and looking askance, a God was produced who was named Sosa no wo no Mikoto. Now Oho-hirume no Mikoto and Tsuki-yumi no Mikoto were both of a bright and beautiful nature, and were therefore made to shine down upon Heaven and Earth. But Sosa no wo's character was to love destruction, and he was accordingly sent down to rule the Nether Land."

I. 13.

In one writing it is said :—" After the sun and moon, the next child which was born was the leech-child. When this child had completed his third year, he was nevertheless still unable to stand upright. The reason why the leech-child was born was that in the beginning, when Izanagi no Mikoto and Izanami no Mikoto went round the pillar, the female Deity was the first to utter an exclamation of pleasure, and the law of male and female was therefore broken. They next procreated Sosa no wo no Mikoto. This God was of a wicked nature, and was always fond of wailing and wrath. Many of the people of the land died, and the green mountains withered. Therefore his parents addressed him, saying : ' Supposing that thou wert to rule this country, much destruction of life would surely ensue. Thou must govern the far-distant Nether Land.' Their next child was the bird-rock-camphor-wood boat of Heaven. They forthwith took this

---

[1] Ne no kuni, lit. the root-country, by which Hades or Yomi is no doubt meant.

[2] See Index—Copper.

boat and, placing the leech-child in it, abandoned it to the
current. Their next child was Kagu tsuchi."[1]   I. 14.

Now Izanami no Mikoto was burnt by Kagu tsuchi, so
that she died.[2] When she was lying down to die, she
gave birth to the Earth-Goddess, Hani-yama-hime,[3] and
the Water-Goddess, Midzu-ha-no-me. Upon this Kagu
tsuchi took to wife Hani-yama-hime, and they had a child
named Waka-musubi.[4] On the crown of this Deity's head
were produced the silkworm and the mulberry tree, and in
her navel the five kinds of grain.[5]

In one writing it is said :—" When Izanami no Mikoto
gave birth to Ho-no-musubi,[6] she was burnt by the child,
and died.[7] When she was about to die, she brought forth
the Water-Goddess, Midzu-ha-no-me, and the Earth-
Goddess, Hani-yama-hime. She also brought forth the
gourd[8] of Heaven."

In one writing it is said :—" When about to give birth
to the Fire-God, Kagu tsuchi, Izanami no Mikoto became
feverish and ill. In consequence she vomited, and the
vomit became changed into a God, who was called
Kana-yama-hiko.[9] Next her urine became changed into
a Goddess, who was called Midzu-ha-no-me. Next her
excrement was changed into a Goddess, who was called
Hani-yama-hime.

In one writing it is said :—" When Izanami no Mikoto
gave birth to the Fire-God, she was burnt, and died. She
was, therefore, buried at the village of Arima in Kumano,
in the province of Kii. In the time of flowers, the inhabitants worship the spirit of this Goddess by offerings of

---

[1] Kagu tsuchi was the God of Fire. Tsu is here probably the genitive
particle, and chi the same honorific word as appears in several other names
of Gods. He was worshipped at Nagusa in Kii.

[2] Lit. ended.   [3] Clay-mountain-lady.

[4] Young-growth.

[5] Hemp, millet, rice, corn, pulse. This is a Chinese form of speech, and
with the mention of the silkworm betrays a recent origin of this tradition.

[6] Fire-growth.   [7] Lit. retired.

[8] The gourd was to hold water to subdue the Fire-God with when he
became violent.

[9] Metal-mountain prince. This legend indicates an acquaintance with
mining.

flowers. They also worship her with drums, flutes, flags, singing and dancing."

In one writing it is said:—"Izanagi no Mikoto and Izanami no Mikoto, having together procreated the Great-eight-island Land, Izanagi no Mikoto said: 'Over the country which we have produced there is naught but morning mists which shed a perfume everywhere!' So he puffed them away with a breath, which became changed into a God, named Shina tohe no Mikoto. He is also called Shina [1] tsu hiko no Mikoto. This is the God of the Wind. Moreover, the child which they procreated when they were hungry was called Uka no mi-tama [2] no Mikoto. Again they produced the Sea-Gods, who were called Wata [3] tsu mi no Mikoto, and the Mountain-Gods, who were called Yama tsu mi, the Gods of the River-mouths, who were called Haya-aki [4]-tsubi no Mikoto, the Tree-Gods, who were called Ku-ku no chi, and the Earth-Goddess, who was called Hani-yasu [5] no Kami. Thereafter they produced all manner of things whatsoever.

When the time came for the Fire-God Kagu tsuchi to be born, his mother Izanami no Mikoto was burnt, and suffered change and departed.[6] Then Izanagi no Mikoto was wroth, and said: 'Oh, that I should have given my beloved younger sister [7] in exchange for a single child!

---

[1] Shina is said to be derived from shi, wind or breath, and na, a short form of naga, long. See Chamberlain's "Kojiki," p. 27. The worship of this God is frequently referred to in the last two books of the Nihongi. See also Satow's "Ancient Japanese Rituals," where a prayer to him is given. Tohe means chief.

[2] Food august-spirit. The Chinese characters transliterated Uka mean storehouse rice.

[3] Wata is an old word for sea ; mi is probably "body."

[4] Haya-aki means swift-autumn ; tsu, of, and bi (or mi) perhaps person or body.

[5] Clay-easy.   [6] i.e. died.

[7] The ancient Japanese word for younger sister was imo, which is also applied to a wife. It may be doubted whether this justifies any adverse inference as to the morals of the Japanese in early times. "Sister" is used as an endearing epithet in the Song of Solomon where the relation is certainly not that of brother and sister. It is true, however, that marriages were allowed between brothers and sisters when of different mothers.

So while he crawled at her head, and crawled at her feet, weeping and lamenting, the tears which he shed fell down and became a Deity. It is this Deity who dwells at Unewo no Konomoto, and who is called Naki-saha-me [1] no Mikoto. At length he drew the ten-span sword with which he was girt, and cut Kagu tsuchi into three pieces, each of which became changed into a God. Moreover, the blood which dripped from the edge of the sword [2] became the multitudinous [3] rocks which are in the bed of the Easy-River [4] of Heaven. This God was the father of Futsu-nushi no Kami. Moreover, the blood which dripped from the hilt-ring of the sword spurted out and became deities, whose names were Mika no Haya-hi [5] no Kami and next Hi no Haya-hi no [6] Kami. This Mika no Haya-hi no Kami was the parent of Take-mika-suchi [7] no I. 17. Kami."

Another version is :—" Mika no haya-hi no Mikoto, next Hi no haya-hi no Mikoto, and next Take-mika-tsuchi no Kami."

" Moreover, the blood which dripped from the point of the sword spurted out and became deities, who were called Iha-saku [8] no Kami, after him Ne-saku no Kami, [9] and next Iha-tsutsu-wo [10] no Mikoto. This Iha-saku no Kami was the father of Futsu-nushi [1] no Kami."

One account says :—" Iha-tsutsu-wo no Mikoto, and next Iha-tsutsu-me no Mikoto."

" Moreover, the blood which dripped from the head of the sword spurted out and became deities, who were called Kura o Kami no Kami, [12] next Kura-yamatsumi no Kami, [13] and next Kura-midzu-ha no Kami. [14]

---

[1] Weep-abundant-female.   [2] Cf. Ch. " Kojiki," p. 32.
[3] Literally, five hundred.
[4] i.e. The Milky Way. Yasu, easy, is probably in error for ya-so, eighty, i.e. manifold, having many reaches.
[5] Jar-swift-sun. So written, but mika is probably a word meaning very or mighty.
[6] Fire-swift-sun. See Ch. " Kojiki," p. 32.   [7] Brave-jar-father.
[8] Rock-splitting-god.   [9] Root-splitting-god.   [10] Rock-elder-male-god.
[11] Futsu is interpreted as " a snapping sound " ; nushi is master.
[12] Dark-god.   [13] Dark-mountain-body-god.   [14] Dark-water-goddess.

D

Thereafter, Izanagi no Mikoto went after Izanami no Mikoto, and entered the land of Yomi.[1] When he reached her they conversed together, and Izanami no Mikoto said : ' My lord and husband, why is thy coming so late? I have already eaten of the cooking-furnace of Yomi.[2] Nevertheless, I am about to lie down to rest. I pray thee, do not thou look on me.' Izanami no Mikoto did not give ear to her, but secretly took his many-toothed comb and, breaking off its end tooth,[3] made of it a torch, and looked at her. Putrefying matter had gushed up, and maggots swarmed. This is why people at the present day avoid using a single light at night, and also avoid throwing away a comb[4] at night. Izanagi no Mikoto was greatly shocked, and said : ' Nay! I have come unawares to a hideous and polluted land.' So he speedily ran away back again. Then Izanami no Mikoto was angry, and said :

[1] The original has "yellow springs," a Chinese expression. Yomi or Yomo is Hades. It is no doubt connected with yo or yoru, night.

[2] This is a feature of many old-world and savage myths. In the legend of the rape of Proserpine by Pluto, as told by Ovid, Jupiter replies to Ceres, who demanded back her daughter—

> ". . . Repetat Proserpina caelum,
> Lege tamen certâ : si nullos contiget illic
> Ore cibos."

But Proserpine already—

> " Puniceum curvâ decerpserat arbore pomum
> Sumta que pallenti septem de cortice grana
> Presserat ore suo."

Compare also the story of Nachikétas from the Taittiríya Brāhmana, and the Katha Upanishad :—

> " Three nights within his (Yama's) mansion stay,
> But taste not, though a guest, his food."
> > Muir's Sanskrit texts, Vol. V., p. 329.

The resemblance of the name Yama of the Indian God of the Lower World to the Japanese Yomi has been noted, and also some points of similarity in the myth of Yami and Yama to that of Izanagi and Izanami. See Lang, " Custom and Myth," p. 171.

[3] End-tooth is in Japanese wo-bashira, i e. male-pillar, for which see above, note to p. 11.

[4] The " Adzuma Kagami " mentions a superstition that any one who picks up a comb which has been thrown away is transformed into another person.

' Why didst thou not observe that which I charged thee ?
Now am I put to shame.' So she sent the eight Ugly
Females of Yomi [1] (*Shikome, called by some Hisame*) to
pursue and stay him. Izanagi no Mikoto therefore drew
his sword, and, flourishing it behind him, ran away.
Then he took his black head-dress and flung it down. I. 19.
It became changed into grapes, which the Ugly Females
seeing, took and ate. When they had finished eating
them, they again pursued Izanagi no Mikoto. Then he
flung down his many-toothed comb, which forthwith
became changed into bamboo-shoots. The Ugly Females
pulled them up and ate them, and when they had done
eating them, again gave chase. Afterwards, Izanami no
Mikoto came herself and pursued him.[2] By this time
Izanagi no Mikoto had reached the Even Pass of
Yomi."

According to one account, Izanagi no Mikoto made
water against a large tree, which water at once turned
into a great river. While the Ugly Females of Yomi were
preparing to cross this river, Izanagi no Mikoto had
already reached the Even Pass of Yomi. So he took a
thousand-men-pull-rock, and having blocked up the path
with it, stood face to face with Izanami no Mikoto, and at
last pronounced the formula of divorce. Upon this,
Izanami no Mikoto said : " My dear Lord and husband, if
thou sayest so, I will strangle to death the people of the
country which thou dost govern, a thousand in one day."
Then Izanagi no Mikoto replied, saying, " My beloved
younger sister, if thou sayest so, I will in one day cause
to be born fifteen hundred." Then he said, " Come no
further, and threw down his staff, which was called
Funado [3] no Kami. Moreover, he threw down his girdle,

---

[1] The " Wamiōsho " mentions a statement that these were used as bogeys
to frighten children with under the name of Gogo-me.

[2] The student of folk-lore will at once recognize this pursuit. Cf. Lang's
" Custom and Myth," pp. 88 and 92 : " A common incident is the throwing
behind of a comb, which turns into a thicket."

[3] Or Kunado, come-not-place. Cf. Ch. " Kojiki," p. 39. This was the God
of roads.

which was called Naga-chi-ha [1] no Kami. Moreover, he threw down his upper garment, which was called Wadzurahi [2] no Kami. Moreover, he threw down his trowsers, which were called Aki-gui [3] no Kami. Moreover, he threw down his shoes, which were called Chishiki [4] no Kami.

Some say that the Even Pass of Yomi is not any place in particular, but means only the space of time when the breath fails on the approach of death. [5]

Now the rock with which the Even Pass of Yomi was blocked is called Yomi-do ni fusagaru Oho-kami. [6] Another name for it is Chi-gayeshi [7] no Oho-kami.

When Izanagi no Mikoto had returned, he was seized with regret, and said, " Having gone to Nay! a hideous and filthy place, it is meet that I should cleanse my body from its pollutions." He accordingly went to the plain of Ahagi at Tachibana in Wodo in Hiuga of Tsukushi, and purified himself. When at length he was about to wash away the impurities [8] of his body, he lifted up his voice and said, " The upper stream is too rapid and the lower stream is too sluggish, I will wash in the middle stream." The God which was thereby produced was called Ya-so-maga-tsu-bi [9] no Kami, and then to remedy these evils

---

[1] Long-road-rock.   [2] Disease or trouble.
[3] This might mean open-bite, but the derivation is very doubtful.
[4] Road-spread-out.
[5] Motoöri treats this suggestion with supreme contempt. He prefers to accept the identification of the " Kojiki " (Ch. K. p. 39) with a place in Idzumo. Other parts of the world also boast entrances to the lower regions. The Chinese have one at Têng-chow, and the Roman and Greek legends need not be more particularly referred to.
[6] Yomi-gate-block-great-God.
[7] Road-turn-back.
[8] Izanagi's ablutions are typical of the ceremonial lustration required after contact with death. A Chinese traveller to Japan in the early centuries of the Christian era noted that " when the funeral is over the whole family go into the water and wash." Ovid makes Juno undergo lustration after a visit to the lower regions, and Dante is washed in Lethe when he passes out of Purgatory. For lustration as a widespread practice, consult Dr. Tylor's ʻʻ Primitive Culture," Vol. II., p. 435, et seqq.
[9] Eighty-evils-of-body. Cf. Ch. " Kojiki," p. 41.

there were produced Deities named Kami-nawo-bi no Kami, and after him Oho-nawo-bi[1] no Kami.

Moreover, the Deities which were produced by his plunging down and washing in the bottom of the sea were called Soko-tsu-wata-tsu-mi[2] no Mikoto and Soko-tsutsu-wo no Mikoto. Moreover, when he plunged and washed in the mid-tide, there were Gods produced who were called Naka[3] tsu wata-dzu-mi no Mikoto, and next Naka-tsutsu-wo no Mikoto.[4] Moreover, when he washed floating on the surface of the water, Gods were produced, who were called Uha-tsu-wata-dzu-mi no Mikoto and next Uha[5]-tsutsu-wo no Mikoto. There were in all nine Gods. The Gods Soko-tsutsu-wo no Mikoto, Naka-tsutsu-wo no Mikoto, and Soko-tsutsu-wo no Mikoto are the three great Gods of Suminoye. The Gods Soko-tsu-wata-dzu-mi no Mikoto, Naka-tsu-wata-dzu-mi no Mikoto, and Uha-tsu-wata-dzu-mi no Mikoto are the Gods worshipped[6] by the Muraji of Adzumi.[7]

Thereafter, a Deity was produced by his washing his

---

[1] Nawo is the root of a verb nawosu, to remedy.

[2] Bottom-sea-of-body.   [3] Middle-sea-god.

[4] Middle-elder-male.   [5] Uha means upper.

[6] As appears from the parallel passage of the " Kojiki," this is a case of ancestor worship, not, it will be observed, of the immediate ancestors, as in China, but of a remote mythical ancestor who is a Deity, as his name indicates.

[7] Adzumi no Muraji is a title corresponding exactly to such English titles as " Duke of Wellington," Adzumi being the name of a place and Muraji a title of honour. It is derived from mura, a village or assemblage, and ushi, master. These titles, called Uji or Kabane, though Kabane is properly the second or honorary element, were in their origin simply official designations, and in the " Nihongi " we frequently meet with cases where the office and the title are united in the same person. They were, however, hereditary, and by degrees the mere honorary element prevailed. It too, ultimately vanished, these titles becoming simply surnames to which no particular distinction was attached. Japanese writers, the author of the " Nihongi " with the rest, have, for want of a more appropriate character, identified them with the Chinese 姓 or surname, which is only true of a period later than the time covered by the " Nihongi." There was also a personal name (na), but the ancient Japanese seem to have had no proper surnames, although the Uji answered the same purpose in a rough way.

left eye, which was called Ama-terasu-no-oho-Kami.[1] Then he washed his right eye, producing thereby a Deity who was called Tsuki-yomi no Mikoto.[2] Then he washed his nose, producing thereby a God who was called Sosa no wo no Mikoto. In all there were three Deities. Then Izanagi no Mikoto gave charge to his three children, saying, " Do thou, Ama-terasu no Oho-kami, rule the plain of High Heaven: do thou, Tsuki-yomi no Mikoto, rule the eight-hundred-fold tides of the ocean plain: do thou, Sosa no wo no Mikoto, rule the world." At this time, Sosa no wo no Mikoto was already of full age. He had, moreover, grown a beard eight spans long. Nevertheless, he neglected to rule the world, and was always weeping, wailing, and fuming with rage. Therefore Izanagi no Mikoto inquired of him, saying, "Why dost thou continually weep in this way?" He answered and said, " I wish to follow my mother to the Nether Land, and it is simply for that reason that I weep." Then Izanagi no Mikoto was filled with detestation of him, and said, " Go, even as thy heart bids thee." So he forthwith drove him away.

In one writing it is said : " Izanagi no Mikoto drew his sword and cut Kagutsuchi into three pieces. One of these

---

[1] The Sun-Goddess.

[2] The Moon-God. Compare with this the Chinese myth of P'an-ku : " P'an-ku came into being in the Great Waste, his beginning is unknown. In dying, he gave birth to the existing material universe. His breath was transmuted into the wind and clouds, his voice into thunder, his left eye into the sun, and his right into the moon : his four limbs and five extremities into the four quarters of the globe and the five great mountains, his blood into the rivers, his muscles and veins into the strata of the earth, his flesh into the soil etc."—Mayer's " Chinese Manual," p. 174. Note here that the Japanese myth gives precedence to the left over the right. This is a Chinese characteristic. Hirata rejects any identification of the two myths, pointing out that the sun is masculine in China and feminine in Japan. This is not conclusive. Such closely related nations as the English and Germans differ as to the sex which they ascribe to the sun, and Lang in his " Myth, Ritual, and Religion," points out that among the Australians, different tribes of the same race have different views of the sex of the sun and moon.

became Ikadzuchi no Kami,[1] one became Oho-yama-tsu-mi[2] no Kami, and one became Taka-wo-Kami.[3] Moreover, it is said : " When he slew Kagutsuchi, the blood gushed out and stained the five hundred[4] rocks which are in the midst of the eighty rivers of Heaven, forming thereby Gods who were called Iha-saku[5] no Kami; next Ne-saku[6] no Kami's child, Iha-tsutsu-wo[7] no Kami ; and next, Iha-tsutsu-me no Kami's child, Futsu-nushi no Kami."

In one writing it is said : " Izanagi no Mikoto cut I. 24. Kagutsuchi no Mikoto into five pieces, which were each changed, and became the five Mountain-Gods. The first piece, viz., the head, became Oho-yama-tsu-mi;[8] the second, viz. the trunk, became Naka[9]-yama-tsu-mi; the third, viz. the hands, became Ha[10]-yama-tsu mi ; the fourth, viz. the loins, became Masa-katsu-yama-tsu-mi;[11] and the fifth, viz. the feet, became Shiki[12]-yama-tsu-mi.

At this time the blood from the wounds spurted out and stained the rocks, trees and herbage. This is the reason that herbs, trees, and pebbles naturally contain the element of fire."

In one writing it is said : " Izanagi no Mikoto, wishing to see his younger sister, went to the temporary burial-place. At this time, Izanami no Mikoto being still as she was when alive came forth to meet him, and they talked together. She spoke to Izanagi no Mikoto and said, ' My august Lord and husband, I beseech thee not to look at me.' When she had done speaking, she suddenly became invisible. It was then dark, so Izanagi no Mikoto lit a single light, and looked at her. Izanami no Mikoto was then swollen and festering, and eight kinds of Thunder-Gods rested on her. Izanagi no Mikoto was shocked, and ran away. Then the thunders all arose and pursued him.

---

[1] The Thunder-God.   [2] Great-mountain-of-person.
[3] High male-God.
[4] The numbers 500, 80, 8, 180, 10,000 are often put vaguely for a large number.
[5] Rock-split.   [6] Root-split.
[7] Rock-elder-male.   [8] Great-mountain-of-person.
[9] Middle.   [10] Spur, *vide* Ch. K., p. 33.
[11] True-conquer or excel.   [12] Foundation.

Now by the roadside there grew a large peach tree,[1] at the foot of which Izanagi no Mikoto concealed himself. He accordingly took its fruit and flung it to the thunders, upon which the thunders all ran away. This was the origin of the practice of keeping off evil spirits by means of peaches. Then Izanagi flung down his staff, saying: ʻ The thunders may not come beyond this.ʼ It (the staff) was called Funado no Kami, and was originally called Kunado no Ohoji.[2]

Of the so-called Eight Thunders, that which was on her head was called the Great Thunder ; that which was on her breast was called the Fire-Thunder ; that which was on her belly was called the Earth-Thunder ; that which was on her back was called the Young-Thunder; that which was on her posteriors was called the Black-Thunder; that which was on her hand was called the Mountain-Thunder ; that which was on her foot was called the Moor-Thunder ; and that which was on her genitals was called the Cleaving-Thunder."

In one writing it is said : " Izanagi no Mikoto followed after Izanami no Mikoto, and, arriving at the place where she was, spoke to her and said : ʻ I have come because I sorrowed for thee.ʼ She answered and said, ʻ We are relations.[3] Do not thou look upon me.ʼ Izanagi no Mikoto would not obey, but continued to look on her. Wherefore Izanami no Mikoto was ashamed and angry, and said, ʻ Thou hast seen my nakedness. Now I will in turn see thine.ʼ Then Izanagi no Mikoto was ashamed, and prepared to depart. He did not, however, merely go away in silence, but said solemnly, ʻ Our relationship is severed.ʼ[4] Again he said, ʻ I will not submit to be beaten

---

[1] Chinese legend also ascribes magical properties to the peach. Si Wang Mu, a fabulous being of the female sex, possessed a peach tree whose fruit conferred the gift of immortality. It has also the virtue of driving off the demons of disease. Staves and bows of peach-tree wood were used in the ceremony of oni-yarahi (sending away demons), performed on the last day of the year.

[2] Come-not-place-great-elder (or ancestor).

[3] Relations. The interlinear kana has *ugara*, i.e. the same uji or house.

[4] From the "Kiujiki" it would appear that this was the formula of divorce.

by a relation.'[1] And the God of the Spittle[2] which he
thereupon spat out was called Haya-tama no wo.[3] Next
the God of his purification was called Yomo-tsu-koto-saka
no wo ;[4] two gods in all. And when he came to contend
with his younger sister at the Even Pass of Yomi, Izanagi
no Mikoto said, ' It was weak of me at first to sorrow
and mourn on account of a relation.'

Then said the Road-wardens of Yomi, ' We have a
message for thee, as follows : ' I and thou have produced
countries. Why should we seek to produce more ? I
shall stay in this land, and will not depart along with thee.'
At this time Kukuri[5]-hime no Kami said something which
Izanagi no Mikoto heard and approved, and she then
vanished away.

But, having visited in person the Land of Yomi, he had I. 26.
brought on himself ill-luck. In order, therefore, to wash
away the defilement, he visited the Aha gate[6] and the
Haya-sufu-na[7] gate. But the tide in these two gates was
exceeding strong. So he returned and took his way
towards Wodo[8] in Tachibana. There he did his ablutions. At this time, entering the water, he blew out and
produced Iha-tsu-tsu[9] no Mikoto ; coming out of the water,
he blew forth and produced Oho-nawo-bi[10] no Kami.
Entering a second time, he blew out and produced Soko-
tsutsu[11] no Mikoto ; coming out he blew forth and produced
Oho-aya-tsu-bi[12] no Kami. Entering again, he blew forth

---

[1] Referring to the threat of slaying 1000 people in one day, and the
counter-threat of making 1500 children to be born in one day.

[2] A Japanese authority says that at the present time spitting is essential
in the purification ceremony. Another says, " This is the reason why at the
present day people spit when they see anything impure." Cf. Tylor's
" Primitive Culture," Vol. I., p. 103 ; Vol. II., p. 441.

[3] Quick-jewel-male.   [4] Yomi-of-thing-divide-male.

[5] Hirata derives this from *kiki*, hear, and *iri*, enter, the meaning be ng
that of mediation.

[6] Now known as the Naruto passage, a strait famous for its rapid tides.

[7] Quick suck-name. In the Bungo Channel.

[8] Little-gate.   ' Rock-of-elder.

[10] Great-remedy-person.   [11] Bottom-elder.

[12] Great-pattern-of-person

and produced Aka-tsutsu [1] no Mikoto, and coming out he blew out and produced the various deities of Heaven and Earth, and of the Sea-plain."

In one writing it is said:—" Izanagi no Mikoto charged his three children, saying, ' Do thou, Ama-terasu no Oho-kami, rule over the plain of High Heaven ; do thou, Tsuki-yomi no Mikoto, be associated with her in the charge of Heavenly matters ; do thou, Sosa no wo no Mikoto, govern the plain of Ocean.'

Now when Ama-terasu no Oho-kami was already in Heaven, she said :—' I hear that in the Central country of reed-plains there is the Deity Uke-mochi no Kami.[2] Do thou, Tsuki-yomi no Mikoto, go and wait upon her.' Tsuki-yomi no Mikoto, on receiving this command, descended and went to the place where Uke-mochi no Kami was. Thereupon Uke-mochi no Kami turned her head towards the land, and forthwith from her mouth there came boiled rice : she faced the sea, and again there came from her mouth things broad of fin and things narrow of fin. She faced the mountains and again there came from her mouth things rough of hair and things soft of hair. These things were all prepared and set out on one hundred tables for his entertainment. Then Tsuki-yomi no Mikoto became flushed with anger, and said :—' Filthy ! Nasty ! That thou shouldst dare to feed me with things disgorged from thy mouth.' So he drew his sword and slew her, and then returned and made his report, relating all the circumstances. Upon this Ama-terasu no Oho-kami was exceedingly angry, and said :—' Thou art a wicked Deity. I must not see thee face to face.' So they were separated by one day and one night, and dwelt apart.

After this Ama-terasu no Oho-kami sent a second time Ame-kuma-bito [3] to go and see her. At this time Uke-mochi no Kami was truly dead already. But on the crown of her head there had been produced the ox and the horse ;

---

[1] Red-elder.   [2] The Goddess of food.
[3] Written " Heaven-bear-man." The real meaning is supposed to be Heaven-cloud (kumo)-man, the clouds being regarded as messengers of the Gods.

on the top of her forehead there had been produced
millet ; over her eyebrows there had been produced the silkworm ; within her eyes there had been produced panic ; in
her belly there had been produced rice; in her genitals there
had been produced wheat, large beans [1] and small beans.[2]

Ame-kuma-bito carried all these things and delivered them
to Ama-terasu no Oho-kami, who was rejoiced, and said : —
' These are the things which the race of visible [3] men will
eat and live.' So she made the millet, the panic, the   I. 28.
wheat, and the beans the seed for the dry fields, and the
rice she made the seed for the water-fields. Therefore she
appointed a Mura-gimi [4] of Heaven, and forthwith sowed
for the first time the rice seed in the narrow fields and in
the long fields of Heaven. That autumn, drooping ears
bent down, eight span long, and were exceedingly pleasant
to look on.

Moreover she took the silkworms in her mouth, and
succeeded in reeling thread from them. From this began
the art of silkworm rearing." [5]

Upon this Sosa no wo no Mikoto made petition, saying :—
" I will now obey thy instructions and proceed to the Nether
Land. Therefore I wish for a short time to go to the Plain of
High Heaven and meet with my elder sister, after which I will
go away for ever." Permission was granted him, and he there-
fore ascended to Heaven.

After this, Izanagi no Mikoto, his divine task having been

---

[1] Soja hispida. Hepburn.

[2] Phaseolus radiatus. Hepburn. Compare with this the Chinese myth of
P'an-ku quoted above. There are Indian and Iranian myths of a similar
character. See " T.R.A.S.," Jan., 1895, p. 202. " Creation from the frag-
ments of a fabulous anthropomorphic being is common to Chaldæans,
Iroquois, Egyptians, Greeks, Tinnehs, Mangaians, and Aryan Indians."
Lang, " Myth, Religion, Ritual," I. 246.

[3] As opposed to the unseen gods.   [4] Village-chief.

[5] The " Kojiki " makes Susa no wo to slay Uke-mochi no Mikoto, but the
" Kiujiki " agrees with the version just given, which is more likely to be the
original form of the story, as it is an explanation of the reason why the sun
and moon are not seen together, and has parallels in myths of other
countries. Ama-terasu no Oho-kami (now called Ten-shō-dai-jin) and
Ukemochi no Kami are the two principal Deities worshipped at Ise. See
Satow's " Handbook of Japan," pp. 175, 176.

accomplished, and his spirit-career about to suffer a change, built himself an abode of gloom in the island of Ahaji, where he dwelt for ever in silence and concealment.

Another account says :—" Izanagi no Mikoto, his task having been accomplished, and his power great, ascended to Heaven and made report of his mission. There he dwelt in the smaller palace of the Sun." (*By smaller palace is meant the palace of a prince.*)

I. 29.

Now at first when Sosa no wo no Mikoto went up to Heaven, by reason of the fierceness of his divine nature there was a commotion in the sea, and the hills and mountains groaned aloud. Ama-terasu no Oho-kami, knowing the violence and wickedness of this Deity, wås startled and changed countenance, when she heard the manner of his coming. She said (to herself) :—" Is my younger brother coming with good intentions ? I think it must be his purpose to rob me of my kingdom. By the charge which our parents gave to their children, each of us has his own allotted limits. Why, therefore, does he reject the kingdom to which he should proceed, and make bold to come spying here ? " So she bound up her hair into knots [1] and tied up her skirts into the form of trowsers. Then she took an august string of five hundred Yasaka [2] jewels, which she entwined around her hair and wrists. Moreover, on her back she slung a thousand-arrow quiver and a five-hundred-arrow quiver. On her lower arm she drew a dread loud-sounding elbow-pad. [3] Brandishing her bow end upwards, [4] she firmly grasped her

I. 30.

---

[1] In male fashion.

[2] This word has given much difficulty to the commentators. It is written with characters which mean " eight feet," and this is accepted by some as the true derivation. Hirata makes it ya, very, sa, a honorific, and aka, bright. Perhaps the best interpretation is simply that which makes it the name of the place where the jewels, or rather beads, were made. Ya-saka would then mean eight-slopes. A place of this name is mentioned more than once in the " Nihongi." See Ch. " Kojiki," p. 46, and Satow's " Rituals."

[3] In Japanese, tomo. This was partly for the protection of the arm against the recoil of the bow-string, and partly in order to produce a terrifying sound when struck by it. Its shape (like a comma) is familiar to us from the well-known tomoye, the symbol so constantly met with in Japanese art, in which two or three tomo are joined together. There it represents the in and yô, or the in, yō and taiki.

[4] In the position for shooting.

sword-hilt, and stamping on the hard earth of the courtyard, sank her thighs into it as if it had been foam-snow,[1] and kicked it in all directions. Having thus put forth her dread manly valour, she uttered a mighty cry of defiance, and questioned him in a straightforward manner. Sosa no wo no Mikoto answered and said:—"From the beginning my heart has no been black. But as in obedience to the stern behest of our parents, I am about to proceed for ever to the Nether Land, how could I bear to depart without having seen face to face thee my elder sister? It is for this reason that I have traversed on foot the clouds and mists and have come hither I. 31. from afar. I am surprised that my elder sister should, on the contrary, put on so stern a countenance."

Then Ama-terasu no Oho-kami again asked him, saying:— "If this be so, how wilt thou make evident the redness of thy heart?"[2] He answered and said:—"Let us, I pray thee, make an oath together. While bound by this oath, we shall surely produce children. If the children which I produce are females, then it may be taken that I have an impure heart. But if the children are males, then it must be considered that my heart is pure."

Upon this Ama-terasu no Oho-kami asked for Sosa no wo no Mikoto's ten-span sword, which she broke into three pieces, and rinsed in the true-well of Heaven. Then chewing them with a crunching noise, she blew them away, and from the true-mist of her breath Gods were born. The first was named Ta-gori-bime, the next Tagi-tsu-bime, and the next Ichiki-shima-bime,[3] three daughters in all.

After this Sosa no wo no Mikoto begged from Ama-terasu no Oho-kami the august string of 500 Yasaka jewels which was entwined in her hair and round her wrists, and rinsed it in the true-well of Heaven. Then chewing it with a crunching noise, he blew it away, and from the true-mist of his breath there were Gods produced. The first was called Masa-ya-a-katsu-

---

[1] i.e. snow of as little consistence as foam.

[2] i. e. The purity of thine intentions.

[3] The first two of these three names are of doubtful meaning. The third is the name of a sacred island in the Inland Sea, near Hiroshima, better known as Miya-jima. Cf. Ch. K., p. 48.

kachi-hayabi-ama no oshi-ho-mimi no Mikoto,[1] and the next
Ama no ho-hi no Mikoto.[2] This is the ancestor of the Idzumo
I. 32. no Omi, and of the Hashi no Muraji.[3] The next was Ama-tsu
hiko-ne no Mikoto.[4] He was the ancestor of the Ohoshi-
kafuchi no Atahe, and of the Yamashiro no Atahe.[5] The next
was Iku-tsu-hiko-ne no Mikoto,[6] and the next Kumano no
kusu-bi[7] no Mikoto—in all five males.[8]

Then Ama-terasu no Oho-kami said :—" Their seed was in
the beginning the august necklace of 500 Yasaka jewels which
belonged to me. Therefore these five male Deities are all my
children." So she took these children and brought them up.
Moreover she said :—" The ten-span sword belonged to thee,
Sosa no wo no Mikoto. Therefore these three female Deities
are all thy children." So she delivered them to Sosa no wo no
I. 33. Mikoto. These are the deities which are worshipped by the
Munagata no Kimi of Tsukushi.

In one writing it is said :—" The Sun-Goddess, aware
from the beginning of the fierce and relentless purpose of
Sosa no wo no Mikoto, said (to herself) when he ascended :
' The coming of my younger brother is not for a good
object. He surely means to rob me of my Plain of Heaven.'
So she made manly warlike preparation, girding upon her
a ten-span sword, a nine-span sword, and an eight-span
sword. Moreover, on her back she slung a quiver, and on
her fore-arm drew a dread loud-sounding elbow-pad. In

Truly-I-conquer-conquer-swiftness-heaven-of-great-great-august-person.
Cf. Ch. K., p. 48. I take mimi to be composed of mi the honorific, and mi,
body, person, which is also the termination of abstract nouns, as fukami,
depth, and in this meaning frequently becomes bi, as in several names of
Deities.

[2] Heaven-great-sun ?

[3] Idzumo no Omi. Omi is a title of rank, probably derived from o, for oho,
great, and mi, person. The Chinese character with which it is written
means minister or vassal. Hashi no Muraji. Muraji is explained above,
p. 27. Hashi, which is also read Hanishi, Hase, or Haji, means clay-worker.
For the origin of this title see below, reign of Suinin, 32nd year.

[4] Heaven prince—honorific particle.

[5] Atahe is a title of nobility, like Omi, Muraji, etc., but lower.

[6] Live-of-prince—honorific particle.   [7] Name of place-of-wondrous-ness.

[8] These five, with the three female children mentioned above, are now
worshipped under the name of Hachi-ō-ji, or the Eight Princes.

her hand she took a bow and arrow, and going forth to meet him in person, stood on her defence. Then Sosa no wo no Mikoto declared to her, saying :—' From the beginning I have had no evil intentions. All that I wished was to see thee, my elder sister, face to face. It is only for a brief space that I have come.' Thereupon the Sun-Goddess, standing opposite to Sosa no wo no Mikoto, swore an oath, saying :—' If thy heart is pure, and thou hast no purpose of relentless robbery, the children born to thee will surely be males.' When she had finished speaking, she ate first the ten-span sword which she had girded on, and produced a child which was called Oki-tsu-shima-bime.[1] Moreover she ate the nine-span sword, and produced a child which was called Tagi-tsu-hime. Moreover she ate the eight-span sword, and produced a child which was called Tagori-hime—in all three female Deities. After this Sosa no wo no Mikoto took the august five-hundred I 34. string of jewels which hung upon his neck, and having rinsed them in the Nuna[2] well of Heaven, another name for which is the true-well of Isa, and ate them. So he produced a child, which was called Masa-ya-a-katsu-kachi-haya-bi-ame no oshi-ho-ne no Mikoto. Next he produced Ama-tsu-hiko-ne no Mikoto, next Iku-tsu-hiko-ne no Mikoto, next Ama no ho-hi no Mikoto, and next Kumano no oshi homi no Mikoto—in all five male Deities. Therefore as Sosa no wo no Mikoto had thus acquired proof of his victory, the Sun-Goddess learnt exactly that his intentions were wholly free from guilt. The three female Deities which the Sun-Goddess had produced were accordingly sent down to the Land of Tsukushi. She therefore instructed them, saying :—' Do ye, three Deities, go down and dwell in the centre of the province, where you will assist the descendants of Heaven,[3] and receive worship from them.' "

In one writing it is said :—" When Sosa no wo no Mikoto was about to ascend to Heaven, there was a Deity whose name was Ha-akaru-tama.[4] This Deity came to

---

[1] Lady of the island of the offing.
[2] Nuna-wi,—perhaps for mana-wi, i.e. true well.
[3] i.e. the Emperors.   [4] Feather-bright-gem.

meet him and presented to him beautiful maga-tama [1] of
Yasaka jewels. So Sosa no wo no Mikoto took these
gems and went up to Heaven. At this time Ama-terasu

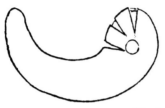

Magatama.

no Oho-kami, suspecting that the intentions of her younger
brother were evil, prepared war and questioned him. Sosa
no wo no Mikoto answered and said :—' Truly the sole
reason of my coming is that I wished to see my elder
sister face to face, and moreover to present to her these
beautiful curved jewels of Yasaka gem. I dare not have
any other purpose.' Then Ama-terasu no Oho-kami asked
him again, saying :—' Wherewithal wilt thou prove to me
whether thy words are true or false ? ' He answered and
said :—' Let thee and me bind ourselves by an oath. If
while we are bound by this oath, the children produced are
females, my heart is to be accounted black, but if they are
males, it is to be thought red.' So they dug three true-
wells of Heaven and stood opposite to one another. Then
Ama-terasu no Oho-kami spoke to Sosa no wo no Mikoto
and said :—' I am now about to give thee the sword which
is in my girdle ; do thou give me the curved jewels of
Yasaka gem which thou hast.' Having thus covenanted
they made a mutual exchange. Then Ama-terasu no
Oho-kami took the curved jewels of Yasaka gem, and
having made them float on the true-well of Heaven, bit
off the heads of the jewels and blew them away. The
Deity which was produced from amidst her breath was
called Ichiki-shima-hime no Mikoto. This is the Goddess
who dwells in Oki-tsu miya. Again, a Deity was produced

I. 35.

---

[1] Maga-tama, curved jewels, are the comma-shaped gems of cornelian or
other stones frequently seen in museums in Japan.

from amidst her breath when she bit through and blew away the middle parts of the jewels. This Deity was called Ta-gori-hime no Mikoto. It is she who dwells in Naka-tsu miya. Again a Deity was produced from amidst her breath when she bit through and blew away the tails of the jewels. This Deity was called Tagi-tsu-hime no Mikoto. It is she who dwells in He-tsu miya.[1] In all there were three female Deities.

Upon this Sosa no wo no Mikoto, taking the sword which he held, and having made it to float on the surface of the True-Well of Heaven, bit off the end of the sword and blew it away. The Deities which were produced from amidst his breath were called Ama no ho-hi no Mikoto, next Masa-ya-a katsu-katsu-no-hayá-hi-ama-no oshi-ho-ne-no Mikoto, next Ama-tsu hiko-ne no Mikoto, next Iku-tsu hiko-ne no Mikoto, and next Kumano no kusu-hi no Mikoto. In all there were five male Deities. Such is the story."

In one writing it is said:—" The Sun-Goddess stood opposite to Sosa no wo no Mikoto, separated from him by the Tranquil River of Heaven,[2] and established a covenant with him, saying, ' If thou hast not a traitorous heart, the I. 36 children which thou wilt produce will surely be males, and if they are males, I will consider them my children, and will cause them to govern the Plain of Heaven.' Hereupon the Sun-Goddess first ate her ten-span sword, which became converted into a child, the Goddess Oki-tsu-shima hime no Mikoto, also called Ichiki-shima hime no Mikoto. Next she ate her nine-span sword, which became converted into a child, the Goddess Tagi-tsu hime no Mikoto. Again she ate her eight-span sword, which became converted into a child, the Goddess Ta-giri hime no Mikoto. Upon this, Sosa no wo no Mikoto took in his mouth the string of 500 jewels which was entwined in the left knot of his hair, and placed it on the palm of his left hand, whereupon it became converted into a male child. He then said:—' Truly

---

[1] Oki-tsu miya means the "shrine of the offing;" Naka-tsu miya, the "middle shrine;" He-tsu miya, the "shrine of the shore." Ichiki-shima is the same as Itsuku shima, the sacred island near Hiroshima in the Inland Sea.
[2] The Milky Way.

I have won.' And the child was therefore called Katsu no haya-hi ama no oshi-ho-mimi no Mikoto. After that he took in his mouth the jewels of the right knot of his hair, and placed them on the palm of his right hand, when they became changed and produced the God Ama no ho-hi no Mikoto. After that he took in his mouth the jewels which hung round his neck and laid them on his left fore-arm, when they became changed and produced the God Ama-tsu hiko-ne no Mikoto. Moreover, from his right fore-arm there was produced the God Iku-tsu hiko-ne no Mikoto. Again from his left foot was produced the God Hi no haya-hi no Mikoto. Again from his right leg was produced Kumano no oshi-homi-no Mikoto, also called Kumano no oshi-sumi no Mikoto. The children produced by Sosa no wo no Mikoto were all male children. Therefore the Sun-Goddess knew exactly that Sosa no wo no Mikoto's intentions had been from the first honest. So these six male children were taken and made the children of the Sun-Goddess, and were caused to govern the Plain of Heaven. The three female Deities born of the Sun-Goddess were made to descend and dwell at Usa-shima in the Reed-plain Central Land.[1] They are now in the middle of the Northern Sea province, and are styled the Michi-nushi no Muchi.[2] These are the Deities which are worshipped by the Kimi of Minuma in Tsukushi."

I. 37.

After this Sosa no wo no Mikoto's behaviour was exceedingly rude. In what way? Ama-terasu no Oho-kami had made august rice-fields of Heavenly narrow rice-fields and Heavenly long rice-fields. Then Sosa no wo no Mikoto, when the seed was sown in spring, broke down the divisions between the plots of rice, and in autumn let loose the Heavenly piebald colts,[3] and made them lie down in the midst of the rice-fields. Again, when he saw that Ama-terasu no Oho-kami was about to celebrate the feast of first-fruits, he secretly voided excrement

---

[1] Ashihara no Naka tsu kuni, i.e. Japan. The phrase Central Land is suspiciously like Chinese.

[2] Province-master—honoured ones or possessors.

[3] Indian myth has a piebald or spotted deer or cow among celestial objects. The idea is probably suggested by the appearance of the stars. It is doubtful whether colt should be singular or plural.

in the New [1] Palace. Moreover, when he saw that Ama-terasu no Oho-kami was in her sacred [2] weaving hall, engaged in weaving the garments of the Gods, he flayed a piebald colt of Heaven, and breaking a hole in the roof-tiles of the hall, flung it in. Then Ama-terasu no Oho-kami started with alarm, and wounded herself with the shuttle. Indignant at this, she straightway entered the Rock-cave of Heaven, and having fastened the Rock-door, dwelt there in seclusion. Therefore constant darkness prevailed on all sides, and the alternation of night and day was unknown.[3]

I. 38.

[1] For the sake of greater purity in celebrating the festival.

[2] The Chinese character here translated sacred is 齋, the primary meaning of which is abstinence, fasting. In the "Nihongi," however, it represents the Japanese word ihahi (pronounced iwai). According to Hirata this contains the same root as imi, avoidance, especially religious avoidance of impurity, and had originally the same meaning. The yu of yu-niha, or sacred plot of ground where rice for the festival of first-fruits was grown, is the same root. But as a strict observance of conditions of cere-monial purity was a chief feature of the Shinto services, this word came to be put for religious rites generally, and the Chinese character is even used, if we may believe the interlinear gloss which renders it by ogami, for Buddhist celebrations. The usual modern meaning of ihahi is blessing, well-wishing, congratulation, where we have got a long way from the original sense of tabu, avoidance.

Ritual purity is of the very essence of Shinto. It applies to food, clothing, and language. There was in later times a special set of terms for certain Buddhist objects and ideas. It was probably to avoid contamination to the ordinary dwelling that special huts were erected for the consummation of marriage, and for childbirth. Death contaminated a house, and therefore a new one had to be erected on the decease of the owner, a practice which was long continued in the case of Imperial Palaces.

[3] Ama-terasu no Oho-kami is throughout the greater part of this narrative an anthropomorphic Deity, with little that is specially characteristic of her solar functions. Here, however, it is plainly the. sun itself which withholds its light and leaves the world to darkness. This inconsistency, which has greatly exercised the native theologians (see Satow's "Revival of Pure Shinto," p. 50, reprint), is not peculiar to Japanese myth. Muir, in the introduction to Vol. V. of his "Sanskrit Texts," says :—" The same visible object was at different times regarded diversely as being either a portion of the inanimate universe, or an animated being and a cosmical power. Thus in the Vedic hymns, the sun, the sky, and the earth are severally considered, sometimes as natural objects governed by particular gods, and sometimes as themselves gods who generate and control other beings." But this difficulty is inherent in all mythologies.

Then the eighty myriads of Gods met on the bank of the Tranquil River of Heaven, and considered in what manner they should supplicate her. Accordingly Omohi-kane [1] no Kami, with profound device and far-reaching thought, at length gathered long-singing birds [2] of the Eternal Land and made them utter their prolonged cry to one another. Moreover he made Ta-jikara-wo [3] no Kami to stand beside the Rock-door. Then Ame no Koyane [4] no Mikoto, ancestor of the Nakatomi no Muraji,[5] and Futo-dama no Mikoto,[6] ancestor of the Imibe [7]

---

[1] Thought-combining or thought-including.

[2] The cock is meant.   [3] Hand-strength-male.

[4] Ko-yane is written with two characters which mean child and roof. Hirata (" Koshiden," Vol. XIII., p. 1) identifies this Deity with Omohi-kane no Mikoto, and endeavours to show that ko is for kokoro, heart. .Ya, he thinks, is many, and ne a honorific. See also Ch. K., p. 56. I agree with Ch. that the meaning is obscure.

[5] Hirata and Motowori have written many pages on the derivation of Nakatomi. The former takes it to be for Naka-tori-mochi, which would give the meaning mediator, these officials being regarded as go-betweens for the Kimi, or sovereign, in his intercourse with the Kami. Perhaps it is safest to follow the Chinese characters which mean "middle-minister," in Japanese Naka-tsu-omi, tsu being a genitive particle. The Nakatomi would then be the ministers of middle rank, as opposed to Prime Ministers on the one hand, and underlings on the other. In historical times their duties were of a priestly character. Worship and government were closely associated in ancient times in more countries than Japan. Matsurigoto, government, is derived from matsuri, worship. It was they who recited the Harahi or purification rituals.

[6] Futo-dama, big-jewel.

[7] Imi-be or imbe is derived from imi, root of imu, to avoid, to shun, to practise religious abstinence, and be, a hereditary corporation. The original function of the Imibe will be understood from the following extract from a Chinese book written not long after the Christian Epoch :—"They (i.e. the Japanese) appoint a man whom they call an 'abstainer.' He is not allowed to comb his hair, to wash, to eat meat, or to approach women. When they are fortunate they make him presents, but if they fall ill, or meet with disaster, they set it down to the 'abstainer's' failure to keep his vows, and together they put him to death." Compare with this the following paragraph from a recent American newspaper.

"AN UNLUCKY MEDICINE MAN.

Big Bob was a prominent member of the tribe, and claimed to be a " tenanimous " man, which, translated from the Chinook, means an Indian doctor. By Indian superstition a " tenanimous " man is held responsible if

no Obito, dug up a five-hundred branched True Sakaki [1] I. 39.
tree of the Heavenly Mt. Kagu.[2]   On its upper branches they
hung an august five-hundred string of Yasaka jewels.   On the
middle branches they hung an eight-hand [3] mirror.

any general calamity befalls the tribe.   Things had not been going well with
the Swinomish Indians for some time.   There was much sickness among
them, and Big Bob was regarded as responsible for it.   So at a meeting of
the tribe four Indians were appointed to execute him.   The day upon which
the murder took place Big Bob was waylaid by four assassins, who seized
him, held him, and cut his throat from ear to ear.   The red men were
arrested and bound over for murder by the Justice of the Peace of Laconner."

In the "Nihongi" times the Imibe occupied a subordinate position in
performing the ceremonies of Shinto, and at a still later period this term
became a mere surname.   *Vide* Satow, "Ancient Rituals," in "J.A.S.T.,"
Vol. VII., Pt. II., p. 126

The Be, or hereditary corporations, were a peculiar institution of Old Japan.
This term has been rather inadequately rendered by clan, tribe, or guild.
But they differed from clans, as it was not even supposed that there was any
tie of blood-relationship between the various classes of members.   And if we
call them guilds we lose sight of their hereditary character, and of the fact
that they were essentially branches of the Government.   Perhaps if we
imagine the staff of one of our dockyards in which the director and officials
should be drawn from the governing class, the artisans being serfs, and the
whole having a more or less hereditary character, we shall have a tolerable
idea of a Be.   The origin of some, as of the Imibe, is lost in antiquity, but
many were instituted in historical times, and for all manner of objects.
There were Be of weavers (Oribe), of figured-stuff weavers (Ayabe), of
executioners (Osakabe), of fishers (Amabe), of farmers (Tanabe), of clay-
workers (Hasebe or Hashibe), and many more.   The sole function of some
was to perpetuate the name of a childless Emperor or Empress.   The local
habitation of these corporations was also called Be, just as our word
admiralty may mean either a body of officials or the building where they
discharge their duties.   This accounts for the frequency with which this
termination occurs in names of places.   A familiar example is Kobe, the
open port in the Inland Sea.   Kobe is for Kami-be, and meant originally the
group of peasants allotted to the service of a Deity (of Ikuta?), and hence
the village where they lived.   A good number of Japanese surnames contain
the same termination.

O-bito is a title of nobility, perhaps for Oho-bito, great man.   It is
represented by a Chinese character which means head or chief.

[1] The Sakaki or Cleyera Japonica, is the sacred tree of the Shinto
religion.   It is used in Shinto religious ceremonies at the present day.

[2] Mt. Kagu is the name of a mountain in Yamato.   It is here supposed to
have a counterpart in Heaven.

[3] In Japanese yata-kagami, which is literally "eight-hand mirror."   The

One writing says Ma-futsu no Kagami.

On its lower branches they hung blue soft offerings and white soft offerings.[1] Then they recited their liturgy together.

Moreover Ama no Uzume[2] no Mikoto, ancestress of the Sarume[3] no Kimi, took in her hand a spear wreathed with Eulalia grass, and standing before the door of the Rock-cave of Heaven, skilfully performed a mimic dance.[4] She took, moreover, the true Sakaki tree of the Heavenly Mount Kagu, and made of it a head-dress, she took club-moss and made of it braces,[5] she kindled fires,[6] she placed a tub bottom upwards,[7] and gave forth a divinely-inspired utterance.[8]

I. 40.

word ta (for te, hand) may here be a measure of length, an explanation which is favoured by the Chinese character used for it in the "Nihongi." The hand is a hand's length, not a hand's breadth, as with us. The yata-kagami would therefore be "a mirror of large size."

There are ancient mirrors in Japan with a number of suzu or bells projecting round them, or of an octagonal shape, and I am disposed to think that the epithet yata has reference to this peculiarity, the corners or projections being taken for handles. Compare the analogous word Yatagarasu (Index).

It is said to be this mirror which is worshipped at Ise as an emblem of the Sun-Goddess. See Satow's "Handbook," second edit., p. 176.

[1] The blue were of hempen cloth, and the white of the paper-mulberry cloth. By blue probably the colour of undyed hempen stuff is meant. The Japanese word awo, blue, is used very loosely. Some take soft in the metaphorical sense of "propitiatory." These offerings are the originals of the Gohei, or strips of paper wreathed round a wand, which are now seen set up in every Shinto shrine.

[2] Terrible female of Heaven.   [3] Monkey-female.

[4] This is said to be the origin of the Kagura or pantomimic dance now performed at Shinto festivals.

[5] The braces or shoulder straps were to support a tray for carrying things, and so assist the arms. The Japanese word is tasuki, which means assistance.

[6] A prototype of the nihabi (courtyard fires) of later Shinto worship.

[7] The "Nihongi" strangely omits to say that, as we learn from the "Kojiki," she danced on this and made it give out a sound.

[8] In Hirata's version of the ancient mythical narrative, he introduces here an incantation said in the "Kiujiki" to have been taught by the Sun-Goddess to Ninigi no Mikoto, but stated in the "Ko-go-jiui" to have come down originally from Uzume no Mikoto. It consists of the syllables Hito-futa-mi-yo-itsu-mu-nana-ya-kokono-tari, which Hirata has tried hard to extract some meaning out of. Hito, he says, is man, futa, the lid, i.e. the door of the rock-cave, miyo is the imperative of miru, to see, this phrase meaning "Look! ye Gods at the door!" and so on. That these words are now

Now Ama-terasu no Oho-kami heard this, and said :—" Since I have shut myself up in the Rock-cave, there ought surely to be continual night in the Central Land of fertile reed-plains. How then can Ama no Uzume no Mikoto be so jolly?" So with her august hand, she opened for a narrow space the Rock-door and peeped out. Then Ta-jikara-wo no Kami forthwith took Ama-terasu no Oho-kami by the hand, and led her out. Upon this the Gods Nakatomi no Kami and Imibe no Kami[1] at once drew a limit by means of a bottom-tied rope[2] (*also* I. 41. *called a left-hand rope*) and begged her not to return again (into the cave).

After this all the Gods put the blame on Sosa no wo no Mikoto, and imposed on him a fine of one thousand tables,[3] and so at length chastised him. They also had his hair plucked out, and made him therewith expiate his guilt.

Another version is :—They made him expiate it by plucking out the nails of his hands and feet.

When this was done, they at last banished him downwards.

In one writing it is said :—" After this Waka-hiru-me[4] no Mikoto was in the sacred weaving-hall, weaving the garments of the Deities. Sosa no wo no Mikoto saw this, and forthwith flaying a piebald colt with a backward flaying, flung it into the interior of the hall. Then Waka-hiru-me no Mikoto was startled, and fell down from the loom, wounding herself with the shuttle which she held in her hand, and divinely departed.[5] Therefore Ama-terasu no Oho-kami spoke to Sosa no wo no Mikoto and said :— ' Thou hast still evil intentions.[6] I do not wish to see thee face to face.' So she entered the Rock-cave of Heaven and

---

simply the numerals from one to ten cannot be denied, but this, he argues, is a later application. The "Kojiki" gives other details of the conduct of this Goddess which the "Nihongi" draws a veil over.

[1] These Gods' names were properly Koyane no Mikoto and Futo-dama no Mikoto (see above), but here the names of their human descendants are substituted.

[2] Shiri-kume-naha, now called shime-naha, a rope made of straw of rice which has been pulled up by the roots. See Ch. K., p. 59.

[3] By tables are meant tables of offerings, as in the illustrations.

[4] Young-Sun-female, a younger sister of the Sun-Goddess.

[5] i.e. died.   [6] Lit. a black heart.

shut the Rock-door. Hereupon all under Heaven was in
continual darkness, and there was no difference of day and
night. Therefore the eighty myriads of Gods met in the

High-market-place of Heaven and made inquiry. Now

there was Omohi-kane no Kami, son of Taka-mi-musubi
no Mikoto, who had a talent for devising plans. He
accordingly considered the matter, and spoke, saying, ' Let
there be made an image of this Goddess, and let prayer

be addressed to it.' They therefore proceeded to appoint Ishi-kori-dome [1] as artisan, who, taking copper of the Mt. Kagu of Heaven, made therefrom a Sun-spear. Moreover, he stripped off in one piece the hide of a true stag, and made of it Heavenly bellows. The Goddess which he fashioned by this means is the Goddess Hi no mahe no Kami, who dwells in the province of Kiï."

In one writing it is said :—" The august Sun Goddess took an enclosed rice-field and made it her Imperial rice-field. Now Sosa no wo no Mikoto, in spring, filled up the channels and broke down the divisions, and in autumn, when the grain was formed, he forthwith stretched round them division ropes.[2] Again when the Sun-Goddess was in her Weaving-Hall, he flayed alive a piebald colt and flung it into the Hall. In all these various matters his conduct was rude in the highest degree. Nevertheless, the Sun-Goddess, out of her friendship for him, was not indignant or resentful, but took everything calmly and with forbearance. I. 43.

When the time came for the Sun-Goddess to celebrate the feast of first-fruits, Sosa no wo no Mikoto secretly voided excrement under her august seat in the New Palace.[3] The Sun-Goddess, not knowing this, went straight there and took her seat. Accordingly the Sun-Goddess drew herself up, and was sickened. She therefore was enraged, and straightway took up her abode in the Rock-cave of Heaven, and fastened its Rock-door.

Then all the Gods were grieved at this, and forthwith caused Ama no nuka-do no Kami, the ancestor of the Be of mirror-makers, to make a mirror, Futo-dama, the ancestor of the Imibe, to make offerings,[4] and Toyo-tama,[5] the ancestor of the Be of jewel-makers, to make jewels. They also caused Yama-tsuchi [6] to procure eighty precious combs of the five-hundred-branched true sakaki tree, and Nu-dzuchi [7] to procure eighty precious combs of the five-hundred-branched suzuki grass. When all these various

---

[1] The meaning is doubtful, as also whether this Deity is a God or a Goddess.

[2] i.e. ropes drawn along the divisions of the rice-fields in token of ownership.   [3] See above, p. 41.

[4] Of cloth.   [5] Rich-jewel.   [6] Mountain-god.   [7] Moor-god.

objects were collected, Ama no Koyane no Mikoto, the
ancestor of the Nakatomi, recited a liturgy in honour of
the Deity. Then the Sun-Goddess opened the Rock-door
and came out. At this time, when the mirror was put into
the Rock-cave, it struck against the door and received a
slight flaw, which remains until this day. This is the
great Deity worshipped at Ise. After this Sosa no wo no
Mikoto was convicted, and fined in the articles required
for the ceremony of purification. Hereupon these were the
things abhorrent of luck of the tips of his fingers, and the
things abhorrent of calamity of the tips of his toes.[1] Again,
of his spittle he made white soft offerings, and of his nose-
mucus he made blue soft offerings, with which the purification service was performed. Finally he was banished
according to the law of Divine banishment."

In one writing it is said :—" After this the Sun-Goddess
had three rice-fields, which were called the Easy[2] Rice-
field of Heaven, the Level Rice-field of Heaven, and the
Village-join[3] Rice-field of Heaven. All these were good
rice-fields, and never suffered even after continuous rain or
drought. Now Sosa no wo no Mikoto had also three
rice-fields, which were called the Pile-field of Heaven,[4]
the River-border[5] Field of Heaven, and the Mouth-
Sharp[6] Field of Heaven. All these were barren places.
In the rains, the soil was swept away, and in droughts
it was parched up. Therefore, Sosa no wo no Mikoto
was jealous and destroyed his elder sister's rice-fields. In
spring, he knocked away the pipes and troughs, filled up
the channels and broke down the divisions. He also
sowed seed over again. In autumn, he set up combs,[7] and

---

[1] No very satisfactory explanation is given by the commentators of this
sentence. Hirata understands the things abhorrent of luck, etc., to be
things required for the purification service.

[2] Easy to cultivate, says the " Shukai " editor.

[3] Mura-ahase, a term of doubtful meaning. Motowori suggests that for
ahase we should read yori. The meaning then would be rice-fields adjoin-
ing the village. Accommodation land, as we should say.

[4] Obstructed with stumps of wood.

[5] Exposed to inundation.   [6] Exposed to drought ?

[7] The " Shiki " explains that combs were stuck up in the rice-fields with

made horses lie down in the rice-fields. Notwithstanding all these wicked doings, which went on incessantly, the Sun-Goddess was not indignant, but treated him always with calmness and forbearance, etc., etc.

When the Sun-Goddess came to shut herself up in the I. 46. Rock-cave of Heaven, all the Gods sent the child of Kogoto Musubi, Ama no Koyane no Mikoto, the ancestor of the Nakatomi no Muraji, and made him recite a liturgy. Hereupon Ama no Koyane no Mikoto rooted up a true Sakaki tree of the Heavenly Mount Kagu and hung upon its upper branches a mirror of eight hands, made by the ancestor of the mirror-makers, Ono-kori-dome, a child of Ama no Nukado; on the middle branches he hung curved [1] jewels of Yasaka gem made by the ancestor of the jewel-makers, Ama no Akaru-dama, a child of Izanagi no Mikoto. On the lower branches he hung tree-fibre [2] made by Ama-no Hi-washi, the ancestor of the Imbe of the province of Aha. Futo-dama no Mikoto, ancestor of the Imbe no Obito, was thereupon made to take these things in his hand, and, with lavish and earnest words of praise, to recite a liturgy.

When the Sun-Goddess heard this, she said:—'Though of late many prayers have been addressed to me, of none has the language been so beautiful as this.' So she opened a little the Rock-door and peeped out. Thereupon the God Ama no Tajikara-wo no Kami, who was waiting beside the Rock-door, forthwith pulled it open, and the radiance of the Sun-Goddess filled the universe. Therefore all the Gods rejoiced greatly, and imposed on Sosa no wo no Mikoto a fine of a thousand tables of (articles of) purifica- I. 47 tion.[3] Of the nails of his hands they made things abhorrent

words of incantation, so that if anyone wrongly claimed the fields he might be destroyed. "The present custom of setting up combs in rice-fields whose ownership is disputed arose perhaps from this."

[1] The curved jewels are the well-known maga-tama, numbers of which have been preserved. They are made of chalcedony, jasper, nephrite, chrysophrase, serpentine, steatite, crystal, etc. Some of these materials are not found in Japan.

[2] Made of the bark of the paper-mulberry.

[3] The word *harahi* or *harahe* not only means purification, but an in-

of luck, and of the nails of his feet they made things abhorrent of calamity. Then they caused Ama no Koyane no Mikoto to take charge of his Great Purification Liturgy, and made him recite it. This is the reason why the people of the world are careful in the disposal of their own nails.[1]

After this, all the Gods upbraided Sosa no wo no Mikoto, saying :—' Thy conduct has been in the highest degree improper. Thou must, therefore, not dwell in Heaven. Nor must thou dwell in the Central Reed-Plain Land. Thou must go speedily to the Bottom Nether Land.'[2] So together they drove him away downwards. Now this was at the time of continuous rains. Sosa no wo no Mikoto bound together green grass, and made of it a broad hat and rain-coat, and in this garb asked a lodging of the assembled Gods. They said :—' Thy behaviour has been filthy and wicked, and therefore thou hast been banished. How canst thou ask of us a lodging ? ' In the end they unanimously repulsed him. Therefore, although the wind and rain were very violent, he was unable to find a resting-place, and went downwards, suffering bitterly. Ever since that time all the world has avoided entering the house of another wearing a broad hat and a grass rain-coat, or bearing a bundle of grass on the back. For a breach of these rules an expiatory fine is certainly imposed. This is an institution which has come down to us from remote antiquity.

After this, Sosa no wo no Mikoto said :—' All the Gods have banished me, and I am now about to depart for ever. Why should I not see my elder sister face to face ; and why take it on me of my own accord to depart without more ado ? ' So he again ascended to Heaven, disturbing Heaven and disturbing Earth. Now Ame no Uzume, seeing this, reported it to the Sun-Goddess. The Sun-Goddess said :— ' My younger brother has no good purpose in coming up.

I. 48.

---

demnity or " damages " paid by an offender. " Expiatory fine " would, perhaps, be a good rendering here. See Index—Purgation.

[1] Referring to a superstition, not confined to Japan, as to cutting the nails on particular days and burying the parings.

[2] Yomi, or Hades.

It is surely because he wishes to rob me of my kingdom. Though I am a woman, why should I shrink?' So she arrayed herself in martial garb, etc., etc.

Thereupon Sosa no wo no Mikoto swore to her, and said :—' If I have come up again cherishing evil feelings, the children which I shall now produce by chewing jewels will certainly be females, and in that case they must be sent down to the Central Land of Reed-Plains. But if my intentions are pure, then I shall produce male children, and in that case they must be made to rule the Heavens. The same oath will also hold good as to the children produced by my elder sister.' In this way the Sun-Goddess first of all chewed her ten-span sword, etc., etc.

Sosa no wo no Mikoto straightway unwound, coil after coil, the complete string of five hundred jewels entwined in the right knot of his hair. The jewels chinked as he rinsed them on the surface of the true well of Heaven. Then he chewed their ends, and laid them on his left palm, thus producing a child, who was called Masa-ya-a-katsu-katsu-haya-hi-ama-no-oshi-ho-ne no Mikoto. After this he chewed the left jewels, and placing them on his right palm, produced a child, who was called Ama-no-ho-hi no Mikoto. He is the ancestor of the Idzumo no Omi, of the Musashi no Miyakko,[1] and of the Hashi no Muraji. There was next produced Ama tsu hikone no Mikoto, the ancestor of the I. 49. Mubaraki[2] no Miyakko and of the Nukada Be no Muraji. Next was produced Iku-me tsu hikone no Mikoto, and next Kumano no Oho-sumi no Mikoto—in all six male Deities. Then Sosa no wo no Mikoto spoke to the Sun-Goddess, and said :—' The reason why I came up a second time was that, having been condemned by the assembled Gods to banishment to the Nether Land, and being about to take my departure thither, I could never bear to become separated from my elder sister without having seen her face to face. Therefore it is truly with a pure heart, and not otherwise, that I came up again. Now that our interview is over, I must return hence for ever to the Nether

---

[1] Or Miya-tsu-ko, originally provincial governors, afterwards hereditary local nobles. [2] In Hitachi.

Land, in obedience to the Divine behest of the assembled Deities. I pray that my elder sister may illuminate the Land of Heaven, and that it may spontaneously enjoy tranquillity. Moreover, I deliver to my elder sister the children which, with a pure heart, I have produced.' Having done so, he returned downwards."

Then Sosa no wo no Mikoto descended from Heaven and proceeded to the head-waters of the River Hi, in the province
I. 50. of Idzumo. At this time he heard a sound of weeping at the head-waters of the river, and he therefore went in search of the sound. He found there an old man and an old woman. Between them was set a young girl, whom they were caressing and lamenting over. Sosa no wo no Mikoto asked them, saying :—" Who are ye, and why do ye lament thus ? " The answer was :—" I am an Earthly Deity, and my name is Ashi-nadzuchi.[1] My wife's name is Te-nadzuchi.[2] This girl is our daughter, and her name is Kushi-nada-hime.[3] The reason of our weeping is that formerly we had eight children, daughters. But they have been devoured year after year by an eight [4]-forked serpent, and now the time approaches for this girl to be devoured. There is no means of escape for her, and
I 51. therefore do we grieve." Sosa no wo no Mikoto said :—" If that is so, wilt thou give me thy daughter ? " He replied, and said :—" I will comply with thy behest and give her to thee." Therefore Sosa no wo no Mikoto on the spot changed Kushi-nada-hime into a many-toothed close-comb, which he stuck in the august knot of his hair. Then he made Ashi-nadzuchi and Te-nadzuchi to brew eight-fold sake, to make eight cupboards, in each of them to set a tub filled with sake,[5] and so to

---

[1] Foot-stroke-elder.

[2] Hand-stroke-elder. These names refer to the caressing of the young girl by her parents.

[3] Kushi-nada-hime. Wondrous Inada-princess.

[4] Eight—in Japanese yatsu. This word is here used as a numeral. But in many places in the old Japanese literature it must be taken in what I regard as its primary sense of " many," " several," as in the word yatagarasu —the many-handed crow—which had really only three claws. In Corean the word yörö, which means many, is, I think, the same root that we have in yöl, ten—words which are probably identical with the Japanese yatsu. The Japanese word yorodzu, myriad, belongs to the same group.

[5] Sake is an intoxicating liquor brewed from rice.

await its coming. When the time came, the serpent actually appeared. It had an eight-forked head and an eight-forked tail; its eyes were red, like the winter-cherry;[1] and on its back firs and cypresses were growing. As it crawled it extended over a space of eight hills and eight valleys. Now when it came and found the sake, each head drank up one tub, and it became drunken and fell asleep. Then Sosa no wo no Mikoto drew the ten-span sword which he wore, and chopped the serpent into small pieces. When he came to the tail, the edge of his sword was slightly notched, and he therefore split open the tail and examined it. In the inside there was a sword. I. 52. This is the sword which is called Kusa-nagi no tsurugi.[2]

In one writing it is said :—" Its original name was Ama no Mura-kumo no tsurugi."[3]

[*It perhaps received this name from the clouds constantly gathering over the place where the serpent was. In the time of the Imperial Prince Yamato-dake its name was changed to Kusa-nagi no tsurugi.*]

Sosa no wo no Mikoto said:—" This is a divine sword. How can I presume to appropriate it to myself?" So he gave it up to the Gods of Heaven.[4]

After this he went in search of a place where he might celebrate his marriage, and at length came to Suga, in the province of Idzumo. Then he spoke, and said :—" My heart is refreshed." Therefore that place is now called Suga.[5] There he built a palace.

One version says :—" Now Take[6] Sosa no wo no Mikoto composed a verse of poetry, saying :—

> Many clouds arise, I. 53.
> On all sides a manifold fence,
> To receive within it the spouses,

---

[1] Hirata thinks that the akakagachi, here translated, on the authority of the " Original Commentary," by " red winter-cherry," was really a kind of snake.

[2] The grass-mower. See Index—Kusa-nagi.

[3] The sword of the gathering clouds of Heaven.

[4] It is hardly necessary to point out the resemblance of this story to that of Perseus and Andromeda, and many others.

[5] Suga means pure, fresh.   [6] Fierce.

> They form a manifold fence—
> Ah ! that manifold fence ! " [1]

Thereupon they had intercourse together,[2] and a child was born named Oho-na-muchi[3] no Kami.

He (Sosa no wo) accordingly spake, and said :—" The masters of my son's Palace[4] are Ashi-nadzuchi and Te-

---

[1] In the original—

> Ya-kumo tatsu
> Idzu-mo ya-he-gaki :
> Tsuma-gome ni
> Ya-he-gaki tsukuru—
> Sono ya-he-gaki wo !

This poem is also given in the " Kojiki " (Ch. K., p. 64), with the slight variant of tsuma-gomi for tsuma-gome in the third line, which makes it intransitive instead of transitive. Idzumo is written with two characters which mean "issuing clouds," as if it were idzuru kumo. The poem no doubt alludes to this meaning and also to the name of the province, but it seems probable that the primary signification of idzumo here is that given in the translation. The true derivation of Idzumo, as the name of the province, is probably idzu, sacred, and mo, quarter. Idzu-mo is for idzure-mo, as so-mo is for sore-mo. It has the same meaning, I think, in a poem given below (" Reign of Kenzō," xv. 11).

This verse of poetry is undoubtedly old, but the regularity of the metre which is a tanka (short poetry) of thirty-one syllables, and its allusive character, point to a somewhat later date than many of the other poems contained in the " Nihongi." The fact that it is here relegated to a note is some corroboration of this view.

The poems in this work are translated so that a line of the English version corresponds to a line of Japanese, but it has not always been possible to preserve the original order of the lines.

[2] The interlinear version has kumi-do ni mito no makuai shite. Kumi-do is no doubt the special nuptial hut above referred to. Mito is " august-place " according to Hirata, and is another word for the kumi-do. This phrase, which is taken from the " Kojiki," probably denotes legitimate nuptial, as opposed to casual intercourse. But the Chinese original has nothing of the sort.

It has been already observed that the erection of a special building for the consummation of the marriage had a ceremonial as well as a practical significance.

[3] Or Oho-na-muji, or Oho-na-mochi, Great-name-possessor. This Deity, one of the most prominent of the Japanese Pantheon, has numerous names (Hirata mentions seven). The derivation is not quite clear. See Ch. K., p. 67.

[4] The same word (miya) means also shrine.

nadzuchi. I therefore grant to these two Deities the designation of Inada no Miya-nushi [1] no Kami."

Having done so, Sosa no wo no Mikoto at length proceeded to the Nether Land.

In one writing it is said:—" Sosa no wo no Mikoto, having descended from Heaven, came to the head-waters of the river Hi, in Idzumo. There he saw Inada-hime, the daughter of Susa no yatsu-mimi,[2] Master of the Shrine of Inada. He had connubial relations with her, and a child was born, styled Suga no yu-yama-nushi [3] Mitsu-na-saro-hiko-yama-shino." [4]

One version has Suga no Kake-na Saka-karu-hiko-ya-shima [5] no Mikoto.

Another has:—" Suga no yu-yama-nushi Mitsu-na-saro-hiko ya-shima-no.[6] The descendant of this God in the fifth generation was Oho-kuni-nushi no Kami." [7]

In one writing it is said:—" At this time Sosa no wo no Mikoto went down and came to the head-waters of the River Ye, in the province of Aki. There was there a God whose name was Ashi-nadzu-te-nadzu.[8] His wife's name was Inada no Miya-nushi Susa no yatsu-mimi. This Deity was just then pregnant, and the husband and wife sorrowed together. So they informed Sosa no wo no Mikoto, saying:—' Though we have had born to us many children, whenever one is born, an eight-forked serpent comes and devours it, and we have not been able to save one. We are now about to have another, and we fear that it also will be devoured. Therefore do we grieve.' Sosa no wo no Mikoto forthwith instructed them, saying :—' You

I. 54.

---

[1] Shrine }
Palace } Master.

[2] Susa, name of place ; yatsu, eight or many ; mi, august ; mi, body or abstract termination.

[3] Master of the hot-spring mountain of Suga.

[4] Three name-monkey (?) prince-mountain-bamboo-grass.

[5] Suga-of-attach-name-pass-light-prince-eight-island.

[6] Eight-island-moor.

[7] Great-country-master-god. Identified by Hirata with Oho-na-muji, also with one of the Shichi-fuku-jin, or Seven Gods of Happiness, named Dai-koku-sama.

[8] Foot-stroke-hand-stroke.

F

must take fruit of all kinds, and brew from it eight jars
of sake, and I will kill the serpent for you.' The two
Gods, in accordance with his instructions, prepared sake.
When the time came for the child to be born, the serpent
came indeed to the door, and was about to devour the
child. But Sosa no wo no Mikoto addressed the serpent,
and said :—' Thou art an Awful Deity. Can I dare to
neglect to feast thee ? ' So he took the eight jars of sake,
and poured one into each of its mouths. The serpent
drank it up and fell asleep. Sosa no wo no Mikoto drew
his sword and slew it. When he came to sever its tail,
the edge of his sword was slightly notched. He split the
tail open and examined it, when he found that inside it
there was a sword. This sword is called Kusa-nagi no
tsurugi. It is now in the village of Ayuchi, in the province
of Ohari. It is this Deity which is in the charge of the
Hafuri [1] of Atsuta. The sword which slew the serpent is
called Worochi no Ara-masa.[2] It is now at Isonokami.[3]

I. 55.

Afterwards the child who was born of Inada no Miya-
nushi Susa no yatsu-mimi, namely Ina-gami Furu-kushi-
nada-hime,[4] was removed to the upper waters of the river
Hi, in the province of Idzumo, and brought up there.
After this Sosa no wo no Mikoto made her his consort,
and had by her a child, whose descendant in the sixth
generation was Oho-na-muchi no Mikoto."

In one writing it is said :—" Sosa no wo no Mikoto
wished to favour [5] Kushi-nada-hime, and asked her of
Ashinadzuchi and Tenadzuchi,[6] who replied, saying :—
' We pray thee first to slay the serpent, and thereafter it
will be good that thou shouldst favour her. This serpent
has rock-firs growing on each of its heads; on each of
its sides there is a mountain; it is a very fearful beast.
How wilt thou set about to slay it ? ' Sosa no wo no
Mikoto thereupon devised a plan. He brewed a poisonous

---

[1] Shintō priests. Atsuta is near Nagoya.
[2] Worochi means serpent ; ara, rough ; masa, true.   [3] In Bizen.
[4] True-hair-touch-wondrous-Inada-princess.
[5] I.e. to take to wife.
[6] Note that the mother as well as the father was consulted.

sake, which he gave it to drink. The serpent became
drunk, and fell asleep. Sosa no wo no Mikoto forthwith
took his sword, called Worochi no Kara-sabi,[1] and severed I. 56.
its head and severed its belly. When he severed its tail,
the edge of the sword was slightly notched, so he split the
tail open and made examination. He found there another
sword, which he called Kusa-nagi no Tsurugi. This
sword was formerly with Sosa no wo no Mikoto. It is
now in the province of Ohari. The sword with which
Sosa no wo no Mikoto slew the serpent is now with the
Kambe[2] of Kibi. The place where the serpent was slain
is the mountain at the upper waters of the river Hi in
Idzumo."

In one writing it is said :—" Sosa no wo no Mikoto's
behaviour was unmannerly. A fine was therefore imposed
on him by all the Gods of a thousand tables, and he was
driven into banishment. At this time, Sosa no wo no
Mikoto, accompanied by his son Iso-takeru[3] no Kami,
descended to the Land of Silla,[4] where he dwelt at Soshi-
mori.[5] There he lifted up his voice and said :—' I will
not dwell in this land.' He at length took clay and made
of it a boat, in which he embarked, and crossed over eastwards until he arrived at Mount Tori-kamu no Take, which
is by the upper waters of the river Hi in Idzumo. Now
there was in this place a serpent which devoured men.
Sosa no wo no Mikoto accordingly took his sword, called
Ama no Haye-kiri,[6] and slew this serpent. Now when he I. 57.

---

[1] Serpent's Kara-blade. Kara is that part of the present province
of Kyöng-syang-do in Corea which lies S.W. of the Naktong River.
But the word is used loosely for all Corea, and in modern times even for
China. See Early Japanese History in " J.A.S.T.," Vol. XVI. Pt. I., p. 43.
It was called Mimana by the Japanese.

[2] The Kambe or Kami-be were the group of peasants charged with the
care of a Shintō shrine.

[3] Fifty-courageous.

[4] The eastern of the three kingdoms into which Corea was formerly
divided.

[5] This is the traditional Kana pronunciation. It is not clear whether this
is the name of a person or a place. Mori may be the Corean moi, mountain.

[6] Fly-cutter.

cut the serpent's tail, the edge of his sword was notched.
Thereupon he split open the tail, and on examination,
found within it a divine sword. Sosa no wo no Mikoto
said:—'I must not take this for my private use.' So he
sent Ama no Fuki-ne no Kami, his descendant in the fifth
generation, to deliver it up to Heaven. This is the sword
now called Kusa-nagi.

Before this, when Iso-takeru no Kami descended from
Heaven, he took down with him the seeds of trees in great
quantity. However, he did not plant them in the land of
Han,[1] but brought them all back again, and finally sowed
them every one throughout the Great Eight-island-country,
beginning with Tsukushi. Thus green mountains were
produced. For this reason Iso-takeru no Mikoto was
styled Isaoshi no Kami.[2] He is the Great Deity who
dwells in the Land of Kii."[3]

In one writing it is stated:—"Sosa no wo no Mikoto
said:—'In the region[4] of the Land of Han there is gold
and silver. It will not be well if the country ruled by my
son should not possess floating riches. So he plucked out
his beard and scattered it. Thereupon Cryptomerias were
produced. Moreover, he plucked out the hairs of his
breast, which became Thuyas.[5] The hairs of his buttocks
became Podocarpi.[6] The hairs of his eye-brows became
Camphor-trees. Having done so, he determined their
uses. These two trees, viz. the Cryptomeria and the
Camphor-tree, were to be made into floating riches;[7] the
Thuya was to be used as timber for building fair palaces;[8]
the Podocarpus was to form receptacles in which the
visible race of man was to be laid in secluded burial-places.
For their food he well sowed and made to grow all the
eighty kinds of fruit.

Now the children of Sosa no wo no Mikoto were named
Iso-takeru no Mikoto, with Oho-ya[9] tsu hime, his younger

I. 58.

---

[1] Corea.   [2] The meritorious God.   [3] Kii or Ki means tree.
[4] Shima usually means island, but in this and other places must be
rendered "region."
[5] A kind of pine.   [6] Maki, a kind of pine.
[7] Ships.   [8] Or Shintō shrines.   [9] Great-house.

sister, and next Tsuma¹-tsu-hime no Mikoto. All these three Deities also dispersed well the seeds of trees, and forthwith crossed over to the Land of Kiï.

Thereafter ·Sosa no wo no Mikoto dwelt on the Peak of Kuma-nari,² and eventually entered the Nether Land." I. 59.

In one writing it is said :—" Oho-kuni-nushi³ no Kami is also called Oho-mono-nushi no Kami,⁴ or else Kuni-dzukuri Oho-na-mochi⁵ no Mikoto, or again Ashi-hara no Shiko-wo,⁶ or Ya-chi-hoko⁷ no Kami, or Oho-kuni-dama⁸ no Kami, or Utsushi-kuni-dama⁹ no Kami. His children were in all one hundred and eighty-one Deities.

Now Oho-na-mochi no Mikoto and Sukuna-bikona no Mikoto, with united strength and one heart, constructed this sub-celestial world. Then, for the sake of the visible race of man as well as for beasts, they determined the method of healing diseases. They also, in order to do away with the calamities of birds, beasts, and creeping things, established means for their prevention and control.¹⁰

¹ Written with a Chinese character which means nail or hoof.

² Probably Mount Kumano in Idzumo. It adjoins the Suga mentioned above as the residence of Sosa no wo. See Index—Kuma-nari.

³ Great-country-master.   ⁴ Great-thing-master.

⁵ Country-make great-name-possessor.

⁶ The ugly male of the reed-plain.   ⁷ Eight thousand spears.

⁸ Great-country-jewel.   ⁹ Apparent-country-jewel.

¹⁰ Calamities (wazahahi) are defined by Hirata as injuries which come to us from the unseen world.

By beasts wild beasts are meant. In addition to the real injuries caused by them, we must remember that in Japan all manner of imaginary effects are attributed to the enchantments of foxes and badgers.

One of the Norito (rituals) mentions calamities of birds flying in by the smoke-hole in the roof—perhaps because their droppings polluted the food which was being cooked.

The term hafu mushi (creeping things) includes both insects and reptiles. The stings of wasps, centipedes, and vipers are doubtless meant. The ancient Japanese houses, slight structures often built in pits, would be especially obnoxious to such calamities. Possibly also the injury to the crops and to domestic animals by insects and snakes may be referred to. It should be remembered, too, that the Japanese suppose many ailments, such as toothache and children's convulsions, to be owing to mushi, and these are no doubt to be included in the hafu mushi no wazahahi. Hirata remarks that it is the opinion of the men of the Western Ocean that by

The people enjoy the protection of these universally until the present day.

Before this Oho-na-mochi no Mikoto spake to Sukuna-bikona no Mikoto, and said :—' May we not say that the country which we have made is well made ? ' Sukuna-bikona no Mikoto answered and said :—' In some parts it is complete and in others it is incomplete.' This conversation had doubtless a mysterious purport.

Thereafter Sukuna-bikona no Mikoto went to Cape Kumano,[1] and eventually proceeded to the Everlasting Land.[2]

Another version is that he went to the island of Aha, where he climbed up a millet-stalk, and was thereupon jerked off, and went to the Everlasting Land.

After this, wherever there was in the land a part which was imperfect, Oho-na-mochi no Kami visited it by himself, and succeeded in repairing it. Coming at last to the province of Idzumo, he spake, and said :—' This Central Land of Reed-plains had been always waste and wild. The very rocks, trees and herbs were all given to violence. But I have now reduced them to submission, and there is none that is not compliant.' Therefore he said finally :— ' It is I, and I alone, who now govern this Land. Is

---

examining ringworm (called in Japanese ta-mushi, i.e. rice-field insect), itch and other diseases under a microscope, it would appear that they are due to the presence of exceedingly small insects. It would also appear, he says, from a work recently published, that the human body is full of such animalcules.

The words "prevention and control" are rendered in the interlinear kana by Majinahi, i.e. witchcraft, including incantations, etc. Possibly the author had in mind the Oho-harahi, which deprecates "calamities of creeping things" and of "high birds." Here is a modern majinahi directed against hafu mushi. If you wish to keep your house free from ants, all you have to do is to put up a notice at the place where they come in, "Admittance, one cash each person." The economical ant goes no further.

Yamada in his dictionary defines majinahi as "the keeping off of calamity by the aid of the supernatural power of Gods and Buddhas."

[1] In Idzumo.

[2] Toko-yo no kuni. The Japanese scholar Arawi identifies this with a province in the East of Japan, now called Hitachi.

there perchance any one who could join with me in governing the world?' Upon this a Divine radiance illuminated the sea, and of a sudden there was something which floated towards him and said :—' Were I not here, how couldst thou subdue this Land? It is because I am here that thou hast been enabled to accomplish this mighty undertaking.' Then Oho-na-mochi no Kami inquired, saying :—' Then who art thou?' It replied and said :—' I am thy guardian spirit, the wondrous spirit.' I. 61. Then said Oho-na-mochi no Kami :—' True, I know there-fore that thou art my guardian spirit, the wondrous spirit. Where dost thou now wish to dwell?' The spirit answered and said :—' I wish to dwell on Mount Mimoro, in the province of Yamato.' Accordingly he built a shrine in that place and made the spirit to go and dwell there. This is the God of Oho-miwa.

The children of this Deity were the Kimi of Kamo and of Oho-miwa,[1] and also Hime-tatara[2] I-suzu-hime no I. 62. Mikoto.

Another version is that Koto-shiro-nushi no Kami, having become transformed into an eight-fathom bear-sea-monster,[3]

---

[1] Descendants are here meant. Kimi is simply Lord.

[2] Tatara is said to be the name of a plant. Isuzu (fifty bells) is the name of the site of the Inner Shrine at Ise.

[3] Sea-monster is in Japanese wani. It is written with a Chinese character which means, properly, crocodile, but that meaning is inadmissible in these old legends, as the Japanese who originated them can have known nothing of this animal. The wani, too, inhabits the sea and not rivers, and is plainly a mythical creature.

Satow and Anderson have noted that the wani is usually represented in art as a dragon, and Toyo-tama-hime (see Index), who in one version of the legend changes into a wani, as her true form, at the moment of child-birth, according to another changes into a dragon. Now Toyo-tama-hime was the daughter of the God of the Sea. This suggests that the latter is one of the Dragon-Kings familiar to Chinese (see Mayers' Manual, p. 142) and Corean fable who inhabit splendid palaces at the bottom of the sea. It is unnecessary here to follow the Dragon-Kings into Indian myth, where they appear under the form of the Nâga Râdja or Cobra-Kings. The reader who wishes to do so should consult Anderson's British Museum Catalogue, p. 50. Chamberlain has remarked that " the whole story of the Sea-God's palace has a Chinese ring about it, and the

had intercourse with Mizo-kuhi[1] hime of the island
of Mishima (some call her Tama-kushi-hime), and
had by her a child named Hime-tatara I-suzu-hime no
Mikoto, who became the Empress of the Emperor Kami-
Yamato Ihare-biko Hohodemi.[2]

Before this time, when Oho-na-mochi no Kami was
pacifying the land, he went to Wobama in Isasa, in the
province of Idzumo. He was just having some food
and drink, when of a sudden there was heard a human
voice from the surface of the sea. He was astonished, but
on seeking for it there was nothing at all to be seen.
After a while a dwarf appeared, who had made a boat of
the rind of a kagami[3] and clothing of the feathers of a

I. 63.

wren.[4] He came floating towards him on the tide, and
Oho-na-mochi no Mikoto taking him up, placed him on
the palm of his hand. He was playing with him, when
the dwarf leaped up, and bit him on the cheek. He
wondered at his appearance, and sent a messenger to
report the matter to the Gods of Heaven. Now when
Taka-mi-musubi no Mikoto heard this, he said :—' The
children whom I have produced number in all one thou-

cassia-tree mentioned in it is certainly Chinese." Is it possible that
wani is for the Corean wang-i, i.e. "the King," i being the Corean
definite particle, as in zeni, fumi, yagi, and other Chinese words which
reached Japan viâ Corea? We have the same change of ng into n in the
name of the Corean who taught Chinese to the Japanese Prince Imperial in
Ojin Tennō's reign. It is Wang-in in Corean, but was pronounced Wani
by the Japanese. Wani occurs several times as a proper name in the
"Nihongi." Bear (in Japanese kuma) is no doubt an epithet indicating
size, as in kuma-bachi, bear-bee or bear-wasp, i.e. a hornet ; kuma-gera, a
large kind of wood-pecker, etc.

[1] Mizo-kuhi means water-channel pile. Tama-kushi is jewel-comb.
[2] Otherwise called Jimmu Tennō. See below, beginning of Book III.
[3] Some plant, very likely having gourd-shaped fruit. Vide Ch. K., p. 85.
[4] The "Kojiki" says goose skins. The wren was no doubt substituted
as more in accordance with the dwarfish stature of Sukuna-bikona.

Dr. Schlegel in his " Problèmes Géographiques" mentions a Chinese
notice of a Han-ming-kuo, the inhabitants of which sew together skins
of birds for clothing. He identifies this country with the Kuriles, where
modern travellers have found this to be the custom. The bird whose
skins are thus used is the Procellaria gracilis (petrel).

sand and five hundred. Amongst them one was very
wicked, and would not yield compliance to my instructions.
He slipped through between my fingers and fell. This
must be that child, let him be loved and nurtured.' This
was no other than Sukuna-bikona no Mikoto." [1]

[1] Sukuna-bikona is a popular God at the present day. Hirata has
devoted two volumes (the " Shidzu no ihaya ") to a glorification of him as
the inventor of medicine and of the art of brewing sake under the name
of Kushi no Kami. The " Kojiki " relates his legend somewhat differently.
See Ch. K., p. 85. Sukuna means small (in modern Japanese few) and
bikona is honorific.

Hirata identifies Sukuna-bikona with Yebisu and Oho-na-mochi with
Daikoku. See Anderson's B. M. Catalogue, p. 36. All these identifica-
tions, of which Hirata is profuse, are somewhat problematical.

BOOK II.

THE AGE OF THE GODS.

PART II.

MASA-YA-A-KATSU-KATSU-HAYA-HI AMA NO OSHI-HO-MI-MI NO MIKOTO, the son of Ama-terasu no Oho-kami, took to wife Taku-hata[1]-chi-chi-hime, daughter of Taka-mi-musubi no Mikoto. A child was born to them named Ama-tsu-hiko-hiko-ho-no-ninigi no Mikoto.[2] Therefore his august grandparent, Taka-mi-musubi no Mikoto, treated him with special affection, and nurtured him with great regard. Eventually he desired to establish his august grandchild Ama-tsu-hiko-ho-ho-ninigi no Mikoto as the Lord of the Central Land of Reed-Plains. But in that Land there were numerous Deities which shone with a lustre like that of fireflies, and evil Deities which buzzed like flies. There were also trees and herbs all of which could speak. Therefore Taka-mi-musubi no Mikoto assembled all the eighty Gods, and inquired of them, saying :—" I desire to have the evil Gods of the Central Land of Reed-Plains expelled and subdued. Whom is it meet that we should send for this purpose? I pray you, all ye Gods, conceal not your opinion." They all said :—" Ama-no-ho-hi no Mikoto is the most heroic among the Gods. Ought not he to be tried? "

Taka-mi-musubi no Mikoto thereupon complied with the general advice, and made Ama-no-ho-hi no Mikoto to go and subdue them. This Deity, however, curried favour with Oho-na-mochi no Mikoto, and three years passed without his making any report. Therefore his son Oho-se-ihi no Mikuma no ushi[3] (also called Take[4]-mikuma no ushi) was sent.

---

[1] Taku-hata, paper-mulberry loom (cloth).

[2] The interpretation of this name is doubtful. See Ch. K., p. 106.

[3] Great-husband-boiled-rice-of-Mikuma of master.

[4] Take, brave, is merely a honorific. It is prefixed to several names of Deities.

He, too, yielded compliance to his father, and never made II. 3.
any report. Taka-mi-musubi no Mikoto therefore again
summoned together all the Gods and inquired of them who
should be sent. They all said :—" Ame-waka-hiko,[1] son of
Ame no Kuni-dama.[2] He is a valorous person. Let him be
tried." Hereupon Taka-mi-musubi no Mikoto gave Ame-waka-
hiko a heavenly deer-bow and heavenly feathered arrows, and
so despatched him. This God also was disloyal, and as soon
as he arrived took to wife Shita-teru-hime,[3] the daughter of
Utsushi-kuni-dama[4] (*also called Taka-hime or Waka-kuni-
dama*). Accordingly he remained, and said :—" I, too, wish to
govern the Central Land of Reed-Plains." He never reported
the result of his mission. At this time, Taka-mi-musubi no
Mikoto, wondering why he was so long in coming and making
his report, sent the pheasant Na-naki[5] to observe. The
pheasant flew down and perched on the top of a many-branched
cassia-tree which grew before Ame-waka-hiko's gate. Now
Ama-no Sagu-me[6] saw this and told Ame-waka-hiko, saying :— II. 4.
" A strange bird has come and is perched on the top of the cassia-
tree." Then Ame-waka-hiko took the heavenly deer-bow and
the heavenly feathered arrows which had been given him by
Taka-mi-musubi no Mikoto, and shot the pheasant, so that it
died. The arrow having passed through the pheasant's breast,
came before where Taka-mi-musubi no Kami was sitting. Then
Taka-mi-musubi no Kami seeing this arrow, said :—" This
arrow I formerly gave to Ame-waka-hiko. It is stained with
blood, it may be because he has been fighting with the Earthly
Deities." Thereupon Taka-mi-musubi no Mikoto took up the
arrow and flung it back down (to earth). This arrow, when it

---

[1] Heaven-young-prince. [2] Heaven-of-country-jewel.
[3] Lower-shine-princess. [4] Real-country-jewel.
[5] Na-naki. This word is written here as if the meaning were "nameless."
But in the " Kojiki " (see Ch. K., p. 95), characters are used which give it the
sense of name-crying, i.e. calling out its own name. The old Japanese for
pheasant is kigishi or kigisu. Comparing this with uguhisu (the Japanese
nightingale), kakesu (the jay), kirigirisu (the grasshopper), karasu (the
crow), and hototogisu (a kind of cuckoo), it becomes evident that kigisu is an
onomatopoetic word. Su is for suru, to do. The Corean for a pheasant is
kiŏng, no doubt also an onomatope.
[6] Heavenly-spying-woman.

fell, hit Ame-waka-hiko on the top of his breast. At this time
Ame-waka-hiko was lying down after the feast of first-fruits,
and when hit by the arrow died immediately. This was the
origin of the general saying, " Fear a returning arrow."

The sound of the weeping and mourning of Ame-waka-hiko's
II. 5. wife Shita-teru-hime reached Heaven. At this time, Ame no
Kuni-dama, hearing the voice of her crying, straightway knew
that her husband, Ame-waka-hiko, was dead, and sent down a
swift wind to bring the body up to Heaven. Forthwith a
mortuary house was made, in which it was temporarily deposited. The river-geese were made the head-hanging
bearers and broom-bearers.

> One version is :—" The barn-door fowls were made head-
> hanging bearers, and the river-geese were made broom-
> bearers."

The sparrows were made pounding-women.

> One version is :—" The river-geese were made head-hang-
> ing bearers and also broom-bearers, the kingfisher was made
> the representative of the deceased, the sparrows were made
> the pounding-women, and the wrens the mourners. Alto-
II. 6. gether the assembled birds were entrusted with the matter."

For eight days and eight nights they wept and sang dirges.[1]

---

[1] We have here a glimpse of the ancient Japanese funeral ceremonies.

"Head-hanging bearers" is a literal translation of the Chinese characters.
The interlinear Kana renders them by the obsolete word kisari-mochi, of
obscure meaning. An ancient commentator says that these were persons
who accompanied the funeral, bearing on their heads food for the dead,
which is perhaps correct. The brooms were probably for sweeping the road
before the procession. The pounding-women pounded the rice for the guests,
and perhaps also for the offerings to the deceased. By mourners are meant
paid mourners.

To these Hirata adds from old books the wata-dzukuri or tree-fibre carders,
the kites (the fibre being to fill up the vacant space in the coffin), and the
fleshers (for food offered to the deceased), an office given to the crow.
Compare also Ch. K., p. 97.

The student of folk-lore will not think it frivolous of me to cite here the
English story of the Death and Burial of Cock Robin, where the birds
officiate in various capacities at a funeral.

"Sang dirges." Hirata condemns this as a Chinese importation. He
prefers the "Kojiki" version, which says that "they made merry," and
explains that this was with the object of recalling the dead to life, perhaps in

Before this, when Ame-waka-hiko was in the Central Land of Reed-Plains, he was on terms of friendship with Aji-suki [1]-taka-hiko-ne no Kami. Therefore Aji-suki-taka-hiko-ne no Kami ascended to Heaven and offered condolence on his decease. Now this God was exactly like in appearance to Ame-waka-hiko when he was alive, and therefore Ame-waka-hiko's parents, relations, wife, and children all said :—" Our Lord is still alive," and clung to his garments and to his girdle, partly rejoiced and partly distracted. Then Aji-suki-taka-hiko-ne no Kami became flushed with anger and said :—" The way of friends is such that it is right that mutual condolence should be made. Therefore I have not been daunted by the pollution, but have come from afar to make mourning. Why then should I be mistaken for a dead person ? " So he drew his sword, Oho-ha-kari,[2] which he had in his girdle, and cut down the mortuary house, which fell to earth and became a mountain. It is now in the province of Mino, by the upper waters of the River Ayumi. This is the mountain of Moyama (mourning moun- II. 7. tain). This is why people take care not to mistake a living for a dead person.

After this, Taka-mi-musubi no Mikoto again assembled all the Gods that they might select some one to send to the Central Land of Reed-Plains. They all said :—" It will be well to send Futsu-nushi [3] no Kami, son of Iha-tsutsu no wo [4] and Iha-tsutsu no me, the children of Iha-saku-ne-saku [5] no Kami."

imitation of the Gods dancing and making merry in order to entice the Sun-Goddess from her rock-cave. Compare the following passage from a Chinese History of the Han (A.D. 25-220) Dynasty.

In Japan " Mourning lasts for some ten days only, during which time the members of the family weep and lament, whilst their friends come singing, dancing and making music."

The mortuary house was required for the temporary disposal of the dead, while the sepulchral mound with its megalithic chamber was being constructed. *Vide* Index—Misasagi.

[1] No satisfactory explanation of this name.   [2] Great-leaf-mower.

[3] Futsu is explained by Hirata as an onomatopoetic word like the modern futtsuri for the abrupt snapping sound produced when anything is cleanly cut or broken off. Nushi means master.

[4] Iha-tsutsu. Iha is rock, tsutsu probably a honorific=elder. Wo is male ; me, female.

[5] Iha-saku means rock-split ; ne-saku, root-split.

Now there were certain Gods dwelling in the Rock-cave of Heaven, viz. Mika no Haya-hi[1] no Kami, son of Idzu no wobashiri[2] no Kami, Hi no Haya-hi no Kami, son of Mika no Haya-hi no Kami, and Take-mika-dzuchi no Kami,[3] son of Hi no Haya-hi no Kami. The latter God came forward and said:—"Is Futsu-nushi no Kami alone to be reckoned a hero? And am I not a hero?" His words were animated by a spirit of indignation. He was therefore associated with Futsu-nushi no Kami and made to subdue the Central Land of Reed-Plains. The two Gods thereupon descended and arrived at the Little Shore[4] of Itasa, in the Land of Idzumo. Then they drew their ten-span swords, and stuck them upside down in the earth, and sitting on their points questioned Oho-na-mochi no Kami, saying:—"Taka-mi-musubi no Mikoto wishes to send down his August Grandchild to preside over this country as its Lord. He has therefore sent us two Gods to clear out and pacify it. What is thy intention? Wilt thou stand aside or no?" Then Oho-na-mochi no Kami answered and said:—"I must ask my son before I reply to you." At this time his son Koto-shiro-nushi no Kami was absent on an excursion to Cape Miho in the Land of Idzumo, where he was amusing himself by angling for fish.

II. 8.   Some say:—"He was amusing himself by catching birds."
He therefore took the many-handed boat of Kumano,
[Another name is the Heavenly Pigeon-boat.]
and placing on board of it his messenger, Inase-hagi,[5] he despatched him, and announced to Koto-shiro-nushi no Kami the declaration of Taka-mi-musubi no Kami. He also inquired what language he should use in answer. Now Koto-shiro-nushi no Kami spoke to the messenger, and said:—"The Heavenly Deity has now addressed us this inquiry.[6] My father

---

[1] Mika is explained by Hirata as the same as ika, terrible; haya-hi means swift sun.

[2] Idzu no wo-bashiri, lit. dread-of-male-run.

[3] Take-mika-dzuchi. Take is brave. Mika-dzuchi is identified with ika-dzuchi, thunder.

[4] Wobama.

[5] Hirata points out the appropriateness of this name, which means "Yes or no?—shanks," to a messenger sent to ask a question.

[6] The Chinese character indicates a communication from an Emperor.

ought respectfully to withdraw, nor will I make any opposition."
So he made in the sea an eight-fold fence of green branches, and
stepping on the bow of the boat, went off.[1] The messenger returned and reported the result of his mission. Then Oho-na-
mochi no Kami said to the two Gods, in accordance with the
words of his son :—" My son, on whom I rely, has already
departed. I, too, will depart. If I were to make resistance all
the Gods of this Land would certainly resist also. But as I
now respectfully withdraw, who else will be so bold as to refuse
submission ? " So he took the broad spear which he had used
as a staff when he was pacifying the land and gave it to the
two Gods, saying :—" By means of this spear I was at last
successful. If the Heavenly Grandchild will use this spear to II. 9.
rule the land, he will undoubtedly subdue it to tranquillity. I
am now about to withdraw to the concealment of the short-of-a-
hundred [2]-eighty road-windings." [3] Having said these words, he
at length became concealed.[4] Thereupon the two Gods put to
death all the rebellious spirits and Deities.

One version says :—" The two Gods at length put to
death the malignant Deities and the tribes of herbs, trees and
rocks. When all had been subdued, the only one who refused submission was the Star-God Kagase-wo.[5] There-

" Went off " is the same character as is translated " withdraw " above.
Hirata understands this of his death. The whole episode is related quite
differently in the " Kojiki." *Vide* Ch. K., p. 101.

Enclosures of bamboo are used at the present day to trap fishes, but it is
not very clear why one is introduced here.

[2] A mere epithet or pillow-word (makura-kotoba) of eighty.

[3] The eighty-road-windings are put for a long journey, i.e. to Yomi or
Hades, or rather for Yomi itself.

[4] i.e. died.

[5] Kagase-wo. Wo means male. Kaga is obviously connected with
kagayaku, to shine. This is the only Star-God mentioned in Japanese myth,
and it may be noted that little honour is shown him. He is described as a
conquered rebel, and has neither Kami nor Mikoto affixed to his name. The
only stars mentioned in the " Kojiki " or " Nihongi " are Venus, the Pleiades,
and the Weaver or Star *a* Lyrae, the latter being connected with a Chinese
legend.

The Weaver-God is literally, if we follow the Chinese character, the God
of Japanese striped stuffs. The interlinear " Kana " gives Shidzuri or
Shidori, from shidzu, cloth, and ori, weave, which is doubtless correct.

fore they sent the Weaver-God Take-ha-dzuchi no Mikoto also, upon which he rendered submission. The two Gods therefore ascended to Heaven."

Ultimately they reported the result of their mission.

Then Taka-mi-musubi no Mikoto took the coverlet which was on his true couch, and casting it over his August Grandchild, Amatsu-hiko-hiko-ho-ninigi no Mikoto, made him to descend. So the August Grandchild left his Heavenly Rock-seat, and with an awful [1] path-cleaving, clove his way through the eight-fold clouds of Heaven, and descended on the Peak of Takachiho of
II. 10. So [2] in Hiuga.

After this the manner of the progress of the August Grandchild was as follows :—From the Floating Bridge of Heaven on the twin summits of Kushibi, he took his stand on a level part of the floating sand-bank. Then he traversed the desert land of Sojishi from the Hill of Hitawo in his search for a country, until he came to Cape Kasasa, in Ata-no-nagaya. A certain man of that land appeared and gave his name as Koto-katsu-kuni-katsu Nagasa.[3] The August Grandchild inquired of him,
II. 11. saying :—" Is there a country, or not ? " He answered, and said : —" There is here a country. I pray thee roam through it at thy pleasure." The August Grandchild therefore went there and took up his abode. Now there was a fair maid in that land whose name was Ka-ashi-tsu-hime.

[Also called Kami Ata-tsu-hime or Ko no hana no saku-ya-hime.[4]]

Take-ha-dzuchi is brave-leaf-elder. It is not clear that this Weaver-God is the same as the Weaver star.

[1] The interlinear gloss has idzu, an obsolete word which means awful, holy, sacred. It is, I would suggest, the same root which appears in the name of the province Idzu-mo and in Idzu-shi in Tajima, also a seat of Shintō worship. Mo means quarter, as in yomo, the four quarters, everywhere, and shi is for ishi, stone. See Index—Idzu.

[2] It is this word which forms the second part of Kumaso, the general name of the tribes which inhabited the south of Kiushiu.

[3] Thing-excel-country-excel. Long-narrow.

[4] These names mean respectively Deer-reed-of-princess, Deity (or upper) Ata-of-princess and Tree-of-flower-of-blossom-princess, i.e. blossoming like the flowers of the trees. The last name is that by which she is called in the " Kojiki " (vide Ch. K., p. 115), and is the one best known.

The August Grandchild inquired of this fair maid, saying :—
" Whose daughter art thou ? " She answered and said :—" Thy
handmaiden [1] is the child of a Heavenly Deity by his marriage
with Oho-yama-tsu-mi Kami."

The August Grandchild accordingly favoured [2] her, whereupon in one night she became pregnant. But the August Grandchild was slow to believe this, and said :—" Heavenly Deity
though I am, how could I cause any one to become pregnant in
the space of one night ? That which thou hast in thy bosom is
assuredly not my child." Therefore Ka-ashi-tsu-hime was
wroth. She prepared a doorless [3] muro [4] (*called utsumuro*), and

---

[1] The use of the character meaning concubine as a pronoun of the first
person fem. is a Chinese idiom. The interlinear Kana version has yakko,
i.e. slave. Oho-yama-tsu-mi means the Great-mountain-body. Possibly it
should be taken here as a common noun, a mountain Deity.

[2] i.e. married her.

[3] It appears from the " Kojiki " that after going in she plastered up the
entrance.

[4] The character 室 which in Chinese means a house, a chamber, is, in
the older Japanese literature, generally, if not invariably, used to represent
the Japanese word muro. Another character used for this purpose is 窨, a
cellar. The muro is distinguished from the ihe, or ordinary dwelling. What
was the muro ? This term is nowadays applied to a gardener's forcing-
house, which in Japan consists of a pit four or five feet deep and roofed over.
Hi-muro means an ice-house. If the ice-houses in Japan (see drawing in
"San-sai-dzu-ye," IV., 19), so denominated, resemble those which I have seen
at Yang-hwa-chin in Corea, they were pits sunk several feet below the surface of the ground and covered with a heavy thatched roof. At the foot of
Mount Ohoyama there was to be seen, some years ago, a large rectangular
pit, three or four feet in depth, with a thatched roof sloping to the ground,
and no walls, which was occupied as a dwelling by the pilgrims to that
mountain. There are also pits in Corea covered with thatch or strong oil-
paper, which are used by the poorest classes as shelters. These are called
um, or um-mak. Pit-dwellers are also mentioned in the old Chinese literature. The references to the muro in the " Kojiki " and " Nihongi " show
that the muro of those days had a similar character. We read of Tsuchi-
gumo (earth-hiders, see Index) living in muro, of a muro being dug, and of
steps (down) to a muro. That they were sometimes of considerable size is
shown by the legend of Jimmu Tennō's reign, which speaks of 160 persons
being in a muro at the same time. The pit was (at least in some cases) not
simply roofed over, but contained a house with a wooden frame lashed
together with cords of a creeping vine (dolichos), the walls having sedges or
reeds for laths, and plastered with a mixture of grass and clay. The roof was

G

entering, dwelt therein. Then she made a solemn declaration, saying :—" If that which is in my bosom is not the offspring of the Heavenly Grandchild, it will assuredly be destroyed by fire, but if it is really the offspring of the Heavenly Grandchild, fire

thatched with reeds. The muro had a door opening inwards, and contained a raised platform for sleeping on. A dwelling closely answering this description was actually unearthed near Akita in Dewa in 1807.

Muro were used in ancient times by the higher as well as by the poorest classes. Sosa no wo no Mikoto is said by the Idzumo Fudoki to have made himself a muro, and Jimmu Tennō's son is represented as sleeping in a great muro. In modern times muro sometimes means simply chamber.

Some writers confound the muro with the ihaya. So far as I am aware, the latter is used only of caverns in the rock, or of the artificial megalithic chambers contained in sepulchral mounds.

Mr. J. Milne, in an extremely interesting paper on the pit-dwellers of Yezo, read before the Asiatic Society of Japan in 1882, argues that certain pits discovered by him in large numbers in the islands of Yezo and Itorup were the dwellings of a pre-Aino race, whose modern representatives are to be found amongst the Kurilsky or their neighbours in Kamschatka and Saghalin. To these he gives the name of Koro-pok-guru, following an Aino tradition communicated to him by Mr. Batchelor.

On the other hand, I am informed by Baron A. von Siebold, who visited several of these groups of pits in Kusiro and the Kurile Islands, that,—

1. Their appearance is, in his opinion, not consonant with the great antiquity assigned to them by Mr. Milne's theory. It was especially noticeable that no large trees or even deep-rooted brushwood were found growing in or between the square pits.

2. They are arranged in a regular order more suggestive of a military encampment than of the abodes of a tribe of savages. They are all of the same size, except a few larger ones, which may have been occupied by officers. An earthwork near one of them was also suggestive of a military occupation.

3. The pits were carefully dug and found to contain fragments of burned wood, unglazed pottery, and what is more remarkable, a small Japanese sword (tantō) of comparatively modern manufacture.

4. The most important evidence, however, is the fact that the sites of these pits correspond in all the cases which Baron von Siebold was able to examine with those of the military encampments established in Yezo and the Kuriles by the Japanese Government about the beginning of the present century as a defence against the Russians. These encampments are marked on a Japanese map presented to Ph. Fr. von Siebold (the father) by a Court astronomer named Mogami Toknai, and published in Siebold's Atlas. The inference is obvious. In fact pit-dwelling in northern climates affords no indication of race. It has been seen that Chinese, Japanese, and Coreans may all be pit-dwellers on occasion, and the practice is by no means confined to this part of the world.

cannot harm it." So she set fire to the muro. The child which was born from the extremity of the smoke which first arose was called Ho no Susori no Mikoto (*he was the ancestor of the Hayato*) ; next the child which was born when she drew back and remained away from the heat was called Hiko-ho-ho-demi no Mikoto ; the child which was next born was called Ho no akari no Mikoto (*he was the ancestor of the Wohari no Muraji*)—in all three children.[1]

II. 12.

A long time after, Ama-tsu-hiko hiko-ho-no-ninigi no Mikoto died, and was buried in the Misasagi[2] of Hiuga no ye in Tsukushi.

In one writing it is said :—" Ama-terasu no Oho-kami gave command unto Ame-waka-hiko, saying :—' The Central Land of Reed-Plains is a region which it is for my child to rule over. Considering, however, that there are there certain rebellious, violent and wicked Deities, do thou therefore go first and subdue it.' Accordingly she gave him the Heavenly deer-bow and the Heavenly true-deer-arrows, and so despatched him. Ame-waka-hiko, having received this command, went down and forthwith married many daughters of the Earthly Deities. Eight years passed, during which he made no report of his mission. Therefore Ama-terasu-no Oho-kami summoned Omohi-kane no Kami (the Thought-combiner) and inquired the reason why he did not come. Now the Thought-combining Deity reflected and in-formed her, saying :—' It will be well to send the pheasant to inquire into this.' Hereupon, in accordance with this God's device, the pheasant was caused to go and spy out the reason. The pheasant flew down and perched on the top of a many-branched cassia-tree before Ame-waka-hiko's

II. 13.

---

[1] The " Kojiki " gives these names differently. Ho no akari means fire-light. The other two are of doubtful interpretation. Perhaps Susori is from the word suso, skirt, and ho-ho-de may mean " go out from flames." This passage shows that the muro was used as an ubu-ya or parturition-house. It was the custom in ancient Japan for women to retire for their confinement to a temporary hut constructed for the purpose. Satow and Dickins found this practice still in vogue in the Island of Hachijō when they visited it in 1878. See " J. A. S. T.," vi. 3.

[2] See Index.

gate, where it uttered a cry, saying :—' Ama-waka-hiko!
wherefore for the space of eight years hast thou still not
made a report of thy mission?' Now a certain Earthly
Goddess, named Ama-no-sagu-me, saw the pheasant, and
said :—' A bird of evil cry is sitting on the top of this tree.
It will be well to shoot it and kill it.' So Ame-waka-hiko
took the Heavenly deer-bow and the Heavenly true deer-
arrow given him by the Heavenly Deity and shot it, upon
which the arrow went through the pheasant's breast, and
finally reached the place where the Heavenly Deity was.
Now the Heavenly Deity seeing the arrow, said :—' This
arrow I formerly gave to Ame-waka-hiko. Why has it come
here?' So she took the arrow, and pronouncing a curse
over it, said :—' If it has been shot with evil intent, let
mischief surely come upon Ama-waka-hiko; but if it has
been shot with a tranquil heart, let no harm befall him.'
So she flung it back. It fell down and struck Ame-waka-
hiko on the top of the breast, so that he straightway died.
This is the reason why people at the present day say,
' Fear a returning arrow.' Now Ame-waka-hiko's wife and
children came down from Heaven and went away upwards
taking with them the dead body. Then they made a
mourning house in Heaven, in which they deposited it and
lamented over it. Before this Ame-waka-hiko was on
friendly terms with Aji-suki-taka-hiko-ne no Kami.
Therefore Aji-suki-taka-hiko-ne no Kami ascended to
Heaven and condoled with them on the mourning, lamenting greatly. Now this God had by nature an exact
resemblance to Ame-waka-hiko in appearance. Therefore
Ame-waka-hiko's wife and children, when they saw him,
rejoiced, and said :—' Our Lord is still alive.' And they
clung to his robe and to his girdle, and could not be thrust
away. Now Aji-suki-taka-hiko ne no Kami became angry,
and said :—' My friend is dead, therefore have I come to
make condolence. Why then should I be mistaken for a
dead man?' So he drew his ten-span sword and cut
down the mourning house, which fell to earth and became
a mountain. This is Moyama (Mount Mourning) in the
province of Mino. This is the reason why people dislike
to be mistaken for a dead person.

Now the glory of Aji-suki-taka-hiko ne no Mikoto was so effulgent that it illuminated the space of two hills and two valleys, and those assembled for the mourning celebrated it in song, saying :—

[Another version is that Aji-suki-taka-hiko-ne no Kami's younger sister, Shita-teru-hime, wishing to make known to the company that it was Aji-suki-taka-hiko ne no Mikoto who illuminated the hills and valleys therefore made a song, saying :—]

> Like the string of jewels
> Worn on the neck
> Of the Weaving-maiden,
> That dwells in Heaven—
> Oh ! the lustre of the jewels
> Flung across two valleys
> From Aji-suki-taka-hiko-ne !^[1]

Again they sang, saying :—

> To the side-pool—
> The side-pool
> Of the rocky stream
> Whose narrows are crossed
> By the country wenches
> Afar from Heaven,
> Come hither, come hither !
> (The women are fair)
> And spread across thy net
> In the side-pool
> Of the rocky stream.^[2]

These two poems are in what is now called a Rustic^[3] measure.

---

[1] The metre is irregular. The " Kojiki " version (see Ch. K., p. 99) is somewhat different. The Weaving-maiden of Heaven is a Chinese personification of the Star a Lyrae. See Mayers' " Chinese Manual," p. 97. This affords some indication of the date of this poem. It must have been written after the Japanese became familiar with Chinese astronomy.

[2] The metre is irregular, the text doubtful, and the meaning and application obscure. I agree with the Japanese critics who think that this poem has no business here. The " Kojiki," which gives the previous one, omits it.

Afar from Heaven is a mere epithet (makura-kotoba) of the country. Heaven here stands for the capital.

[3] Probably because hina, country or rustic, is a prominent word in the latter of these two poems.

After this Ama-terasu no Oho-kami united Yorodzu-hata Toyo-aki-tsu-hime, the younger sister of Omohi-kane no Kami to Masa-ya-a-katsu-katsu-no-haya-hi no Ama no Oshi-ho-mimi no Mikoto, and making her his consort, caused them to descend to the Central Land of Reed-Plains. At this time Katsu-no-haya-hi no Ama no Oshi-ho-mimi no Mikoto stood on the floating bridge of Heaven, and glancing downwards, said :—'Is that country tranquillized yet? No! it is a tumble-down land, hideous to look upon.' So he ascended, and reported why he had not gone down. Therefore, Ama-terasu no Oho-kami further sent Taka-mika-tsuchi no Kami and Futsu-nushi no Kami first to clear it. Now these two Gods went down and arrived at Idzumo, where they inquired of Oho-na-mochi no Mikoto, saying : -- ' Wilt thou deliver up this country to the Heavenly Deity or not?' He answered and said : — ' My son, Koto-shiro-nushi is at Cape Mitsu for the sport of bird-shooting. I will ask him, and then give you an answer.' So he sent a messenger to make inquiry, who brought answer and said :—' How can we refuse to deliver up what is demanded by the Heavenly Deity?' Therefore Oho-na-mochi no Kami replied to the two Gods in the words of his son. The two Gods thereupon ascended to Heaven and reported the result of their mission, saying :— ' All the Central Land of Reed-Plains is now completely tranquillized.' Now Ama-terasu no Oho-kami gave command, saying :—' If that be so, I will send down my child.' She was about to do so, when in the meantime, an August Grandchild was born, whose name was called Ama-tsu-hiko-hiko-ho-no-ninigi no Mikoto. Her son represented to her that he wished the August Grandchild to be sent down in his stead. Therefore Ama-terasu no Oho-kami gave to Ama-tsu-hiko-hiko-ho no ninigi no Mikoto the three treasures, viz. the curved jewel of Yasaka gem, the eight-hand mirror, and the sword Kusanagi, and joined to him as his attendants Ame no Koyane no Mikoto, the first ancestor of the Naka-tomi, Futo-dama no Mikoto, the first ancestor of the Imbe, Ame no Uzume no Mikoto, the first ancestor of the Sarume,[1] Ishi-kori-dome no Mikoto,

---

[1] Lit. monkey-eye.

the first ancestor of the mirror-makers, and Tamaya no Mikoto, the first ancestor of the jewel-makers, in all Gods of five Be. Then she commanded her August Grandchild, saying:—'This Reed-plain-1500-autumns-fair-rice-ear Land is the region which my descendants shall be lords of. Do thou, my August Grandchild, proceed thither and govern it. Go! and may prosperity attend thy dynasty, and may it, like Heaven and Earth, endure for ever.' When he was about to descend, one, who had been sent in advance to clear the way, returned and said:—' There is one God who dwells at the eight-cross-roads of Heaven, the length of whose nose is seven hands, the length of whose back is more than seven fathoms. Moreover, a light shines from his mouth and from his posteriors. His eye-balls are like an eight-hand mirror and have a ruddy glow like the Aka-kagachi.' Thereupon he sent one of his attendant Deities II. 17. to go and make inquiry. Now among all the eighty myriads of Deities there was not one who could confront him and make inquiry. Therefore he specially commanded Ame no Uzume, saying:—' Thou art superior to others in the power of thy looks. Thou hadst better go and ques-tion him.' So Ame no Uzume forthwith bared her breasts and, pushing down the band of her garment below her navel, confronted him with a mocking laugh. Then the God of the cross-ways asked her, saying: —'Ame no Uzume! What meanest thou by this behaviour?' She answered and said:—' I venture to ask who art thou that dost thus remain in the road by which the child of Ama-terasu no Oho-kami is to make his progress?' The God of the cross-ways answered and said:—' I have heard that the child of Ama-terasu no Oho-kami is now about to de-scend, and therefore I have come respectfully to meet and attend upon him. My name is Saruta-hiko no Oho-kami.'[1] Then Ame no Uzume again inquired of him, saying:— ' Wilt thou go before me, or shall I go before thee?' He answered and said:—" I will go before and be his harbinger.' Ame no Uzume asked again, saying:— " Whither wilt thou go and whither will the August Grand-child go?' He answered and said:—' The child of the

---

[1] In later times a phallic Deity.

Heavenly Deity will proceed to the peak of Kushifuru of
Takachiho in Hiuga in the Land of Tsukushi, and I will

go to the upper waters of the River Isuzu at Sanada in Ise.
He accordingly said :—' Thou art the person who didst
discover me. Thou must therefore escort me and com-

Saruta-hiko and Uzume.

plete thy task.' Ame no Uzume returned and reported
these circumstances. Thereupon the August Grandchild,
leaving the Heavenly rock-seat, and thrusting apart the
eight-piled clouds of Heaven, clove his way with an awful
way-cleaving, and descended from Heaven. Finally, as

had been arranged, the August Grandchild arrived at the peak of Kushifuru of Takachiho in Hiuga, in the land of Tsukushi. And Saruta-hiko no Kami forthwith proceeded to the upper waters of the River Isuzu at Sanada in Ise. Ame no Uzume no Mikoto, in accordance with the request made by Saruta[1] hiko no Kami, attended upon him. Now the August Grandchild commanded Ame no Uzume no Mikoto, saying :—' Let the name of the Deity whom thou didst discover be made thy title.' Therefore he conferred on her the designation of Sarume no Kimi.[2] So this was the origin of the male and female Lords of Sarume being both styled Kimi." [3]

In one writing it is said :—" The Heavenly Deity sent II. 19. Futsu-nushi no Kami and Take-mika-tsuchi no Kami to tranquillize the Central Land of Reed-Plains. Now these two Gods said :—' In Heaven there is an Evil Deity called Ama-tsu-mika-hoshi, or Ame no Kagase-wo. We pray that this Deity may be executed before we go down to make clear the Central Land of Reed-Plains.' At this time Iwahi-nushi[4] no Kami received the designation of Iwahi no Ushi. This is the God which now dwells in the land of

---

[1] Monkey-field.   [2] Lord of Sarume.

[3] The " Kojiki " says that it was the females alone who had this title. In either case, the inference is that it was unusual for women to have such names or titles, Motowori's opinion to the contrary notwithstanding.

The Sarume were primarily women who performed comic dances (sarumahi or monkey-dances) in honour of the Gods. They are mentioned along with the Nakatomi and Imbe as taking part in the festival of first-fruits and other Shintō ceremonies. These dances were the origin of the Kagura and Nō performances. Another function of the Sarume is that indicated in the part taken by Uzume no Mikoto when the Gods enticed the Sun-Goddess out of her rock-cave. She is there said to have been divinely inspired. This divine inspiration has always been common in Japan. The inspired person falls into a trance, or hypnotic state, in which he or she speaks in the character of some God. Such persons are now known as Miko, defined by Hepburn as ' a woman who, dancing in a Miya, pretends to hold communication with the Gods and the spirits of the dead,' in short a medium. There are also strolling mediums, as in England, women of a low class, who pretend to deliver messages from deceased friends or relatives. See Lowell's " Esoteric Shinto," in the " J. A. S. T.," and Index—Inspiration.

[4] Master of religious abstinence or worship.

Katori in Adzuma.[1] After this the two Deities descended
and arrived at the Little Shore of Itasa in Idzumo, and
asked Oho-na-mochi no Kami, saying :—'Wilt thou
deliver up this country to the Heavenly Deity, or no?'
He answered and said :—' I suspected that ye two gods were
coming to my place. Therefore I will not allow it.' Thereupon Futsu-nushi no Kami forthwith returned upwards, and
made his report. Now Taka-mi-musubi no Mikoto sent
the two Gods back again, and commanded Oho-na-mochi
no Mikoto, saying :—' Having now heard what thou hast
said, I find that there is profound reason in thy words.
Therefore again I issue my commands to thee more circum-
stantially, that is to say :—Let the public matters which
thou hast charge of be conducted by my grandchild, and
do thou rule divine affairs. Moreover, if thou wilt dwell
in the palace of Ama no Hi-sumi,[2] I will now build it for
thee. I will take a thousand fathom rope[3] of the (bark of
the) paper mulberry, and tie it in 180 knots. As to the
dimensions of the building of the palace,[4] its pillars shall
be high and massy, and its planks broad and thick. I will
also cultivate thy rice-fields for thee, and, for thy provision
when thou goest to take pleasure on the sea, I will make
for thee a high bridge, a floating bridge, and also a
Heavenly bird-boat. Moreover, on the Tranquil River of
Heaven I will make a flying-bridge. I will also make for
thee white shields[5] of 180 seams, and Ame no Ho-hi no
Mikoto shall be the president of the festivals in thy honour.'
Hereupon Oho-na-mochi no Kami answered and said :—
' The instructions of the Heavenly Deity are so courteous
that I may not presume to disobey his commands. Let
the August Grandchild direct the public affairs of which I
have charge. I will retire and direct secret matters.' So
he introduced Kunado no Kami to the two Gods, saying :—

---

[1] A general name for the eastern part of Japan.

[2] Heaven-sun-corner.

[3] The rope was for measuring the site, say some. Or it may have been for
lashing together the timbers of the building.

[4] Or shrine.

[5] Shields are frequently mentioned in the " Norito " among offerings to the
Gods.

' He will take my place and will yield respectful obedience.
I will withdraw and depart from here.' He forthwith
invested him with the pure Yasaka jewels, and then became
concealed for ever.[1] Therefore Futsu-nushi no Kami appointed Kunado no Kami[2] as guide, and went on a circuit II. 21.
of pacification. Any who were rebellious to his authority
he put to death, while those who rendered obedience
were rewarded. The chiefs of those who at this time
rendered obedience were Oho-mono-nushi[3] no Kami and
Koto-shiro-nushi no Kami. So they assembled the eighty
myriads of Gods in the High Market-place of Heaven, and
taking them up to Heaven with them, they declared their
loyal behaviour. Then Taka-mi-musubi no Mikoto commanded Oho-mono-nushi no Kami, saying:—' If thou dost
take to wife one of the Deities of Earth, I shall still consider that thy heart is disaffected. I will therefore now give
thee my daughter Mi-ho-tsu hime to be thy wife. Take with
thee the eighty myriads of Deities to be the guards of my
August Grandchild to all ages. So she sent him down
again. Thereupon Ta-oki-ho-ohi no Kami, ancestor of the
Imbe of the Land of Kii, was appointed hatter,[4] Hiko-sachi
no Kami was made shield-maker,[5] Ma-hitotsu no Kami[6]
was made metal-worker, Ame no Hi-washi[7] no Kami was
appointed tree-fibre maker, and Kushi-akaru-dama no Kami
ewel-maker.[8]   II. 22.

Taka-mi-musubi no Kami accordingly gave command,
saying:—' I will set up a Heavenly divine fence[9] and a

---

[1] i.e. died.   [2] The Deity of roads.   [3] Great-thing-master.
[4] Kasa-nuhi, i.e. broad-hat-sewer.
[5] Tate-nuhi, lit. shield-sewer.
[6] The one-eyed God. It is curious that the Smith-God of Japan, like the
Cyclops of Greek fable, should have but one eye. The "Kojiki" calls him
Ama-tsu Mara, as to which see Index. Also Ch. K., p. 55.
[7] Sun-eagle. Tree-fibre is yufu. It was the fibre for weaving made of
the inner bark of the paper-mulberry, and perhaps also included hemp. All
these objects were used in Shintō ceremonies.
[8] Kushi means comb; akaru, shining; dama (for tama), jewel.
[9] In Japanese, himorogi. The "Shiki" says that this is the same thing which
is now called a shrine, but admits that its meaning is not clear. The usual
interpretation is that the himorogi is a fence of sakaki (the sacred tree)

Heavenly rock-boundary wherein to practise religious abstinence [1] on behalf of my descendants. Do ye, Ame no Koyane no Mikoto and Futo-dama [2] no Mikoto, take with you the Heavenly divine fence, and go down to the Central Land of Reed-Plains. Moreover, ye will there practise abstinence [3] on behalf of my descendants.' So she attached the two Deities to Ame no Oshi-ho-mi-mi no Mikoto and sent them down. It was when Futo-dama no Mikoto was sent that the custom first began of worshipping this Deity with stout straps [4] flung over weak shoulders when taking the place of the Imperial hand. From this, too, the custom had its origin, by which Ame no Koyane no Mikoto had charge of divine matters. Therefore he was

planted round the enclosure consecrated for Shintō worship. But this interpretation is not without difficulty. In Suinin Tennō's reign we hear of a himorogi which was brought over from Corea and preserved as a sacred treasure. This could hardly have been a hedge. Another interpretation makes the himorogi an offering, and interprets the " Kuma " himorogi of the passage just referred to as an offering of bear's paws, one of the eight dainties of ancient Chinese literature. But it is not easy to see how this should be preserved as a sacred treasure.

The derivation does not help us much. Hi is no doubt sun, used metaphorically, as in hi-kagami, sun-mirror or sacred-mirror ; hiko, sun-child (prince); hime, sun-female (princess). This is fairly well represented by the Chinese character 神 in the text. The remainder of the word, viz. morogi, is probably moro, a word of multitude, all, many, and gi (for ki), wood. There is a proper name, Take-morogi, where morogi is written with characters which imply this derivation. Hi-moro-gi is therefore a sacred row or group of sticks of some sort or another.

I may mention a suspicion that the himorogi may be connected, perhaps by way of a survival, with a time when the Japanese Deities were a row of posts roughly carved into human shape. See above, p. 3.

[1] This and other passages show that the Shintō place of worship might be merely a piece of ground enclosed for the purpose. The modern word for a Shintō shrine, viz. ya-shiro, house-enclosure or house-area, suggests the same inference. See Satow, " Japanese Rituals," in " T.A.S.J.," Vol. VII., Pt. II., p. 115. It will be remembered that the Roman templum and the Greek τέμενος had originally a similar signification.

[2] The ancestor of the Imbe, or abstainers.

[3] Including avoidance of ceremonial impurities, and hence used for religious worship generally. See above, note to p. 41.

[4] For supporting a tray on which the offerings were placed. See " T.A.S.J.," Vol. VII., p. 112.

made to divine by means of the Greater Divination, and thus to do his service.[1]

At this time Ama-terasu no Oho-kami took in her hand II. 23· the precious mirror, and, giving it to Ame no Oshi-ho-mi-mi no Mikoto, uttered a prayer, saying :—' My child, when thou lookest upon this mirror, let it be as if thou wert looking on me. Let it be with thee on thy couch and in thy hall, and let it be to thee a holy[2] mirror.' Moreover, she gave command to Ame no Ko-yane no Mikoto and to Futo-dama no Mikoto, saying :—' Attend to me, ye two Gods! Do ye also remain together in attendance and guard it well.' She further gave command, saying :—' I will give over to my child the rice-ears of the sacred garden,[3] of which I partake in the Plain of High Heaven.' And she straightway took the daughter of Taka-mi-musubi no Mikoto, by name Yorodzu-hata-hime, and uniting her to Ame no Oshi-ho-mi-mi no Mikoto as his consort, sent her down. Therefore while she was still in the Void of Heaven,[4] she gave birth to a child, who was called Ama-tsu-hiko-ho no ninigi no Mikoto. She accordingly desired to send down this grandchild instead of his parents. Therefore on him she bestowed Ame no Ko-yane no Mikoto, Futo-dama no Mikoto, and the Deities of the various Be,[5] all without exception. She gave him, moreover, the things belonging to his person,[6] just as above stated.

After this, Ame no Oshi-ho-mi-mi no Mikoto went back again to Heaven. Therefore Ama-tsu-hiko-ho no ninigi no

---

[1] The Greater Divination was by observing the cracks in a deer's shoulder-blade which had been exposed to fire. This is also a practice of the Chinese and Mongols, but in China it is more common to use the shell of a tortoise for this purpose, as is sometimes done in Japan also. See Legge's "Chinese Classics," Vol. III., p. 335, 336. Ban Nobutomo has devoted a work in two volumes to this subject, entitled 正 卜 考.

[2] The same word as is used above for religious abstinence.

[3] The yu-niha, in which rice was grown under conditions of strict ceremonial purity for the festival of first-fruits.

[4] Not the Takama no hara, or Plain of High Heaven, but the Oho-sora or Great Void, the space between Heaven and Earth. She was on her way downwards.

[5] The hatter, shield-maker, etc., mentioned above.

[6] The regalia, or mirror, sword and jewel are doubtless meant.

Mikoto descended to the peak of Takachiho of Kushibi in Hiuga. Then he passed through the Land of Munasohi,[1] in Sojishi, by way of the Hill of Hitawo, in search of a country, and stood on a level part of the floating sandbank. Thereupon he called to him Koto-katsu-kuni-katsu-Nagasa, the Lord of that country, and made inquiry of him. He answered and said :—' There is a country here. I will in any case obey thy commands.' Accordingly the August Grandchild erected a palace-hall and rested here. Walking afterwards by the sea-shore, he saw a beautiful woman. The August Grandchild inquired of her, saying:—' Whose child art thou ? ' She answered and said :—' Thy handmaiden is the child of Oho-yama-tsu-mi no Kami. My name is Kami-ataka-ashi-tsu-hime, and I am also called Ko-no-hana-saku-ya-hime.' Then she said:—' I have also an elder sister named Iha-naga-hime.'[2] The August Grandchild said :—' I wish to make thee my wife. How will this be ? ' She answered and said :—' I have a father, Oho-yama-tsu-mi no Kami, I pray thee ask him. The August Grandchild accordingly spake to Oho-yama-tsu-mi no Kami, saying:—' I have seen thy daughter and wish to make her my wife.' Hereupon Oho-yama-tsu-mi no Kami sent his two daughters with one hundred tables of food and drink to offer them respectfully. Now the August Grandchild thought the elder sister ugly, and would not take her. So she went away. But the younger sister was a noted beauty. So he took her with him and favoured her, and in one night she became pregnant. Therefore Iha-naga-hime was greatly ashamed, and cursed him, saying :—' If the August Grandchild had taken me and not rejected me, the children born to him would have been long-lived, and would have endured for ever like the massy rocks. But seeing that he has not done so, but has married my younger sister only, the children born to him will surely be decadent like the flowers of the trees.' ''

One version is :—" Iha-naga-hime, in her shame and

---

[1] Above, p. 70, we have Muna-kuni or desert land.

[2] Rock-long-princess. Ko-no-hana-saku-ya-hime is the " Princess who blossoms like the flowers of the trees."

resentment, spat and wept. She said :—' The race of
visible mankind shall change swiftly like the flowers of
the trees, and shall decay and pass away.' This is the
reason why the life of man is so short.

After this, Kami-ataka-ashi-tsu-hime saw the August
Grandchild, and said :—' Thy handmaiden has conceived
a child by the August Grandchild. It is not meet that it
should be born privately.' The August Grandchild said :
—' Child of the Heavenly Deity though I am, how could I
in one night cause anyone to be with child ? Now it cannot be my child.' Kono-hana-saku-ya-hime was exceedingly ashamed and angry. She straightway made a doorless muro, and thereupon made a vow, saying :—' If the
child which I have conceived is the child of another Deity,
may it surely be unfortunate. But if it is truly the offspring of the Heavenly Grandchild, may it surely be alive and
unhurt.' So she entered the muro, and burnt it with fire.
At this time, when the flames first broke out, a child was
born who was named Ho-no-susori no Mikoto ; next when
the flame reached its height, a child was born who was
named Ho-no-akari no Mikoto. The next child which was
born was called Hiko-ho-ho-demi no Mikoto,[1] and also
Ho-no-wori no Mikoto."

In one writing it is said :—" When the flames first be-
became bright, a child was born named Ho-no-akari no
Mikoto ; next, when the blaze was at its height, a child was
born named Ho-no-susumi[2] no Mikoto, also called Ho-no-
suseri no Mikoto ; next, when she recoiled from the blaze,
a child was born named Ho-no-ori-hiko-ho-ho-demi no
Mikoto—three children in all. The fire failed to harm them,
and the mother, too, was not injured in the least. Then
with a bamboo knife she cut their navel-strings.[3] From
the bamboo knife which she threw away, there eventually

II. 25.

---

[1] Ho-ho-demi no Mikoto. The word Mikoto is here written with a different
and more honourable character than in the case of his two brothers, for the
reason that this Deity was the direct ancestor of the Mikados. See above,
p. 3.

[2] Flame-advance.

[3] A note to the Shukai edition mentions a local custom of severing the
umbilical cord with a bamboo or copper knife. Another custom is not to use

sprang up a bamboo grove. Therefore that place was called Taka-ya.[1]

Now Kami-ataka-ashi-tsu-hime by divination fixed upon a rice-field to which she gave the name Sanada, and from the rice grown there brewed Heavenly sweet sake, with which she entertained him. Moreover, with the rice from the Nunada rice-field she made boiled rice and entertained him therewith."[2]

In one writing it is said :—" Taka-mi-musubi no Mikoto took the coverlet which was on the true couch and wrapped in it Ama-tsu-hiko-kuni-teru-hiko-ho no ninigi no Mikoto, who forthwith drew open the rock-door of Heaven, and thrusting asunder the eight-piled clouds of Heaven, descended. At this time Ama-no-oshi-hi no Mikoto, the ancestor of the Oho-tomo[3] no Muraji, taking with him Ame-kushi-tsu Oho-kume, the ancestor of the Kume Be,[4] placed on his back the rock-quiver of Heaven, drew on his

a knife, but to bite it through, a thin garment being interposed. It should be breathed on seven times with warm breath before being tied.

Superstition and Ritual have a preference for knives of some more primitive material than iron. Medea shears her magic herbs "curvamine falcis ahenæ," and Zipporah performs the rite of circumcision with a sharp stone. But a more prosaic explanation of the present passage is suggested by a surgeon friend. There is less hæmorrhage when a blunt instrument is used.

[1] Bamboo-house.

[2] This incident is the mythical counterpart of the annual festival of Nihinahe or nihi-name, now celebrated on November 23rd, when the new season's rice is offered to the Gods and partaken of by the Emperor for the first time. It was grown in plots of ground (yu-niha), the position of which was fixed upon by divination and prepared under strict conditions of ceremonial purity. Nihi means new, n represents no, the genitive particle, and ahe means feast. Name means to taste.

The modern name of this festival is Shin-jō-sai. There is a similar one in China. In ancient times there was no distinction made between this and the Oho-nihe or Oho-name, when the Emperor at his accession offered rice to the Gods (now called the Daijōye), both being called Oho-nihe. The prayer read at the Nihi-name is given among the norito in the Yengishiki, and Hirata devotes the last three vols. of the " Koshiden " to this subject.

[3] Great escort, i.e. of the Emperor.

[4] I quite endorse Chamberlain's shrewd suggestion that this Kume is " nothing more nor less than an ancient mispronunciation of the Chinese word chün (軍), the modern Japanese gun, army, troops." The Oho-tomo were the Imperial guards. *Vide* Ch. K., p. 112.

forearm a dread loud-sounding elbow-pad,[1] and grasped in his hand a Heavenly vegetable-wax-tree bow and a Heavenly feathered arrow, to which he added an eight-eyed sounding-arrow.[2] Moreover he girt on his mallet-headed sword,[3] and taking his place before the Heavenly Grand- II. 27. child, proceeded downwards as far as the floating bridge of Heaven, which is on the two peaks of Kushibi of Takachiho in So in Hiuga. Then he stood on a level part of the floating sand-bank and passed through the desert land

Stone Mallets.

of Sojishi by way of Hitawo in search of a country until he came to Cape Kasasa in Ata no Nagaya. Now at this place there was a God named Koto-katsu-kuni-katsu-Nagasa. Therefore the Heavenly Grandchild inquired of this God, saying :—' Is there a country ? ' He answered and said : — ' There is.' Accordingly he said :—' I will yield it up to thee in obedience to thy commands.' Therefore the Heavenly Grandchild abode in that place. This Koto-katsu-kuni-katsu no Kami

---

[1] See above, p. 34.

[2] Or nari-kabura. Giles says they were discharged by bandits as a signal to begin an attack. "Eight-eyed" means that there were several holes in the head, the air passing through which produced a humming sound. Parker says that the nari-kabura is not Chinese, but an invention of the Huns.

[3] From the way in which these swords are associated with "stone-mallet" swords in the Jimmu Tennō narrative (see also Ch. K., pp. 112, 142), I am disposed to think that they were of stone, and probably identical with the mallet-shaped objects called raiko shown in Plate XI. of Kanda's "Stone Implements of Japan," from which the illustration is taken. They were, no doubt, lashed to wooden handles, and used as weapons.

H

was the child of Izanagi no Mikoto, and his other name is Shiho-tsu-tsu-no oji." [1]

In one writing it is said:—" The Heavenly Grandchild favoured Ataka-ashi-tsu-hime, the daughter of Oho-yama-tsu-mi no Kami. In one night she became pregnant, and eventually gave birth to four children. Therefore Ataka-ashi-tsu-hime took the children in her arms, and, coming forward, said:—' Ought the children of the Heavenly Grandchild to be privately nurtured? Therefore do I announce to thee the fact for thy information.' At this time the Heavenly Grandchild looked upon the children, and, with a mocking laugh, said:—' Excellent—these princes of mine! Their birth is a delightful piece of news!' Therefore Ataka-ashi-tsu-hime was wroth, and said:— ' Why dost thou mock thy handmaiden?' The Heavenly Grandchild said:—' There is surely some doubt of this, and therefore did I mock. How is it possible for me, Heavenly God though I am, in the space of one night to cause anyone to become pregnant? Truly they are not my ɪchildren.' On this account Ataka-ashi-tsu-hime was more and more resentful. She made a doorless muro, into which she entered, and made a vow, saying:—' If the children which I have conceived are not the offspring of the Heavenly Grandchild, let them surely perish. But if they are the offspring of the Heavenly Grandchild, let them suffer no hurt.' So she set fire to the muro and burnt it. When the fire first became bright, a child sprang forth and announced himself, saying:—' Here am I, the child of the Heavenly Deity, and my name is Ho-no-akari no Mikoto. Where is my father?' Next, the child who sprang forth when the fire was at its height also announced himself, saying:—' Here am I, the child of the Heavenly Deity, and my name is Ho-no-susumi no Mikoto. Where are my father and my elder brother?' Next, the child who sprang forth when the flames were becoming extinguished also announced himself, saying:—' Here am I, the child of the Heavenly Deity, and my name is Ho-no-ori no Mikoto. Where are my father and my elder brothers?' Next, when she recoiled from the heat, a child sprang forth, and

II. 28.

_____
[1] Old man of the sea.

also announced himself, saying :—' Here am I, the child of the Heavenly Deity, and my name is Hiko-ho-ho-demi no Mikoto. Where are my father and my elder brothers?' After that, their mother, Ataka-ashi-tsu-hime, came forth from amidst the embers, and approaching, told him, saying :—' The children which thy handmaiden has brought forth, and thy handmaiden herself, have of our own accord undergone the danger of fire,[1] and yet have suffered not the smallest hurt. Will the Heavenly Grandchild not look on them?' He answered and said :—' I knew from the first that they were my children, only, as they were conceived in one night, I thought that there might be suspicions, and I wished to let everybody know that they are my children, and also that a Heavenly Deity can cause pregnancy in one night. Moreover, I wished to make it evident that thou dost possess a wonderful and extraordinary dignity, and also that our children have surpassing spirit. Therefore it was that on a former day I used words of mockery.' "

In one writing it is said :—" Ame no Oshi-ho-ne no Mikoto took to wife Taku-hata-chichi-hime Yorodzu-hata [2] hime no Mikoto, daughter of Taka-mi-musubi no Mikoto."

Another version says :—" Honoto-hata-hime-ko-chichi-hime no Mikoto, daughter of Taka-mi-musubi no Mikoto." She bore to him a child named Ama-no-ho-no-akari no Mikoto. Next she bore Ama-tsu-hiko-ne-ho-no-ninigi-ne no Mikoto. The child of Ama-no-ho-no-akari no Mikoto was called Kaguyama no Mikoto. He is the ancestor of the Ohari no Muraji.   II. 29.

When Taka-mi-musubi no Mikoto was sending down the Heavenly Grandchild Ho-no-ninigi no Mikoto to the Central Land of Reed-Plains, she commanded the eighty myriads of Gods, saying :—" In the Central Land of Reed-

---

[1] The ordeal by fire is here alluded to. In later times the ordeal of boiling water was also practised. Both customs are kept up by Shintō devotees in modern times. See Lowell's " Esoteric Shintō," in the " T.A.S.J." A picture in Hokusai's " Mangwa " represents two in persons the garb of Buddhist priests passing through the ordeal of fire.

[2] Myriad looms, or rather webs. The currency of ancient Japan consisted of pieces of cloth. Hence Yorodzu-hata means wealthy.

Plains, the rocks, tree-stems and herbage have still the power of speech. At night, they make a clamour like that of flames of fire; in the day-time they swarm up like the flies in the fifth month, etc., etc." Now Taka-mi-musubi no Mikoto gave command, saying :—" I formerly sent Ame-waka-hiko to the Central Land of Reed-Plains, but he has been long absent, and until now has not returned, perhaps being forcibly prevented by some of the Gods of the Land." She therefore sent the cock-pheasant Na-naki to go thither and spy out the reason. This pheasant went down, but when he saw the fields of millet and the fields of pulse he remained there, and did not come back. This was the origin of the modern saying, "The pheasant special messenger." Therefore she afterwards sent the hen-pheasant Na-naki, and this bird came down and was hit by an arrow shot by Ame-waka-hiko, after which she came up and made her report, etc., etc. At this time Taka-mi-musubi no Mikoto took the coverlet which was upon the true couch, and having clothed therewith the Heavenly Grandchild Ama-tsu-hikone Ho-no-ninigi-ne no Mikoto, sent him downwards, thrusting asunder the eight-piled clouds of Heaven. Therefore this God was styled Ame-kuni-nigishi-hiko-ho-ninigi no Mikoto. Now the place at which he arrived on his descent is called the Peak of Sohori-yam a of Takachiho in So in Hiuga. When he proceeded therefore on his way, etc., etc.,[1] he arrived at Cape Kasasa in Ata, and finally ascended the Island of Takashima in Nagaya. He went round inspecting that land, and found there a man whose name was Koto-katsu-kuni-katsu Nagasa. The Heavenly Grandchild accordingly inquired of him, saying :—" Whose land is this?" He answered and said :—" This is the land where Nagasa dwells. I will, however, now offer it to the Heavenly Grandchild." The Heavenly Grandchild again inquired of him, saying :—" And the maidens who have built an eight-fathom palace on the highest crest of the waves and tend the loom with jingling wrist jewels, whose daughters are they?" He answered and said :—" They are the daughters of Oho-yama-tsu-mi no Kami. The elder is named Iha-naga-hime, and the younger is named Kono-

II. 30.

---

[1] These etc's mark intentional omissions.

hana saku-ya-hime, also called Toyo-ata-tsu hime, etc., etc."
The August Grandchild accordingly favoured Toyo-ata-tsu
hime, and after one night she became pregnant. The August
Grandchild doubting this, etc., etc. Eventually she gave
birth to Ho-no-suseri no Mikoto ; next she bore Ho-no-ori
no Mikoto, also called Hiko-hoho-demi no Mikoto. Proof
having been given by the mother's vow, it was known exactly
that they were truly the offspring of the Heavenly Grandchild.
Toyo-ata-tsu hime however was incensed at the Heavenly
Grandchild, and would not speak to him. The Heavenly
Grandchild, grieved at this, made a song, saying :—

> The sea-weed of the offing—
> Though it may reach the shore :
> The true couch
> Is, alas ! impossible.
> Ah ! ye dotterels of the beach !¹

In one writing it is said :—" The daughter of Taka-mi-
musubi no Mikoto, Ama-yorodzu-taku-hata chi-hata hime."

II. 31.

One version is :—" Yorodzu-hata-hime ko-dama-yori-
hime no Mikoto was the child of Taka-mi-musubi no
Mikoto. This Goddess became the consort of Ame no
Oshi-hone no Mikoto, and bore to him a child named Ama-
no Ki-ho-ho-oki-se no Mikoto."

One version is :—" Katsu no haya-hi no Mikoto's child
was Ama no Oho-mimi no Mikoto. This God took to wife
Nigutsu hime, and had by her a child named Ninigi no
Mikoto."

One version is :—" The daughter of Kami-mi-musubi no
Mikoto, Taku-hata chi-hata hime, bore a child named Ho-
no-ninigi no Mikoto."

One version is :—" Ama no Kise no Mikoto took to wife
Ata-tsu hime, and had children, first Ho-no-akari no
Mikoto, next Ho-no-yo-wori no Mikoto, and next Hiko-ho-
ho-demi no Mikoto."

In one writing it is said :—" Masa-ya-a-katsu-katsu-no-
haya-hi Ama no Oshi-ho-mimi no Mikoto took to wife Ama

---

¹ A regular tanka (short poem) of 31 syllables. The meaning is : " The
weeds of the deep sea may drift to the shore, but between thy couch and
mine an impassable gulf is fixed. I appeal to you, ye dotterels of the beach!
Is it not so ? "

no yorodzu-taku-hata-chi-hata hime, daughter of Taka-mi-
musubi no Mikoto, and by her as consort had a child
named Ama-teru-kuni-teru Hiko-ho no akari no Mikoto.
He is the ancestor of the Ohari no Muraji. The next child
was Ama-no-nigishi-kuni-no-nigishi Ama-tsu-hiko-ho-no
ninigi no Mikoto. This God took to wife Kono hana saku-
ya-hime no Mikoto, daughter of Oho-yama-tsu-mi no Kami,
and by her as consort had first a child named Ho-no-susori
no Mikoto, and next Hiko-hoho-demi no Mikoto."

The elder brother Ho-no-susori no Mikoto had by nature a
sea-gift; the younger brother Hiko-ho-ho-demi no Mikoto had
by nature a mountain-gift.[1] In the beginning the two brothers,
the elder and the younger, conversed together, saying :—" Let
us for a trial exchange gifts." They eventually exchanged
them, but neither of them gained aught by doing so. The elder
brother repented his bargain, and returned to the younger
brother his bow and arrows, asking for his fish-hook to be given
back to him. But the younger brother had already lost the
elder brother's fish-hook, and there was no means of finding it.
He accordingly made another new hook which he offered to his
elder brother. But his elder brother refused to accept it, and
II. 32. demanded the old hook. The younger brother, grieved at this,
forthwith took his cross-sword[2] and forged[3] from it new fish-
hooks, which he heaped up in a winnowing tray, and offered to his
brother. But his elder brother was wroth, and said :—" These
are not my old fish-hook : though they are many, I will not
take them." And he continued repeatedly to demand it vehe-
mently. Therefore Hiko-hoho-demi no Mikoto's grief was
exceedingly profound, and he went and made moan by the shore
of the sea. There he met Shiho-tsutsu[4] no Oji.[5] The old
man inquired of him saying :—" Why dost thou grieve here ? "
He answered and told him the matter from first to last. The
old man said :—" Grieve no more. I will arrange this matter
for thee." So he made a basket without interstices, and placing

---

[1] A talent for fishing and a talent for hunting.
[2] The interlinear gloss has tachi, or simply sword.
[3] This points to iron as the material of both swords and fish-hooks at the
time when this story became current. The Homeric fish-hook was of horn
—βοὸς κέρας ἀγραύλοιο. See Index — Bronze Age.
[4] Salt-sea-elder.   [5] Grandfather or old-man.

in it Hoho-demi no Mikoto, sank it in the sea. Forthwith he found himself at a pleasant strand, where he abandoned the basket, and, proceeding on his way, suddenly arrived at the palace of the Sea-God. This palace was provided with battlements and turrets, and had stately towers. Before the gate there was a well, and over the well there grew a many-branched cassia-tree,[1] with wide-spreading boughs and leaves. Now Hiko-hoho-demi no Mikoto went up to the foot of this tree and loitered about. After some time a beautiful woman appeared, and, pushing open the door, came forth. She at length took a II. 33. jewel-vessel and approached. She was about to draw water, when, raising her eyes, she saw him, and was alarmed. Returning within, she spoke to her father and mother, saying :—" There is a rare stranger at the foot of the tree before the gate." The God of the Sea thereupon prepared an eight-fold cushion and led him in. When they had taken their seats, he inquired of him the object of his coming. Then Hiko-hoho-demi no Mikoto explained to him in reply all the circumstances. The Sea-God accordingly assembled the fishes, both great and small, and required of them an answer. They all said :—" We know not. Only the Red-woman[2] has had a sore mouth for some time past and has not come." She was therefore peremptorily summoned to appear, and on her mouth being examined the lost hook was actually found.

After this, Hiko-hoho-demi no Mikoto took to wife the Sea-God's daughter, Toyo-tama[3]-hime, and dwelt in the sea-palace. For three years he enjoyed peace and pleasure, but still had a longing for his own country, and therefore sighed deeply from time to time. Toyo-tama-hime heard this and told her father, II. 34. saying :—" The Heavenly Grandchild often sighs as if in grief. It may be that it is the sorrow of longing for his country." The God of the Sea thereupon drew to him Hiko-hoho-demi no

---

[1] A castle-gate with a tree growing before it, and a well at its bottom which serves as a mirror, are the stock properties of several old-world stories. The following is from Lang's "Custom and Myth," p. 91 :—"Then the Giant's dochter came to the palace where Nicht Nought Nothing was, and she went up into a tree to watch for him. The gardener's dochter going to draw water in the well, saw the shadow," etc.

[2] Aka-me, a name of the Tai (pagrus).   [3] Rich-jewel.

Mikoto, and addressing him in an easy, familiar way, said :—
" If the Heavenly Grandchild desires to return to his country
I will send him back." So he gave him the fish-hook which he
had found, and in doing so instructed him, saying :—" When
thou givest this fish-hook to thy elder brother, before giving to
him call to it secretly, and say, " A poor hook." He further
presented to him the jewel of the flowing tide and the jewel of
the ebbing tide, and instructed him, saying :—" If thou dost dip
the tide-flowing jewel, the tide will suddenly flow, and therewithal thou shalt drown thine elder brother. But in case thy
elder brother should repent and beg forgiveness, if, on the contrary, thou dip the tide-ebbing jewel, the tide will spontaneously
ebb, and therewithal thou shalt save him. If thou harass him
in this way, thy elder brother will of his own accord render
submission."

When the Heavenly Grandchild was about to set out on his
return journey, Toyo-tama-hime addressed him, saying :—" Thy
handmaiden is already pregnant, and the time of her delivery is
not far off. On a day when the winds and waves are raging, I
will surely come forth to the sea-shore, and I pray thee that
thou wilt make for me a parturition house,[1] and await me
there."

When Hiko-hoho-demi no Mikoto returned to his palace, he
complied implicitly with the instructions of the Sea-God, and
the elder brother, Ho-no-susori no Mikoto, finding himself in
the utmost straits, of his own accord admitted his offence, and
II. 35. said :—" Henceforward I will be thy subject to perform mimic
dances for thee. I beseech thee mercifully to spare my life."
Thereupon he at length yielded his petition, and spared him.[2]
This Ho-no-susori no Mikoto was the first ancestor of the
Kimi of Wobashi in Ata.

After this Toyo-tama-hime fulfilled her promise, and, bringing
with her her younger sister, Tama-yori-hime, bravely confronted
the winds and waves, and came to the sea-shore. When the
time of her delivery was at hand, she besought Hiko-hoho-demi
no Mikoto, saying :—" When thy handmaiden is in travail, I

---

[1] See above, p. 73.

[2] Ever since the time of Cain and Abel, folk-lore has had a curious par-
tiality for the younger of two brothers. The Jimmu legend contains several
instances of this.

pray thee do not look upon her." However, the Heavenly Grandchild could not restrain himself, but went secretly and peeped in. Now Toyo-tama-hime was just in childbirth, and had changed into a dragon.[1] She was greatly ashamed, and said :—" Hadst thou not disgraced me, I would have made the sea and land communicate with each other, and for ever pre-

vented them from being sundered. But now that thou hast disgraced me, wherewithal shall friendly feelings be knit together ? " So she wrapped the infant in rushes, and abandoned it on the sea-shore. Then she barred the sea-path, and passed away.[2] Accordingly the child was called Hiko-nagisa-take-u-gaya-fuki-ahezu[3] no Mikoto.

A long time after, Hiko-hoho-demi no Mikoto died, and was buried in the Misasagi on the summit of Mount Takaya in Hiuga.

In one writing it is said :—" The elder brother Ho-no- II. 36. susori no Mikoto had acquired a mountain-gift. Now the elder and younger brothers wished to exchange gifts, and therefore the elder brother took the bow which was of the gift of the younger brother, and went to the mountain in quest

---

[1] In the accompanying illustration from a Japanese book (printed 1746), the Sea-King and his daughter are represented as combining the Dragon with the human form. See above, p. 61.

[2] " There are many examples of the disappearance of the bride or bridegroom in consequence of the infringement of various mystic rules." Lang's " Custom and Myth," p. 81.

[3] Prince-beach-brave-cormorant-rush-thatch-unfinished. The application of the latter part of the name will appear from one of the variant myths given below. See also Ch. K., p. 127.

of wild animals. But never a trace of game did he see. The younger brother took the fish-hook of his elder brother's gift, and with it went a-fishing on the sea, but caught none at all, and finally lost his fish-hook. Then the elder brother restored his younger brother's bow and arrows, and demanded his own fish-hook. The younger brother was sorry, and of the cross-sword which he had in his girdle made fish-hooks, which he heaped up in a winnowing tray, and offered to his elder brother. But the elder brother refused to receive them, saying :—' I still wish to get the fish-hook of my gift.' Hereupon Hiko-hoho-demi no Mikoto, not knowing where to look for it, only grieved and made moan. He went to the sea-shore, where he wandered up and down lamenting. Now there was an old man, who suddenly came forward, and gave his name as Shiho-tsuchi no Oji. He asked him, saying :—' Who art thou, my lord, and why dost thou grieve here?' Hiko-hoho-demi no Mikoto told him all that had happened. Whereupon the old man took from a bag a black comb, which he flung upon the ground. It straightway became changed into a multitudinous[1] clump of bamboos. Accordingly he took these bamboos and made of them a coarse basket with wide meshes, in which he placed Hiko-hoho-demi no Mikoto, and cast him into the sea."

One version says :—" He took a katama without interstices, and made of it a float, to which he attached Hoho-demi by a cord and sunk him." [*The term katama means what is now called a bamboo-basket.*]

Now there is in the bottom of the sea a natural " Little-shore of delight." Proceeding onwards, along this shore, he arrived of a sudden at the palace of Toyo-tama-hiko, the God of the Sea. This palace had magnificent gates and towers of exceeding beauty. Outside the gate there was a well, and beside the well was a cassia-tree. He approached the foot of this tree, and stood there. After a while a beautiful woman, whose countenance was such as is not anywhere to be seen, came out from within, followed by a bevy of attendant maidens. She was drawing water in a

[1] Lit. 500.

jewel-urn, when she looked up and saw Hoho-demi no
Mikoto. She was startled, and returning, told the God, her
father, saying:—'At the foot of the cassia-tree without
the gate, there is a noble stranger of no ordinary build. If
he had come down from Heaven, he would have had on
him the filth of Heaven; if he had come from Earth, he
would have had on him the filth of Earth. Could he be
really the beautiful prince of the sky?'

One version says:—"An attendant of Toyo-tama-hime
was drawing water in a jewel-pitcher, but she could not
manage to fill it. She looked down into the well, when
there shone inverted there the smiling face of a man. She
looked up and there was a beautiful God leaning against a
cassia-tree. She accordingly returned within, and informed
her mistress.

Hereupon Toyo-tama-hiko sent a man to inquire,
saying:—'Who art thou, O stranger, and why hast thou
come here?' Hoho-demi no Mikoto answered and said:—
'I am the grandchild of the Heavenly Deity,' and ultimately went on to give the reason of his coming.

Then the God of the Sea went out to meet him. He
made him obeisance, and led him within, where he inquired
courteously of his welfare, and gave him to wife his
daughter, Toyo-tama-hime. Therefore he remained and
dwelt in the palace of the sea. Three years passed, after
which Hoho-demi no Mikoto sighed frequently, and Toyo-
tama-hime asked him, saying:—'Does the Heavenly
Grandchild perchance wish to return to his native land?'
He answered and said:—'It is so.' Toyo-tama-hime
forthwith told the God her father, and said:—'The
noble guest who is here wishes to return to the upper
country.' Hereupon the God of the Sea assembled all the II. 38.
fishes of the sea, and asked of them the fish-hook. Then
one fish answered and said:—'The Red-woman¹ (*also
called the Red Tahi*) has long had an ailment of the mouth.
I suspect that she has swallowed it.' So the Red-woman
was forthwith summoned, and on looking into her mouth, the
hook was still there. It was at once taken and delivered
to Hiko-hoho-demi no Mikoto, with these instructions:—

¹ See above, p. 93.

' When thou givest the fish-hook to thy elder brother, thou must use this imprecation : " The origin of poverty : the beginning of starvation : the root of wretchedness." Give it not to him until thou hast said this. Again, if thy brother cross the sea, I will then assuredly stir up the blasts and billows, and make them overwhelm and vex him.' Thereupon he placed Hoho-demi no Mikoto on the back of a great sea-monster, and so sent him back to his own country.

At another time, before this, Toyo-tama-hime spoke in an easy, familiar way, and said :—' Thy handmaid is with child. Some day, when the winds and waves are boisterous, I will come forth to the sea-shore, and I pray thee to construct for me a parturition-house, and to await me there.'

After this, Toyo-tama-hime fulfilled her promise to come, and spake to Hoho-demi no Mikoto, saying :—' To-night thy handmaiden will be delivered. I pray thee, look not on her.' Hoho-demi no Mikoto would not hearken to her, but with a comb [1] he made a light, and looked at her. At this time Toyo-tama-hime had become changed into an enormous sea-monster of eight fathoms, and was wriggling about on her belly. She at last was angry that she was put to shame, and forthwith went straight back again to her native sea, leaving behind her younger sister Tama-yori-hime as nurse to her infant. The child was called Hiko-nagisa-take-u-gaya-fuki-ayezu no Mikoto, because the parturition-house by the sea-shore was all thatched with cormorants' feathers, and the child was born before the tiles had met. It was for this reason that he received this name." [2]

One version says :—" Before the gate there was a beautiful well, and over the well there grew a cassia-tree with an hundred branches. Accordingly Hiko-hoho-demi no Mikoto sprang up into that tree and stood there. At this time, Toyo-tama-hime, the daughter of the God of the Sea, came with a jewel-bowl in her hand and was about to draw water, when she saw in the well the reflection of a

[1] See above, p. 24.

[2] There is a superstition that a woman in childbirth gained relief by holding a cormorant's feather in her hand. A cowrie (ko-yasu-gai) is used for the same purpose, no doubt on account of its shape. See above, p. 95.

man. She looked up and was startled, so that she let fall the bowl, which was broken to pieces. But without regard for it, she returned within and told her parents, saying :— ' I have seen a man on the tree which is beside the well. His countenance is very beautiful, and his form comely. He is surely no ordinary person.' When the God, her father, heard this, he wondered. Having prepared an eight-fold cushion, he went to meet him, and brought him in. When they were seated, he asked the reason of his coming, upon which he answered and told him all his case. Now the God of the Sea at once conceived pity for him, and summoning all the broad of fin and narrow of fin, made inquiry of them. They all said :—' We know not. Only the Red-woman has an ailment of the mouth and has not come.' [Another version is :—' The Kuchi-me [1] has an ailment of the mouth.'] So she was sent for in all haste, and on searching her mouth, the lost fish-hook was at once found. Upon this the God of the Sea chid her, saying :—' Thou Kuchime ! Henceforward thou shalt not be able to swallow a bait, nor shalt thou be allowed to have a place at the table of the Heavenly Grandchild.' This is the reason why the fish kuchime is not among the articles of food set before the Emperor.

When the time came for Hiko-hoho-demi no Mikoto to take his departure, the God of the Sea spake to him, saying :—' I am rejoiced in my inmost heart that the Heavenly Grandchild has now been graciously pleased to visit me. When shall I ever forget it ? ' So he took the jewel which II. 40. when thought of makes the tide to flow, and the jewel which when thought of makes the tide to ebb, and joining them to the fish-hook, presented them, saying :—' Though the Heavenly Grandchild may be divided from me by eight-fold windings (of road), I hope that we shall think of each other from time to time. Do not therefore throw them away.' And he taught him, saying :—' When thou givest this fish-hook to thy elder brother, call it thus :—' A hook of poverty, a hook of ruin, a hook of downfall.' When thou hast said all this, fling it away to him with thy back turned, and deliver it not to him face to face. If thy elder

[1] Kuchi-me means " mouth-female."

brother is angry, and has a mind to do thee hurt, then produce the tide-flowing jewel and drown him therewith. As soon as he is in peril and appeals for mercy, bring forth the tide-ebbing jewel and therewith save him. If thou dost vex him in this way, he will of his own accord become thy submissive vassal.' Now Hiko-hoho-demi no Mikoto, having received the jewels and the fish-hook, came back to his original palace, and followed implicitly the teaching of the Sea-God. First of all he offered his elder brother the fish-hook. His elder brother was angry and would not receive it. Accordingly the younger brother produced the tide-flowing jewel, upon which the tide rose with a mighty overflow, and the elder brother was drowning. Therefore he besought his younger brother, saying :—' I will serve thee as thy slave. I beseech thee, spare my life.' The younger brother then produced the tide-ebbing jewel, whereupon the tide ebbed of its own accord, and the elder brother was restored to tranquillity. After this the elder brother changed his former words, and said :—' I am thy elder brother. How can an elder brother serve a younger brother ? ' Then the younger brother produced the tide-flowing jewel, which his elder brother seeing, fled up to a high mountain. Thereupon the tide also submerged the mountain. The elder brother climbed a lofty tree, and thereupon the tide also submerged the tree. The elder brother was now at an extremity, and had nowhere to flee to. So he acknowledged his offence, saying :—' I have been in fault. In future my descendants for eighty generations shall serve thee as thy mimes in ordinary. [One version has ' dog-men.'] I pray thee, have pity on me.' Then the younger brother produced the tide-ebbing jewel, whereupon the tide ceased of its own accord. Hereupon the elder brother saw that the younger brother was possessed of marvellous powers, and at length submitted to serve him.

On this account the various Hayato descended from Ho no susori no Mikoto to the present time do not leave the vicinity of the enclosure of the Imperial Palace, and render service instead of barking dogs.[1]

II. 41.

---

[1] The Hayato constituted the Imperial Guard. The literal meaning of the

This was the origin of the custom which now prevails of not pressing a man to return a lost needle." [1]

In one writing it is said:—"The elder brother, Ho no susori no Mikoto, was endowed with a sea-gift, and was therefore called Umi no sachi-hiko : [2] the younger brother, Hiko-hoho-demi no Mikoto, was endowed with a mountain-gift, and was therefore called Yama no sachi-hiko. When- II. 42. ever the wind blew and the rain fell, the elder brother lost his gain, but in spite of wind and rain the younger brother's gain did not fail him. Now the elder brother spoke to the younger brother, saying :—' I wish to make trial of an exchange of gifts with thee.' The younger brother consented, and the exchange was accordingly made. Thereupon the elder brother took the younger brother's bow and arrows, and went a-hunting to the mountain : the younger brother took the elder brother's fish-hook, and went on the sea a-fishing. But neither of them got anything, and they came back empty-handed. The elder brother accordingly restored to the younger brother his bow and arrows, and demanded back his own fish-hook. Now the younger brother had lost the fish-hook in the sea, and he knew not how to find it. Therefore he made other new fish-hooks, several thousands in number, which he offered to his elder brother. The elder brother was angry, and would not receive them, but demanded importunately the old fish-hook, etc., etc. Then the younger brother went to the sea-shore and wandered about, grieving and making moan. Now

name (for haya-bito) is falcon-man. They were from the provinces of Satsuma and Ohosumi. The Hayato are mentioned repeatedly in the reigns of Temmu and Jitō, not, I think, before that time.

The Yengi-shiki (regulations of the Yengi, 901-923 period) says that on the first day of the year, at coronations, and when foreign envoys were received, twenty upper class hayato were to attend, twenty "new-comer" hayato, and 132 ordinary hayato. These were to take their posts in detachments to right and left outside the Palace Gate. When the officials first entered, or got up from their seats, the "new-comer" hayato raised three barks, and there was more barking or howling, sometimes loud and sometimes low, at other stages of the ceremony.

[1] The Japanese word hari means both needle and fish-hook. There is no such ambiguity in the Chinese characters used here.

[2] Sea-gift-prince.

there was there a river wild-goose which had become en-
tangled in a snare, and was in distress. He took pity on it,
and loosing it, let it go. Shortly after there appeared Shiho
tsutsu no Oji. He came and made a skiff of basket-work
without interstices, in which he placed Hoho-demi no
Mikoto and pushed it off into the sea, when it sank
down of its own accord, till of a sudden there appeared the
Pleasant Road. So he went on along this road, which in
due course led him to the palace of the Sea-God. Then the
Sea-God came out himself to meet him, and invited him to
enter. He spread eight layers of sea-asses'[1] skins, on which
he made him to sit, and with a banquet of tables of a hundred, which was already prepared, he fulfilled the rites of
hospitality. Then he inquired of him in an easy manner:—
' Wherefore has the Grandchild of the Heavenly Deity been
graciously pleased to come hither?' "

[One version has :—" A little while ago my child came
and told me that the Heavenly Grandchild was mourning
by the sea-shore. Whether this be true or false I know
not, but perhaps it may be so."]

Hiko-hoho-demi no Mikoto related to him all that had
happened from first to last. So he remained there, and
the Sea-God gave him his daughter Toyo-tama-hime to
wife. At length, when three years had passed in close and
warm affection, the time came for him to depart. So the
Sea-God sent for the tahi, and on searching her mouth found
there the fish-hook. Thereupon he presented the fish-hook
to Hiko-hoho-demi no Mikoto, and instructed him thus:—
' When thou givest this to thy elder brother thou must
recite the following :—" A big hook, an eager hook, a poor
hook, a silly hook." After saying all this, fling it to him with
a back-handed motion.' Then he summoned together the
sea-monsters, and inquired of them, saying :—' The Grandchild of the Heavenly Deity is now about to take his departure homewards. In how many days will you accomplish this service?' Then all the sea-monsters fixed each a
number of days according to his own length. Those of

II. 43.

---

[1] The interlinear gloss has michi. One of the marine carnivora is meant,
probably the seal.

them which were one fathom long of their own accord said :
—' In the space of one day we will accomplish it.' The one-
fathom sea-monsters were accordingly sent with him as his
escort.   Then he gave him two precious objects, the tide-
flowing jewel and the tide-ebbing jewel, and taught him how
to use them.   He further instructed him, saying :—' If thy
elder brother should make high fields, do thou make puddle
fields ; if thy elder brother make puddle fields, do thou make
high fields.   In this manner did the Sea-God in all sincerity lend him his aid.   Now Hiko-hoho-demi no Mikoto,
when he returned home, followed implicitly the God's instructions, and acted accordingly.   When the younger
brother produced the tide-flowing jewel, the elder brother
forthwith flung up his hands in the agony of drowning.
But when, on the other hand, he produced the tide-ebbing
jewel, he was relieved, and recovered.   After that Hi no
susori no Mikoto pined away from day to day, and
lamented, saying :—' I have become impoverished.'   So he
yielded submission to his younger brother.

Before this Toyo-tama-hime spake to the Heavenly II. 44.
Grandchild, saying :—' That which thy handmaid has
conceived is the offspring of the Heavenly Grandchild.
How could I give birth to it in the midst of the ocean ?
Therefore when the time of my delivery comes, I will surely
betake myself to my lord's abode, and it is my prayer that
thou shouldst build me a house by the sea-side and
await me there.'   Therefore Hiko-ho-ho-demi no Mikoto,
as soon as he returned to his own country, took cormorants'
feathers, and with them as thatch, made a parturition-house.
But before the tiling of the house was completed, Toyo-
tama-hime herself arrived, riding on a great tortoise, with
her younger sister Tama-yori-hime, and throwing a
splendour over the sea.   Now the months of her pregnancy
were already fulfilled, and the time of her delivery was
urgent.   On this account she did not wait till the
thatching of the house was completed, but went straight in
and remained there.   Then she spake quietly to the
Heavenly   Grandchild, saying : — ' Thy   handmaid is
about to be delivered.   I pray thee do not look on her.'
The Heavenly Grandchild wondered at these words, and

1

peeped in secretly, when behold, she had become changed into a great sea-monster of eight fathoms. Now she was aware that the Heavenly Grandchild had looked in upon her privacy, and was deeply ashamed and resentful. When the child was born, the Heavenly Grandchild approached and made inquiry, saying :—' By what name ought the child to be called ? ' She answered and said :—' Let him be called Hiko-nagisa-take-u-gaya-fuki-ahezu no Mikoto.' [1] Having said so, she took her departure straight across the sea. Then Hiko-hoho-demi no Mikoto made a song, saying :—

> Whatever befals me,
> Ne'er shall I forget my love
> With whom I slept
> In the island of wild-ducks—
> The birds of the offing." [2]

II. 45.   Another account says :—" Hiko-ho-ho-demi no Mikoto took other women and made them wet-nurses, bathing-women, boiled-rice-chewers, and washerwomen. [3] All these various Be were provided for the respectful nurture of the infant. The provision at this time, by means of other women, of milk for the nurture of the august child was the origin of the present practice of engaging temporarily wet-nurses to bring up infants.

After this, when Toyo-tama-hime heard what a fine boy her child was, her heart was greatly moved with affection, and she wished to come back and bring him up herself. But she could not rightly do so, and therefore she sent her younger sister Tama-yori-hime to nurture him. Now when Toyo-tama-hime sent Tama-yori-hime, she offered (to Hoho-demi no Mikoto) the following verse in answer :—

> Some may boast
> Of the splendour
> Of red jewels,

---

[1] See above, p. 95.

[2] The order of the lines in the original is exactly the reverse of the above. Metre, regular tanka.

The word for " my love " is imo, which in ancient Japanese is used indifferently for wife and younger sister. See above, p. 22.

[3] Evidently the narrator is here describing the staff of the Imperial nursery of the day.

But those worn by my Lord—
It is they which are admirable.[1]

These two stanzas, one sent, and one in reply, are what are termed age-uta."[2]

In one writing it is said :—" The elder brother, Ho no susori no Mikoto had a sea-gift, while the younger brother, Ho no ori no Mikoto, had a mountain gift, etc., etc.

The younger brother remained by the sea-shore grieving II. 46. and making moan, when he met with Shiho-tsutsu no Oji, who inquired of him, saying :—' Why dost thou grieve in this way ? ' Ho no ori no Mikoto answered and said, etc., etc.

The old man said :—' Grieve no longer. I will devise a plan.' So he unfolded his plan, saying :—' The courser on which the Sea-God rides is a sea-monster eight fathoms in length, who with fins erect stays in the small orange-tree house. I will consult with him.' So he took Ho no ori no Mikoto with him, and went to see the sea-monster. The sea-monster then suggested a plan, saying :—' I could bring the Heavenly Grandchild to the Sea-Palace after a journey of eight days, but my King has a courser, a sea-monster of one fathom, who will without doubt bring him thither in one day. I will therefore return and make him come to thee. Thou shouldst mount him, and enter the sea. When thou enterest the sea, thou wilt in due course find there " the Little-shore of delight." Proceed along this shore and thou wilt surely arrive at the palace of my King. Over the well at the palace gate there is a multitudinous branching cassia-tree. Do thou climb up on to this tree and stay there.' Having so said, he entered into the sea, and departed. Accordingly the Heavenly Grandchild, in compliance with the sea-monster's words, remained there, and waited for eight days, when there did indeed appear to him a sea-monster of one fathom. He mounted on it, and entered the sea, where he followed in every particular the former sea-monster's advice. Now there appeared an attendant of Toyo-tama-hime, carrying a jewel-vessel, with

---

[1] The " Kojiki " gives a different version of this poem. *Vide* Ch. K., p. 128.
[2] Ageru means to exalt, hence to praise, and age-uta may be rendered " complimentary poetry."

which she was about to draw water from the well, when she espied in the bottom of the water the shadow of a man. She could not draw water, and looking up saw the Heavenly Grandchild. Thereupon she went in and informed the King, saying :—' I had thought that my Lord alone was supremely handsome, but now a stranger has appeared who far excels him in beauty.' When the Sea-God heard this, he said :—' I will try him and see.' So he prepared a threefold dais. Thereupon the Heavenly Grandchild wiped both his feet at the first step of the dais. At the middle one he placed both his hands to the ground ; at the inner one he sat down at his ease¹ upon the cushion covering the true couch. When the Sea-God saw this, he knew that this was the grandchild of the Heavenly Deity, and treated

II. 47. him with more and more respect, etc., etc.

The Sea-God summoned the Akame and the Kuchime, and made inquiry of them. Then the Kuchime drew a fish-hook from her mouth and respectfully delivered it to him. [*The Akame is the Red Tahi and the Kuchime is the Nayoshi.*]² The Sea-God then gave the fish-hook to Hiko-hoho-demi no Mikoto, and instructed him, saying :—' When thy elder brother's fish-hook is returned to him, let the Heavenly Grandchild say :—" Let it be to all thy descendants, of whatever degree of relationship, a poor hook, a paltry poor hook." When thou hast thus spoken, spit thrice, and give it to him. Moreover, when thy elder brother goes to sea a-fishing, let the Heavenly Grandchild stand on the sea-shore and do that which raises the wind. Now that which raises the wind is whistling. If thou doest so, I will forthwith stir up the wind of the offing and the wind of the shore, and will overwhelm and vex him with the scurrying waves.' Ho no ori no Mikoto returned, and obeyed implicitly the instructions of the God. When a day came on which the elder brother went a-fishing, the younger brother stood on the shore of the sea, and whistled. Then there arose a sudden tempest, and the elder brother was forthwith overwhelmed and harassed. Seeing no means of

---

¹ i.e. with legs crossed, which is less respectful than the usual squatting posture.　　　　² Mullet.

saving his life, he besought his younger brother from afar, saying :—' Thou hast dwelt long in the ocean-plain, and must possess some excellent art. I pray thee teach it to me. If thou save my life, my descendants of all degrees of relationship shall not leave the neighbourhood of thy precinct, but shall act as thy mime-vassals.' Thereupon the younger brother left off whistling, and the wind again returned to rest. So the elder brother recognized the younger brother's power, and freely admitted his fault. But the younger brother was wroth, and would hold no converse with him. Hereupon the elder brother, with nothing but his waistcloth on, and smearing the palms of his hands and his face with red earth, said to his younger brother :— II. 48. ' Thus do I defile my body, and make myself thy mime for ever.' So kicking up his feet, he danced along and practised the manner of his drowning struggles. First of all, when the tide reached his feet, he did the foot-divination ;[1] when it reached his knees, he raised up his feet ; when it reached his thighs, he ran round in a circle ; when it reached his loins, he rubbed his loins ; when it reached his sides, he placed his hands upon his breast ; when it reached his neck, he threw up his hands, waving his palms. From that time until now, this custom has never ceased.

Before this, Toyo-tama-hime came forth, and when the time came for her delivery, she besought the Heavenly Grandchild, saying, etc., etc.

The Heavenly Grandchild did not comply with her request, and Toyo-tama-hime resented it greatly, saying :—' Thou didst not attend to my words, but didst put me to shame. Therefore from this time forward, do not send back again any of the female servants of thy handmaid who may go to thy place, and I will not send back any of thy servants who may come to my place.' At length she took the coverlet of the true couch and rushes, and wrapping her child in them, laid him on the beach. She then entered the sea and went away. This is the reason why there is no communication between land and sea." II. 49.

One version says :—" The statement that she placed the

---

[1] i e. shuffled with his feet, as when performing this kind of divination.

child on the beach is wrong. Toyo-tama-hime no Mikoto departed with the child in her own arms. Many days after, she said :—' It is not right that the offspring of the Heavenly Grandchild should be left in the sea,' so she made Tama-yori-hime to take him, and sent him away. At first, when Toyo-tama-hime left, her resentment was extreme, and Ho no ori no Mikoto therefore knew that they would never meet again, so he sent her the verse of poetry which is already given above."

Hiko-nagisa-take-u-gaya-fuki-ahezu no Mikoto took his aunt Tama-yori-hime as his consort, and had by her in all four male children, namely, Hiko-itsu-se[1] no Mikoto, next Ina-ihi[2] no Mikoto, next Mi-ke-iri-no[3] no Mikoto, and next Kamu-yamato-Ihare-biko no Mikoto. Long after, Hiko-nagisa-take-u-gaya-fuki-ahezu no Mikoto died, in the palace of the western country, and was buried in the Misasagi on the top of Mount Ahira in Hiuga.

One writing says :—" His first child was Hiko-itsu-se no Mikoto, the next Ina-ihi no Mikoto, the next Mi-ke-iri-no no Mikoto, and the next Sano no Mikoto, also styled Kamu[4]-yamato-Ihare-biko no Mikoto. Sano was the name by which he was called when young. Afterwards when he had cleared and subdued the realm, and had control of the eight islands, the title was added of Kamu-yamato Ihare-biko no Mikoto."

In one writing it is said :—" His first child was Itsu-se no Mikoto, the next Mikeno no Mikoto, the next Ina-ihi no Mikoto, and the next Ihare-biko no Mikoto, also styled Kamu-yamato Ihare-biko Hoho-demi no Mikoto."

In one writing it is said :—" First he had Hiko-itsuse no Mikoto, next Ina-ihi no Mikoto, next Kamu-yamato Ihare biko Hoho-demi no Mikoto, next Waka-mi-ke-no no Mikoto."

In one writing it is said :—" First he had Hiko-itsu-se no Mikoto, next Ihare-biko Hoho-demi no Mikoto, next Hiko Ina-ihi no Mikoto, next Mi-ke-iri-no no Mikoto."

---

[1] Prince-five-reaches.   [2] Boiled rice.
[3] Three-hairs-enter-moor.   [4] Or Kami.

BOOK III.

THE EMPEROR KAMI-YAMATO IHARE-BIKO.[1]

(*JIMMU TENNŌ.*)

THE Emperor Kami Yamato Ihare-biko's personal name was

[1] Emperor is as near an equivalent as possible of the Chinese 天皇. Both are foreign words. The Japanese interlinear gloss is Sumera Mikoto "supreme majesty," sumera having the same root as suberu, "to unite as a whole"; hence, "to have general control of." See Satow, "Rituals," "T.A.S.J.," VII., ii., p. 113.

Yamato, see above, note to p. 13.

Ihare is the name of a district of Yamato ; Hiko means prince.

Jimmu (divine valour) is a posthumous name. These names for the earlier Mikados were invented in the reign of Kwammu (782—806), after the "Nihongi" was written, but it is necessary to mention them, as they are in universal use by Japanese writers.

In this narrative we have probably a legendary echo of a real movement of population from Kiushiu eastwards to Yamato, at some time before the Christian epoch, but it is not safe to go further than this. The details are manifestly fictitious, some of them, as the quotations from Chinese books put into the mouth of Jimmu Tennō, demonstrably so.

Granting for a moment that the narrative of the Conquest of Yamato by Jimmu Tennō is substantially true, the question arises, Of what race were the tribes whom he found there ? I would suggest that they may have been the Southern Wa mentioned in the "Shan hai king," a very ancient Chinese book, as being, along with the Northern Wa, subject to the kingdom of Yen. The Chinese in ancient times had a notion that Yamato lay to the south of Kiushiu. Yen, a kingdom of Northern China, had an independent existence from B.C. 1122 to B.C. 265. Chamberlain has pointed out that the ancient legends of Japan are connected with three distinct centres—Idzumo, Yamato, and Tsukushi, which is some indication that these places were also centres of governmental authority. The names given to the chieftains subdued by Jimmu Tennō are unmistakably Japanese, as are also those of the places which they inhabited. I cannot agree with Chamberlain in deriving Yamato, Ki, Shima, etc., from Aino words, when obvious Japanese explanations are available. There is another Yamato in Chikugo, where the Aino derivation is surely out of place. I have no desire, however, to dispute all his Aino derivations of place names

Hiko-hoho-demi. He was the fourth child [1] of Hiko-nagisa-take-u-gaya-fuki-ahezu no Mikoto. His mother's name was Tama-yori-hime, daughter of the Sea-God. From his birth, this Emperor was of clear intelligence and resolute will. At the III. 2. age of fifteen he was made heir to the throne. When he grew up, he married Ahira-tsu-hime, of the district of Ata in the province of Hiuga, and made her his consort. By her he had Tagishi-mimi no Mikoto and Kisu-mimi no Mikoto.

When he reached the age of forty-five, he addressed his elder brothers and his children, saying:—"Of old, our Heavenly Deities Taka-mi-musubi no Mikoto, and Oho-hiru-me no Mikoto, pointing to this land of fair rice-ears of the fertile reed-plain, gave it to our Heavenly ancestor, Hiko-ho no ninigi no Mikoto. Thereupon Hiko-ho no ninigi no Mikoto, throwing open the barrier of Heaven and clearing a cloud-path, urged on his superhuman course until he came to rest. At this time the world was given over to widespread desolation. It was an age of darkness and disorder. In this gloom, therefore, he fostered justice, and so governed this western border.[2] Our Imperial ancestors and Imperial parent, like gods, like sages, accumulated happiness and amassed glory. Many years elapsed. From the date when our Heavenly ancestor descended until now it is over III. 3. 1,792,470 years.[3] But the remote regions do not yet enjoy the blessings of Imperial rule. Every town has always been allowed to have its lord, and every village its chief, who, each one for himself, makes division of territory and practises mutual aggression and conflict.

Now I have heard from the Ancient of the Sea,[4] that in the East there is a fair land encircled on all sides by blue mountains. Moreover, there is there one who flew down riding in a Heavenly Rock-boat. I think that this land will undoubtedly

in this part of Japan, and I think it very probable that the first Japanese who settled here drove out a population of Aino race.

[1] Primogeniture was evidently not recognized in Japan at the time this story was written.

[2] i.e. Kiushiu.

[3] This is in imitation of the great number of years ascribed to the reigns of the early Chinese monarchs.

[4] Shiho tsutsu no oji.

be suitable for the extension of the Heavenly task,[1] so that its glory should fill the universe. It is, doubtless, the centre of the world.[2] The person who flew down was, I believe, Nigihaya-hi.[3] Why should we not proceed thither, and make it the capital ? "

All the Imperial Princes answered, and said :—" The truth of this is manifest. This thought is constantly present to our minds also. Let us go thither quickly." This was the year Kinoye Tora (51st) of the Great Year.[4]

III. 4.

B.C. 667.

In that year, in winter, on the Kanoto Tori day (the 5th) of the 10th month, the new moon of which was on the day Hinoto Mi, the Emperor in person led the Imperial Princes and a naval force on an expedition against the East. When he arrived at the Haya-suhi gate,[6] there was there a fisherman who came riding in a boat. The Emperor summoned him, and then inquired of him, saying :—" Who art thou ? " He answered and said :—" Thy servant is a Country-God, and his name is Utsuhiko.[7] I angle for fish in the bays of ocean. Hearing that the son of the Heavenly Deity was coming, therefore I forthwith came to receive him." Again he inquired of him, saying :— " Canst thou act as my guide ? " He answered and said : —" I will do so." The Emperor ordered the end of a pole of shihi wood[8] to be given to the fisher, and caused him to be taken and pulled into the Imperial vessel, of which he was made pilot.

[1] i.e. for the further development of the Imperial power.

[2] The world is here the six quarters, N., S., E., W., Zenith, Nadir. This is, of course, Chinese, as indeed is this whole speech.

[3] Nigi-haya-hi means soft-swift-sun.

[4] The great year is the Chinese cycle of sixty years. This system of reckoning time is described in Legge's " Classics," Chalmers' " Essay in prolegomena to Shooking," " Japanese Chronological Tables," by E.M.S., Bramsen's " Chronological Tables," Mayers' " Chinese Manual," etc. It was not in use to record years before the Christian era even in China, and could hardly have been known in Japan before the introduction of writing in the 5th century, A.D. It is needless to add that such dates are, in this part of the " Nihongi," purely fictitious.

[5] The days of the month are throughout the " Nihongi " given in this clumsy fashion. I have not thought it necessary to follow the example, except in this one instance.

[6] The Quick-suck-gate or Bungo Channel, so called from its rapid tides.

[7] Rare-prince.   [8] Quercus cuspidata.

A name was specially granted him, and he was called Shihi-ne-tsu-hiko.[1] He was the first ancestor of the Yamato no Atahe. Proceeding on their voyage, they arrived at Usa[2] in the Land of Tsukushi. At this time there appeared the ancestors of the Kuni-tsu-ko[3] of Usa, named Usa-tsu-hiko and Usa-tsu-hime. They built a palace raised on one pillar[4] on the banks of the River Usa, and offered them a banquet. Then, by Imperial command, Usa-tsu-hime was given in marriage to the Emperor's attendant minister Ama no tane[5] no Mikoto. Now Ama no tane no. Mikoto was the remote ancestor of the Nakatomi Uji.[6]

11th month, 9th day. The Emperor arrived at the harbour of Oka[7] in the Land of Tsukushi.

12th month, 27th day. He arrived at the province of Aki, where he dwelt in the Palace of Ye.

The year Kinoto U, Spring, 3rd month, 6th day. Going onwards, he entered the land of Kibi,[8] and built a temporary palace, in which he dwelt. It was called the Palace of Takashima. Three years passed, during which time he set in order the helms[9] of his ships, and prepared a store of provisions. It was his desire by a single effort to subdue the Empire.

The year Tsuchinoye Muma, Spring, 2nd month, 11th day. The Imperial forces at length proceeded eastwards, the prow of one ship touching the stern of another. Just when they reached Cape Naniha they encountered a current of great swiftness. Whereupon that place was called Nami-haya (wave-swift) or

---

[1] Prince of shihi root.

[2] Usa is now a district (kōri) in the province of Buzen. Tsukushi is used by old writers both for the whole island of Kiushiu and for the northern part of it.

[3] Or Kuni no miyakko, local hereditary nobles.

[4] Vide Ch. K., p. 130, and "Night of the Gods," p. 224, where a curious coincidence with an Irish legend is noted. "In Mailduin's voyage he came to an island called Aenchoss, that is One-foot, so called because it was supported by a single pillar in the middle." The "Kojiki" and a note to the "Nihongi" have for one pillar, "one foot." Possibly there is here a reminiscence of a nomadic tent life.

[5] Heavenly seed.

[6] i.e. house, or noble family.   [7] In Chikuzen.

[8] Including the present provinces of Bizen, Bittchiu, and Bingo.

[9] Or oars.

Nami-hana (wave-flower). It is now called Naniha,[1] which is a corruption of this.

3rd month, 10th day. Proceeding upwards against the stream, they went straight on, and arrived at the port of Awo-kumo no Shira-date, in the township of Kusaka, in the province of Kafuchi.[2]

III. 7.

Summer, 4th month, 9th day. The Imperial forces in martial array marched on to Tatsuta. The road was narrow and precipitous, and the men were unable to march abreast, so they returned and again endeavoured to go eastward, crossing over Mount Ikoma. In this way they entered the inner country.[3]

Now when Naga-sune-hiko[4] heard this, he said:—"The object of the children of the Heavenly Deity in coming hither is assuredly to rob me of my country." So he straightway levied all the forces under his dominion, and intercepted them at the Hill of Kusaka. A battle was engaged, and Itsuse no Mikoto was hit by a random arrow on the elbow. The Imperial forces were unable to advance against the enemy. The Emperor was vexed, and revolved in his inmost heart a divine plan, saying:—" I am the descendant of the Sun-Goddess, and if I proceed against the Sun to attack the enemy, I shall act contrary to the way of Heaven. Better to retreat and make a show of weakness. Then sacrificing to the Gods of Heaven and Earth, and bringing on our backs the might of the Sun-Goddess, let us follow her rays and trample them down. If we do so, the enemy will assuredly be routed of themselves, and we shall not stain our swords with blood." They all said :—" It is good." Thereupon he gave orders to the army, saying:—"Wait a while, and advance no further." So he withdrew his forces, and the enemy also did not dare to attack him. He then retired to the port of Kusaka, where he set up shields, and made a warlike show. Therefore the name of this port was changed to Tatetsu,[5] which is now corrupted into Tadetsu.

Before this, at the battle of Kusaka, there was a man who

III. 8.

---

[1] Naniha is now a poetical name for Ohosaka. The current referred to is no doubt the tide on the bar at the river-mouth, a most dangerous place for small craft in bad weather.

[2] Pronounced Kawachi.   [3] Yamato.

[4] Prince Longshanks. Naga-sune is the name of a place.

[5] Shield-port or shield-ferry.

hid in a great tree, and by so doing escaped danger. So pointing to this tree, he said :—" I am grateful to it, as to my mother." Therefore the people of the day called that place Omo no ki no Mura.[1]

5th month, 8th day. The army arrived at the port of Yamaki in Chinu [*also called Port Yama no wi*]. Now Itsuse no Mikoto's arrow wound was extremely painful. He grasped his sword, and striking a martial attitude, said :—" How exasperating it is that a *man* should die of a wound received at the hands of slaves, and should not revenge it ! " The people of that III. 9. day therefore called the place Wo no minato.[2]

Proceeding onwards, they reached Mount Kama in the Land of Kiï, where Itsuse no Mikoto died in the army, and was therefore buried at Mount Kama.

6th month, 23rd day. The army arrived at the village of Nagusa, where they put to death the Tohe[3] of Nagusa. Finally they crossed the moor of Sano, and arrived at the village of Kami[4] in Kumano. Here he embarked in the rock-boat of Heaven, and leading his army, proceeded onwards by slow degrees. In the midst of the sea, they suddenly met with a violent wind, and the Imperial vessel was tossed about. Then Ina-ihi no Mikoto exclaimed and said :—" Alas ! my ancestors were Heavenly Deities, and my mother was a Goddess of the Sea. Why do they harass me by land, and why moreover do they harass me by sea? " When he had said this, he drew his sword and plunged into the sea, where he became changed into the God Sabi-mochi.[5]

III. 10.   Mike Irino no Mikoto, also indignant at this, said :— " My mother and my aunt are both Sea-Goddesses : why do they raise great billows to overwhelm us ? " So treading upon the waves, he went to the Eternal Land.[6] The Emperor was now alone with the Imperial Prince Tagishi-mimi no Mikoto. Leading his army forward, he arrived at Port Arazaka in Kumano [*also called Nishiki Bay*], where he put to death the Tohe of Nishiki. At this time the Gods belched up

---

[1] Mother-tree-village.   [2] Port Man (vir).
[3] Tohe seems to have been a word for chieftain.
[4] Or it may be of the Deity of Kumano.
[5] i.e. the blade-holder.   [6] Toko-yo no Kuni.

a poisonous vapour, from which everyone suffered. For this reason the Imperial army was again unable to exert itself. Then there was there a man by name Kumano no Takakuraji, who unexpectedly had a dream, in which Ama-terasu no Oho-kami spoke to Take-mika-tsuchi no Kami,[1] saying :—" I still hear a sound of disturbance from the Central Land of Reed-Plains. Do thou again go and chastise it." Take-mika-tsuchi no Kami answered and said :—" Even if I go not, I can send down my sword, with which I subdued the land, upon which the country will of its own accord become peaceful." To this Ama-terasu no Kami assented. Thereupon Take-mika-tsuchi no Kami addressed Takakuraji, saying :—" My sword, which is called Futsu no Mitama, I will now place in thy storehouse. Do thou take it and present it to the Heavenly Grandchild." Takakuraji said " Yes," and thereupon awoke. The next morning, as instructed in his dream, he opened the storehouse, and on looking in, there was indeed there a sword which had fallen down (from Heaven), and was standing upside down[2] on the plank floor of the storehouse. So he took it and offered it to the Emperor. At this time the Emperor happened to be asleep. He awoke suddenly, and said :—" What a long time I have slept !" On inquiry he found that the troops who had been affected by the poison had all recovered their senses and were afoot. The Emperor then endeavoured to advance into the interior, but among the mountains it was so precipitous that there was no road by which they could travel, and they wandered about not knowing whither to direct their march. Then Ama-terasu no Oho-kami instructed the Emperor in a dream of the night, saying :—" I will now send thee the Yata-garasu,[3] make it thy guide through the land." Then there did

III. 11.

---

[1] The Thunder-God.   [2] i.e. point upwards.

[3] Yata-garasu. The Chinese characters used here mean " The crow with a head eight feet long." But this is a case where we must put aside the Chinese characters, and attend solely to the Japanese word which they are meant to represent. This is undoubtedly yata-garasu, as we know from the "Kojiki" and from the traditional Kana rendering. Much has been written about this bird by Motowori and other Shintō scholars, which is, I venture to think, wholly wide of the mark. The clue to its meaning is afforded by the "Wamiō-shō," a Chinese-Japanese vocabulary of the tenth century, which says, on the authority of the " Shiki," still more ancient commentaries on the " Nihongi,"

indeed appear the Yata-garasu flying down from the Void.
The Emperor said:—"The coming of this crow is in due
accordance with my auspicious dream. How grand! How
splendid! My Imperial ancestor, Ama-terasu no Oho-kami,
desires therewith to assist me in creating the hereditary
institution." [1]

III. 12. At this time Hi no Omi [2] no Mikoto, ancestor of the Ohotomo [3] House, taking with him Oho-kume [4] as commander of
the main body, guided by the direction taken by the crow,
looked up to it and followed after, until at length they arrived
at the district of Lower Uda. Therefore they named the
place which they reached the village of Ukechi [5] in Uda.

that the Yang-wu or Sun-crow is in Japanese yata-garasu. The Yang-wu is a
bird with three claws, and of a red colour, which, according to Chinese myth,

inhabits the sun. If we accept this identification, the meaning of the epithet yata becomes
clear. It means eight hands, or, as ya in ancient
Japanese meant also many or several, many
hands, a sufficiently accurate description for
popular myth of the Yang-wu with its three
claws. The late M. Terrien de La-Couperie,
in his "Western Origin of Early Chinese
Civilization," says that "the first allusion to
the three-legged crow supposed to roost in
the sun occurs in the "Li Sao" of Kiü-yuen,
the poet of Ts'u, 314 B.C. in China. A three-
legged bird in various forms was figured on
coins of Pamphylia and Lycia of older times.
Comte Goblet d'Alviella has reproduced some of
them in his interesting work on "La Migration
des Symboles," 1891, p. 222. See a paper on
the Hi no maru in "T.A.S.J.," Vol. XXII., p. 27,
and Ch. K., p. 136. The guidance of con-

Sun-crow.

querors or colonists to their destination by a supernatural bird or beast
is a familiar feature of old-world story. See Lang, "Custom and Myth,"
II, 71.

[1] The sovereignty.   [2] Hi means sun ; Omi, minister.

[3] Oho-tomo means "great companion." The Oho-tomo were the Imperial
guards.

[4] Oho-kume, as Chamberlain points out, probably means simply a great
force. But when the "Kojiki" and "Nihongi" were written, this meaning
was forgotten, and it was supposed to be a man's name.

[5] Ugatsu means to pierce, and the name was given because they penetrated
the mountains to this place. All these derivations are very fanciful.

At this time, by an Imperial order, he commended Hi no Omi no Mikoto, saying :—" Thou art faithful and brave, and art moreover a successful guide. Therefore will I give thee a new name, and will call thee Michi no Omi."[1]

Autumn, 8th month, 2nd day. The Emperor sent to summon Ukeshi the Elder and Ukeshi the Younger. These two were chiefs of the district of Uda. Now Ukeshi the Elder did not come. But Ukeshi the Younger came, and making obeisance at the gate of the camp, declared as follows :—" Thy servant's elder brother, Ukeshi the Elder, shows signs of resistance. Hearing that the descendant of Heaven was about to arrive, he forthwith raised an army with which to make an attack. But having seen from afar the might of the Imperial army, he was afraid, and did not dare to oppose it. Therefore he has secretly placed his troops in ambush, and has built for the occasion a new palace, in the hall of which he has prepared engines. It is his intention to invite the Emperor to a banquet there, and then to do him a mischief. I pray that his treachery be noted, and that good care be taken to make preparation against it." The Emperor straightway sent Michi no Omi no Mikoto to observe the signs of his opposition. Michi no Omi no Mikoto clearly ascertained his hostile intentions, and being greatly enraged, shouted at him in a blustering manner :—" Wretch ! thou shalt thyself dwell in the house which thou hast made." So grasping his sword, and drawing his bow, he urged him and drove him within it. Ukeshi the Elder being guilty before Heaven, and the matter not admitting of excuse, of his own accord trod upon the engine and was crushed to death. His body was then brought out and decapitated, and the blood which flowed from it reached above the ankle. Therefore that place was called Uda no Chi-hara.[2] After this Ukeshi the Younger prepared a great feast of beef and sake,[3] with which he entertained the

III. 13.

---

[1] The Minister of the Road. [2] The bloody plain of Uda.

[3] We might be inclined to infer from this (what was probably the case) that the Ancient Japanese lived more on animal food than their descendants in modern times. But there is much room for suspicion that this statement s nothing more than a reminiscence of a passage in a history of the Later Han dynasty of China, which speaks of beef and sake being presented to the Emperor Kwang Wu Ti, who came to the throne A.D. 25.

Imperial army. The Emperor distributed this flesh and sake to the common soldiers, upon which they sang the following verses :—

> In the high $\left\{ \begin{array}{l} \text{castle} \\ \text{tree} \end{array} \right\}$ of Uda
> I set a snare for woodcock,
> And waited,
> But no woodcock came to it ;
> A valiant whale came to it.[1]
> *   *   *   *
> *   *   *   *

III. 14.

This is called a Kume [2] song. At the present time, when the Department of Music performs this song, there is still the [3] measurement of great and small by the hand, as well as a distinction of coarse and fine in the notes of the voice. This is by a rule handed down from antiquity.

After this the Emperor wished to inspect the Land of Yoshino, so taking personal command of the light troops, he made a progress round by way of Ukechi mura in Uda.

III. 15.

When he came to Yoshino, there was a man who came out of a well. He shone, and had a tail. The Emperor inquired of him, saying :—" What man art thou ? "   He answered and said :—" Thy servant is a local Deity, and his name is Wi-hikari." [4]   He it is who was the first ancestor of the Yoshino no Obito. Proceeding a little further, there was another man with a tail, who burst open a rock and came forth from it. The Emperor inquired of him, saying :—" What man art thou ? " He answered and said :—" Thy servant is the child of Iha-oshi-

---

[1] Ki in the first line of this poem means probably both tree and castle. The words are put into the mouth of Ukeshi the Elder, who found a whale (the Emperor) in his springe instead of the harmless woodcock he expected. The wild boar is now called the yama-kujira or mountain-whale, and is perhaps the animal intended here.

I confess that I can make no satisfactory sense of the remainder of this poem. The version given by Chamberlain (Ch. K., p. 140), following Moribe, is as good as any, but it seems to me very conjectural. It should be noted, however, that this part of the poem contains an indication of the polygamous customs of the Japanese at this time in the use of two words signifying respectively elder wife (konami) and younger wife (uhanari). The " Nihongi" omits the interjectional refrain given in the " Kojiki."

[2] Kume means no doubt "soldier" in this passage.

[3] Beating time is perhaps meant.   [4] Well-brightness.

wake." [1] It is he who was the first ancestor of the Kuzu [2] of Yoshino.

Then skirting the river, he proceeded westward, when there appeared another man, who had made a fish trap and was catching fish. On the Emperor making inquiry of him, he answered and said :—" Thy servant is the son of Nihe-motsu." [3] He it is who was the first ancestor of the U-kahi of Ata. [4]

9th month, 5th day. The Emperor ascended to the peak of Mount Takakura in Uda, whence he had a prospect over all III. 16. the land. On Kuni-mi [5] Hill there were descried eighty bandits. Moreover at the acclivity of Me-zaka [6] there was posted an army of women, and at the acclivity of Wo-zaka [7] there was stationed a force of men. At the acclivity of Sumi-zaka [8] was placed burning charcoal. This was the origin of the names Me-zaka, Wo-zaka and Sumi-zaka.

Again there was the army of Ye-shiki, [9] which covered all the village of Ihare. All the places occupied by the enemy [10] were strong positions, and therefore the roads were cut off and obstructed, so that there was no room for passage. The Emperor, indignant at this, made prayer on that night in person, and then fell asleep. The Heavenly Deity appeared to him in a dream, and instructed him, saying:—" Take earth from within the shrine [11] of the Heavenly Mount Kagu, and of it make eighty Heavenly platters. Also make sacred jars [12] and III. 17. therewith sacrifice to the Gods of Heaven and Earth. Moreover pronounce a solemn imprecation. If thou doest so, the

---

[1] Rock-push-divide.

[2] Kuzu were local chiefs. They are mentioned again in Ōjin's reign.

[3] Food-holder or purveyor.

[4] U-kahi means cormorant-keepers. Fishing with cormorants is still practised in Japan.

[5] Land-view.   [6] Women's acclivity.

[7] Men's acclivity. The terms Me-zaka and Wo-zaka are now applied to two roads or stairs leading up to the same place, one of which (the women's) is less precipitous than the other.

[8] Sumi-zaka means charcoal acclivity.

[9] Shiki the Elder.   [10] Lit. Robber-slaves or prisoners.

[11] A shrine, like a templum, might be merely a consecrated plot of ground. Kagu-yama is a mountain in Yamato.

[12] Idzube. The platters were for rice, the jars for sake. See Satow's "Rituals" in "J.A.S.T.," VII., ii., p. 109.

K

enemy will render submission of their own accord." The
Emperor received with reverence the directions given in his
dream, and proceeded to carry them into execution.

Now Ukeshi the Younger again addressed the Emperor,
saying :—" There are in the province of Yamato, in the village
of Shiki, eighty Shiki bandits. Moreover, in the village of
Taka-wohari [*some say Katsuraki*] there are eighty Akagane[1]
bandits. All these tribes intend to give battle to the Emperor,
and thy servant is anxious in his own mind on his account.
It were now good to take clay from the Heavenly Mount
Kagu, and therewith to make Heavenly platters with which to
sacrifice to the Gods of the Heavenly shrines and of the Earthly
shrines. If after doing so, thou dost attack the enemy, they
may be easily driven off." The Emperor, who had already
taken the words of his dream for a good omen, when he now
heard the words of Ukeshi the Younger, was still more pleased
in his heart. He caused Shihi-netsu-hiko[2] to put on ragged
garments and a grass hat, and to disguise himself as an old man.
He also caused Ukeshi the Younger to cover himself with a
winnowing tray, so as to assume the appearance of an old
woman, and then addressed them, saying :—" Do ye two proceed to the Heavenly Mount Kagu, and secretly take earth from
its summit. Having done so, return hither. By means of
you I shall then divine whether my undertaking will be
successful or not. Do your utmost and be watchful."

III. 18.   Now the enemy's army filled the road, and made all passage
impossible. Then Shihi-netsu-hiko prayed, and said :—" If it
will be possible for our Emperor to conquer this land, let the
road by which we must travel become open. But if not, let
the brigands surely oppose our passage." Having thus spoken
they set forth, and went straight onwards. Now the hostile
band, seeing the two men, laughed loudly, and said :—" What
an uncouth old man and old woman !" So with one accord
they left the road, and allowed the two men to pass and proceed
to the mountain, where they took the clay and returned with
it. Hereupon the Emperor was greatly pleased, and with this

---

[1] Akagane means red metal, i.e. copper, but the text is doubtful. The
" Kiujiki" has a different reading.
[2] See above, p. 111.

clay he made eighty platters, eighty Heavenly small jars and
sacred jars,[1] with which he went up to the upper waters of the
River Nifu and sacrificed to the Gods of Heaven and of Earth.
Immediately, on the Asa-hara plain by the river of Uda, it
became as it were like foam on the water, the result of the curse
cleaving to them.[2]

Moreover the Emperor went on to utter a vow, saying :—" I
will now make ame[3] in the eighty platters without using water.
If the ame is formed, then shall I assuredly without effort and
without recourse to the might of arms reduce the Empire to
peace." So he made ame, which forthwith became formed of
itself.[4]

Again he made a vow, saying :—" I will now take the sacred
jars and sink them in the River Nifu. If the fishes, whether
great or small, become every one drunken and are carried down
the stream, like as it were to floating maki[5] leaves, then shall
I assuredly succeed in establishing this land. But if this be
not so, there will never be any result." Thereupon he sank III. 19.
the jars in the river with their mouths downward. After a
while the fish all came to the surface, gaping and gasping as
they floated down the stream. Then Shihi-netsu-hiko, seeing
this, represented it to the Emperor, who was greatly rejoiced,
and plucking up a five-hundred-branched masakaki tree of the

[1] The reader who wishes to realize what the ancient pottery of Japan was
like should visit the British Museum and inspect the Gowland collection.
There is also a collection in the Uyeno Museum in Tokio. Ninagawa
Noritane's work entitled " Kwan-ko-dzu-setsu " gives very good drawings of
ancient pottery. The common Japanese name for this ware is Giōgi-yaki,
Giōgi being the name of a Buddhist priest who lived 670-749, and who is
credited with the invention of the potter's wheel. But the wheel was certainly known in Japan long before his time. This very passage contains an
evidence of this fact. Both the Chinese characters and the Japanese word
ta-kujiri given in the ancient commentary for the small jars here mentioned
mean "hand-made," leading to the conclusion that this was exceptional.
Indeed, nearly all the pottery of the Nihongi period which has come down to
us is wheel-made.

[2] Foam on water is a favourite emblem of the transitoriness of human
life.

[3] Ame (sweetness) is usually made of millet, malted, and is nearly identical
in composition with what our chemists call " malt extract." It is a favourite
sweetmeat in the far East.

[4] Cf. Judges vi. 36.   [5] Podocarpus macrophylla.

upper waters of the River Nifu, he did worship therewith to all the Gods. It was with this that the custom began of setting sacred jars.[1]

At this time he commanded Michi no Omi no Mikoto, saying:—"We are now in person[2] about to celebrate a public[3] festival to Taka-mi-musubi no Mikoto, and I appoint thee Ruler of the festival, and grant thee the title of Idzu-hime.[4] The earthen jars which are set up shall be called the Idzube or sacred jars, the fire shall be called Idzu no Kagu-tsuchi or sacred-fire-elder, the water shall be called Idzu no Midzu-ha no me or sacred-water-female, the food shall be called Idzu-uka no me or sacred-food-female, the firewood shall be called Idzu no Yama-tsuchi or sacred-mountain-elder, and the grass shall be called Idzu no No-tsuchi or sacred-moor-elder."

III. 20.   Winter, 10th month, 1st day. The Emperor tasted[5] the food of the Idzube, and arraying his troops set forth upon his march. He first of all attacked the eighty bandits at Mount Kunimi, routed and slew them. It was in this campaign that the Emperor, fully resolved on victory, made these verses, saying :—

> Like the Shitadami
> Which creep around
> The great rock
> Of the Sea of Ise
> Where blows the divine wind —
> Like the Shitadami,
> My boys! my boys!
> We will creep around,
> And smite them utterly,
> And smite them utterly.[6]

---

[1] A note says that they were set up in the courtyard.

[2] The Mikado deputed most of his priestly functions to the Nakatomi.

[3] The ancient commentary gives the Japanese word utsushi, i.e. manifest, visible. This suggests that there was a distinction between esoteric and exoteric in the Shintō rites of this time.

[4] Idzu-hime means dread or sacred princess. The "Tsūshō" commentator says that the persons entrusted with this function were usually women, as may be seen in the case of the priestesses of Ise, Kamo, and Kasuga. But as no women were available at this time, Michi-no-Omi was given a feminine title for the occasion.

[5] The interlinear Kana has tatematsuri, i.e. offered. The reference is to the feast of Nihiname described above. See p. 86.

[6] The shitadami is a small shell of the turbinidæ class. Its introduction

In this poem, by the great rock is intended the Hill of Kunimi.

After this the band which remained was still numerous, and their disposition could not be fathomed. So the Emperor privately commanded Michi no Omi no Mikoto, saying :—" Do thou take with thee the Oho-kume, and make a great muro at the village of Osaka.[1] Prepare a copious banquet, invite the enemy to it, and then capture them." Michi no Omi no Mikoto thereupon, in obedience to the Emperor's secret behest, dug a muro at Osaka, and having selected his bravest soldiers, stayed therein mingled with the enemy. He secretly arranged with them, saying :—" When they have got tipsy with sake, I will strike up a song. Do you, when you hear the sound of my song, all at the same time stab the enemy." Having III. 21. made this arrangement they took their seats, and the drinking-bout proceeded. The enemy, unaware that there was any plot, abandoned themselves to their feelings, and promptly became intoxicated. Then Michi no Omi no Mikoto struck up the following song :—

> At Osaka
> In the great muro-house,
> Though men in plenty
> Enter and stay,
> We the glorious
> Sons of warriors,
> Wielding our mallet-heads,
> Wielding our stone-mallets,
> Will smite them utterly.[2]

Now when our troops heard this song, they all drew at the

here does not seem very appropriate. Perhaps the meaning is " in number like the turbinidæ." Cf. Ch. K., p. 143. The " Shukai " editor thinks that the shitadami represent the bandits. The great rock is, perhaps, the Miyôto-seki at Futami, so often represented in Japanese pictures. See Anderson's Catalogue, p. 320, or Satow and Hawes' Handbook, p. 150.

[1] In Yamato. To be distinguished from the city of Ohosaka.

[2] The muro-ya is a pit-dwelling (see above, p. 71). The poem speaks of mallet-heads, but the text which follows of mallet-headed swords. I have little doubt that the former is the true phrase, and that stone weapons are referred to. The stone-mallets are unmistakably the weapons figured above (p. 87). The mallet-heads and stone-mallets are perhaps the same thing under different names.

same time their mallet-headed swords, and simultanously slew the enemy, so that there were no eaters left.[1] The Imperial army were greatly delighted; they looked up to Heaven and laughed. Therefore he made a song, saying :—

> Though folk say
> That one Yemishi
> Is a match for one hundred men,
> They do not so much as resist.[2]

The practice according to which at the present time the Kume sing this and then laugh loud, had this origin.

Again he sang, saying :—

> Ho ! now is the time ;
> Ho ! now is the time ;
> Ha ! Ha ! Psha !
> Even now
> My boys !
> Even now
> My boys ![3]

All these songs were sung in accordance with the secret behest of the Emperor. He had not presumed to compose
III. 22. them of his own motion.

Then the Emperor said :—" It is the part of a good general when victorious to avoid arrogance. The chief brigands have now been destroyed, but there are ten bands of villains of a similar stamp, who are disputatious. Their disposition cannot

---

[1] That is, none were left alive.

The Yemishi are the Ainos, or more correctly Ainus, of whom a remnant of some ten thousand souls now inhabit the island of Yezo. When the " Nihongi " was written they still occupied a large part of the main island of Japan, and in earlier times, as we gather from the evidence of place-names (See Chamberlain's Essay published by the Imperial University), they ex- tended west even of Yamato. But it would not be safe to draw any con- clusion from their mention in this poem. The writer of the " Nihongi " is in the habit of fitting ancient poetry into his narrative in a very arbitrary manner. The " Kojiki " omits it. Yemishi or Yebisu is also applied to barbarous tribes generally, and this is probably its primary meaning. It ought, perhaps, to be added to the group of onomatopoetic words ending in *su* or *shi*, mentioned at p. 65, the *b* or *m* having the same function as these letters in the words barbarian, babble, murmur, etc. See Index—Yemishi.

[2] Nothing could well be more primitive than this. The metre is irregular, and, like all Japanese poetry, there is no rhyme, quantity or regular recur- rence of accent to distinguish it from prose.

be ascertained. Why should we remain for a long time in one place? By so doing we could not have control over emergencies." So he removed his camp to another place.

11th month, 7th day. The Imperial army proceeded in great force to attack the Hiko [1] of Shiki. First of all the Emperor sent a messenger to summon Shiki the Elder, but he refused to obey. Again the Yata-garasu was sent to bring him. When the crow reached his camp it cried to him, saying:—" The child of the Heavenly Deity sends for thee. Haste! haste!" Shiki the Elder was enraged at this, and said:—" Just when I heard that the conquering Deity of Heaven was coming and was indignant at this, why shouldst thou, a bird of the crow tribe, utter such an abominable cry?" So he drew his bow and aimed at it. The crow forthwith fled away, and next proceeded to the house of Shiki the Younger, where it cried, saying:— " The child of the Heavenly Deity summons thee. Haste! haste!" Then Shiki the Younger was afraid, and, changing countenance, said:—" Thy servant, hearing of the approach of the conquering Deity of Heaven, is full of dread morning and evening. Well hast thou cried to me, O crow." He straightway made eight leaf-platters,[2] on which he disposed food, and entertained the crow. Accordingly, in obedience to the crow, he proceeded to the Emperor and informed him, saying:—" My elder brother, Shiki the Elder, hearing of the approach of the child of the Heavenly Deity, forthwith assembled eighty bandits and provided arms, with which he is about to do battle with thee. It will be well to take measures against him without delay." The Emperor accordingly assembled his generals and inquired of them, saying:—" It appears that Shiki the Elder has now rebellious intentions. I summoned him, but again he will not come. What is to be done?" The generals said:—" Shiki the Elder is a crafty knave. It will be well, first of all, to send Shiki the Younger to make matters clear to him, and at the same time to make explanations to Kuraji the Elder and Kuraji the Younger. If after that they still refuse submission, it will not be too late to take warlike measures against them." Shiki the Younger was accordingly sent to explain to them

III. 23.

---

[1] Princes.
[2] Or trays, made of the leaves of Kashiha, a kind of evergreen oak.

their interests. But Shiki the Elder and the others adhered to their foolish design, and would not consent to submit. Then Shihi-netsu-hiko advised as follows :—" Let us first send out our feebler troops by the Osaka road. When the enemy sees them he will assuredly proceed thither with all his best troops. We should then straightway urge forward our robust troops, and make straight for Sumi-zaka.[1] Then with the water of the River Uda we should sprinkle the burning charcoal, and suddenly take them unawares, when they cannot fail to be routed." The Emperor approved this plan, and sent out the feebler troops towards the enemy, who, thinking that a powerful force was approaching, awaited them with all their power. Now up to this time, whenever the Imperial army attacked, they invariably captured, and when they fought they were invariably victorious, so that the fighting men were all wearied out. Therefore the Emperor, to comfort the hearts of his leaders and men, struck off this verse :—

III. 24.

> As we fight,
> Going forth and watching
> From between the trees
> Of Mount Inasa,
> We are famished.
> Ye keepers of cormorants
> (Birds of the island),
> Come now to our aid.[2]

In the end he crossed Sumi-zaka with the stronger troops, and, going round by the rear, attacked them from two sides and put them to the rout, killing their chieftains Shiki the Elder and the others.

12th month, 4th day. The Imperial army at length attacked Naga-sune-hiko and fought with him repeatedly, but was unable to gain the victory. Then suddenly the sky became overcast, and hail fell. There appeared a wondrous kite of a golden colour which came flying and perched on the end of the Emperor's bow. The lustre of this kite was of dazzling

---

[1] The charcoal acclivity.

[2] The metre is nearly regular naga-uta, which consists of alternate lines of five and seven syllables, with an additional line of seven syllables at the end. The cormorant-keepers were appealed to to supply fish for the army's food.

brightness, so that its appearance was like that of lightning.
In consequence of this all Naga-sune-hiko's soldiers were
dazzled and bewildered so that they could not fight stoutly.   III. 25.
Nagasune was the original name of the village, whence it
became the name of a man. But in consequence of the
Imperial army obtaining the favourable omen of the Kite, the
men of that time called it Tobi no mura.[1] It is now called
Tomi, which is a corruption of this.

Ever since Itsuse no Mikoto was hit by an arrow at the
battle of Kusaka and died, the Emperor bore this in mind, and
constantly cherished resentment for it. On this campaign it
was his desire to put all to death, and therefore he composed
these verses, saying :—

> My mouth tingles
> With the ginger planted
> At the bottom of the hedge
> By the glorious
> Sons of warriors—
> I cannot forget it ;
> Let us smite them utterly.

Again he sang, saying :—

> In the millet-field
> Is one stem of odorous garlic :—
> The glorious
> Sons of warriors
> Binding its stem
> And binding its shoots
> Will smite it utterly.

Then again letting loose his army, he suddenly attacked him.
In general, all these songs composed by the Emperor are
termed *kume uta*, in allusion to the persons who took and sang
them.

Now Naga-sune-hiko sent a foot-messenger, who addressed
the Emperor, saying :—" There was formerly a child of the

---

[1] Kite-village.

[2] "As the taste of ginger remains in the mouth for a long time after it is
eaten, so do my feelings of resentment for my brother's death remain present
to my mind. I cannot forget it, so let us revenge it by destroying the enemy
utterly."

The word for shoots is *me*, which also means *females.* This is no
doubt intentional. Naga-sune-hiko is to be destroyed with all his family.

Heavenly Deity, who came down from Heaven to dwell here, riding in a Rock-boat of Heaven. His name was Kushi-dama Nigi-haya-hi no Mikoto. He took to wife my younger sister

III. 26   Mi-kashiki-ya-bime [1] [*also called Naga-sune-hime, or Tomi-ya-hime*] [2] of whom he at length had a child, named Umashi-ma-te [3] no Mikoto. Therefore did I take Nigi-haya-hi no Mikoto for my Lord, and did service to him. Can it be that there are two seeds of the children of the Heavenly Deity? Why should any one else take the name of Child of the Heavenly Deity and therewith rob people of their dominions? I have pondered this in my heart, but have as yet failed utterly to believe it." The Emperor said :—"There are many other children of the Heavenly Deity. If he whom thou has taken as thy Lord were truly a child of the Heavenly Deity, there would be surely some object which thou couldst show to us by way of proof." Naga-sune-hiko accordingly brought a single Heavenly-feathered-arrow of Nigi-haya-hi no Mikoto, and a foot-quiver, [4] and exhibited them respectfully to the Emperor. The Emperor examined them, and said :—"These are genuine." Then in his turn he showed to Naga-sune-hiko the single Heavenly-feathered-arrow and quiver which he wore. When Naga-sune-hiko saw the Heavenly token he became more and more embarrassed. But the murderous weapons were already prepared, and things were in such a state that he was unable to pause in his career. Therefore he adhered to his misguided scheme, and would not alter his purpose.

Nigi-haya-hi no Mikoto, knowing from the first that the Heavenly Deity had simply generously bestowed the Empire on the Heavenly Grandchild, and that in view of the perverse disposition of Naga-sune it would be useless to instruct him

III. 27.   in the relation of Heaven to Man, [5] put him to death. He then came with his army and made submission. The Emperor, who from the first had heard that Nigi-haya-hi no Mikoto had come down from Heaven, finding that he now had actually performed faithful service, accordingly praised him, and was gracious to him. He was the ancestor of the Mono no Be House. [6]

---

[1] Three-cook-house-princess.   [2] Wealth-house.   [3] Sweet-true-hand.

[4] A foot-soldier's quiver is meant.   [5] i.e. of Lord and Vassal.

[6] The Mononobe were soldiers. Here, however, the hereditary chiefs only are meant, the Mononobe no Muraji.

The year Tsuchi no to Hitsuji, Spring, 2nd month, 20th B.C. 662.
day. The Emperor commanded his generals to exercise the
troops. At this time there were Tsuchi-gumo [1] in three places,
viz. :—The Tohe [2] of Nihiki at Tada no Oka-zaki [3] in the
district of Sofu, the Kose Hofuri at Wani no Saka-moto,[4] and
the Wi-Hofuri [5] at Hosomi no Nagara no Oka-zaki. All of these,

[1] The Tsuchi-gumo are mentioned in four or five passages of the
"Nihongi" and one passage of the "Kojiki," all of which belong to the
highly legendary period of Japanese history. We gather from them that
the Tsuchi-gumo were usually, though not invariably, outlaws who defied the
Imperial authority. They had Japanese names, and inhabited such long-
settled parts of Japan as Yamato, Harima, and even Kiushiu. There is
nothing, if we put aside the mention of Yemishi at p. 124, to suggest that
they were not of Japanese race. The "short bodies," etc., of the "Nihongi"
description I take to be nothing more than a product of the popular
imagination working on the hint contained in the name Tsuchi-gumo, which
is literally "earth spider." Some etymologists prefer the derivation which
connects *kumo* (or *gumo*) with *komori*, to hide, thus making tsuchi-gumo
the "earth-hiders." But this is probably a distinction without a difference,
these two words containing the same root, and the animal which we call
the spider, i.e. spinner, being in Japan termed the "hider," an epithet of
which no one who has observed its habits will dispute the appropriateness.
An ancient Japanese book says Tsuchi-gumo is a mere nickname, to be
compared therefore with our clod-hopper or bog-trotter.

In one of the passages above referred to, the Tsuchi-gumo are described
as inhabiting a rock-cave, but in others they are said to live in muro or
pit-dwellings, and this is obviously the origin of the name.

There are several notices of Tsuchi-gumo in the ancient "Fudoki," or
"County Histories," but they are probably mere echoes of the older legends
related in the "Nihongi" and "Kojiki," and in any case they add nothing of
importance to our information about them. It may be noted, however, that
Hiuga and Higo are mentioned in them as habitats of bands of these outlaws.

An amusing expansion by a modern writer of the spider conception of the
Tsuchi-gumo will be found at p. 140 of Anderson's B.M. Catalogue. See
also Ch. K., p. 141, and Index.

A little work called "Kek-kio-kō," in a collection entitled "Haku-butsu-
sō-sho," published by the Japanese Imperial Museum, has brought together
all the available information respecting Muro and Tsuchi-gumo.

[2] Chiefs.

[3] Oka-zaki means hill-spur, and is perhaps to be so understood here, and
not as a proper name.

[4] Saka-moto (acclivity bottom) may be also a description and not a proper
name.

[5] Hofuri is a kind of Shintō priest. It is unlikely that persons not of
Japanese race should be so called.

trusting to their valour, refused to present themselves at Court. The Emperor therefore sent detachments separately, and put them all to death. There were, moreover, Tsuchi-gumo at the village of Taka-wohari, whose appearance was as follows :— They had short bodies, and long arms and legs. They were of the same class as the pigmies. The Imperial troops wove nets of dolichos, which they flung over them and then slew III. 28. them. Wherefore the name of that village was changed to Katsuraki.[1] It is in the land of Ihare. Its ancient name was Kataru, or Katatachi. When our Imperial forces routed the enemy, a great army assembled and filled that country. Its name was accordingly changed to Ihare.[2]

Another account says that when the Emperor on a previous occasion tasted the food of the sacred jars, he moved forward his army on an expedition towards the West. At this time the eighty bandits of Katsuraki were encamped together there. A great battle with the Emperor followed, and they were at length destroyed by the Imperial army. Therefore that place was called the village of Ihare.[3] Again, the place where the Imperial troops made a warlike stand was called Takeda.[4] The place where he built a castle was named Kita.[5] Moreover, the place where the enemy fell in battle, their dead bodies prostrate, with their forearms for pillows, was called Tsura-maki-da.[6]

The Emperor, in Autumn, the 9th month of the previous year, secretly took clay of the Heavenly Mount Kagu, with which he made eighty platters, and thereafter performing abstinence in person, sacrificed to all the Gods. He was thereby at length enabled to establish the world[7] in peace. Therefore he called the place where the clay was taken Hani-yasu.[8]

[1] Dolichos Castle.

[2] The interlinear Kana gives for "fill," ihameri, a word which I do not know.

[3] The " original commentary" says that the Japanese word corresponding to the Chinese characters rendered "encamp" is ihami, a word not otherwise known to me.

[4] Brave-field.   [5] Castle-field.   [6] Face-pillow-field.

[7] "World" is not quite a merely rhetorical expression for the Empire of Japan. Hirata justifies Hideyoshi's invasion of Corea on the grounds that the sovereigns of Japan are de jure lords of the whole earth.

[8] Clay-easy or clay-peace.

3rd month, 7th day. The Emperor made an order,[1] say- III. 29.
ing :—" During the six years that our expedition against the
East has lasted, owing to my reliance on the Majesty of
Imperial Heaven, the wicked bands have met death. It is
true that the frontier lands are still unpurified, and that a
remnant of evil is still refractory. But in the region of the
Central Land there is no more wind and dust. Truly we
should make a vast and spacious capital, and plan it great
and strong.[2]

At present things are in a crude and obscure condition, and
the people's minds are unsophisticated. They roost in nests
or dwell in caves.[3] Their manners are simply what is customary.
Now if a great man were to establish laws, justice could not
fail to flourish. And even if some gain should accrue to
the people, in what way would this interfere with the Sage's[4]
action? Moreover, it will be well to open up and clear the
mountains and forests, and to construct a palace. Then I may
reverently assume the Precious Dignity, and so give peace to III. 30.
my good subjects. Above, I should then respond to the
kindness of the Heavenly Powers in granting me the Kingdom,
and below, I should extend the line of the Imperial descendants
and foster rightmindedness. Thereafter the capital may be
extended so as to embrace all the six cardinal points, and the
eight cords may be covered so as to form a roof.[5] Will this
not be well?

When I observe the Kashiha-bara[6] plain, which lies

---

[1] This whole speech is thoroughly Chinese in every respect, and it is
preposterous to put it in the mouth of an Emperor who is supposed to have
lived more than a thousand years before the introduction of Chinese learning
into Japan. The strange thing is that it is necessary to make this remark.
Yet there are still writers who regard this part of the " Nihongi " as
historical.

[2] The Kana rendering is mi-araka, "an august shrine" or "an august
palace." This would imply a different reading, 社 instead of 壯.

[3] The reader must not take this as any evidence of the manners and
customs of the Ancient Japanese. It is simply a phrase suggested by the
author's Chinese studies.

[4] Meaning the Emperor's action.

[5] The character for roof 宇 also means the universe. The eight cords,
or measuring tapes, simply mean "everywhere."

[6] Kashiha is an evergreen oak, the Quercus dentata. Hara means plain.

S.W. of Mount Unebi, it seems the Centre of the Land. I must set it in order." Accordingly he in this month commanded officers to set about the construction of an Imperial Residence.

Year Kanoye Saru, Autumn, 8th month, 16th day. The Emperor, intending to appoint a wife, sought afresh [1] children of noble families. Now there was a man who made representation to him, saying:—"There is a child who was born to Koto-shiro-nushi no Kami by his union with Tama-kushi-hime, daughter of Mizo-kuhi-ni no Kami of Mishima. Her name is Hime-tatara-i-suzu-hime no Mikoto. She is a woman of remarkable beauty." The Emperor was rejoiced, and on the 24th day of the 9th month he received Hime-tatara-i-suzu-hime no Mikoto and made her his wife.

Year Kanoto Tori, Spring, 1st month, 1st day. The Emperor assumed the Imperial Dignity in the Palace of Kashiha-bara. This year is reckoned the first year of his reign.[2] He honoured his wife by making her Empress. The children born to him by her were Kami-ya-wi-mimi no Mikoto and Kami-nunagaha mimi no Mikoto.

Therefore [3] there is an ancient saying in praise of this, as follows:—" In Kashiha-bara in Unebi, he mightily established his palace-pillars on the foundation of the bottom-rock, and reared aloft the cross roof-timbers to the Plain of High Heaven.[4]

This afterwards became a proper name. Here it is perhaps simply a description.

[1] He had already a consort, but she was apparently not considered a wife.

[2] Japanese History is often said to begin with this year. The fact is that nothing which really deserves the name of history existed for nearly a thousand years more. This date is very much like that given for the foundation of Rome by Romulus, B.C. 753. The very calendar by which the reckoning was made was not invented or known in Japan until many centuries after. See Bramsen's " Chronological Tables," and "Early Japanese History " in " T.A.S.J."

[3] As above remarked, the author often introduces this word without much reason.

[4] It was a mark of Shrines or Imperial Palaces to have the rafters at each end of the roof projecting upwards for several feet beyond the roof-tree, as in the illustration. These were called Chigi. See Ch. K., p. 311. Shintō temples at the present day are thus distinguished. What would those Japanese

The name of the Emperor who thus began to rule the Empire was Kami Yamato Ihare-biko Hohodemi."

On the day on which he first began the Heavenly institution, Michi no Omi no Mikoto, the ancestor of the Ohotomo House, accompanied by the Oho-kume Be, was enabled, by means of a secret device received from the Emperor, to use incantations and magic formulæ so as to dissipate evil influences. The use of magic formulæ had its origin from this.

2nd year, Spring, 2nd month, 2nd day. The Emperor ascer- B.C. 659. tained merit and dispensed rewards. To Michi no Omi no

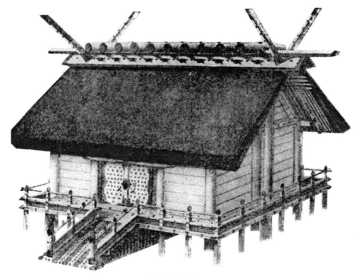

Shrine at Ise.

Mikoto he granted a site for a house in which to dwell at the village of Tsuki-zaka, thereby showing him special favour.

Moreover, he caused the Oho-kume to dwell at a place on the river-bank, west of Mount Unebi, now called Kume no mura.[1] Such was the origin of this name. Utsu-hiko was made Miyakko of the land of Yamato. Moreover, he gave to Ukeshi III. 33. the younger the village of Takeda, constituting him' Agata-

Euhemerists who think Takama ga hara (the Plain of High Heaven) to be the name of a country, make of this passage?

[1] i.e. the village of the kume or soldiers.

nushi[1] of Takeda. He was the ancestor of the Mohi-tori[2] of Uda. Shiki the younger, whose personal name was Kuro-haya, was made Agata-nushi of Shiki. Moreover, he appointed a man called Tsune to be Miyakko of the Land of Katsuraki. The Yata-garasu was also included in the ranks of those who received rewards. His descendants are the Agata-nushi of Katsurano and the Tonomori[3] Be.

4th year, Spring, 2nd month, 23rd day. The Emperor issued the following decree :—" The spirits of our Imperial ancestors reflecting their radiance down from Heaven, illuminate and assist us. All our enemies have now been subdued, and there is peace within the seas. We ought to take advantage of this to perform sacrifice to the Heavenly Deities, and therewith develop filial duty."

He accordingly established spirit-terraces amongst the Tomi hills, which were called Kami-tsu-wono no Kaki-hara and Shimo-tsu-wono no Kaki-hara.[4] There he worshipped his Imperial ancestors, the Heavenly Deities.[5]

31st year, Summer, 4th month, 1st day. The Imperial palanquin[6] made a circuit, in the course of which the Emperor ascended the Hill Waki Kamu no Hotsuma. Here, having viewed the shape of the land on all sides, he said :—" Oh ! what a beautiful country we have become possessed of ! Though a blessed land of inner-tree-fibre,[7] yet it resembles a dragon-fly licking its hinder parts." From this it first received the name of Akitsu-shima.[8]

[1] Ruler of district.

[2] The Mohi-tori, afterwards mondori or mondo, were originally the officials charged with the water supply of the Palace. The designation Mondo no Kami remained until quite recent times.

[3] Tonomori, guardian of a palace or shrine.

[4] These names mean respectively the Persimmon plain of Upper Little-moor and the Persimmon plain of Lower Little-moor. The " spirit terraces " (a Chinese phrase) seems meant for the plots of ground consecrated for Shintō worship. See above, p. 81.

[5] The union of the offices of priest and king is to be noted all through this narrative.

[6] It is considered respectful to speak of the Imperial car or palanquin when the Emperor himself is meant.

[7] The inner-tree-fibre is the inner bark of the paper mulberry, used for weaving into cloth. It is here an ornamental epithet.

[8] The real meaning of Aki-tsu-shima is the " region of harvests." See

Of old, Izanagi no Mikoto, in naming this country, said :—
" Yamato is the Land of Ura-yasu :¹ it is the Land of Hoso-
hoko no Chi-taru :² it is the Land of Shiwa-Kami-Ho-tsu-ma." ³

Afterwards Oho-namuchi no Oho-kami named it the Land III. 35,
of Tama-gaki no Uchi-tsu-kuni.⁴

Finally, when Nigi-haya-hi no Mikoto soared across the
Great Void in a Heaven-rock-boat, he espied this region and
descended upon it. Therefore he gave it a name and called it
Sora-mitsu-Yamato.⁵

42nd year, Spring, 1st month, 3rd day. He appointed Prince B.C. 619.
Kami-nunagaha-mimi no Mikoto Prince Imperial.

76th year, Spring, 3rd month, 11th day. The Emperor died B.C. 585.
in the palace of Kashiha-bara. His age was then 127.⁶ The
following year, Autumn, the 12th day of the 9th month, he was
buried in the Misasagi ⁷ N.E. of Mount Unebi.

above, p. 13. It has nothing to do with akitsu, the dragon-fly This insect
may often be seen with its tail touching its mouth, so that its body forms a
ring. The appearance of the province of Yamato, which is a plain surrounded by a ring of mountains, suggested the simile in the text. Later
historians have converted this into a comparison of Japan to a dragon-fly
with outstretched wings.

¹ Bay-easy. Explained to mean " which has peace within its coasts."
² Slender-spears-thousand-good. " Well supplied with weapons," say the
commentators.
³ Rock-ring-upper-pre-eminent-true (land).
⁴ Jewel-fence-within-land.
⁵ Sky-saw-Yamato. But Sora-mitsu really means " that fills the sky," i.e.
that reaches to the farthest horizon. These names are merely poetical
inventions. They were never in actual use.
⁶ The " Kojiki " makes him 137.
⁷ The Misasagi are still to be seen in large numbers in Japan, especially
in the Gokinai or five metropolitan provinces. They are particularly
numerous in Kahachi and Yamato.

In the most ancient times, say the Japanese antiquarians, the Misasagi or
tombs of the Mikados were simple mounds. At some unknown period,

Misasagi, side view.

however, perhaps a few centuries before the Christian epoch, a highly
specialized form of tumulus came into use for this purpose, and continued
for several hundreds of years without much change. It consists of two

L

mounds, one having a circular, the other a triangular base, merging into each other after the manner shown in the illustration, the whole being surrounded by a moat, or sometimes by two concentric moats with a narrow strip of land between. The interment took place n the circular mound, the other probably serving as a platform on which were performed the rites in honour of the deceased. Seen from the side the appearance is that of a saddle-hill, the circular mound being somewhat higher than the other. There are sometimes two smaller mounds at the base of the larger ones, filling up the angle where they meet. The slope of the tumulus is not

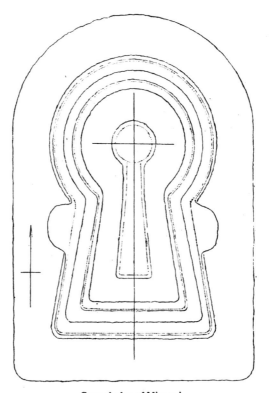

Ground plan of Misasagi.

regular, but is broken up by terraces, on which are placed in rows, a few inches apart, curious cylinders made of baked clay shaped in a mould, and measuring from 1 to 2 feet in height, and from 6 to 14 inches in diameter. They are buried in the earth, their upper rims being just level with the surface.

In some, perhaps in most cases, the Misasagi contains a large vault of great unhewn stones without mortar. The walls of the vault converge gradually towards the top, which is roofed in by enormous slabs of stone weighing many tons each. The entrance was by means of a gallery roofed with similar stones.

Sarcophagi of stone or pottery have been found in some Misasagi.

The above description is quoted from an article by the present writer in Chamberlain's "Things Japanese." I would ask travellers in China and Corea to compare with it any ancient tumuli which they may discover in those countries.

I learn from Mr. W. Gowland, who has visited the spot recognized officially as the Misasagi of Jimmu Tennō, that there are here two enclosures, the inner of which contains two low mounds each about 18 feet in diameter and 2 feet in height. A Chokushi or Imperial Envoy visits this Misasagi annually on the 3rd April with offerings of products of mountain, river, and sea, viz., tahi, carp, sea-weed, salt, water, sake, mochi (a preparation of rice), warabi (fern flour ?), pheasants and wild ducks.

The site of Jimmu's tomb is a question even with Japanese antiquaries, and European scholars may be pardoned if they are somewhat sceptical about it. *Vide* "San-rio-shi" (山 陵 志), p. 9.

BOOK IV.

THE Emperor Kami-Nunagaha-mimi was the third child of the Emperor Kami-Yamato-Ihare-biko Hohodemi. His mother's name was Hime-tatara-Isuzu no Mikoto, the eldest daughter of Koto-shiro-nushi no Kami.

This Emperor was of distinguished manners and appearance. As a child he possessed the vigour of manhood ; when he grew to manhood, his form was gigantic. He excelled in warlike accomplishments, and his will was resolute in the extreme.

IV. 2.   When he reached the age of forty-eight, the Emperor Kami-Yamato-Ihare-biko died. Now Kama-Nunagaha-mimi no Mikoto's disposition was profoundly filial, and his grief and longing knew no bounds. He made the funeral ceremonies his especial care.

His elder half-brother,[2] Tagishi-mimi no Mikoto, was now advanced in years,[3] and had a long experience of matters of

---

[1] This book contains the reigns of eight emperors, and covers a period of 483 years, giving an average of over sixty years for each reign. This is far too much for real history, especially when we consider the ages to which these sovereigns are said to have reached. Kôshô lived to the age of 114, Kôan to 137, and so on. Most of it is not even legendary. The account of the period previous to the accession of Suizei seems to contain a genuine ancient tradition, but the rest is plainly fictitious and the invention of some one imbued with Chinese ideas.

Kami means upper or lord ; Nunagaha is the name of a river ; mimi means august body.

Suizei means quiet, tranquil.

[2] The word employed indicates that the mother of this prince was not of full rank, but there is no such stigma as is implied by our word " bastard."

[3] As he was present with his younger brother at a council held by the Emperor Jimmu before starting on his expedition to the East, B.C. 667, we

state. Therefore he was again charged with the conduct of affairs, and the Emperor treated him as an intimate friend. This prince, however, was of a perverse disposition, and his natural bent was opposed to justice. During the period of sincere seclusion [1] his authority at last became independent, and concealing his malicious purposes, he plotted the destruction of his two younger brothers.

Now in the year Tsuchinoto U of the cycle, Winter, the 11th month, Kami-Nunagaha-mimi no Mikoto and his elder brother Kami-Ya-wi-mimi no Mikoto learnt privately his intentions and effectively prevented him. When the business of the misasagi was ended, they caused Yumi Be no Waka-hiko to make a bow, and Yamato no Kanuchi [2] Ama-tsu-ma-ura [3] to make a true-deer arrow-point, and the Ya [4] Be to prepare arrows. When the bow and arrows were ready, Kami-Nunagaha-mimi no Mikoto wished therewith to shoot IV. 3. to death Tagishi-mimi no Mikoto, who happened just then to be in a great muro at Kataoka, lying alone on a great couch. Then Kami-Nunagaha-mimi no Mikoto spake to Kami-Ya-wi

may suppose that he was at that time twenty years of age at least. We are now in B.C. 585, so that he must have been over 100.

[1] i.e. of mourning.

[2] Yumi-be is the Be of bow-makers ; Kanuchi, smith.

[3] Ama-tsu-ma-ura. This name is obviously identical with that of the smith-god, Ama-tsu-mara, mentioned in the "Kojiki" (see Ch. K., p. 55), upon which Chamberlain remarks, " Obvius hujus nominis sensus foret ' Cælestis Penis.' " Ma-ura means literally true-heart, or inwards, and hence came to be used as a decent term for penis, corresponding somewhat to our word "nakedness." In modern times it is a very vulgar word. This is Hirata's view. Another derivation connects it with Mâra, the Indian God of lust, sin, and death.

If Ama-tsu-ma-ura or mara stood alone, we might be disposed with Motowori to pass it by as a proper name of doubtful derivation. But Hirata (" Koshiden " v. 48) quotes from old books three other names of deities which contain this element, viz. Oho (great) mara no Mikoto, Ama-tsu-aka (red) mara no Mikoto and Ama-teru (shining) mara take-wo (brave male) no Mikoto. He thinks it sufficient to say that as these are the names of Gods, a phallic interpretation is inadmissible, but in this European scholars will hardly agree with him. There is a Mara no Sukune in the Japanese peerage of the ninth century, known as the Seishiroku. See Index— Phallic worship.

[4] Ya, arrow.

no Mikoto, saying:—"The right time has now arrived. In words, secrecy is to be prized: in deeds, caution is advisable. Therefore, we have never had any partner in our conspiracy, and the enterprise of to-day is to be carried out by thee and me alone. I will first open the door of the muro. Do thou then shoot him." They accordingly went forward and entered in together.

Kami-Nunagaha-mimi no Mikoto pushed open the door, while Kami-Ya-wi-mimi no Mikoto's arms and legs trembled so that he was unable to let fly the arrow. Then Kami-Nunagaha-mimi no Mikoto snatched the bow and arrows which his elder brother held and shot Tagishi-mimi no Mikoto. The first shot struck him on the breast, the second on the back, and so at length he killed him. Hereupon Kami-Ya-wi-mimi no Mikoto was troubled and submitted himself, yielding the sovereignty to Kami-Nunagaha-mimi no Mikoto, saying :— "I am thy elder brother.[1] But I am timid and weak, and unfit for effective action. On the present occasion thou hast specially displayed divine valour, and hast thyself put to death our chief enemy. Is it not expedient that thou shouldst illuminate the Celestial station[2] and take over the functions of

IV. 4. our Imperial ancestors? I will be thy assistant and will attend to the worship of the Gods of Heaven and Earth." He was the first ancestor of the Oho no Omi.

B.C. 581. 1st year, Spring, 1st month, 8th day. Kami-Nunagaha-mimi no Mikoto assumed the rank of Emperor. He made his capital at Katsuraki. It was called the palace[3] of Takaoka. He honoured the Empress by granting her the title of Kwō-dai-gō or Grand Empress.[4] This was the year Kanoye Tatsu of the cycle.

B.C. 580. 2nd year, Spring, 1st month. Isuzu-yori-bime was appointed Empress.

One writing says :—" Kaha-mata-bime, daughter of the Agata-nushi of Shiki."

---

[1] In this and other passages of the "Nihongi," there is a sort of recognition of a right of primogeniture, but cases are numerous where the eldest son is ignored or set aside without very strong reason in favour of a brother, widow, or younger son of the deceased sovereign.

[2] i.e. the rank of Emperor.

[3] Capital and palace are interchangeable terms in this narrative.

[4] Equivalent to Empress Dowager. This is a Chinese title.

One writing says:—"Itori-hime, daughter of Ohohimoro, Agata-nushi of Kasuga."

She was the Emperor's aunt. The Empress bore a son, the Emperor Shiki-tsu-hiko-tama-demi.

4th year, Summer, 4th month. Kami-Ya-wi-mimi no Mikoto B.C. 578. died, and was buried on the Northern side of Mount Unebi.

25th year, Spring, 1st month, 7th day. The Imperial Prince B.C. 557. Shiki-tsu-hiko-tama-demi no Mikoto was made heir to the IV. Imperial throne.

33rd year, Summer, 5th month. The Emperor took ill, and B.C. 549. on the 10th day of the same month, he died, at the age of eighty-four.

THE EMPEROR SHIKI-TSU-HIKO-TAMA-DEMI.

(ANNEI[1] TENNŌ.)

The Emperor Shiki-tsu-hiko-tama-demi was the eldest child of the Emperor Kami-Nunagaha-mimi. His mother's name was Isuzu-yori-bime no Mikoto, the younger daughter of Koto-shiro-nushi no Kami.. This Emperor had been made Prince Imperial in the 25th year of the Emperor Kami-Nunagaha-mimi. He was then twenty-one[2] years of age. In the 5th month, Summer, of the 33rd year of his reign, the Emperor Kami-Nunagaha-mimi died. In the 7th month of that year, on the 3rd day of the month, the Prince Imperial assumed the Imperial Dignity.

1st year,[3] Winter, 10th month, 11th day. The Emperor B.C. 548. Kami-Nunagaha-mimi was buried in the Misasagi on Tsukida Hill in Yamato.

The Emperor honoured the Empress with the title of Kwō-dai-gō.

---

[1] Annei means peace.

[2] The editor of the Shukai edition alters this to eleven, in order to agree with other passages. But when the whole chronology is utterly fanciful, there is no use attempting to make it consistent.

[3] For purposes of chronology, these reigns begin with the next year following the previous Emperor's death. The first year of Annei's reign is therefore B.C. 548, although his predecessor died B.C. 549.

This was the year Midzunoto Ushi of the cycle.

B.C. 547.   2nd year. The capital was removed to Katashiho. It was called the Palace of Ukiana.

B.C. 546.   3rd year, Spring, 1st month, 5th day. Nuna-soko-naka-tsu

IV. 6. hime no Mikoto was appointed Empress.

> Others call her Nuna-so hime.
>
> One writing says :—" Kaha-tsu hime, daughter of Haye, Agata-nushi of Shiki."
>
> One writing says :—" Daughter of Ohoma no Sukune." [1]

Before this, his consort had given birth to two Imperial princes. The first was called Ikishi-mimi no Mikoto, the second, the Emperor Oho-Yamato-hiko-suki-tomo.

> One version says :—" She bore three princes, the first of whom was called Toko-tsu-hiko-iro-ne ; the second, the Emperor Oho-Yamato-hiko-suki-tomo ; and the third, Shiki-tsu-hiko no Mikoto."

B.C. 538.   11th year, 1st month, 1st day. Oho-Yamato-hiko-suki-tomo no Mikoto was made Prince Imperial. His younger brother, Shiki-tsu-hiko no Mikoto was the first ancestor of the Wi-tsu-kahi no Muraji.

B.C. 511.   38th year, Winter, 11th month, 6th day. The Emperor died at the age of 57.[2]

THE EMPEROR OHO-YAMATO-HIKO-SUKI-TOMO.

(*ITOKU*[3] *TENNŌ*.)

IV. 7.   The Emperor Oho-Yamato-hiko-suki-tomo was the second child of the Emperor Shiki-tsu-hiko-tama-demi. His mother's name was Nuna-soko-naka-tsu-hime, grandchild of Koto-shiro-nushi no Kami, and daughter of the Prince[4] of Kamo. He was made Prince Imperial in the 11th year, Spring, the 1st month

---

[1] A title, derived by Yamada from Sukuna, small, and e or ye, elder brother.

[2] The " Kojiki " makes him 49.

[3] Admirable virtue.

[4] Prince is here 王, a lower rank than 皇 子 or Imperial Prince.

of the Emperor Shiki-tsu-hiko-tama-demi's reign. He was then 16 years of age. In the 38th year of that reign, Winter, the 12th month, the Emperor Shiki-tsu-hiko-tama-demi died.[1]

1st year, Spring, 2nd month, 4th day. The Prince Imperial B.C. 510. assumed the Imperial Dignity.

Autumn, 8th month, 1st day. The Emperor Shiki-tsu-hiko-tama-demi was buried in the Misasagi above Mihodo no wi, south of Mount Unebi.

9th month, 14th day. The Empress was honoured with the title of Grand Empress. This was the year Kanoto U of the cycle.

2nd year, Spring, 1st month, 5th day. The capital was B.C. 509. removed to Karu.[2] It was called the Palace of Magariwo.

2nd month, 11th day. Ama-toyo-tsu-hime no Mikoto was made Empress.

> One version has :—" Idzumi hime, daughter of Oto-wite, son of Haye, Agata-nushi of Shiki."
> One version has :—" Ihi-hime, daughter of Futo-ma- IV. 8. waka-hiko, Agata-nushi of Shiki."

This Empress was the mother of the Emperor Mi-matsu-hiko-Kayeshine.

> One version has :—" The Emperor's younger brother by the mother's side,[3] Takeshi-hiko-kushi-tomo se no Mikoto." [4]

22nd year, Spring, 2nd month, 12th day. Mi-matsu-hiko- B.C. 489. Kayeshine no Mikoto was made Prince Imperial. He was then 18 years of age.

34th year, Autumn, 9th month, 8th day. The Emperor B.C. 477. died.

---

[1] These repetitions seem intended to conceal the want of any real information about this period.

[2] In Yamato.

[3] The Japanese word for brother by the mother's side is hara-kara, " of the same belly," as to which a paper by the present writer on the " Family in Ancient Japan," contributed to the Japan Society's Journal, may be consulted.

[4] It is not clear what is meant by this.

THE EMPEROR MI-MATSU-HIKO-KAYESHINE.

(*KŌSHŌ*[1] *TENNŌ*.)

The Emperor Mi-matsu-hiko-Kayeshine was the eldest son of the Emperor Oho-Yamato-hiko-suki-tomo. The name of the Empress, his mother, was Ama-toyo-tsu-hime no Mikoto. She was the daughter of Ikishi-mimi no Mikoto. The Emperor had been made Prince Imperial in Spring, the second month of the 22nd year of the reign of the Emperor Oho-Yamato-hiko-suki-tomo. The Emperor Oho-Yamato-hiko-suki-tomo died in autumn, the ninth month of the 34th year of his reign. On the 13th day of the 10th month of the following year, the Emperor Oho-Yamato-hiko-suki-tomo was buried in the Misasagi over the Masago Valley to the south of Mount Unebi.

IV. 9.   1st year, Spring, 1st month, 9th day. The Prince Imperial
B.C. 475. assumed the Imperial Dignity.

Summer, 4th month, 5th day. The Empress was honoured with the title of Grand Empress.[2]

7th month. The capital was removed to Wakigami.[3] It was called the Palace of Ikegokoro. This year was the year Hinoye Tora of the cycle.

B.C. 447. 29th year, Spring, 1st month, 3rd day. Yoso-tarashi-hime was appointed Empress.

> One version says :—" Nunaki-tsu hime, daughter of Haye, Agata-nushi of Shiki."
> One version has :—" Oho-wi-hime, daughter of Toyo-aki-sata-wo of the Land of Yamato."

The Empress gave birth to Ama-tarashi-hiko-kuni-oshi-bito no Mikoto, and to the Emperor Yamato-tarashi-hiko-kuni-oshi-bito.

B.C. 408. 68th year, Spring, 1st month, 14th day. Yamato-tarashi-hiko-kuni-oshi-bito no Mikoto was made Prince Imperial. He

---

[1] Filial piety manifested.   [2] Kwō-dai- ō.

[3] In Yamato.

was twenty years of age. Ama-tarashi-hiko-kuni-oshi-bito no
Mikoto was the first ancestor of the Wani no Omi.

83rd year, Autumn, 8th month, 5th day. The Emperor B.C. 393.
died.

THE EMPEROR YAMATO-TARASHI-HIKO-KUNI-OSHI-BITO.

(*KŌAN* [1] *TENNŌ.*)

The Emperor Yamato-tarashi-hiko-kuni-oshi-bito was the IV. 10.
second child of the Emperor Mi-matsu-hiko-kayeshine. His
mother's name was Yoso-tarashi-hime. She was the younger
sister of Okitsu Yoso, the ancestor of the Ohari no [2] Muraji.

The Emperor was made Prince Imperial in Spring, the 1st
month of the 68th year of the reign of the Emperor Mi-matsu-
hiko-kayeshine. The Emperor Mi-matsu-hiko-kayeshine died
in Autumn, the 8th month of the 83rd year of his reign.

1st year, Spring, 1st month, 7th day. The Prince Imperial B.C. 392.
assumed the Imperial Dignity.

Autumn, 8th month, 1st day. The Empress was honoured
with the title of Grand Empress. This year was the year
Tsuchi no to Ushi of the cycle.

2nd year, Winter, 10th month. The capital was removed to B.C. 391.
Muro. It was called the Palace of Akitsushima.

26th year, Spring, 2nd month, 14th day. The Emperor B.C. 367.
appointed his niece, [3] Oshi-bime, Empress.

> One version has:—" Naga-hime, daughter of Haye,
> Agata-nushi of Shiki."
> One version has :—" Isaka-hime, daughter of Isaka-hiko,
> Agata-nushi of Tohochi."

The Empress was the mother of the Emperor Oho-Yamato-
neko-hiko-futo-ni.

38th year, Autumn, 8th month, 14th day. The Emperor Mi- B.C. 355.
matsu-hiko-kayeshine was buried in the Misasagi on Mount
Hakata in Wakigami.

76th year, Spring, 1st month, 5th day. Oho-Yamato-neko- IV. 11.
B.C. 317.

---

[1] Filial piety-peace.   [2] Or Owari.   [3] A brother's daughter.

hiko-futo-ni no Mikoto was made Prince Imperial. He was then twenty-six years of age.

B.C. 291.   102nd year, Spring, 1st month, 9th day. The Emperor died.

THE EMPEROR OHO-YAMATO-NEKO[1]-HIKO-FUTO-NI.

(KŌREI[2] TENNŌ.)

The Emperor Oho-Yamato-neko-hiko-futo-ni was the eldest child of the Emperor Yamato-tarashi-hiko-kuni-oshi-bito. His mother's name was Oshi-bime. He had been appointed Prince Imperial in Spring, the 1st month of the 76th year of the reign of the Emperor Yamato-tarashi-hiko-kuni-oshi-bito. In Spring, the 1st month of the 102nd year of his reign, the Emperor Yamato-tarashi-hiko-kuni-oshi-bito died. In Autumn, the 9th month, 13th day, the Emperor Yamato-tarashi-hiko-kuni-oshi-bito was buried in the Misasagi on Tamade Hill.

Winter, 12th month, 4th day. The Prince Imperial removed the capital to Kuroda.[3] It was called the Palace of Ihodo.

B.C. 290.   1st year, Spring, 1st month, 12th day. The Prince Imperial assumed the Imperial Dignity. He honoured the Empress with the title of Grand Empress. This year was the year Kanoto Hitsuji of the cycle.

IV. 12.   2nd year, Spring, 2nd month, 11th day. Hoso-bime no Mi-
B.C. 289. koto was appointed Empress.

> One version has :—" Kasuga no Chichi-haya-yamaka-hime."
>
> One version has :—" Mashita-bime, daughter of Toso, Agata-nushi of Tohochi."

The Empress was the mother of the Emperor Oho-Yamato-neko-hiko-kuni-kuru. A concubine named Yamato no kuni-ka-hime [*also called Haye-irone*] was the mother of Yamato-to-to-

---

[1] Several of the Emperors' names have the element Yamato-neko (neko is a honorific), and one Emperor styles himself Yamato-neko in an edict, although this was not his name. It may be suspected that Yamato-neko was at one time a general title for the sovereigns of Japan.

[2] Filial piety-spirit.   [3] In Yamato.

hi-momo-so bime no Mikoto and of Hiko-i-saseri-hiko no Mikoto [*also called Kibi-tsu-hiko no Mikoto*], and Yamato-toto-waka-ya-bime no Mikoto.

Another concubine Haye-iroto was the mother of Hiko-sajima no Mikoto and of Waka-take-hiko no Mikoto. The younger of these, namely, Waka-take-hiko no Mikoto, was the first ancestor of the Kibi no Omi.[1]

36th year, Spring, 1st month, 1st day. Hiko-kuni-kuru no   B.C. 255.
Mikoto was made Prince Imperial.

76th year, Spring, 2nd month, 8th day. The Emperor died. B.C. 215.

THE EMPEROR OHO-YAMATO-NEKO-HIKO-KUNI-KURU.   IV. 13.

(*KŌGEN[2] TENNŌ.*)

The Emperor Oho-Yamato-neko-hiko-kuni-kuru was the eldest child of the Emperor Oho-Yamato-neko-hiko-futo-ni. His mother's name was Hoso-bime, daughter of Oho-me,[3] Agata-nushi of Shiki. He had been created Prince Imperial in Spring, the 1st month of the 36th year of the reign of the Emperor Oho-Yamato-neko-hiko-futo-ni. He was then nineteen years of age. The Emperor Oho-Yamato-neko-hiko-futo-ni died in Spring, the 2nd month of the 76th year of his reign.

1st year, Spring, 1st month, 14th day. The Prince Imperial   B.C. 214.
assumed the Imperial Dignity. He honoured the Empress with the title of Grand Empress. This year was the year Hinoto I of the cycle.

4th year, Spring, 3rd month, 11th day. The capital was   B.C. 211.
removed to Karu. It was called the Palace of Sakahibara.

6th year, Autumn, 9th month, 6th day. The Emperor Oho-   B.C. 209.
Yamato-neko-hiko-futo-ni was buried in the Misasagi on Muma-zaka[4] at Kataoka.

---

[1] The "Kojiki" genealogies differ a good deal. One must be wrong ; and both, doubtless, leave much to be desired in accuracy.

[2] Filial-duty-origin.

[3] Great-eyes.

[4] The horse-acclivity.

B.C. 208. 7th year, Spring, 2nd month, 2nd day. Uchi-shiko-me no Mikoto was appointed Empress. She had three children, two boys and one girl. The name of the eldest was Oho-hiko no Mikoto; of the second, the Emperor Waka-Yamato-neko-hiko Oho-hihi; and of the third, Yamato-toto-hime no Mikoto.

One version has :—" The Emperor's brother by the mother's side was Sukuna-biko-wo-kokoro[1] no Mikoto."

IV. 14. A concubine named Ika-shiko-me no Mikoto was the mother of Hiko-futo-woshi-makoto no Mikoto. The next concubine, named Hani-yasu-hime, daughter of Awotama of Kahachi, was the mother of Take-hani-yasu no Mikoto.

The elder brother Oho-hiko no Mikoto was the first ancestor of the Abe no Omi, the Kashihade[2] no Omi, the Ahe no Omi, the Sasaki-yama no Kimi, the Tsukushi no Miyakko, the Koshi no Miyakko and the Iga no Omi, in all seven families.

IV. 15. Hiko-futo-woshi-makoto no Mikoto was the grandfather of Takechi no Sukune.

B.C. 193. 22nd year, Spring, 1st month, 14th day. Waka-Yamato-neko-hiko-oho-hihi no Mikoto was made Prince Imperial. He was sixteen years of age.

B.C. 158. 57th year, Autumn, 9th month, 2nd day. The Emperor died.

THE EMPEROR WAKA-YAMATO-NEKO-HIKO-OHO-HIHI.

(*KAIKWA*[3] *TENNŌ*.)

The Emperor Waka-Yamato-neko-hiko-oho-hihi was the second child of the Emperor Oho-Yamato-neko-hiko-kuni-kuru. His mother's name was Uchi-shikome, the ancestor of the Hodzumi no Omi, and younger sister of Uchi-shiko-wo no Mikoto.

The Emperor had been created Prince Imperial in Spring, the 1st month of the 22nd year of the reign of the Emperor Oho-Yamato-neko-hiko-kuni-kuru. He was then sixteen years of age.

---

[1] Small-prince-manly-heart.　　　　[2] This word means steward.
[3] Civilization.

The Emperor Oho-Yamato-neko-hiko-kuni-kuru died in Autumn, the 9th month of the 57th year of his reign.

In Winter, the 11th month, 12th day, the Prince Imperial assumed the Imperial Dignity.

1st year, Spring, 1st month, 4th day. The Empress was B.C. 157. honoured with the title of Grand Empress.

Winter, 10th month, 13th day. The capital was removed to Kasuga. It was called the Palace of Isa-kaha. This year IV. 16. was the year Kinoye Saru of the cycle.

5th year, Spring, 2nd month, 6th day. The Emperor Oho- B.C. 153. Yamato-neko-hiko-kuni-kuru was buried in the Misasagi on the island of Tsurugi-ike.[1]

6th year, Spring, 1st month, 14th day. Ika-shiko-me no B.C. 152. Mikoto was appointed Empress. [*She was his father's concubine.*] The Empress was the mother of the Emperor Mimaki-iri-hiko-i-niye.

The Emperor had previously taken to himself as concubine Taniha no Takano-hime. She was the mother of Hiko-yu-musumi no Mikoto. [*Also called Hiko-komosu no Mikoto.*] There was a subordinate concubine named Oke-tsu-hime, younger sister of Oke-tsu no Mikoto, the ancestor of the Wani no Omi. She was the mother of Prince [2] Hiko-imasu.

28th year, Spring, 1st month, 5th day. Mimaki-iri-hiko no IV. 17. Mikoto was created Prince Imperial. He was nineteen years B.C. 130 of age.

60th year, Summer, 4th month, 9th day. The Emperor B.C. 98. died.

Winter, 10th month, 3rd day. He was buried in the Saka-moto Misasagi at Isa-kaha in Kasuga.

One version has :—" The Misasagi of Saka no kami."[3]

His age was then 115.

---

[1] Ike means a pond or artificial lake.

[2] Where Prince stands alone without the word Imperial before or after it, it represents the Chinese character 王, which in the " Nihongi " is applied sometimes to the kings or princes of Corea, but more usually to Japanese princes who did not belong to the family of the reigning sovereign.

[3] It is difficult to say whether Saka-moto and Saka no kami are proper names or merely descriptions. They mean respectively the " bottom of the acclivity " and the " top of the acclivity."

BOOK V.

THE EMPEROR MIMAKI-IRI-BIKO-I-NIYE.

(SŪJIN[1] TENNŌ.)

THE Emperor Mimaki-iri-biko-i-niye was the second child of the Emperor Waka-yamato-neko-hiko-oho-hi-hi. His mother's name was Ika-shiko-me, daughter of Oho-he-so-ki no Mikoto, the ancestor of the Mononobe House.[2]

The Emperor was created Prince Imperial at the age of nineteen. He was of a quick intelligence, and in his boyhood was fond of manly devices. When he grew up to manhood, he was of wide culture and circumspect in his behaviour. He honoured profoundly the Gods of Heaven and Earth. His mind was constantly directed to the management of the Celestial Institution.[3]

The Emperor Waka-yamato-neko-hiko-oho-hihi died in Summer, the 4th month of the 60th year of his reign.

B.C. 97. 1st year, Spring, 1st month, 13th day. The Prince Imperial assumed the Imperial Dignity. He honoured the Empress with the title of Grand Empress.

2nd month, 16th day. Mimaki-hime was appointed Empress. Before this she had given birth to the Emperor Iku-me-iri-hiko-i-sachi, Kuni-kata-hime no Mikoto, Chichi-tsuku Yamato-hime no Mikoto, Yamato-hiko no Mikoto, and Ika-tsuru-hiko no Mikoto. By a concubine, Tohotsu Ayume ma-kuwashi-hime, daughter of Araka, the Tohe of the Land of Kiï, he had Toyo-suki-iri-hiko no Mikoto, and a subordinate concubine named Ohari no Oho-ama.

One version has :—" Ya-saka-furu-ama-irohe, daughter of Oho-umi no-Sukune."

V. 2.

---

[1] Sūjin means "honouring the Gods."   [2] In Japanese Uji.
[3] The sovereignty.

bore to him Ya-saka-iri-hiko no Mikoto, Nunaki-iri-bime no Mikoto, and Toho-chi-ni-iri-bime no Mikoto.

This year was the year Kinoye Saru of the cycle.

3rd year, Autumn, 9th month. The capital was removed to Shiki. It was called the Palace of Midzu-gaki. B.C. 95.

4th year, Winter, 10th month, 13th day. The Emperor issued a decree, saying:—"When our Imperial ancestors gloriously assumed the Supreme Rank, was it for the benefit of themselves alone? It was doubtless in order that they might thereby shepherd men and spirits,[1] and regulate the Empire. Therefore it was that from generation to generation they were able to extend their unfathomable merit, and in their day to spread abroad their perfect virtue. B.C. 94.

We, having now received at their hands the mighty inheritance, lovingly nourish our good subjects. In so doing, let us follow obediently in the footsteps of our Imperial ancestors, and long preserve the unbounded felicity. And ye too, Our Ministers and functionaries, should you not co-operate with all loyalty in giving peace to the Empire?"[2] V. 3.

5th year. There was much pestilence throughout the country, and more than one half the people died. B.C. 93.

6th year. The people took to vagabondage, and there was rebellion, the violence of which was such that by worth alone it could not be assuaged.[3] B.C. 92.

Therefore, rising early in the morning and being full of awe until the evening, the Emperor requested punishment[4] of the Gods of Heaven and Earth.

Before this the two Gods Ama-terasu no Oho-kami and Yamato no Oho-kuni-dama[5] were worshipped together within the Emperor's Great Hall. He dreaded, however, the power of these Gods, and did not feel secure in their dwelling together. Therefore he entrusted Ama-terasu no Oho-kami to Toyo-suki-iri-bime no Mikoto to be worshipped at the village

---

[1] The Kana has simply hito, men.

[2] This decree is a mere cento of Chinese phrases.

[3] i.e., by the virtues of the Sovereign commanding the respect and obedience of the people.

[4] In accordance with the Chinese notion that national calamities are owing to the faults of the Emperor.

[5] The numen of the great land of Yamato.

M

of Kasanuhi in Yamato, where he established the sacred en-
v. 4. closure of Shiki. Moreover, he entrusted Yamato-oho-kuni-
dama no Kami to Nunaki-iri-bime no Mikoto to be worshipped.
But Nunaki-iri-bime no Mikoto was bald and lean, and therefore unfit to perform the rites of worship.

b.c. 91.   7th year, Spring, 2nd month, 15th day. The Emperor
decreed as follows :—" Of old our Imperial ancestors greatly
extended the vast foundation, and under the later Emperors
the institution became more and more exalted. The royal influence spread and flourished. But now that it has devolved upon
Us, numerous calamities have unexpectedly befallen it. It is to
be feared that from the absence of good Government in the Court,
We have incurred the blame of the Gods of Heaven and Earth.
Would it not be well to commit the matter to the Sacred
Tortoise ¹ and thereby ascertain the cause of the calamity ? "

Accordingly, the Emperor hereupon proceeded to the plain
of Kami-asachi, where he assembled the 80 myriads of Deities,
and inquired of them by means of divination. At this time the
Gods inspired Yamato-to-to-hi-momoso-hime no Mikoto to say
as follows :—" Why is the Emperor grieved at the disordered
state of the country ? If he duly did us reverent worship it
would assuredly become pacified of itself." The Emperor in-
v. 5. quired, saying :—" What God is it that thus instructs me ? "
The answer was :—" I am the God who dwells within the
borders of the land of Yamato, and my name is Oho-mono-
nushi no Kami."

Now, having obtained this divine message, the Emperor
worshipped as he was told, but without effect. Then, having
bathed and practised abstinence, and purified the interior of
the Hall, he prayed, saying :—" Is Our observance of due ceremonies towards the Gods not yet complete? This non-
acceptance is cruel. We pray that We may be further instructed
in a dream, and the divine favour thereby consummated."

That night he had a dream. A man of noble appearance
stood opposite to him in the door of the hall, and, announcing
himself as Oho-mono-nushi no Kami, said :—" Let the

---

¹ The ancient Japanese divination was by roasting deer's shoulder-blades
and observing the cracks thus caused, not by the shell of a tortoise, which is
the Chinese practice.

Emperor grieve no more for the disorder of the country. This is my will. If thou wilt cause me to be worshipped by my child, Oho-tata-neko, then will there be peace at once. Moreover the lands beyond the sea will of their own accord render submission."

Autumn, 8th month, 7th day. Yamato-to-to-kami-asachi-hara-ma-guhashi-hime, Oho-mina-kuchi-no Sukune, the ancestor of the Hodzumi no Omi, and the Kimi of Wo-umi in Ise had all three the same dream, which they reported to the Emperor, saying :—" Last night we had a dream in which there appeared a man of noble aspect, who admonished us, saying :— ' Let Oho-tata-neko no Mikoto be appointed master of the worship of Oho-mono-nushi-no-oho-kami, and let Ichi-shi no V. 6. Naga-ochi be appointed master of the worship of Yamato no Oho-kuni-dama no Kami. Then assuredly the Empire will have profound peace.' "

The Emperor, when he learned the words of the dream, was more and more delighted in his heart. By a proclamation to the Empire he sought for Oho-tata-neko, who was accordingly found in the village of Suye, in the district of Chinu,[1] and sent to the Emperor, who forthwith proceeded in person to the plain of Kami-asachi, and assembled all the Princes and Ministers, and the eighty Be. He then inquired of Oho-tata-neko, saying :— "Whose child art thou ? " He answered and said :—"My father's name is Oho-mono-nushi no Oho-kami. My mother's name is Ikudama-yori-bime, daughter of Suye-tsu mimi."

Also called Kushi-hi-kata-ame-hi-kata, daughter of Take-chinu-tsumi.

The Emperor said :—" Now we shall be prosperous." So he ascertained by divination that it would be lucky to send Ika-shiko-wo to distribute offerings to the Gods. He also divined that it would be unlucky to take advantage of this opportunity to worship other Gods.[2]

11th month, 8th day.[3] The Emperor took the articles[4] for

---

[1] In Idzumi.   [2] Than the two above mentioned.

[3] The original has cyclical characters which would make it the 56th day of the month. I have adopted an emendation which does not make obvious nonsense. But where the whole series of dates is fictitious, it is hardly worth while noticing minor inaccuracies of this kind.

[4] Of pottery.

the worship of the Gods which he ordered Ika-shiko-wo to have made by the hands of the eighty Mononobe, and appointed Oho-tata-neko Master of the worship of Oho-mono-nushi no Oho-kami. Moreover he made Nagaochi Master of the worship of Yamato no Oho-kuni-dama no Kami.

After that, he divined that it would be lucky to worship the other Gods. So he took the opportunity of separately worshipping the assemblage of eighty myriads of Deities. He also settled which were to be Heavenly shrines and which Earthly shrines, and allotted land and houses for the service of the Gods. Thereupon the pestilence first ceased; the country at length had peace, the five kinds of grain were produced, and the peasantry enjoyed abundance.

B.C. 90.   8th year, Summer, 4th month, 6th day. A man of the village of Takahashi, named Ikuhi, was appointed Brewer to the Great Deity.

Winter, 12th month, 20th day. The Emperor caused Oho-tata-neko to worship the Great Deity. On this day, Ikuhi, in person, presented to the Emperor sacred sake, with a song, as follows :—

> This sacred sake
> Is not my sacred sake :
> 'Tis sacred sake brewed
> By Oho-mono-nushi,
> Of Yamato,
> How long ago !
> How long ago ! [1]

Having thus sung, they feasted in the Shrine of the God. As soon as the feast was over, the various high officials sang as follows :—

V. 8.
> The Hall of Miwa
> (Of sweet sake fame),
> Even its morning door
> We would go forth from—
> The door of the Hall of Miwa.

Hereupon the Emperor sang as follows :—

---

[1] "How long ago" is in Japanese Ikuhisa, an obvious allusion to the Brewer's name, Ikuhi, in short a pun.

The Hall of Miwa
(Of sweet sake fame),
Even its morning-door
I would push open—
The door of the Hall of Miwa.[1]

So the door of the Shrine of the God was thrown open, and the Emperor proceeded on his way.

He who was called Oho-tata-neko was the first ancestor of the Kimi of Miwa.

9th year, Spring, 3rd month, 15th day. The Emperor had a dream in which a divine person appeared to him and instructed him, saying:—" Take eight red shields and eight red spears and do worship to the God of Sumi-zaka. Take moreover eight black shields and eight black spears and do worship to the God of Oho-zaka." B.C. 89.

Summer, 4th month, 16th day. In accordance with the instruction he had received in the dream, he worshipped the Gods of Sumi-zaka and Oho-zaka.[2]

10th year, Autumn, 7th month, 24th day. He proclaimed to the company of Ministers, saying:—" For the guidance of the people, the chief thing is education. Now that I have performed due rites to the Gods of Heaven and Earth, all calamity has become spent. The distant savages, however, do not receive our calendar because they are yet unaccustomed to the civilizing influences of our rule. We will, therefore, select some of our company of Ministers and despatch them to the four quarters, so that they may cause our Will to be known." B.C. 88. V. 9.

9th month, 9th day. The Emperor sent Oho-hiko no Mikoto to the northern region, he sent Takenu-kaha wake to the Eastern Sea,[3] he sent Kibi[4]-tsu-hiko to the Western road,

---

[1] The sentiment of these poems seems to be the same as that of our own " We won't go home till morning."

Metre irregular.

[2] However unhistorical all this may be, one thing clearly appears from it, viz., that in the early days of Japan the king and high priest were identical. Both the civil and religious functions, however, might be equally delegated.

[3] In the original Tō-kai, whence Tōkaidō, East-sea-road, the great highway from Kioto to the East and also the provinces lying to each side of it.

[4] Kibi is the ancient name for Bizen, Bingo, and Bittchiu, which lie west of Yamato.

he sent Tamba no chi-nushi no Mikoto to Tamba. On this occasion he addressed them, saying:—"If there be any who do not receive our instructions, prepare war and smite them." Having said so, he granted them all alike seals and ribbons,[1] and appointed them generals.

27th day. Oho-hiko no Mikoto arrived at the top of the Wani acclivity. Now there was there a maiden who sang as follows:—

> One version has:—"Oho-hiko-no Mikoto arrived at the Hira-zaka acclivity, in Yamashiro. Now there was by the road-side a young woman who sang as follows:"—

> Ah! Prince Mimaki-iri!
> Unaware that some are stealthily
> Preparing to cut
> The thread of thine own life,
> Thou amusest thyself like a lady!

Another version is:—

> Unaware that some are preparing
> To slay thee,
> On the watch
> At the great gate,
> Thou amusest thyself like a lady![2]

Wondering at this, Oho-hiko inquired of the maiden, saying:—"What are these words that thou sayest?" She answered and said:—"I was saying nothing: I was only singing." So she sang over again the above song, and suddenly disappeared. Oho-hiko accordingly returned and reported these circumstances to the Emperor. Upon this Yamato-toto-hi momo so bime no Mikoto, the Emperor's aunt by the father's side, a shrewd and intelligent person, who could foresee the future, understood what was portended by this song, and told the Emperor that it was a sign that Take-hani-yasu-hiko[3] was about to plot treason against him. "I have heard," she said, "that Ata-bime, Take-hani-yasu-hiko's wife, came secretly and took earth

---

[1] The seals and ribbons are Chinese, and could not have been used as emblems of office in Japan at this time. The word for general is Shōgun, so familiar at a later period of Japanese History.

[2] The text of this poem is very doubtful. The "Kojiki" has a third version. Prince Mimaki-iri is the Emperor.

[3] A half-brother of the Emperor. He lived in Yamashiro.

from Mount Kako[1] in Yamato, which she wrapped in her neckerchief and prayed, saying :—'This earth represents the Land of Yamato,' and turned it upside down. By this I know that there will be troubles. If thou dost not speedily take measures, it will assuredly be too late." Hereupon he recalled all the generals and consulted with them. No long time after, Take-hani-yasu-hiko and his wife Ata-bime conspired to revolt, and arrived suddenly with an army which they had raised. They came each by different roads, the husband by way of Yamashiro, the wife by Oho-saka. They intended to join their forces and attack the capital. Then the Emperor sent Isaseri-hiko no Mikoto to attack the force led by Ata-bime. He accordingly intercepted it at Oho-saka and put it all to a great rout. Ata-bime was killed, and her troops were all slain. Afterwards he sent Oho-hiko and Hiko-kuni-fuku, the ancestor of the Wani no Omi, towards Yamashiro to attack Take-hani-yasu. Here they took sacred jars and planted them at the top of the acclivity of Takasuki in Wani.[2] Then they advanced with their best troops and ascended Mount Nara and occupied it. Now when the Imperial forces were encamping, they trod level the herbs and trees, whence that mountain was given the name of Mount Nara.[3] Then abandoning Mount Nara, they proceeded as far as the River Wakara. Hani-yasu-hiko was encamped on both sides of the river, and the two armies challenged each other. Therefore the men of that time changed the name of the river, and called it the River Idomi,[4] which is now corrupted into Idzumi.

Hani-yasu-hiko, standing on the bank of this river, inquired of Hiko-kuni-fuku, saying :—"Why hast thou raised an army and come hither?" He answered and said :—"Thou, in opposition to Heaven, and regardless of right, dost intend to overturn the Royal chamber.[5] Therefore I have raised a loyal army to punish thy revolt. This is the Emperor's command." Hereupon there was a struggle who should shoot first. Hani-yasu-hiko shot first at Hiko-kuni-fuku, but missed him. Then

---

[1] The same as Mount Kagu above referred to.
[2] i.e. they sacrificed to the Gods before entering on the campaign.
[3] Narasu means to make level.
[4] Challenge River.   [5] We would say the throne.

Hiko-kuni-fuku aimed at Hani-yasu-hiko, hit him in the breast, and killed him. His troops lost courage and retreated. They were consequently pursued and driven in rout to the north of the river. More than half had their heads cut off, and of dead bodies there was a plentiful overflow. Therefore that place was named Hafu-sono.[1]

Again the troops fled in fear and their excrements were voided on their breeches. So they took off their armour and ran. Knowing that they could not escape, they bowed their heads to the ground, and said, "Our Lord." Therefore the men of that time called the place where the armour was taken off " Ka-wara," [2] and the place where the breeches were defiled they called Kuso-bakama.[3] It is now called Kusuba, which is a corruption of this word.

V. 13. Moreover the place where they bowed their heads was called A-gimi.[4]

After tkis Yamato-toto-hi-momo-so-bime no Mikoto became the wife of Oho-mono-nushi no Kami. This God, however, was never seen in the day-time, but came at night. Yamato-toto-hime no Mikoto said to her husband :—" As my Lord is never seen in the day-time, I am unable to view his august countenance distinctly ; I beseech him therefore to delay a while, that in the morning I may look upon the majesty of his beauty." The Great God answered and said :—" What thou sayest is clearly right. To-morrow morning I will enter thy toilet-case and stay there. I pray thee be not alarmed at my form." Yamato-toto-hime no Mikoto wondered secretly in her heart at this. Waiting until daybreak, she looked into her toilet-case. There was there a beautiful little snake,[5] of the length and thickness of the cord of a garment. Thereupon she was frightened, and uttered an exclamation. The Great God was ashamed, and changing suddenly into human form, spake to his wife, and

---

[1] Afureru is " to overflow," sono means garden. Hafu is more probably for hafuri, sacrifice.

[2] An old word for " armour." [3] " Excrement-breeches."

[4] Our Lord. See above.

[5] This is one of numerous evidences of serpent-worship in Ancient Japan. The interlinear Kana for snake is worochi, where the last syllable is a honorific.

said :—" Thou didst not contain thyself, but hast caused me shame : I will in my turn put thee to shame." So treading the Great Void, he ascended to Mount Mimoro. Hereupon Yamato-toto-hime no Mikoto looked up and had remorse. She flopped down on a seat and with a chopstick stabbed herself in the pudenda so that she died. She was buried at Oho-chi. Therefore the men of that time called her tomb the Hashi no haka.[1] This tomb was made by men in the day-time, V. 14. and by Gods at night. It was built of stones carried from Mount Oho-saka. Now the people standing close to each other passed the stones from hand to hand, and thus transported them from the mountain to the tomb. The men of that time made a song about this, saying :—

> If one passed from hand to hand
> The rocks
> Built up
> On Oho-saka,[2]
> How hard 'twould be to send them ![3]

Winter, 10th month, 1st day. The Emperor gave command to his Ministers, saying :—" The rebels have now all yielded themselves to execution and there is peace in the home district.[4] But the savage tribes abroad[5] continue to be tumultuous. Let the generals of the four roads now make haste to set out." On the 22nd day, the four generals set out on their journeys simultaneously.

---

[1] The Chopstick Tomb.

[2] The great acclivity.

[3] The tombs of men of rank at this period of Japanese History consisted of a round mound of earth varying in size according to the station of the person interred, and containing a vault of megalithic stones, with an entrance gallery similar to those of the Imperial Misasagi, but of much smaller size. Many of these are still to be seen in Japan, especially in the provinces near Yamato. Of course it is utterly impossible to pass from hand to hand stones of the size used in constructing these tombs.

[4] The original is Kinai, more familiarly known as Gokinai, and comprising the provinces of Yamato, Yamashiro, Settsu, Kawachi, and Idzumi.

[5] Lit. outside the sea. This is a Chinese expression which must not be taken too literally. The Ainos may be referred to. But the whole passage seems inspired by recollections from Chinese literature, and is probably entirely fictitious.

B.C. 87. 11th year, Summer, 4th month, 28th day. The generals of the four roads reported to the Emperor the circumstances of their pacification of the savages. This year strange tribes came in great numbers and there was tranquillity throughout the land.

B.C. 86. 12th year, Spring, 3rd month, 11th day. The following decree was issued :—"Ever since we received the Celestial Dignity and undertook the guardianship of the ancestral shrines, Our light has been subject to obscuration, and Our influence has been wanting in placidity. Consequently there has been disaccord in the action of the male and female principles of nature, heat and cold have mixed their due order, epidemic disease has been rife, and calamities have befallen

V. 15. the people. But now in order to be absolved from Our offences and to rectify Our errors, we have reverently worshipped the Gods of Heaven and Earth. We have also dispensed Our instructions and thus pacified the savage tribes, and by force of arms have chastised those who refused submission. In this way authority has been maintained, while below there are no retired people.[1] Education[2] is widespread ; the multitude take delight in their industries ;[3] strange tribes come employing several interpreters ; the countries beyond the sea offer allegiance. At this time We think it fit to make a new recension of the people, and to acquaint them with grades of seniority, and the order of forced labour."

Autumn, 9th month, 16th day. A census of the people was begun and taxes were imposed anew. These are called the men's bow-end tax and the women's finger-end tax.[4] Therefore the Gods of Heaven and Earth were harmonious. The wind

---

[1] By "retired people " are probably meant those who have concealed themselves in order to escape from oppression. The phrase occurs in the " Confucian Analects " (Legge, p. 200), where, however, it is used of a voluntary retirement from the world.

[2] The "education" is not juvenile education, but the education of the people by the good example of the monarch, with, perhaps, an occasional discourse from the throne.

[3] From "authority" to "industries" is copied from a Chinese History of the Han Dynasty. The whole decree is utterly impossible as a document of Japanese History at this period. It is as Chinese as it can be.

[4] That is, a tax of animals' skins and game to be paid by the men, and of textile fabrics to be levied on women. See Ch. K., p. 182.

and rain came in their season, the hundred kinds of grain formed duly. Families did not become extinct, population was sufficient. Profound peace prevailed in the Empire. Therefore he received the title of " The Emperor, the august founder of the country."

17th year, Autumn, 7th month, 1st day. The following decree was issued :—

B.C. 81.
V. 16.

" Ships are of cardinal importance to the Empire. At present the people of the coast, not having ships, suffer grievously by land-transport. Therefore, let every province be caused to have ships built."

Winter, 10th month. The building of ships was begun.

48th year, Spring, 1st month, 10th day. The Emperor gave command to Toyoki no Mikoto and Ikume no Mikoto, saying :—" Ye, my two children, are alike in Our affection, and We know not which of you to make Our successor. Do each of you dream, and We will form an augury from your dreams." Hereupon the two princes, having received this command, performed their ablutions and prayed. In their sleep each of them had a dream. The next dawn the elder brother, Toyoki no Mikoto, reported to the Emperor the story of his dream, saying :—" I myself ascended Mount Mimoro, and turning to the East, eight times I flourished a spear, and eight times dealt blows with a sword."

B.C. 50.

The younger brother, Ikume no Mikoto, reported the story of his dream, saying :—" I myself ascended to the summit of Mount Mimoro, and stretched a cord to the four quarters with which to drive away the sparrows which fed upon the grain." _

The Emperor compared the dreams, and spake to his two sons, saying :—" The elder of you turned to the East only, and it is therefore meet that he should rule the Eastern Land. But the younger looked down generally over the four quarters, and he ought therefore to succeed to Our Dignity."

Summer, 4th month, 19th day. Ikume no Mikoto was appointed Prince Imperial, and Toyoki no Mikoto was made ruler of the Eastern Land. He was the first ancestor of the Kimi of Kami-tsuke [1] and of the Kimi of Shimotsuke.

Now Kōdzuke.

B c. 38.   60th year, Autumn, 7th month, 14th day.   The Emperor
V. 17.   addressed his ministers, saying :—" Take-hi-teru no Mikoto
    Another version is Take-hina-tori or Ama-no-hina-
    tori.
brought from Heaven the divine treasures and stored them in
the Temple of the Great God at Idzumo.   I wish to see them."
Accordingly Take-moro-sumi, the ancestor of the Yata-be no
Miyakko, was sent for them
    One writing says :—" Also called Oho-moro-sumi."
that he might lay them before the Emperor.   Now at this time
Idzumo Furune, the ancestor of the Idzumo no Omi, held
charge of the divine treasures.   He had gone to the Land of
Tsukushi and did not come to meet him.   His younger brother,
Ihi-iri-ne, accordingly received the Imperial command and
entrusted them to his younger brother, Umashi-Kara[1]-hisa and
his son Uka-tsuku-nu, and so rendered them up to the Emperor.
Now when Idzumo Furune returned from Tsukushi and heard
that the divine treasures had been rendered up to the Court, he
rebuked his younger brother Ihi-iri-ne, saying :—" Thou shouldst
have waited for some days.   What wert thou afraid of that thou
didst so lightly part with the divine treasures ? "   On this account
V. 18.   he still, after years and months had passed, cherished wrath
against his younger brother and had a mind to slay him.   So
he deceived his younger brother, saying :—" Of late the *mo*[2]
plant grows plentifully in the Yamiya pool.   Pray let us go
together and see it."   So he followed his elder brother and
went there.   Before this, the elder brother had secretly made
a wooden sword, in appearance like a real sword, which at this
time he himself wore.   The younger brother was girt with a
real sword.   When they both came to the head of the pool,
the elder brother said to the younger :—" The water of the
pool is limpid and cool; pray let us both bathe in it."   The
younger brother agreed to his elder brother's proposal, and·
they each took off the sword which he wore and laid it on

----

[1] Note the occurrence of Kara, the name of a Corean Kingdom, in a
proper name at a time when it was not supposed that Japan had relations
with Corea.

[2] Defined as "a water plant with round leaves and stems which vary in
length according to the depth of the water." It is edible.

the bank of the pool. Having bathed in the water, the elder
brother came first to land, and taking the younger brother's
real sword, girded it on himself. Afterwards the younger
brother, surprised, took up his elder brother's wooden sword,
but on coming to mutual blows, the younger brother was
unable to draw the wooden sword. So the elder brother smote
his younger brother, Ihi-iri-ne, and killed him. Therefore the
men of that day made a song, saying,—

> The sword girt on
> By the warrior of Idzumo
> (Where many clouds arise [1])—
> There is the sheath enwound with creepers,
> But, alas ! there is no blade.

Hereupon Umashi-Kara-hisa and Uka-tsuku-nu proceeded to
Court, where they reported this affair in detail. Accordingly,
Kibi-tsu-hiko and Takenu-kaha-wake were sent to put to death
Idzumo Furune. Therefore the Omi of Idzumo, in dread of
this, desisted for a while from the worship of the Great God.

Now a man of Higami, in Tamba, named Hika-tohe, made
a representation to the Prince Imperial, Iku-me no Mikoto,
saying :—" One of my children is a young infant. Yet of his own V. 19.
accord he has said this :—' These are the Gods worshipped by
the men of Idzumo—Idzumo of the gem-like water-plant [2] and
the sunken stone [3]—viz. the true-kind-beautiful-august-mirror,
the pinion-flapping-beautiful-august-God, the bottom-treasure-
august-treasure-master ; the august-spirit-plunged-in-the-water-
of-the-mountain-stream, the peacefully-wearing (jewels?)-august-
deity, the bottom-treasure-august-treasure-master.' [4] These do
not seem like the words of a young infant. May they have
been spoken by divine inspiration ? "

Hereupon the Prince Imperial reported to the Emperor, who
accordingly caused them to be worshipped.

62nd year, Autumn, 7th month, 2nd day. The following B.C. 36.
edict was issued :—

" Agriculture is the great foundation of the Empire. It is

---

[1] See above, p. 54.
[2] The *mo*, above referred to.
[3] Perhaps a precious stone found at the bottom of rivers.
[4] The Shiki says that this is the description of two deities only.

that upon which the people depend for their subsistence.[1] At present the water of Hanida of Sayama in Kahachi is scarce, and therefore the peasants of that province are remiss in their husbandry. Open up therefore abundance of ponds and runnels, and so develop the industry of the people."

Winter, 10th month. The Yosami pond was made.

11th month. The Karusaka pond and the Sakahori pond were made.

One version has :—" These three ponds were made when the Emperor dwelt in the Palace of Kuhama."

65th year, Autumn, 7th month. The Land of Imna[2] sent Sonaka-cheulchi and offered tribute. Imna is more than 2000 ri to the north of Tsukushi, from which it is separated by the sea. It lies to the south-west of Ké-rin.

In the 68th year of his reign, Winter, the 12th month, 5th day, the Emperor died at the age of 120.[3]

In the following year, Autumn, the 8th month, 11th day, he was buried in the Misasagi above the road at Yamanobe.

---

[1] The above two sentences are copied word for word from a Chinese history.

[2] The traditional Japanese pronunciation of this name is Mimana. I have followed here, as elsewhere, the Corean pronunciation of Corean proper names. On any estimate of the length of the ri, the distance given is far too great.

Imna or Mimana is also known as Kara. It is a small kingdom lying to the S.W. of the River Naktong.

Kérin, in Japanese Kirin, is another name for Silla (in Japanese Shinra or Shiragi). See " Early Japanese History " in " J.A.S.T.," p. 43.

Sonaka-cheulchi looks like a genuine Corean name.

[3] The age given here is inconsistent with other data found in the " Nihongi" itself, and with the " Kojiki," which makes him 168 at the time of his death.

BOOK VI.

THE EMPEROR IKU-ME-IRI-HIKO-I-SACHI.

(*SUININ* [1] *TENNŌ.*)

THE Emperor Iku-me-iri-hiko-i-sachi was the third child of the Emperor Mimaki-iri-hiko-iniye. The Empress his mother was called Mimaki-hime. She was the daughter of Oho-hiko no Mikoto. The Emperor was born in the Palace of Midzu-gaki in the 29th year of the Emperor Mimaki, the 50th year of the cycle, Spring, the 1st month, the 1st day. From his birth he was of a distinguished appearance; when he grew to manhood, he had superior talent and large principles. His disposition was to be guided implicitly by truth and to avoid dissimulation.

The Emperor loved him, and retained him near his own person. At the age of twenty-four,[2] in accordance with the prognostic of a dream, he made him Prince Imperial.

The Emperor Mimaki-iri-hiko-iniye died in Winter, the 12th month of the 68th year of his reign.

1st year, Spring, 2nd day. The Prince Imperial assumed B.C. 29. the Imperial Dignity.

Winter, 10th month, 11th day.[3] The Emperor Mimaki was VI.2. buried in the Misasagi over the road at Yamanobe.

11th month, 2nd day. The Empress was granted the

---

[1] Dispense-benevolence.

[2] This does not agree with what precedes. He was born in the 29th year of his father's reign, and made Prince Imperial in the 48th. He would therefore be only twenty, and not twenty-four. Note that the Japanese always count both the year of birth and the current year in their calculations of age.

[3] This does not agree with the date on the previous page.

honorary title of Grand Empress. This was the year Midzu-noye Tatsu of the cycle.

B.C. 28. 2nd year, Spring, 2nd month, 9th day. Saho-hime was appointed Empress. She gave birth to Homu-tsu-wake no Mikoto. From his birth the Emperor loved him, and kept him near his own person. When he grew to manhood, he could not speak.

Winter, 10th month. The capital was removed to Maki-muku. It was called the Palace of Tamaki. In this year the man of Imna, Sonaka cheulchi,[1] asked permission to return to his country. Therefore gifts were liberally bestowed on him, and there were entrusted to him as a present for the King of Imna 100 pieces of red silk. But the Silla people waylaid and robbed him, and at this time began the enmity between the two countries.[2]

One account says:—"In the reign of the Emperor Mimaki, there was a man with horns on his forehead[3] who came riding in a ship and anchored in the Bay of Kebi in the land of Koshi. Therefore that place was called Tsunoga.[4] He was asked what countryman he was. He replied, saying:—'I am the son of the King of Great Kara.

VI. 3. My name is Tsunoga arashito, and I am also called Ushiki arishichi kanki.[5] It having come to my ears that there is in the Land of Japan a sage Emperor, I wished to offer

---

[1] Corean pronunciation. The Japanese would be Sonaka shichi.

[2] There is probably some historical foundation for this. But the chronology must be wrong. According to the Tongkam, Kara (Imna) was not formed into a kingdom until A.D. 42, and hostilities between Kara and Silla are first mentioned in that work in A.D. 94. They were also at war in 97, 115, 116, and 203. See "Early Japanese History" in "J.A.S.T.," p. 44.

[3] The ancient Chinese Emperors are so depicted.

[4] Now Tsuruga in Echizen. A derivation from Tsuno-nuka (horn-fore-head) seems intended.

[5] The Chinese characters in the text are probably intended to be read with their Japanese pronunciation, and I have accordingly in this instance followed the traditional Kana rendering. If the Corean pronunciation were followed, we should read Tonoka Arasăteung and Usaki ari cheulchi kanki. The Shiki says that kanki is a Silla rank equal to the Japanese senior 3rd rank. From a passage in Keidai Tennō's reign, year 23, it would appear that Arashito, or Arasăteung, was the name of some office or dignity.

him my allegiance and came to Anato.'[1] Now in that land there was a man named Itsutsu-hiko, who spoke to thy servant, saying:—'I am the King of this land, and there is no other king but me. Do not thou therefore proceed further.' But when I observed him closely and saw what manner of man he was, I knew surely that he was not a king. So I departed again from that place, and not knowing the road, anchored at one island and bay after another, going round by way of the Northern Sea and passing the Land of Idzumo until I arrived here."

It so happened that at this time the Emperor died, so he was detained and served the Emperor Ikume for three years.

Then the Emperor inquired of Arashito, saying:—"Dost thou wish to return to thy country?" He answered and said:—"I earnestly desire to do so." The Emperor then addressed Arashito, saying:—"If thou hadst not lost thy way, thou wouldst certainly have arrived here sooner—in time to serve the late Emperor. Do thou, therefore, change the name of thy country. In future take the august name VI. 4. of the Emperor Mimaki and make it the name of thy country. So he gave Arashito red silk stuffs and sent him back to his native land. This was the reason why the name of that country is called Mimana.[2] Hereupon Arashito took the red silk which had been given him, and stored it in the magazine of his country. The people of Silla hearing this, raised an army and proceeding thither robbed him of all the red silk. This was the beginning of the enmity between these two countries."

One writing says:—"In the beginning, when Tsunoga Arashito was still in his own land, he went into the country with an ox loaded with implements of husbandry. The ox suddenly disappeared, and seeking for it by its tracks, he found that the foot-prints ceased in a certain village. Now there was here an old man who said:—'The ox which thou art in search of entered this village, and the

---

[1] Anato, lit. hole-door, is the ancient name of Nagato (long-door) or Chōshiu. The door is the Strait of Shimonoseki.

[2] Imna, according to the Corean pronunciation of the characters.

village chiefs said :—" With the implements which he is carrying let us fell the ox. We must surely prepare to slay and eat him. If the owner comes in search of him, we shall indemnify him with something." So they slew and ate him. If thou art asked what thing thou desirest as the price of the ox, do not ask for treasures, but say that thou wishest to have the God worshipped by the village. Tell them so.' Presently the village chiefs came and said :—' What dost thou desire as the price of thy ox ? ' And he replied as the old man had instructed him. Now the God whom they worshipped was a white stone. So they gave the white stone to the owner of the ox, and he accordingly brought it away with him and placed it in his bed-chamber. This divine stone became changed into

VI. 5. a beautiful maiden, upon which Arashito was greatly re-joiced, and wished to be united to her. But while he was away in another place, the maiden suddenly disappeared. Arashito was greatly alarmed, and inquired of his wife, saying :—' Whither has the maiden gone ? ' She replied and said :—' She has gone towards the East.' So he went in search of her, and at length, drifting far over the sea, he thus arrived in our country. The maiden whom he sought came to Naniha, where she became the Deity of the Himegoso shrine. Then proceeding to the district ot Kusaki, in the Land of Toyo, she afterwards became the Deity of the Himegoso shrine. She is worshipped in both these places."

B.C. 27. 3rd year, Spring, 3rd month. The Silla prince, Ama no hi-hoko,[1] arrived. The objects which he brought were—one Ha-buto gem, one Ashi-daka gem, one red-stone Ukaka gem, one Idzushi short sword, one Idzushi spear, one sun-mirror, one Kuma-himorogi,[2] seven things in all. These were stored in the Land of Tajima,[3] and made divine things for ever.

---

[1] This means " The sun-spear of Heaven," and is purely Japanese. It cannot be a Corean name

[2] Kuma-himorogi. See above, p. 82.

[3] In the district of Idzu-shi (which I take to be for Idzu-ishi, sacred stone), a name which is suggestive of stone-worship. The " Kojiki " mentions eight objects, not at all the same, however, and calls them the Eight Great

One version says:—" In the beginning, Ama no hi-hoko, VI. 6. riding in a ship, anchored at the land of Harima, where he dwelt in the village of Shisaha. Then the Emperor sent to Harima Ohotomo nushi, the ancestor of the Miwa no Kimi, and Nagaochi, the ancestor of the Yamato no Atahe, and inquired of Ama no hi-hoko, saying :—' Who art thou, and to what country dost thou belong?' Ama no hi-hoko answered and said :—' I am the son of the King of Silla. Hearing that in the Land of Japan there was a sage monarch, I gave my country to my younger brother, Chiko,[1] and have come to offer my allegiance and to bring tribute of the following objects, viz.—a Ha-boso[2] gem, an Ashi-daka gem, an Ukaka red-stone (or Akashi) gem, an Idzushi short sword, an Idzushi spear, a sun-mirror, a Kuma-himorogi, and an Isasa sword—eight objects in all.' So the Emperor gave orders to Ama no hi-hoko, saying :— ' Do thou dwell in either of these two villages—Shisaha in the land of Harima, or Idesa in the island of Ahaji, at thy pleasure.' Then Ama no hi-hoko addressed the Emperor, saying :—' In regard to a dwelling-place for thy servant, if the celestial favour is bestowed on him so far as to grant thy servant the place of his desire, thy servant will himself proceed to, and visit the various provinces, and he hopes that he may be granted the place which is agreeable to his mind.' This was agreed to. Thereupon Ama no hi-hoko, ascending the river Uji, went northwards, until he arrived at the village of Ana, in the province of Ohomi.

Afterwards, he proceeded onwards, from the province of Ohomi, through the province of Wakasa, and going westward arrived at the province of Tajima. So there he

---

Deities of Idzushi. *Vide* Ch. K., p. 261. Possibly the Idzushi short sword and the Idzushi spear were stone weapons. This passage is one of several evidences that Japan owes to Corea one element of the Shintō religion. The " Yengi-shiki " mentions several Corean Gods as being worshipped in Japan. The " Kojiki " mixes up this legend with that of Arashito given above. Indeed both are probably founded on the same occurrence.

[1] I can't find any king of this name in Silla History.

[2] Ha-boso means leaf-slender and Ashi-daka leg-high They are probably names of places.

fixed his dwelling-place. Therefore the potters of Kagami no hasama,[1] in the province of Ohomi, are the servants of Ama no hi-hoko. Accordingly Ama no hi-hoko took to wife Matawo, the daughter of Futomimi, a man of Idzushi in Tajima, who bore to him Tajima Morosuke, who was the father of Tajima no Hinaraki, who was the father of Kiyohiko, who was the father of Tajima-mori."

B.C. 26. 4th year, Autumn, 9th month, 23rd day. The Empress's elder brother by the mother's side, Prince Sahohiko, plotted treason and tried to endanger the State. Therefore he watched for an occasion when the Empress was enjoying her leisure, and addressing her, said as follows:—" Whom dost thou love best—thy elder brother or thy husband?" Upon this, the Empress, ignorant of his object in making this inquiry, straightway answered and said:—" I love my elder brother." Then he enticed the Empress, saying:—" If one serves a man by beauty, when the beauty fades, his affection will cease.[2] There are now many beautiful women in the Empire. They will come one after another and seek affection. How, then, canst thou trust always to thy beauty? It is my wish, therefore, to ascend to the immense felicity,[3] and of a certainty to rule over the Empire along with thee. So making high our pillows,[4] we shall complete a long hundred years. Would not this be delightful? I beg thee, therefore, to slay the Emperor for me." So he took a dagger, and giving it to the Empress, said:— " Gird on this dagger among thy garments, and when the Emperor goes to sleep, do thou stab him in the neck, and thus kill him." Upon this the Empress trembled in her heart within, and knew not what she should do. But in view of the determination of the Prince, her elder brother, she felt that remonstrance would be useless. Therefore she took the dagger, and having herself nowhere to deposit it, she placed it in her garments, intending all the while to remonstrate with her elder brother.

B.C. 25. 5th year, Winter, 10th month, 1st day. The Emperor pro-

---

[1] Mirror-valley.   [2] A Chinese saying.
[3] i.e. to take possession of the throne.
[4] A Chinese metaphor meaning "in security."

ceeded to Kume, where he dwelt in Taka-miya."[1] Now the Emperor took his noon-day sleep with the Empress's knees as his pillow. Up to this time the Empress had accomplished nothing, but thought vainly to herself:—"This would be the time to do that which the Prince, my elder brother, plotted." And she wept tears which fell on the Emperor's face. The Emperor woke up and addressed the Empress, saying :—"To-day We have had a dream. A small brocade-coloured snake coiled itself round Our neck and a great rain arose from Saho, which coming hither wet Our face. What does this portend ?" The Empress thereupon, knowing that she could not conceal the plot, in fear and awe bowed herself to the earth, and informed the Emperor fully of the circumstances of the Prince, her elder brother's, treason. Accordingly she addressed him, saying : —"Thy handmaiden was unable to resist the purpose of the Prince, her elder brother, and yet could not be false to the gratitude due to the Emperor. If I confessed I destroyed the Prince, my elder brother. If I said nothing, I over-turned the temples of the earth and of grain,[2] so that on the one hand there was fear, and on the other there was grief. Whether I looked up or down there was lamenta- VI. 9. tion, whether I advanced or retired there was weeping and wailing. Night and day I was disturbed in mind, and could find no way to give information. Only to-day when Your Majesty went to sleep with his handmaiden's knee as a pillow, she thought—'If I were mad enough to accomplish the pur-pose of my elder brother, at this very time the deed could be done without difficulty.' With this thought still in my mind, the tears flowed spontaneously. So I raised my sleeve to wipe away the tears, and they overflowed from the sleeve and moistened Your Majesty's face. Therefore the dream of to-day must have been an effect of this thing. The small brocade-coloured snake is nothing else than the dagger which was given me : the great rain which arose suddenly is nothing else than thy handmaiden's tears." Then the Emperor addressed the Empress, saying :—"This is not thy crime," and raising a force from the neighbouring district, he commanded Yatsunada, the

---

[1] Taka-miya means high-palace or shrine.
[2] A Chinese expression for the State.

remote ancestor of the Kimi of Kôdzuke, to slay Saho-hiko. Now Saho-hiko withstood him with an army, and hastily piling up rice-stalks made thereof a castle, which was so solid that it could not be breached. This is what was called a "rice-castle."[1] A month passed, and yet it did not surrender. Hereupon the Empress, grieved at this, said:—"Even though I am Empress, with what countenance can I preside over the Empire, after bringing to ruin the Prince, my elder brother?" Accordingly, she took in her arms the Imperial Prince Homutsu wake no Mikoto, and entered the rice-castle of the Prince, her elder brother. The Emperor increased his army still more, and having surrounded the castle on all sides, proclaimed to those within it, saying:—"Send forth quickly the Empress and the Imperial Prince." But they would not send them out. So the General Yatsunada set fire to the castle. Then the Empress, taking in her bosom the Imperial child, crossed over the castle and came out from it. Therewithal she besought the Emperor, saying:—"The reason why thy handmaiden at first fled into her elder brother's castle was in the hope that her elder brother might be absolved from guilt for the sake of her and of her child. But now he has not been absolved, and I know that I am guilty. Shall I have my hands tied behind my back? There is nothing left for me but to strangle myself. But even though I, thy handmaiden, die, I cannot bear to forget the favour shown me by the Emperor. I pray, therefore, that the Empress's palace, which I had charge of, may be granted to fair mates for thee. In the land of Tamba there are five ladies, all of virtuous minds, the daughters of the Prince, who is Michi no Ushi[2] of Tamba.

Prince Michi no Ushi was a grandson of the Emperor Waka-Yamato-Neko oho-hi-hi, and son of Prince Hiko-imasu.

VI. 10.

---

[1] The Japanese word for rice-castle is inaki. It may be doubted whether there ever was any such castle as that described here. Artless attempts at derivation furnish a considerable portion of the old myths and legends of Japan. Inaki is the term used for the Imperial granaries in the provinces, and was also applied to their custodians. It therefore became a title of nobility which is frequently met with in the later history.

[2] Lit. master of the road.

One version has :—" Son of Prince Hiko-yu-musubi-kuma."

Let them be placed in the side courts to complete the number of the consort chambers." To this the Emperor agreed.[1] Then the fire blazed up, and the castle was destroyed. The troops all ran away, and Saho-hiko and his younger sister died together inside the castle. Thereupon the Emperor commended the good service of General Yatsunada, and granted him the name of Yamato-hi-muke take-hi-muke-hiko [2] Yatsunada.

7th year, Autumn, 7th month, 7th day. The courtiers repre-sented to the Emperor as follows :—" In the village of Taima [3] there is a valiant man called Kuyehaya of Taima. He is ot great bodily strength, so that he can break horns and straighten out hooks. He is always saying to the people :—' You may search the four quarters, but where is there one to compare with me in strength ? O that I could meet with a man ot might, with whom to have a trial of strength, regardless of life or death.' "

B.C. 23.
VI. 11.

The Emperor, hearing this, proclaimed to his ministers, saying :—" We hear that Kuyehaya of Taima is the champion of the Empire. Might there be any one to compare with him ? "

One of the ministers came forward and said :—" Thy servant hears that in the Land of Idzumo there is a valiant man named Nomi no Sukune. It is desirable that thou shouldst send for him, by way of trial, and match him with Kuyehaya."

That same day the Emperor sent Nagaochi, the ancestor of the Atahe of Yamato, to summon Nomi no Sukune. There-upon Nomi no Sukune came from Idzumo, and straightway he and Taima no Kuyehaya were made to wrestle together. The two men stood opposite to one another. Each raised his foot and kicked at the other,[4] when Nomi no Sukune broke with a kick the ribs of Kuyehaya and also kicked and broke his loins and thus killed him. Therefore the land of Taima no Kuyehaya was seized, and was all given to Nomi no Sukune. This was

But did not act on it till nine years later !
[2] Yamato-sun-facing brave-sun-facing prince.
[3] In Yamato.
[4] The wrestling seems to have been of the nature of a Greek παγκράτιοι, or the French savate.

the cause why there is in that village a place called Koshi-ore-da, i.e. the field of the broken loins.

Nomi no Sukune remained and served the Emperor.

15th year, Spring, 2nd month, 10th day. The five women of Tamba were sent for and placed in the side-court. The name of the first was Hibasu-hime, of the second Nuba-tani-iri-hime, of the third Matonu-hime, of the fourth Azami-ni-iri-hime, and of the fifth Takano-hime.[1]

Autumn, 8th month, 1st day. Hibasu-hime no Mikoto was appointed Empress, and the Empress's three younger sisters were made concubines. Only Takano-hime, on account of the ugliness of her form, was sent back to her own country. Accordingly in her shame at being sent back, when she came to Kadono, she purposely tumbled from the carriage and was killed. Therefore that place received the name of Ochi-kuni.[2] The present name, Oto-kuni, is a corruption of this. The Empress Hibasu-hime no Mikoto had three sons and two daughters. The eldest was called Ini-shiki-iri-hiko no Mikoto, the second Oho-tarashi-hiko no Mikoto, the third Oho-nakatsu-hime no Mikoto, the fourth Yamato-hime no Mikoto, and the fifth Wakaki-ni-iri-biko no Mikoto. The concubine Nuba-tani-iri-hime gave birth to Nuteshi-wake no Mikoto and Ika-tarashi-bime no Mikoto. The next concubine Azami-ni-iri-bime gave birth to Ike-haya-wake no Mikoto and Waka-asa-tsu-hime no Mikoto.

23rd year, Autumn, 9th month, 2nd day. The Emperor addressed his ministers, saying:—"Prince Homutsu-wake is now thirty years of age.[3] His beard is eight span long, yet he weeps like an infant, and never speaks. What can be the reason of this?" So he caused Commissioners to consider the matter.

Winter, 10th month, 8th day. The Emperor stood before the Great Hall, with the Imperial Prince Homutsu-wake in attendance on him. Now there was a swan which crossed the Great Void, uttering its cry. The Imperial Prince looked up,

---

[1] The "Kojiki" (vide Ch. K., p. 197) makes only four princesses, and in another passage only two.   [2] Fall-country.

[3] The "Kojiki" makes this Prince born at the time of Saho-hiko's rebellion, i.e. in the fifth year of Suinin Tennō's reign. The "Nihongi" is less precise, but it is plain from the narrative that he cannot have been thirty at this time.

and seeing the swan, said :—" What thing is this?" The Emperor, observing that the Imperial Prince had gained his speech on seeing the swan, was rejoiced, and commanded his courtiers, saying :—" Which of you will catch this bird and present it to me?" Thereupon, Amano Yukaha Tana, the ancestor of the Tottori[1] no Miyakko, addressed his Majesty, saying :—" Thy servant will surely catch it, and present it to thee." So the Emperor declared to Yukaha Tana, saying :—" If thou present this bird to me, I will certainly reward thee liberally." Now, Yukaha Tana, looking from afar towards the quarter whither the swan had flown, followed in search of it to Idzumo and there captured it.

Some say " To the land of Tajima."

VI. 14.

11th month, 2nd day. Yukaha Tana presented the swan to the Emperor. Homutsu-wake no Mikoto played with this swan and at last learned to speak. Therefore, Yukaha Tana was liberally rewarded, and was granted the title of Tottori no Miyakko.[2] In consequence there was further established the Be of bird-catchers, the Be of bird-feeders,[3] and the Homu-tsu Be.

25th year, Spring, 2nd month, 8th day. The Emperor com-

B.C. 5.

manded the five Daibu,[4] Takenu Kaha-wake, ancestor of the Abe no Omi, Hiko-kuni-fuku,[5] ancestor of the Wani no Omi, Oho-kashima, ancestor of the Nakatomi no Muraji, Tochine, ancestor of the Mononobe no Muraji, and Take-hi, ancestor of the Ohotomo no Muraji, saying :—" The sagacity of our pre-decessor on the throne, the Emperor Mimaki-iri-hiko-iniye, was displayed in wisdom : he was reverential, intelligent and capable. He was profoundly unassuming, and his disposition was to cherish self-abnegation. He adjusted the machinery of Government, and did solemn worship to the Gods of Heaven

VI. 15.

and Earth. He practised self-restraint and was watchful as to

---

[1] Tottori for tori-tori, i.e. bird-catcher, is the name of a number of places in Japan, notably of the capital of the province of Inaba.

[2] Lord of the bird-catchers. The Chinese character for title is 姓, which means properly family name, surname. But, as this instance shows, such appellations were primarily official designations. Then they became hereditary titles, and in the last place were attenuated into mere surnames.

[3] Tori-kahi-be. [4] Daibu, great man, is a general term for high officials.

[5] Both these men are named in Sūjin Tennō's reign, 10th year, eighty-five years before.

his personal conduct. Every day he was heedful for that day. Thus the weal of the people was sufficient, and the Empire was at peace. And now, under Our reign, shall there be any remissness in the worship of the Gods of Heaven and Earth?"[1]

3rd month, 10th day. Ama-terasu no Oho-kami was taken from Toyo-suki-iri-hime no Mikoto,[2] and entrusted to Yamato-hime no Mikoto. Now Yamato-hime no Mikoto sought for a place where she might enshrine the Great Goddess. So she proceeded to Sasahata in Uda. Then turning back from thence, she entered the land of Ohomi, and went round eastwards to Mino, whence she arrived in the province of Ise.

VI. 16.

Now Ama-terasu no Oho-kami instructed Yamato-hime no Mikoto, saying:—"The province of Ise, of the divine wind,[3] is the land whither repair the waves from the eternal world, the successive waves. It is a secluded and pleasant land. In this land I wish to dwell." In compliance, therefore, with the instruction of the Great Goddess, a shrine was erected to her in the province of Ise. Accordingly an Abstinence Palace was built at Kaha-kami in Isuzu. This was called the palace of Iso. It was there that Ama-terasu no Oho-kami first descended from Heaven.

One story is that the Emperor made Yamato-hime no Mikoto to be his august staff,[4] and offered her to Ama-terasu no Oho-kami. Thereupon Yamato-hime no Mikoto took Ama-terasu no Oho-kami, and having enshrined her at Idzu-kashi no Moto in Shiki,[6] offered sacrifice to her. Thereafter, in compliance with the Goddess's instructions, she, in Winter, the 10th month of the year Hinoto

---

[1] This speech is thoroughly Chinese. It contains numerous phrases borrowed from the Chinese classics.

[2] She had been appointed B.C. 92, eighty-seven years before.

[3] This is a stock epithet (makura kotoba) of this province.

[4] Abstinence Palace or Worship Palace. "On the accession of an Emperor, an unmarried Princess of the Imperial House was selected for the service of the Shrine of Ise, or if there was no such unmarried Princess, then another Princess was fixed upon by divination and appointed worship-princess (齋 王). The Worship-Palace was for her residence." Shintō miômoku ruijiushô, III. 23. See above, note to p. 41.

[5] i e. assistant or deputy.

[6] In Yamato. Idzu means sacred ; kashi is the name of a tree ; moto means bottom.

Mi,[1] on the 18th day, removed to the Palace[2] of Watarahi in the province of Ise.   At this time the Great God of VI. 17. Yamato inspired Ohominakuchi no Sukune, the ancestor of the Hodzumi no Omi, and admonished (the Emperor by his mouth), saying :—" At the time of the Great Beginning, it was covenanted that Ama-terasu no Oho-kami should govern all the Plain of Heaven, and that her august Imperial descendants should hold absolute rule over the eighty spiritual beings of the Central Reed-plain Land. My personal tenure of the governance of the great land is already at an end.   But although the worship of the Gods in Heaven and Earth was maintained by the late Emperor Mimaki, he failed to search out the root of the matter in its details ; he was wanting in thoroughness, and stopped short at the leaves and branches.   Therefore that Emperor was short-lived.[3]   For this reason do thou, our august descendant, now show regret for the shortcomings of the late Emperor and be watchful in regard to the ceremonies of worship.   If thou dost so, the life of thine augustness will be long, and moreover the Empire will have peace."

Now when the Emperor heard these words, he caused Fukayu nushi, the ancestor of the Nakatomi no Muraji, to use divination in order to discover who should be appointed to conduct the worship of the Great God of Yamato. Thereupon Nunaki-waka-hime no Mikoto answered to the divination, and was consequently appointed.   A sacred plot of ground was fixed on in the village of Anashi, and worship performed at Point[4] Naga-oka of Oho-chi.   But this Nunaki-waka-hime no Mikoto's body was already all emaciated, so that she was unable to do sacrifice, and therefore Nagaochi no Sukune, ancestor of the Yamato no Atahe, was made to offer the sacrifices.

26th year, Autumn, 8th month, 3rd day.   The Emperor B.C. 4.

---

[1] Corresponding to the 26th year of Suinin Tennō's reign, or B.C. 4.

[2] Or shrine.

[3] He died at the age of 120, or 168 if we take the "Kojiki" as an authority.   This is one of numerous indications that the chronology of this period is worthless.

[4] The word misaki (point) is used both of a promontory and of a spur of a hill.   Naga-oka is long-hill.

commanded the Mononobe, Tochine no Oho-muraji,[1] saying :—

VI. 18.   " We have repeatedly despatched messengers to the Land of Idzumo to inspect the divine treasures of that Land, but we have had no clear report. Do thou go thyself to Idzumo, and having made inspection, attest them." So Tochine no Oho-muraji, having examined and attested the divine treasures, made a clear report thereof to His Majesty. He was accordingly appointed to the charge of the divine treasures.

B.C. 3.   27th year, Autumn, 8th month, 7th day. The Department of Worship was made to ascertain by divination what implements of war would be lucky as offerings to the Gods. Consequently bows, arrows, and cross-swords were deposited in the shrines of all the Gods. The land and houses consecrated to their service were fixed anew, and they were sacrificed to in due season. The practice of offering weapons in sacrifice to the Gods of Heaven and Earth probably had its origin at this time. This year granaries were erected in the village of Kume.[2]

B C. 2.   28th year, Winter, 10th month, 5th day. Yamato-hiko no Mikoto, the Emperor's younger brother by the mother's side, died.

11th month, 2nd day. Yamato-hiko was buried at Tsukizaka in Musa. Thereupon his personal attendants were assembled, and were all buried alive upright in the precinct of the misasagi. For several days they died not, but wept and wailed day and night. At last they died and rotted. Dogs and crows gathered and ate them.

VI. 19.   The Emperor, hearing the sound of their weeping and wailing, was grieved in heart, and commanded his high officers, saying :—" It is a very painful thing to force those whom one has loved in life to follow him in death. Though it be an ancient custom, why follow it, if it is bad ? From this time forward, take counsel so as to put a stop to the following of the dead."[3]

---

[1] Great-village-elder. This word is nearly equivalent to Prime Minister.

[2] As explained above, Kume is probably a variant of the Chinese word for army. There is at present a village of this name in Yamato, but it was no doubt originally the barrack quarter, and the storehouses here referred to were to contain grain for the food of the army. The original commentary gives miyake as the Japanese name for these granaries. At a later period the miyake were local government offices.

[3] The " Kojiki " (Ch. K., p. 174) says that this was the first time a hedge of

30th year, Spring, 1st month, 6th day. The Emperor
commanded Inishiki no Mikoto and Oho-tarashi-hiko no

men was set up round a tumulus. But the "Nihongi's" statement that it
was an old custom must be correct.

This custom is too much in accordance with what we know of other races
in the barbaric stage of culture to allow us to doubt that we have here a
genuine bit of history, though perhaps the details may be inaccurate, and
the chronology is certainly wrong. In an ancient Chinese notice of Japan
we read that "at this time (A.D. 247) Queen Himeko died. A great mound
was raised over her, and more than a hundred of her male and female
attendants followed her in death."

Funeral human sacrifice for the service of the dead is described by Dr.
Tylor ("Primitive Culture," i. 458) as "one of the most wide-spread, distinct,
and intelligible rites of animistic religion. Arising in the lower barbaric
stage, it develops itself in the higher, and thenceforth continues or dwindles
in survival." He proceeds to quote numerous examples of it from all parts
of the world, and from many ages of history.

It is well known to have existed among the Manchu Tartars and other
races of North-Eastern Asia until modern times. The Jesuit missionary
Du Halde relates that the Emperor Shunchi, of the T'sing dynasty (died
1662), inconsolable for the loss of his wife and infant child, "signified by his
will that thirty men should kill themselves to appease her manes, which ceremony the Chinese look upon with horror, and was abolished by the care of
his successor"—the famous Kanghi.

Another missionary, Alvarez Semedo, in his history of the Tartar invasion, says :—"The Tartarian King vowed to celebrate his Father's Funerals
with the lives of two hundred thousand of the inhabitants of China. For it
is the custome of the Tartars, when any man of quality dieth, to cast into
that fire which consumes the dead corpse as many Servants, Women and
Horses with Bows and Arrows as may be fit to atend and serve them in the
next life."

This custom was also practised in China in the most ancient times, though
long condemned as barbarous. Confucius disapproved of it. An ode in
the "Sheking" (Legge, iv. i. 198) laments the death of three brothers who
were sacrificed at the funeral of Duke Muh, B.C. 621. When the Emperor
She Hwang-ti died, B.C. 209, his son Urh said, "My father's palace ladies
who have no children must not leave the tomb," and compelled them all to
follow him in death. Their number was very great. For other cases see a
paper by Mayers in the Journal of the North China Branch of the Asiatic
Society, new Series, xii.

A King of Kokuryö in Corea died A.D. 248. He was beloved for his
virtues, and many of his household wished to die with him. His successor
forbade them to do so, saying that it was not a proper custom. Many of
them, however, committed suicide at the tomb. "Tongkam," iii. 20.

In A.D. 502, Silla prohibited the custom of burying people alive at the

Mikoto, saying :—" Do ye each tell me the thing ye would dearly like to have." The elder Prince said :—" I should like to have a bow and arrows." The younger Prince said :—" I should like to have the Imperial Dignity." Thereupon the Emperor commanded, saying :—" Let the desire of each of you be complied with." So a bow and arrows were given to Inishiki no Mikoto, and a decree was addressed to Oho-tarashi hiko no Mikoto, saying :—" Thou must succeed to Our Dignity."

A.D. 3.   32nd year, Autumn, 7th month, 6th day. The Empress Hibasu-hime no Mikoto died.

One version has Hibasu ne no Mikoto.

Some time before the burial, the Emperor commanded his Ministers, saying :—" We have already recognized that the practice of following the dead is not good. What should now be done in performing this burial ? " Thereupon Nomi no Sukune came forward and said :—" It is not good to bury living men upright at the tumulus of a prince. How can such a practice be handed down to posterity ? I beg leave to propose an expedient which I will submit to Your Majesty." So he sent messengers to summon up from the Land of Idzumo a hundred men of the clay-workers' Be. He himself directed the men of the clay-workers' Be to take clay and form therewith

VI. 20.   shapes of men, horses, and various objects, which he presented to the Emperor, saying :—" Henceforward let it be the law for future ages to substitute things of clay for living men, and to set them up at tumuli." Then the Emperor was greatly rejoiced, and commanded Nomi no Sukune, saying :—" Thy expedient hath greatly pleased Our heart." So the things of clay were first set up at the tomb of Hibasu-hime no Mikoto. And a

funerals of the sovereigns. Before this time five men and five women were put to death at the King's tomb. " Tongkam," v. 5.

Cases of suicide at the tomb of a beloved lord or sovereign have not been uncommon in Japan even in modern times. There was one in 1868.

The Japanese, like the Chinese, make no distinction between voluntary deaths and human sacrifices. Both are called jun-shi, a term which means " following in death." Indeed, as we may see by the Indian Suttee, it is often hard to draw the line between these two forms of what is really the same custom.

name was given to these clay objects. They were called *Hani-wa.*[1]

Another name is *Tatemono.*[2]

Then a decree was issued, saying :—" Henceforth these clay figures must be set up at tumuli : let not men be harmed."
The Emperor bountifully rewarded Nomi no Sukune for this service, and also bestowed on him a kneading-place, and appointed him to the official charge of the clay-workers' Be. His original title was therefore changed, and he was called Hashi no Omi. This was how it came to pass that the Hashi no Muraji superintend the burials of the Emperors.[3]

The said Nomi no Sukune was the first ancestor of the Hashi no Muraji.[4]   VI. 21.

34th year, Spring, 3rd month, 2nd day. The Emperor made A.D. 5. a progress to Yamashiro. At this time his courtiers represented to him that there was in that country a beautiful person named Kambata no Tohe.[5] She was very handsome, and was the daughter of Fuchi of Ohokuni in Yamashiro. Hereupon the Emperor, spear in hand, made a vow, saying :—" I must be united to this beautiful person." On his way he saw an omen.

---

[1] Clay-rings.   [2] Things set up.

[3] The date ascribed to this incident cannot be depended on. At least Chinese accounts speak of the custom of human sacrifices at the burial of a sovereign as in full force in Japan so late as A.D. 247. Probably all the events of this part of Japanese history are very much antedated. But of the substantial accuracy of the narrative there can be no doubt. Some of these clay figures (known as tsuchi-ningiô) are still in existence, and one may be seen in the British Museum, where it constitutes the chief treasure of the Gowland collection. The Uyeno Museum in Tokio also possesses specimens, both of men and horses. None, however, remain in situ at the tombs. The hani-wa (clay-ring) cylinders which may now be seen embedded in the earth round all the principal misasagi are so numerous that they can hardly have all been surmounted by figures. But they are of the same workmanship and of the same date, and no doubt some of them are the pedestals of images, the above-ground part of which has been long ago destroyed by the weather or by accident.

A similar substitution of straw or wooden images for living men took place in China in ancient times, though by a curious inversion of ideas, the former practice is described as leading to the latter. See Legge's " Chinese Classics, Mencius," p. 9.

[4] Hashi (clay-worker) is also read hanishi, hashibe, or hasebe.

[5] As above stated, Tohe means chief.

When he was arriving at his lodging,[1] a large tortoise came out from the river. The Emperor raised his spear and thrust at

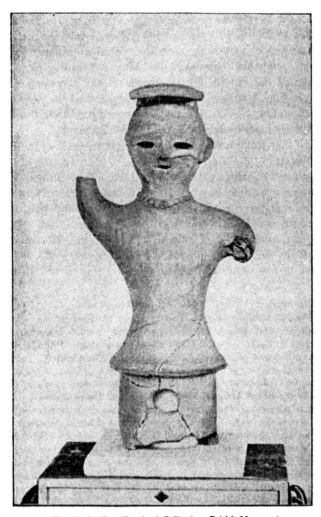

Tsuchi-ningiô. (Gowland Collection, British Museum.)

the tortoise, when it suddenly became changed into a white stone. Then the courtiers said:—" If one were only to think

[1] Literally, travelling-palace.

this out, it must prognosticate something." So Kambata no Tohe was sent for, and lodged in the hinder palace. She was the mother of Iha-tsuku-wake no Mikoto, who was the ancestor of the Kimi of Miho. Before this he had taken to wife Kari-hata-tohe, who bore him three sons. The first was called Oji-wake no Mikoto, the second Ika-tarashi-hiko no Mikoto, and the third I-take-wake no Mikoto.

Ika-tarashi-hiko no Mikoto was the first ancestor of the Kimi VI. 22. of Ishida.

35th year, Autumn, 9th month. Inishiki no Mikoto was A.D. 6. sent to the province of Kahachi to construct the pond of Takashi, and the pond of Chinu.

Winter, 10th month. He made the pond of Saki in Yamato, and the pond of Tomi. In this year, the various provinces were commanded extensively to excavate ponds and channels,[1] to the number of eight hundred and more. Much attention was thus paid to husbandry. Therefore the people enjoyed abundance, and the Empire was at peace.

37th year, Spring, 1st month, 1st day. Oho-tarashi-hiko no A.D. 8. Mikoto was made Prince Imperial.

39th year, Winter, 10th month. Inishiki no Mikoto, while A.D. 10. dwelling in the palace at Kahakami of Udo in Chinu, made a thousand swords. Therefore those swords were called the Kahakami set.

Another name was the Naked[2] Companions.

They were deposited in the shrine of Iso no kami. After this VI. 23. the Emperor gave orders to Inishiki no Mikoto, and made him to have charge of the divine treasures of the shrine of Iso no kami.

One version is:—" Whilst the Imperial Prince Inishiki dwelt at Kahakami of Udo in Chinu, he sent for a smith by name Kahakami, and made a thousand swords. At this time, the shield-makers' Be, the Japanese-figured-cloth-workers' Be, the sacred-bow-shavers' Be, the sacred-arrow-makers' Be,[3] the Oho-anashi Be, the Hatsu-kashi[4]

---

[1] For irrigation.   [2] So called because worn without a sheath.
[3] See above, p. 178.
[4] These are the names of villages. The " Shukai " editor suggests that they were allotted to the Prince for his support.

Be, the jewel-workers' Be, the Kami-osaka Be,[1] the Hi-oki[2] Be, and the sword-wearers' Be—the Be of ten articles altogether—were granted to the Imperial Prince Inishiki.

These thousand swords were deposited in the village of Osaka. They were afterwards removed from Osaka and deposited in the shrine of Iso no kami. At this time the God made a request, saying :—' Let the person named Ichikaha, of the family of the Omi of Kasuga, be made to attend to them.' Therefore by the Emperor's command, Ichikaha was caused to attend to them. He was the first ancestor of the Mononobe[3] no Obito."

VI. 24.

A.D. 58. 87th year, Spring, 2nd month, 5th day. Inishiki no Mikoto spake to his younger sister, Oho-naka-tsu-hime no Mikoto, saying :—" I am old, and unable to have charge of the divine treasures. Henceforward thou must have charge of them." Oho-naka-tsu-hime refused, saying :—" I am a feeble woman. How can I ascend to the divine storehouse of Heaven ? "

Inishiki no Mikoto said :—" Although the divine storehouse[4] is high, I can make for the divine storehouse a ladder. How, then, should it be hard to ascend to the storehouse ? " Hence the proverbial saying, " You can ascend even to the divine storehouse of Heaven, if you only plant a ladder." This was its origin. Ultimately Oho-naka-tsu-hime no Mikoto gave them to Mononobe no Tochine no Oho-muraji, and made him to have charge of them. Therefore the Mononobe no Muraji retain charge of the divine treasures of Iso no kami up to the present time. The above was the origin of this practice.

Formerly in the Land of Tamba, in the village of Kuwada, there was a man whose name was Mikaso. Now, in Mikaso's house there was a dog, by name Ayuki. This dog bit a wild animal called the *mujina*,[5] and killed it. In the animal's belly there was found a magatama of Yasaka gem. This gem was

---

[1] Osaka was the place where the swords were stored.

[2] Hi-oki means "daily offerings."

[3] The Mononobe were Imperial life guards.

[4] One of these storehouses, dating from the 8th century, may still be seen at Tōdaiji, Nara. It is raised on pillars some ten feet above the ground.

[5] A kind of badger.

accordingly offered to the Emperor, and is now in the shrine of
Iso no kami.   VI. 25.

88th year, Autumn, 7th month, 10th day. The Emperor A.D. 59.
commanded the Ministers, saying:—"We hear that the
divine treasures which the Silla Prince Ama no hihoko brought
with him when he first came here are now in Tajima. They
were originally made divine treasures because the people of that
province saw that they were admirable. We desire to see
these treasures." That same day messengers were despatched
with the Imperial commands to Kiyo-hiko, great-grandson of
Ama no hihoko, directing him to present them to the Emperor.
Thereupon, Kiyo-hiko, when he received the Imperial orders,
brought the divine treasures himself, and laid them before His
Majesty. There was one Ha-buto gem, one Ashi-daka gem,
one Uka no Akashi (red-stone) gem, one sun-mirror, and one
Kuma-himorogi.[1] But there was one short sword called Idzushi,[2]
which it suddenly occurred to Kiyo-hiko not to offer to the
Emperor; so he concealed it in his clothing, and wore it himself. The Emperor, unaware of the circumstance of the concealment of the short sword, and wishing to be gracious to
Kiyo-hiko, sent for him and gave him sake in the palace.
Then the short sword appeared from among his garments and
became visible. The Emperor saw it, and himself asked
Kiyo-hiko, saying:—"What short sword is that in thy clothing?" Then Kiyo-hiko, seeing that he was unable to conceal
the short sword, explained that it belonged to the divine
treasures which he was laying before the Emperor. So the
Emperor said to Kiyo-hiko:—"How is it possible for this
divine treasure to be separated from its kind?" So he took it
out and presented it to the Emperor, and all were deposited in
the Sacred Treasury. Afterwards, when the Sacred Treasury
was opened and inspected, the short sword had spontaneously
disappeared. Accordingly, a messenger was sent to Kiyo-hiko,
who inquired of him, saying:—"The short sword which thou
hast presented to the Emperor has suddenly disappeared.
Has it perchance come to thy place?" Kiyo-hiko answered, VI. 26.
and said:—"Last night the short sword came of its own
accord to thy servant's house; but this morning it has dis-

---

[1] Cf. above, p. 168.   [2] Sacred-stone.

appeared." The Emperor was struck with awe, and made no further endeavour to find it. Afterwards the Idzushi short sword went of its own accord to the Island of Ahaji, where the people of the island considered it a God, and erected for the short sword a shrine, in which it is worshipped until this day.

Formerly there was a man, who riding in a ship, cast anchor in the land of Tajima. He was therefore asked, saying:— "Of what country art thou?" He answered and said:—"I am a son of the king of Silla, and my name is Ama no hihoko. So he dwelt in Tajima, and took to wife Mata no wo, daughter of Mahetsu mimi [One version has Mahetsu mi and another Futo-mimi] of that province, who bore to him Tajima Morosuke, the grandfather of Kiyo-hiko.

A.D. 61.   90th year, Spring, 2nd month, 1st day. The Emperor commanded Tajima Mori to go to the Eternal Land[1] and get the fragrant fruit that grows out of season, now called the Tachibana.[2]

A.D. 70.   99th year, Autumn, 7th month, 14th day. The Emperor died in the Palace of Maki-muku at the age of 140,[3] and in Winter, the 12th month, the 10th day, was buried in the misasagi of Fushimi, in Suga-hara.

VI. 27.   The next year, Spring, the 3rd month, the 12th day, Tajima Mori arrived from the Eternal Land, bringing of the fragrant fruit that grows out of season eight sticks and eight bundles.[4]

Thereupon Tajima Mori wept and lamented, saying:—

"Receiving the Celestial Court's command,
Afar I went to a remote region:

---

[1] Tajima Mori was apparently selected for this mission on account of his descent from a king of Silla. But the Tokoyo no Kuni, or Eternal Land, can hardly have been Corea, where the Orange is little, if at all, grown in the present day. It was more likely China.

[2] The Orange, vide Ch. K., p. 198.

[3] The chronology, as usual, will not bear investigation.

[4] The meaning of the characters which I have thus rendered is doubtful. The corresponding passage in the "Kojiki" is corrupt and equally obscure. I do not feel sure that Motoöri has cleared it up quite satisfactorily, in spite of the amount of recondite learning he has brought to bear on it. Cf. Ch. K., p. 199.

Ten thousand ri I crossed the waves,
Distantly I passed over the weak water.[1]
This Eternal Land
Is no other than the mysterious realm of Gods and Genii
To which ordinary mortals cannot attain ;
Therefore in going thither and returning
Ten years have naturally passed.
Beyond my expectation, I braved alone the towering billows,
Turning my way again towards my own land.
Thus, trusting in the spirits of the Emperors,
I hardly accomplished my return.
But now the Emperor is dead,
I am unable to report my mission.
Though I should remain alive,
What more would it avail me ?"[2]

Then turning his face towards the misasagi of the Emperor, he wept aloud, and so of himself he died. When the ministers heard of it they all shed tears.

Tajima Mori was the first ancestor of the Miyake[3] no Muraji.

[1] Said by the Chinese to be north of Fuyu (in Manchooria). It does not support ships.

[2] The sentiment and diction of this speech are thoroughly Chinese. It is not exactly poetry, but nearly so.

[3] Miyake, written with characters which mean "three storehouses." Mi, however, is more probably the honorific prefix.

BOOK VII.

THE EMPEROR OHO-TARASHI-HIKO-OSHIRO-WAKE.

(*KEIKŌ[1] TENNO*.)

THE Emperor Oho-tarashi-hiko-oshiro-wake was the third child of the Emperor Iku-me-iri-hiko-isachi. The Empress his mother was named Hibasu-hime no Mikoto. She was the daughter of Prince Michi no ushi of Tamba. The Emperor Iku-me-iri-hiko-isachi, in the 37th year of his reign, raised him to the rank of Prince Imperial. He was then twenty-one years of age. In the 99th year of his reign, Spring, the second month, the Emperor Iku-me-iri-hiko-isachi died.

A.D. 71.   1st year, Autumn, 7th month, 11th day. The Prince Imperial assumed the Imperial Dignity. The chronological epoch was altered accordingly. This year was the year Kanoto Hitsuji (8th) of the Cycle.

A.D. 72.   2nd year, Spring, 3rd month, 3rd day. The elder lady[2] of Inabi in Harima was appointed Empress.

Another version has:—" The younger lady of Inabi in Harima."

VII. 2.   She had two sons, the first of whom was named the Imperial Prince Oho-usu, and the second Wo-usu no Mikoto.

In one writing it is said:—" The Empress bore three sons. The third was named the Imperial Prince Waka-Yamato-neko."

The Imperial Prince Oho-usu and Wo-usu no Mikoto were born as twins[3] on the same day with the same placenta. The

---

[1] Great road or great conduct.   [2] Oho-iratsume.

[3] There seems to have been a question which of twins was to be considered the elder. One idea was that the last born should be senior, because he occupied the higher place in the womb.

Emperor, wondering at this, informed the mortar.[1] Therefore he gave these two Princes the names of Great Mortar (Oho-usu) and Little Mortar (Wo-usu). Now this Wo-usu no Mikoto was also called Yamato Woguna and again Yamato-dake no Mikoto.[2] Whilst a child he had a manly spirit ; when he arrived at manhood his beauty was extraordinary. He was a rod in height, and his strength was such that he could lift a tripod.[3]

3rd year, Spring, 2nd month, 1st day. Divination was made A.D. 73. as to whether the Emperor should make a progress to the Land of Kii to perform sacrifices to all the Gods of Heaven and Earth. It was found to be unlucky, and the Imperial car was accordingly countermanded. Ya-nushi-oshiho-dake-wo-goro

---

[1] The Chinese character used here is 碓, which properly means a pestle, and is more particularly applied to that arrangement of a mortar and pestle in which the latter is set on a pivot and worked by the foot. This is called the Kara-usu in Japan. Here, however, is one of those cases where we must put aside the Chinese character and be guided by the Japanese word, which is unquestionably *usu*, a term applied to any arrangement for hulling or grinding grain. The usu is properly the mortar rather than the pestle (*kine*), but it is used for the combination of both, and for querns or hand-mills, which are also in use in Japan.

The usu here referred to is probably of the kind shown in the annexed illustration. Stone pestles resembling in shape that in the right hand upper corner are among the stone implements figured in Kanda's work on this subject.

Hardy, in his " Manual of Buddhism," p. 158, says :—"The eastern pestle is found in every house, and is connected with as many superstitions and ceremonies as the besom among the old wives of Europe."

Pestle and Mortar.

The " Shukai" editor suggests that by Great Mortar and Little Mortar the lower and upper stones of the hand-mill were meant. But there is no reason to doubt the statement below (A.D. 610) that hand-mills were first introduced in Suiko's reign.

[2] Woguna means boy, Yamato-dake means hero of Yamato. It is by the last of these names that he is best known to posterity.

[3] A Chinese phrase.

no Mikoto [one version has Take-wi-goro] was sent and caused

VII. 3. to do sacrifice. Hereupon Ya-nushi-oshiho-dake-wo-goro no Mikoto went thither, and stayed at Kashihara in Abi, where he sacrificed to the Gods of Heaven and Earth. He lived here for nine years, and took to wife Kage-hime, the daughter of Uji-hiko, who was the ancestor of the Ki no Atahe.[1] She was the mother of Takechi no Sukune.

A.D. 74. 4th year, Spring, 2nd month, 11th day. The Emperor made a progress to Mino. His courtiers represented to him, saying :—
" In this province there is a handsome woman named Oto-hime, of perfect beauty. She is the daughter of the Imperial Prince Yasaka Irihiko." The Emperor wished to obtain her to be his consort, and went to the house of Oto-hime.[2] Oto-hime, hearing that the Emperor was coming in his carriage, straightway concealed herself in a bamboo-grove. Hereupon the Emperor provisionally caused Oto-hime to go and reside in the Kuguri Palace, and letting loose carp in a pond, amused himself by looking at them morning and evening. Now Oto-hime wished to see the carp sporting, so she came secretly and stood over the pond. The Emperor forthwith detained her, and had intercourse with her. Hereupon Oto-hime thought :—" The way of a husband and wife is the prevailing rule both now and of old time. But for me it is not convenient." So she besought the Emperor, saying :—" Thy handmaiden's disposition is averse to the way of conjugal

VII. 4. intercourse. Unable to withstand the awe of the Imperial commands, she has been placed for a while within the curtain. But it gives her no pleasure. Her face too is hideous, and she is unworthy of being added to the side courts. Thy handmaiden, however, has an elder sister, by name Yasaka Iri-hime, of a beautiful countenance, and also of a virtuous disposition. Let her be placed in the hinder palace." The Emperor assented, and having summoned Yasaka Iri-hime, made her his consort. She bore to him seven sons and six daughters. The name of

---

[1] In this passage the province now known as Kii is called indifferently *Ki* or *Kii*.

[2] Oto-hime means simply " younger lady." There are frequent cases in the " Nihongi " where a woman seems to have no other name than "elder lady " or " younger lady."

the first was the Emperor Waka-tarashi-hiko, of the second the Imperial Prince Iho-ki Iri-hiko, of the third the Imperial Prince Oshi-wake, of the fourth the Imperial Prince Waka-Yamato-neko, of the fifth the Imperial Prince Oho-su-wake, of the sixth the Imperial Princess Nunoshi, of the seventh the Imperial Princess Nunaki, of the eighth the Imperial Princess Ihoki no Iri-hime, of the ninth the Imperial Princess Kako-yori-hime, of the tenth the Imperial Prince Isaki no Iri-hiko, of the eleventh the Imperial Prince Kibi no Ye-hiko, of the twelfth the Imperial Princess Takaki no Iri-hime, and of the thirteenth the Imperial Princess Oto-hime.

Again he took as consort the Lady[1] Midzuha, younger sister of Ihaki-wake, of the Miho House, who bore to him the Imperial Princess Ihono. His next consort, named Ikaha-hime, bore to him the Imperial Prince Kami-kushi[2] and the Imperial Prince Inase no Iri-hiko. The elder of these two, the Imperial Prince VII 5 Kami-kushi, was the first ancestor of the Miyakko of Sanuki. The younger, the Imperial Prince Inase no Iri-hiko, was the first ancestor of the Harima no Wake.[3] His next consort was named Takada-hime, daughter of Kogoto of the Abe House, who bore to him the Imperial Prince Take-kuni Kori-wake. He was the first ancestor of the Wake of Mimura, in the Province of Iyo. His next consort, named Oho-tane-hime, of Kami-naga in Hiuga, bore the Imperial Prince Hiuga no Sotsu-hiko. He was the first ancestor of the Kimi of Amu.[4] His next consort, named Sotake-bime, bore the Imperial Prince Kuni-chi-wake, the Imperial Prince Kuni-se-wake [one version has the Imperial Prince Miya-chi-wake] and the Imperial Prince Toyoto-wake. The elder of these, the Imperial Prince Kuni-chi-wake, was the first ancestor of the Wake of Minuma. The youngest brother, the Imperial Prince Toyo-to-wake, was the first ancestor of the Wake of the Province of Hi.[5]

Now the children of the Emperor, male and female, from VII. 6. first to last, numbered eighty in all. With the exception, however, of Yamato-dake no Mikoto, the Emperor Waka-

---

[1] Iratsume. [2] Divine-comb.
[3] Wake, separation, branch, was a title which implied descent from the Imperial line.
[4] In Nagato. [5] Now Hizen and Higo in Kiushiu.

tarashi-hiko and the Imperial Prince Ihoki no Iri-hiko, the other seventy and odd children were all granted fiefs[1] of provinces and districts, and each proceeded to his own province. Therefore, those who at the present time are called Wake of the various provinces are the descendants of these separated (wakare) Princes.[2]

In this month, the Emperor, hearing that the daughters of Kambone, Mino no Miyakko, the elder's name being Ane-toho-ko, and the younger's being Oto-toho-ko, were both of distinguished beauty, sent Oho-usu no Mikoto with orders to examine the countenance of these women. Now Oho-usu no Mikoto had secret intercourse with them, and did not report his mission. For this reason the Emperor was wrath with Oho-usu no Mikoto.

Winter, the 11th month, 1st day. The Emperor returned from Mino and removed the capital to Maki-muku. This was called the palace of Hi-shiro.

A.D. 82.   12th year, Autumn, 7th month. The Kumaso[3] rebelled, and did not bring tribute.

VII. 7.   8th month, 15th day. The Emperor made a progress to Tsukushi.[4]

9th month, 5th day. On arriving at Saha in Suwo, the Emperor, standing with his face to the south,[5] addressed his Ministers, saying:—"To the southwards, smoke rises abundantly. There must certainly be brigands there." So he halted, and sending in advance Take-moro-gi, ancestor of the Omi of Oho, Unade, ancestor of the Omi of Kusaki, and Natsu-bana, ancestor of the Kimi of the Mononobe, made them to reconnoitre. Now there was here a woman, by name

---

[1] This points to something like a feudal system. But the analogy to European feudalism must not be too closely pressed. Cf. Ch. K., p. 203.

[2] This omits to notice that *Wake* is a much older term.

[3] The country of the Kumaso was the southern part of the island of Kiushiu corresponding to the present provinces of Hiuga, Ohosumi, and Satsuma. Kuma and So are the names of two tribes.

[4] Tsukushi is used in two senses. It sometimes stands for the whole island of Kiushiu, sometimes for only the northern part of it, viz. the two provinces of Chikugo and Chikuzen.

[5] The Emperor of China stands with his face to the south on state occasions. But here it seems only to mean that the Emperor looked southwards.

Kamu-nashi-hime, whose followers were exceedingly numerous. She was the chieftain of that whole country. When she heard that the Emperor's messengers had arrived, she broke off branches of the hard wood of Mount Shitsu. On the upper branch [1] she hung an eight-span sword, on the middle branch she hung an eight-hand mirror, and on the lower branch a Yasaka jewel. She also hoisted a white flag on the bow of her ship, and having come to meet them, addressed them, saying :— " I beseech you, do not have recourse to arms. None of my people, I assure you, are rebellious. They will presently submit themselves to virtue.[2] But there are mischievous brigands. The name of one is Hanatari.[3] He has assumed an unauthorized title. In the mountains and valleys he has called men together, and is encamped at Kahakami in Usa. Another is called Mimi-tari.[4] He is a mischievous brigand, rapacious, frequently plundering the people. He dwells at Kahakami in Mike. The third is called Asa-hagi. He has VII. 8. secretly assembled a following, and dwells at Kahakami in Takaha. The name of the fourth is Tsuchi-wori-wi-wori.[5] He lives concealed at Kahakami[6] in Midori no, and relying solely on the difficulties of the mountains and rivers, plunders the people greatly. All the places to which these four have betaken themselves are strong places. Each of them therefore makes his relations chiefs of one place, and they all say they will not obey the Imperial command. I pray you attack them suddenly, and fail not. "

Hereupon Take-moro-gi and the others first enticed the followers of Asa-hagi, and gave them presents of trowsers of red material and all manner of curious objects. Then having made them beckon to the four unsubmissive men, who came accompanied by their followers, they seized them and put them all to death.

The Emperor ultimately pursued his journey to Tsukushi, and arrived at the district of Nagawo in the province of Buzen,

---

[1] It was the ancient custom in Japan to deliver letters or presents fastened to branches of trees.

To the Emperor's virtuous influence.   [3] Nose-depend.
[4] Ear-depend.   [5] Earth-break-well-break.
[6] Kaha-kami means the upper course of a river.

where he erected a travelling palace and dwelt there. There-fore the name of that place was called Miyako.[1]

Winter, 10th month. He arrived in the Land of Ohokida. The form of this region is wide and beautiful. Therefore it was called Ohokida.[2]

When he came to the village of Hayami, there was there a woman named Haya-tsu-hime. She was chieftain[3] of one place. When she heard that the Imperial car was coming, she went out in person to meet the Emperor, and reported to him, saying:—" In this mountain there is a great cavern called the Rat's Cave. There are two Tsuchi-gumo[4] who dwell in this cave. One is called Awo,[5] and the other Shira.[6] Again at Negino, in the district of Nawori, there are three Tsuchi-gumo. The name of the first is Uchi-zaru,[7] of the second Yata,[8] and of the third Kunimaro.[9] These five men are alike mighty of frame, and moreover have numerous followers. They all say that they will not obey the Imperial command. If their coming is insisted on, they will raise an army and offer resist-ance." The Emperor, provoked by this, could not advance on his journey. So he halted at the village of Kutami, where he erected a temporary palace muro, and dwelt therein. Then he consulted with his Ministers, saying:—" Let us now put in motion a numerous army and slay the Tsuchi-gumo. If, fearing the might of our arms, they should conceal themselves in the mountains and moors, they will assuredly do future mischief." Accordingly he gathered camellia trees, and made of them mallets for weapons. Then selecting his bravest soldiers, he gave them the mallet-weapons. Therewith they pierced through the mountains, cleared away the grass, and attacking the Tsuchi-gumo of the cave,[10] defeated them at Kahakami in Inaba. The whole band were killed, and their blood flowing reached to the ancle. Therefore the men of that day called

VII. ç.

---

[1] Capital.   [2] Great field.

[3] The reader will observe that there are numerous cases of the " monstrous regiment of women " in these old legends.

[4] See above, p. 129.   [5] Green or blue.   [6] White.

[7] Strike-monkey.   [8] Eight-fields.

[9] Country-fellow. Note again that the Tsuchi-gumo have Japanese names, and inhabit old-settled parts of Japan.

[10] The interlinear gloss has iha-muro, rock-muro.

the place where the camellia mallets were made Tsubaki-no-ichi,[1] and the place where the blood flowed they called Chida.[2] Then, in order to attack Uchi-zaru, he crossed straight over Mount Negi. At this time the arrows of the enemy, shot cross- VII. 10. wise from the mountain, fell like rain in front of the Imperial army. The Emperor retreated to Shiro-hara, where he made divination on the river-bank, and accordingly arraying his troops, he first attacked Yata on the moor of Negi, and defeated him. Upon this Uchi-zaru felt that he could not gain the victory, and prayed that his submission should be accepted. This, however, was refused, and they all flung themselves into a ravine and were killed. In the beginning, when the Emperor was about to attack the enemy, he made a station on the great moor of Kashihawo. On this moor there was a stone six feet in length, three feet in breadth, and one foot five inches in thickness. The Emperor prayed, saying:—"If we are to succeed in destroying the Tsuchi-gumo, when we kick this stone, may we make it mount up like a Kashiha leaf." Accordingly he kicked it, upon which, like a Kashiha leaf, it arose to the Great Void. Therefore that stone was called Homishi.[3] The Gods whom he prayed to at this time were the God of Shiga, the God of the Mononobe of Nawori, and the God of the Nakatomi of Nawori—these three Gods.

11th month. He arrived at the Land of Hiuga, and erected a travelling palace, wherein he took up his residence. This was called the palace of Takaya.

12th month, 5th day. Counsel was held how they should attack the Kumaso. Hereupon the Emperor addressed his Ministers, saying:—"We have heard that in the Land of the Kumaso there are two men named Atsukaya and Sakaya, who are the leaders of the Kumaso. Their followers are exceedingly VII. 11. numerous, and are called the eighty Kumaso braves. It will be better not to touch their spear-points. For if we raise a small force, it will be insufficient to exterminate the brigands, while if a large army is put in motion, the people will suffer harm. Is there no means of subduing this country without active measures, and without resorting to the might of arms?" Then

---

[1] Camellia market.   [2] Blood-field.
[3] For fumi-ishi, i.e. kicking-stone.

one of the ministers stood forward and said :—" A Kumaso brave has two daughters, the elder named Ichi-fukaya, and the younger Ichi-kaya. Their beauty is perfect, and their hearts are brave. Offer valuable presents, and under the pretence of bestowing them beneath thy standard, take advantage of this to gain intelligence of the enemy, and attack them unawares. So without ever a sword-edge being stained with blood, the enemy will surely yield themselves up." The Emperor gave command, saying :—" Let it be so." Thereupon the presents were offered, and the two women, deceived by them, were bestowed beneath the tent. The Emperor straightway had intercourse with Ichi-fukaya, and made a show of affection for her. Then Ichi-fukaya told the Emperor, saying :—" Be not anxious lest the Kumaso should not submit. Thy handmaiden has an excellent plan. Let me have one or two soldiers to follow me." She then returned to her home, and prepared much strong sake, which she made her father drink. He became drunk and lay down to sleep. Ichi-fukaya then secretly cut her father's bowstring. Thereupon one of the soldiers who had escorted her came up and killed the Kumaso brave. The Emperor was provoked by such excessively unfilial conduct and put Ichi-fukaya to death. But Ichi-kaya he gave to the

VII. 12. Miyakko of the Land of Ki.

A.D. 83. 13th year, Summer, 5th month. The Kumaso country having been all subdued, the Emperor accordingly dwelt in the palace of Takaya. When he had lived there six years, there was a beautiful woman in that country named Mihakashi-hime.[1] So he took her and made her his concubine. She bore to him the Imperial Prince Toyo-kuni-wake. He was the first ancestor of the Miyakko of the Land of Hiuga.

A.D. 87. 17th year, Spring, 3rd month, 12th day. The Emperor made a progress to the district of Koyu,[2] where he visited the little moor of Nimo. Then looking down towards the east, he said to his courtiers :—" This country faces directly the quarter of the Rising Sun." Therefore he named that country Hiuga.[3] On this day he mounted upon a great stone in the middle of the moor, and feeling a longing for the capital, made this poetry :—

---

[1] The lady of the august sword. [2] In Hiuga.
[3] For Hi-muka, i.e. sun-fronting.

Oh ! how sweet !

From the quarter of my home,   VII. 13.

Clouds arising come hither !

Yamato

Is the most secluded of lands.

Yamato

Retired behind Mount Awo-gaki,

Which encompasses it in its folds,

Is beautiful.

Let those whose lives are sound

Stick (in their hair) by way of headdress

Branches of the white evergreen oak

Of Mount Heguri—

(Fold within fold).

This child ! [1]

This is called a song of longing for one's country.

18th year, Spring, 3rd month. The Emperor, when about to   A.D. 88.
turn his way towards the capital, made a tour of inspection to
the Land of Tsukushi.[2] He first arrived at Hina-mori. There
was at this time on the bank of the River Ihase a crowd of
men assembled. The Emperor, looking down on them from
afar, addressed his courtiers, saying :—" Who are these men
who are assembled ? Are they an enemy ? " So he sent two
men, Hinamori the Elder and Hinamori the Younger, to
see. Now Hinamori the Younger returned and reported,
saying :—" Idzumi-hime, the Kimi of Muro-kata, is about to   VII. 14
offer your Majesty a banquet, and therefore have people
gathered together."

Summer, 4th month, 3rd day. The Emperor arrived at the
district of Kuma. In this place there were two brothers called
Kuma-tsu-hiko.[3] The Emperor first sent to summon Kuma
the Elder to him. Accordingly he came along with the
messenger. Then he summoned Kuma the Younger, but he
would not come. Therefore he sent soldiers and put him to
death.

[1] The text and interpretation of this poem present considerable difficulty,
and the above rendering is in parts only tentative. The "Kojiki" makes three
distinct poems of it, and attributes them to Yamato-dake no Mikoto. Cf.
Ch. K., p. 219. Awo-gaki means green-fence. " Fold within fold " is a mere
epithet, or makura-kotoba, of Mount Heguri.

[2] Tsukushi is here evidently the northern part of the island.

[3] Prince of Kuma.

11th day. Proceeding by the sea route, he anchored at a small island in Ashikita, where he partook of food. Then he told Wo-hidari, ancestor of the Yama no Ahiko,[1] to give him some cold water. Just at this time there was no water in the island, and he did not know what to do. So looking up, he prayed to the Gods of Heaven and the Gods of Earth, when suddenly a cool spring bubbled forth from the side of a cliff. This he drew and put before the Emperor. Therefore that island was called Midzushima.[2] That spring still exists in the cliff of Midzushima.

5th month, 1st day. Setting sail from Ashikita, he proceeded to the Land of Hi.[3] Here the sun went down, and the night being dark, they did not know how to reach the shore. A fire was seen shining afar off, and the Emperor commanded the helmsman, saying :—" Make straight for the place where the fire

VII. 15. is." So he proceeded towards the fire, and thus was enabled to reach the shore. The Emperor made inquiry respecting the place where the fire was, saying :—" What is the name of this village ? " The people of the land answered and said :— " Toyomura, in the district of Yatsushiro." Again he made inquiry respecting the fire :—" Whose fire is this ? " But no owner could be found, and thereupon it was known that it was not a fire made by man. Therefore that country was called Hi no Kuni.[4]

. 6th month, 3rd day. He crossed over from the district of Takaku to the village of Tamakina. At this time he killed a Tsuchi-gumo of that place called Tsudzura.

16th day. He arrived at the Land of Aso.[5] The level tracts of that Land were wide and far-reaching, but no dwellings of men were to be seen. The Emperor said :—" Are there any people in this country ? " Now there were two Deities, one called Aso-tsu-hiko, and the other Aso-tsu-hime, who suddenly assuming human form, sauntered forward and said :—" We

---

[1] Ahiko appears to be a title similar to Atahe, Sukune, etc. It is derived by the Japanese commentators from a, I, my, and hiko, prince.

[2] Water-island.   [3] Now Hizen and Higo.

[4] The Land of Fire.

[5] The name Aso is preserved in Mount Aso, a very curious volcanic mountain in the province of Higo.

two are here. How can it be said that there are no men?"
Therefore that place was called Aso.[1]

Autumn, 7th month, 4th day.   He arrived at Mike[2] in the
further Land of Tsukushi,[3] where he dwelt in the temporary
Palace of Takata.   Now there was here a fallen tree 970 rods
in length. The hundred functionaries passed backwards and VII. 16.
forwards stepping on this tree.   The people of that day made
a song, saying:—

> The morning hoar-frost [4]
> August tree pole-bridge !
> The Lords of the Presence
> Pass over it—
> The august tree pole-bridge !

The Emperor inquired, saying:—"What tree is this?"
There was there an old man who said:—"This tree is a
Kunugi tree.[5] Before it fell down, when the rays of the
morning sun fell on it, it overshadowed the Hill of Kishima;
when the rays of the evening sun fell on it, it covered Mount
Aso." The Emperor said:—"This tree is a divine tree.
Therefore let this country be called the Land of Mike."[6]

7th day. He reached the district of Yame, where, crossing VII. 17.
Mount Mahe, he looked down to the south upon Aha no Saki,
and spake, saying:—"The peaks and glens of this mountain
follow each other fold upon fold. They are exceedingly
beautiful. May it be that a God dwells in this mountain?"
Then Saru-ohomi,[7] the Agata-nushi of Minuma, represented to
the Emperor, saying:—"There is a female Deity named Yame-
tsu hime, who dwells always among these mountains." This is
therefore the reason why this country is called the Land of
Yame.

8th month. He arrived at the village of Ikuha,[8] where he

---

[1] Aso is a dialectical variation for nanzo or nazo, how or why.
[2] August tree.   [3] Now Chikugo.
[4] Morning hoar-frost is a makura-kotoba. The only connection between
it and the rest of the poem is that hoar-frost melts, and that ke (for ki) tree
is also the first syllable of kesu, to melt. The Presence is of course the
Imperial Presence.
[5] Quercus Serrata, Hepburn.   [6] August tree.
[7] Monkey-great-sea.   [8] In Chikugo.

P

partook of food. On this day the stewards left behind the drinking cup. Wherefore the men of that day called the place where the drinking cup had been forgotten Ukuha. The present name Ikuha is a corruption of this. In old times the common people of Tsukushi called a drinking-cup Ukuha.

A.D. 89. 19th year, Autumn, 9th month, 20th day. The Emperor arrived from Hiuga.

A.D. 90. 20th year, Spring, 2nd month, 4th day. The Princess Ihono was made to sacrifice to Ama-terasu no Oho-kami.

A.D. 95. 25th year, Autumn, 7th month, 3rd day. Takechi no Sukune was commissioned to inquire into the geography of the various provinces of the Northern [1] and Eastern [2] circuits and the condition of the people.

A.D. 97. 27t year, Spring, 2nd month, 12th day. Takechi no Sukune returned from the East Country and informed the Emperor, saying :—" In the Eastern wilds there is a country VII. 18. called Hitakami.[3] The people of this country, both men and women, tie up their hair in the form of a mallet, and tattoo their bodies. They are of fierce temper, and their general name is Yemishi. Moreover, their land is wide and fertile. We should attack them and take it."

Autumn, 8th month. The Kumaso again rebelled, and made unceasing inroads on the frontier districts.

Winter, 10th month, 13th day. Yamato-dake no Mikoto was sent to attack the Kumaso. He was at this time sixteen years of age. Thereupon Yamato-dake no Mikoto said :—" I desire to take with me some good archers. Where are there any good archers ? " Some one told him, saying :— " In the province of Mino there is a good archer named Oto-hiko-gimi." Thereupon Yamato-dake no Mikoto sent Miyado-hiko, a man of Katsuraki, and summoned to him Oto-hiko-gimi. Therefore Oto-hiko-gimi came and brought with him Ishiura no Yokotachi, Tako no Inaki,[4] and Chichika no Inaki of the province of Ohari, and followed Yamato-dake no Mikoto on his expedition.

[1] Including Mutsu and Dewa.
[2] Or Adzuma, the region round what is now Tokio.
[3] Sun-height. So called from its eastern position. Hi-tachi, sun-rise, is a name of similar purport.
[4] One of the lower ranks of the local nobility.

12th month. Having arrived at the Land of Kumaso, he inquired into the state of things, and the character of the country in respect of facilities of access. Now the Kumaso had a leader named Torishi-kaya, also called the Brave of Kahakami, who assembled all his relations in order to give VII. 19. them a banquet. Hereupon Yamato-dake no Mikoto let down his hair, and disguising himself as a young girl, secretly waited until the banquet should be given by the Brave of Kahakami. Then with a sword girded on him underneath his inner garment, he entered the banqueting muro of the Brave of Kahakami and remained among the women. The Brave of Kahakami, enchanted with the beauty of the young girl, forthwith took her by the hand, and made her sit beside him. He also offered her the cup, and made her drink, and thus amused himself with her. By and by the night grew late, and the company fewer. Also the Brave of Kahakami became intoxicated. Hereupon Yamato-dake no Mikoto drew the sword which he had in his inner garments, and stabbed the Brave of Kahakami in the breast, but did not kill him outright. The Brave of Kahakami, bowing down his head to the ground, said :—" Wait a little. I have something to say." Then Yamato-dake no Mikoto stayed his sword and waited. The Brave of Kahakami addressed him, saying :—"Who is thine Augustness ? " He answered and said :—" I am the child of the Emperor Oho-tarashi-hiko, and my name is Yamato Woguna." The Brave of Kahakami again spake to him, saying :—" I am the strongest man in all this land, and therefore none of the men of this time can excel me in might, and none refuses to be my follower. I have met with many valiant men, but none as yet could match the Prince. Therefore this despicable robber, from his filthy mouth, offers thine Augustness a title. Wilt thou accept it ? " He said :—" I will accept it." So he spake to him, saying :—" Henceforward in speaking of the Imperial Prince, let him be styled the Imperial Prince Yamato-dake." [1] When he had done speaking Yamato-dake pierced his breast through and killed him. Therefore up to the present day he is styled Yamato-dake no Mikoto. This was the origin of it.

---

[1] The champion of Japan.

Afterwards he despatched Oto-hiko and the others, who slew all that band, leaving not a chewer,[1] and when this was done, he returned by sea to Yamato. Arriving at Kibi, he crossed the Ana Sea. In this place there was a malignant Deity, whom he forthwith slew. Again, turning northwards, he arrived at Naniha,[2] where he killed the malignant Deity of the Kashiha ferry.

A.D. 98. 28th year, Spring, 2nd month, 1st day. Yamato-dake no Mikoto reported to the Emperor how he had subdued the Kumaso, saying :—" Thy servant, trusting in the Emperor's Divine Spirit,[3] by force of arms, at one blow, suddenly slew the Kumaso chieftain and reduced that whole country to peace. In this way the Western Land is now quiet, and the people are undisturbed. Only the God of the Ferry of Ana in Kibi and the God of the Ferry of Kashiha at Naniha, both, with mischievous intent, sent forth a poisonous vapour, by which travellers were plagued. Both of them formed centres of calamity. Therefore I killed all those evil Deities, and have thrown open the roads by land and water alike." The Emperor upon this commended the good service done by Yamato-dake no Mikoto, and bestowed extraordinary affection on him.

A.D. 110. 40th year, Summer, 6th month. There was wide rebellion of the Eastern wilds, and the frontier was in a state of tumult.

Autumn, 7th month, 16th day. The Emperor addressed his Ministers, saying :—" The Eastern country is now in an unquiet state, and turbulent Deities have sprung up in numbers. Moreover the Yemishi have rebelled to a man and frequently carry off the people. Whom shall I send to still this disturbance?" But none of the Ministers knew whom to send. Then Yamato-dake no Mikoto addressed the Emperor, saying :—" Thy servant it was who formerly performed the labour of the expedition to the West. This campaign must be the business of the Imperial Prince Oho-usu." But the Imperial Prince Oho-usu was afraid, and ran to conceal himself among the grass. Accordingly a messenger was sent to fetch him. Hereupon the Emperor chid him, saying :—" If thou dost not

---

[1] i.e. a living soul.   [2] The modern Ohosaka.
[3] Very nearly the Latin *numen*.

wish it, shall We insist on sending thee? Why all this alarm, VII. 21.
whilst thou hast not yet confronted the enemy?" Accordingly
he eventually granted him Mino as a fief, and so he went to
his government. He was the first ancestor of the two houses
of the Kimi of Muketsu and the Kimi of Mori. Upon this
Yamato-dake no Mikoto, striking a martial attitude, said:—
"Not many years have passed since I subdued the Kumaso.
Now the Yemishi of the East have made a fresh rebellion.
When shall we arrive at a universal peace? Thy servant,
notwithstanding that it is a labour to him, will speedily quell
this disturbance." So the Emperor took a battle-axe,[1] and
giving it to Yamato-dake no Mikoto, said:—"We hear that
the Eastern savages are of a violent disposition, and are much
given to oppression : their hamlets have no chiefs, their villages
no leaders, each is greedy of territory, and they plunder one
another. Moreover, there are in the mountains malignant
Deities, on the moors there are malicious demons, who beset
the highways and bar the roads, causing men much annoyance.
Amongst these Eastern savages the Yemishi are the most
powerful, their men and women live together promiscuously,
there is no distinction of father and child. In winter they
dwell in holes, in summer they live in nests. Their clothing
consists of furs, and they drink blood.[2] Brothers are suspicious of one another. In ascending mountains they are like
flying birds; in going through the grass they are like fleet
quadrupeds. When they receive a favour, they forget it, but
if an injury is done them they never fail to revenge it. Therefore they keep arrows in their top-knots and carry swords VII. 22.
within their clothing. Sometimes they draw together their
fellows and make inroads on the frontier. At other times they
take the opportunity of the harvest to plunder the people. If
attacked, they conceal themselves in the herbage ; if pursued,
they flee into the mountains. Therefore ever since antiquity
they have not been steeped in the kingly civilizing influences.

[1] Motoöri points out this as an instance where the desire to imitate his
Chinese models has caused the author of the ".Nihongi" to introduce
Chinese things which have no business in a Japanese narrative. The
"Kojiki" says it was a spear of holly eight fathoms long.

[2] The "Liki" speaks of the ancient Chinese living on fruits and the flesh of
wild beasts and drinking their blood.

Now We mark that thou art mighty of stature and thy countenance is of perfect beauty, thou hast strength sufficient to raise tripods, thy fierceness is like thunder and lightning, wherever thou dost turn thy face, there is none to stand before thee; whenever thou dost attack thou dost surely conquer. This we know, that whereas in outward form thou art Our child, in reality thou art a God. Truly Heaven, commiserating Our want of intelligence and the disturbed condition of the country, has ordained that thou shouldst order the Heavenly institution, and save the monarchy from extinction. Moreover, this Empire is thy Empire, and this Dignity is thy Dignity. I adjure thee to exercise profound policy and far-reaching foresight in searching out iniquity and watching against crises. Admonish with majesty; comfort with kindness. Avoid having recourse to arms, and thou wilt naturally inspire loyal obedience. So by cunning words thou mayst moderate the violent Deities, and by a display of armed force sweep away malignant demons." [1]

Then Yamato-dake no Mikoto received the battle-axe, and, bowing twice, addressed the Emperor, saying:—"But few years have elapsed since my former expedition to the West, when, trusting in the might of the Imperial spirit, I, with a sword three feet in length, conquered the land of Kumaso, and VII. 23. the rebel chiefs yielded themselves to punishment. Now again, trusting in the spirits [2] of the Gods of Heaven and Earth, and in reliance on the Imperial might, I am proceeding to the frontier. I will admonish them by gentle teaching, and if any remain unsubmissive, I will smite them with arms." So he again bowed twice. Then the Emperor commanded Kibi no Take-hiko and Ohotomo no Take-hi no Muraji to follow Yamato-dake no Mikoto. He also appointed Nana-tsuka-hagi his steward.

---

[1] This speech cannot be received as a document of Japanese history. It is a cento of reminiscences of Chinese literature.

[2] Numina.

[3] Hirata says that Japanese surnames were taken from offices or avocations, names of places, parents' names, circumstances, or objects. I suppose he would have included under circumstances such personal peculiarities as that which suggested the name Nana-tsuka-hagi, literally "Seven-span-shanks."

Winter, 10th month, 2nd day. Yamato-dake no Mikoto set
out on his journey.

7th day. He turned aside from his way to worship at
the shrine of Ise. Here he took leave of Yamato-hime[1] no
Mikoto, saying:—" By order of the Emperor, I am now proceeding on an expedition against the East to put to death
the rebels, therefore I am taking leave of thee." Hereupon
Yamato-hime no Mikoto took the sword Kusa-nagi and gave it
to Yamato-dake no Mikoto, saying:—" Be cautious, and yet
not remiss."

This year Yamato-dake no Mikoto first reached Suruga.
The brigands of this place made a show of obedience, and said,
deceivingly:—" On this moor there are large deer in very great
plenty. Their breath is like the morning mist, their legs are
like a dense wood. Do thou go and hunt them." Yamato-
dake no Mikoto believed these words, and, going into the
middle of the moor, sought for game. The brigands, desiring
to kill the Prince, set fire to the moor. But the Prince, seeing VII. 24.
that he had been deceived, produced fire by means of a fire-
drill,[2] and, kindling a counter-fire, succeeded in making his
escape.

> One version says:—" The sword Mura-kumo,[3] which
> the Prince wore, wielded itself, and mowed away the
> herbage near the Prince, thus enabling him to escape.
> Therefore that sword was called Kusa-nagi."[4]

The Prince said:—" I was almost betrayed." So he burnt
all that robber-band and exterminated them. Therefore that
place was called Yaketsu.[5]

Next he marched on to Sagami, whence he desired to proceed to Kadzusa. Looking over the sea, he spake with a loud
voice, and said:—" This is but a little sea:[6] one might even

---

[1] She was appointed priestess B.C. 5, and we are now at A.D. 110, by the
common chronology.

[2] The interlinear gloss and the " Kojiki" (Ch. K., p. 211) have hi-uchi, or
fire-striker, by which a flint and steel is doubtless meant. A fire-drill was
known to the ancient Japanese, as appears from the " Kojiki"(Ch. K., p. 104)
and other authorities, and it is actually in use at present to produce fire for
sacred purposes. See a paper by Satow, in " J.A.S.T.," VI. 223.

[3] Assembled-clouds.   [4] The herbage mower.
[5] Port or ferry of burning.   [6] The bay of Yedo.

jump over it." But when he came to the middle of the sea a storm suddenly arose, and the Prince's ship was tossed about, so that he could not cross over. At this time there was a concubine in the Prince's suite, named Oto-tachibana-hime. She was the daughter of Oshiyama no Sukune of the Hodzumi House. She addressed the Prince, saying :—"This present uprising of the winds and rushing of the waves, so that the Prince's ship is like to sink, must be due to the wishes of the God of the Sea. I pray thee let me go into the sea, and so let the person of thy mean handmaiden be given to redeem the life of the Prince's Augustness." Having finished speaking, she plunged into the billows. The storm forthwith ceased, and the ship was enabled to reach the shore. Therefore the people of that time called that sea Hashiri-midzu.[1]

VII. 25.   Hereupon Yamato-dake no Mikoto, going by way of Kadzusa, changed his route, and entered the Land of Michi no oku.

At this time a great mirror was hung upon the Prince's ship. Proceeding by the sea route, he went round to Ashi no ura and crossed aslant to Tama no ura.[2] When he arrived at the Yemishi frontier, the chiefs of the Yemishi, Shima-tsu-kami and Kuni-tsu-kami,[3] encamped at the harbour of Take, with the intention of making resistance. But when they saw the Prince's ship from afar, they feared his majesty and power, and knew in their hearts that they could not gain the victory over him. They all flung away their bows and arrows, bowed down towards him, and said :—"When we look upon thy face, we see that it is more than human. Art thou perchance a Deity? We desire to know thy name." The Prince answered and said:—"I am the son of a Deity of visible men." Hereupon the Yemishi were all filled with awe. They gathered up their skirts and, plunging into the waves, of their own accord assisted the Prince's ship to reach the shore. Then, with their hands bound behind them, they submitted themselves for punishment. He therefore pardoned their offence, and having made prisoners their chieftains, caused them to be his personal attendants. The Yemishi having been

---

[1] Running-water.   [2] In Shimōsa.
[3] Literally, Gods of the Islands and Gods of the Continent.

subdued, he returned from the country of Hitakami, and proceeding to the south-west, passed through Hitachi, and arrived
at the Land of Kahi, where he dwelt in the palace of Sakawori. VII. 26.
At this time a light was kindled and he partook of food. On
this night he made a song, in which he inquired of those in
attendance on him, saying :—

> Since I passed Tsukuba,
> And Nihibari,
> How many nights have I slept ?

None of his attendants was able to answer him. Now there
was a man who had charge of the lights, who made a song, in
continuation of the Prince's, saying :—

> Counting the days—
> Of nights there are nine nights,
> Of days there are ten days.

Therefore the Prince commended his intelligence and liberally
rewarded him.[1]

Now while he was residing in this palace, he granted to
Take-hi, the ancestor of the Ohotomo no Muraji, the Yuki[2] Be.
Thereupon Yamato-dake no Mikoto said :—"All the wicked
chiefs of the Yemishi have submitted to the punishment of their
crimes. Only in the Land of Shinano and the Land of Koshi
there are a considerable number who are not yet obedient to
the civilizing influence." So from Kahi he turned towards the
north, and passing through Musashi and Kōdzuke, he went
westward as far as the Usuhi-saka.[3] Now Yamato-dake no VII..27.
Mikoto always thought with regret of Oto-tachibana-hime.
Therefore, when he ascended to the summit of Usuhi and
looked down towards the south-east, he sighed three times, and
said, " Alas ! my wife ! " Therefore the 'provinces east of the
mountains were given the name of Adzuma.[4]

Here he sent Kibi no Takehiko by a different road to the
Land of Koshi, and caused him to examine the character of the
country as regards means of access, and also whether the people
were tractable or not. So Yamato-dake no Mikoto advanced

---

[1] Cf. Ch. K., p. 214.　　　　[2] Quiver.
[3]. Now known as the Usuhi Tōge (pass) on the Nakasendō road.
[4] Aga tsuma means my wife.

into the province of Shinano. This is a Land of high mountains and profound valleys. Verdant summits are piled up ten
thousand fold, so that for men with staff in hand they are hard
to ascend. The cliffs are precipitous, and are girt with flying
bridges.[1] Many thousand are the hill-ranges, where even with
slackened reins the horse makes no progress. Yet Yamato-dake
no Mikoto, bursting through the smoke, and braving the mists,
distantly crossed Mount Oho-yama. He had already reached
the summit when he became hungry and had food on the mountain. The God of the mountain plagued the Prince. He
assumed the form of a white deer and stood before him. The
Prince, wondering at this, took a stick of garlic, and jerked it
VII. 28. at the white deer, striking it in the eye and killing it.[2] Here
the Prince suddenly lost his way and could find no issue.
Then a white dog came of its own accord, and made a show of
guiding the Prince. Following the dog, he proceeded on his
way, and succeeded in coming out into Mino. Kibi no Take-
hiko, coming out from Koshi, met him. Before this when any
one crossed the Shinano pass, he inhaled so much of the breath
of the Deity that he became ill and lay down. But after the
white deer was killed, the travellers who crossed that mountain chewed garlic,[3] and smearing with it men, kine, and
horses, preserved them from being affected by the Deity's
breath.

Yamato-dake no Mikoto, having returned back again to
Ohari, straightway took to wife a daughter of the Ohari
House, by name Miyazu-hime, and tarried there until the next
month. Here he heard that on Mount Ibuki in Afumi there
was a savage Deity. So he took off his sword, and leaving it in
the house of Miyazu-hime, went on afoot. When he arrived at
Mount Ibuki, the God of the mountain took the shape of a
VII. 29. great serpent, and posted himself on the road. Hereupon

---

[1] Kake-hashi, a bridge supported on poles driven into the side of a cliff.
Common in some mountainous parts of Japan.

[2] Ch. K., 213.

[3] "Another popular device (in Scotland) for frightening away witches and
fairies was to hang bunches of garlic about the farms." "Auld Licht Idylls,"
by J. M. Barrie.

Dennys, in his "Folk-lore of China," mentions several cases of the use
of garlic or onions to keep away evil spirits.

Yamato-dake no Mikoto, not knowing that it was the master God who had become a serpent, said to himself:—" This serpent must be the Savage Deity's messenger. Having already slain a master God, is a messenger worth hunting after ? " Accordingly he strode over the serpent and passed on. Then the God of the mountain raised up the clouds, and made an icy rain to fall. The tops of the hills became covered with mist, and the valleys involved in gloom. There was no path which he could follow. He was checked and knew not whither to turn his steps. However, braving the mist, he forced his way onwards, and barely succeeded in finding an issue. He was still beside himself like a drunken man. He therefore sat down beside a spring at the foot of the mountain, and, having drunk of the water, recovered his senses. Therefore that spring was called the Wi-same [1] spring.

It was at this time that Yamato-dake no Mikoto first became ill. The disease gradually increased and he returned to Ohari. Here he did not enter the house of Miyazu-hime, but passed on to Ise and reached Otsu.[2] Formerly, in the year when Yamato-date no Mikoto was proceeding eastwards, he halted on the shore at Otsu and partook of food. At that time he took off a sword which he laid down at the foot of a fir-tree. Eventually he went away forgetting it. When he now came to this place, the sword was still there. Therefore he made a song, saying :—

> Oh ! thou single pine-tree !
> That art right opposite
> To Ohari—
> Ah me—thou single pine-tree !
> If thou wert a man,
> Garments I would clothe thee with,
> A sword I would gird on thee.

When he came to the moor of Nobo, his sufferings became VII. 30. very severe. So he made an offering of the Yemishi whom he had captured to the Shrine of the God.[3] He therefore sent Kibi no Take-hiko to report to the Emperor, saying :—" Thy servant having received the command of the Celestial Court, undertook a distant expedition to the wilds of the East, where

---

[1] Sit-sober.
[2] Not Ôtsu on the southern shore of Lake Biwa, but a place in Ise.
[3] As slaves.

by the favour of the Gods, and trusting in the mighty power of the Emperor, I made the rebellious to submit themselves for punishment, and the violent deities to become moderate. Therefore I rolled up my armour, laid aside my weapons, and was returning peacefully. It was my hope on such a day at such an hour to report my mission to the Celestial Court.[1] But the life allotted me by Heaven has unexpectedly approached an end. Passing swiftly as a four-horse carriage passes a crack in the road, it may not be stayed. Alone I lay me down on the waste moor with none to say a word to me. But why should I regret the loss of this body? My only grief is that I cannot meet thee."

Having said so, he died on the moor of Nobo. He was then thirty years of age. When the Emperor heard it, he could not sleep peacefully on his couch, nor was the taste of food sweet to him. Night and day his voice was choked with grief: with tears and lamentations he beat his breast. Therefore he exclaimed aloud, saying :—" Oh! Our son, Prince Wo-usu! Formerly when the Kumaso revolted he was still a boy. But for a long time he bore the labour of campaigning. Afterwards he was constantly at Our side, supplying Our deficiencies. Then when the troubles with the Eastern savages arose, there was no one else whom We could send to smite them, so in spite of Our affection for him, We sent him into the country of the enemy. No day passed that we did not think of him. Therefore morning and evening We longingly awaited the day of his return. Oh! what a calamity! Oh! what a crime! While We least expected it, we suddenly lost Our child. Henceforth with whom to help us shall we manage the vast institution?"

So he commanded his ministers and through them instructed the functionaries[2] to bury him in the misasagi of Nobo Moor in the Land of Ise.

Now Yamato-dake no Mikoto, taking the shape of a white bird, came forth from the misasagi, and flew towards the Land of Yamato. The Ministers accordingly opened the coffin, and looking in, saw that only the empty clothing remained, and

VII. 31.

---

[1] This sentence is in the " Shukai " edition introduced at the end of this speech.

[2] Lit. the hundred bureaus.

that there was no corpse. Thereupon messengers were sent to
follow in search of the white bird. It stopped on the plain of
Kotobiki in Yamato. Accordingly in that place a misasagi
was erected. The white bird flew on again until it reached
Kahachi, where it rested in the village of Furuchi, and in this
place also a misasagi[1] was erected. Therefore the men of VII. 32.
that day called these three misasagi " the white bird misasagi."[2]
At last it soared aloft to Heaven, and there was nothing buried
but his clothing and official cap. The Emperor, wishing to
perpetuate the fame of his services, established the Takeru[3]
Be. This was in the 43rd year of the Emperor's reign.

51st year, Spring, 1st month, 7th day. The Emperor A.D. 121.
summoned his Ministers, and feasted them for several days.
Now the Imperial Prince Waka-tarashi-hiko no Mikoto and
Takechi no Sukune did not come to the Banqueting Court.
The Emperor sent for them and asked the reason. Therefore
they represented to the Emperor, saying:—"On a day of
festival, the Ministers and functionaries must have their minds
bent on jollity, and they do not think of the State. In view of
the possibility of there being madmen, who might watch for
an unprotected space in the ramparts, we remain on guard
beneath the Gate[4] and provide against emergencies." Then
the Emperor spake and said:—"Splendid!" So he showed
them an extraordinary affection.

Autumn, 8th month, 4th day. Waka-tarashi-hiko no
Mikoto was appointed Prince Imperial. On this day Takechi
no Sukune was appointed Prime Minister.

The cross-sword Kusanagi, which was at first worn by VII. 33.
Yamato-dake no Mikoto, is now in the shrine of Atsuta in the
district of Ayuchi, in the province of Ohari. Now the Yemishi
who had been presented to the shrine brawled day and night,
and were disrespectful in their goings out and comings in.
Then Yamato-hime no Mikoto said:—"These Yemishi should
not be allowed near the shrine." Accordingly she sent them up

---

[1] I have seen this tumulus. It is a very large double mound surrounded
by a moat.

[2] Shira-tori no Misasagi. Many of the tumuli are favourite resorts of the
white egret, whence doubtless the name.

[3] Or Take, brave.   [4] Mikado means "august gate."

to the Court, where they were made to settle beside Mount Mimoro. Ere long they cut down all the trees of the sacred mountain. They shouted and bawled in the neighbouring villages and threatened the people. The Emperor, hearing this, summoned his Ministers, and said :—" The Yemishi who were placed beside the sacred mountain have by nature the hearts of beasts. They cannot be allowed to dwell in the inner country." So he caused them to be stationed without the home provinces, in any places which they pleased. They were the ancestors of the present Saheki[1] Be of the five provinces of Harima, Sanuki, Iyo, Aki, and Aha.

VII. 34.
In the beginning Yamato-dake no Mikoto took the Imperial Princess Futachi-iri-hime, and made her his consort.[2] She bore Prince Ineyori-wake, next the Emperor Tarashi-naka-tsu-hiko,[3] next Nuno oshi-iri-hime no Mikoto, and next Prince Waka-take. The eldest of these, Prince Ineyori-wake, was the first ancestor of the two families of the Kimi of Inu-gami and of the Kimi of Takebe. Another consort, named Kibi no Anato no Take-hime, daughter of Kibi no Take-hiko, bore to him Prince Take-miko and Prince Towoki-wake. The elder of these, Prince Take miko, was the first ancestor of the Kimi of Aya in Sanuki. Prince Towoki-wake was the first ancestor of the Kimi of Wake in Iyo. His next consort, Oto-tachibana hime, daughter of Oshiyama no Sukune, of the Hodzumi House, bore to him Prince Waka-take-hiko.

VII. 35.
A.D. 122.
52nd year, Summer, 5th month, 4th day. The Empress Harima no Oho-iratsume died.

Autumn, 7th month, 7th day. Ya-saka-iri-hime no Mikoto was appointed Empress.

A.D. 123.
53rd year, Autumn, 8th month, 1st day. The Emperor commanded his Ministers, saying :—" When will Our longing for Our son cease? We desire to make a tour of inspection to the region subdued by Prince Wo-usu." In this month he

---

[1] The Chinese characters for Saheki mean "Assistant-Chief." It is apparently a Chinese word and not Japanese, and therefore it seems out of place in the history of a period long previous to the introduction of Chinese learning. But, however unhistorical this narrative may be, it goes to prove that there is an Aino element in the Japanese nation.

[2] She was his aunt.   [3] Chiuai Tennô.

mounted into his carriage and made a progress to Ise ; where, turning aside, he entered the East Sea provinces.

Winter, 10th month. He arrived at the province of Kadzusa, whence by the sea-route he crossed over to the harbour of Aha.

At this time the Emperor, hearing the cry of a fish-hawk, wished to see the bird's form. So he went out upon the sea in search of it, and caught clams. Hereupon the ancestor of the Kashihade no Omi,[1] by name Ihaka Mutsukari, made shoulder-straps of bulrushes, and preparing a hash of the clams, put it before the Emperor. Therefore he commended the service rendered by the Omi Ihaka Mutsukari, and granted him the Stewards' Ohotomo Be.

12th month. The Emperor returned from the Eastern country and dwelt in Ise. This was called the Kambata Palace.

54th year, Autumn, 9th month, 19th day. From Ise the Emperor returned to Yamato, and dwelt in the Palace of Makimuku. VII. 36. A.D. 124.

55th year, Spring, 2nd month, 5th day. Prince Hiko-sa-jima was appointed Governor-general of the fifteen provinces of the Tô-san-dô.[2] He was a grandson of Toyoki no Mikoto. But when he arrived at the village of Anashi in Kasuga he fell ill and died. A.D. 125.

At this time the people of the Eastern Land, grieved that the Prince did not arrive, secretly purloined his body, and buried it in the land of Kōdzuke.[3]

56th year, Autumn, 8th month. The Emperor commanded Prince Mimoro-wake, saying :—" Thy father, Prince Hiko-sajima, was unable to proceed to his governorship and died prematurely. Therefore do thou undertake the absolute rule of the Eastern Land." So Mimoro-wake no Mikoto, having received the Emperor's commands, and being also desirous of accomplishing his father's work, straightway proceeded thither, and undertook the government. He had already attained to a A.D. 126.

---

[1] Stewards.   [2] East-mountain-road.

[3] Several ancient tumuli near the village of Ohomuro in this province are perhaps the tombs of this dynasty of governors. They are described in a paper by Satow, in " T.A.S.J.," Vol. VIII., p. 327.

good administration when the Yemishi made a disturbance.
So he raised an army and attacked them. Then the Yemishi
chieftains, Ashi-furi-he, Oho-ha-furi-he, and Tohotsu Kura-ho-
he bowed their heads to the ground and came; they made
deep obeisance and accepted punishment, offering him all their
territory without exception. Therefore he pardoned those who
surrendered, and put to death those who would not submit.
On this account the Eastern Land was for a long time free
from trouble. Therefore his descendants are to this day in
the Eastern Land.

A.D. 127.   57th year, Autumn, 9th month. The Pool of Sakate was
VII. 37.   constructed, and the embankment planted with bamboos.

Winter, 10th month. It was commanded that every province should erect granaries of the labourers' Be.[1]

A D. 128.   58th year, Spring, 2nd month, 11th day. The Emperor
made a progress to the Land of Ohomi, and dwelt in Shiga for
three years. This was called the Palace of Taka-Anaho.

A.D. 130.   60th year, Winter, 11th month, 7th day. The Emperor
died in the Palace of Taka-Anaho at the age of 106.

THE EMPEROR WAKA-TARASHI-HIKO.

(*SEIMU*[2] *TENNŌ.*)

The Emperor Waka-tarashi-hiko was the fourth child of the
Emperor Oho-tarashi-hiko-oshiro-wake. The name of the
Empress his mother was Ya-saka-iri-hime no Mikoto, daughter
of the Imperial Prince Ya-saka-iri-hiko. He was appointed
Prince Imperial in the 46th year of the Emperor Oho-tarashi-
hiko, being then aged twenty-four years. In the 60th year of
his reign, Winter, the 11th month, the Emperor Oho-tarashi-
hiko died.

A.D. 131.   1st year, Spring, 1st month, 5th day. The Prince Imperial
assumed the Imperial Dignity. This year was the year Kanoto
Hitsuji (8th) of the Cycle.

A.D. 132.   2nd year, Winter, 11th month, 10th day. The Emperor

---

[1] Cf. Ch. K., p. 205.   Accomplish-functions.

Oho-tarashi-hiko was buried in the misasagi over the road at Yamanobe in the province of Yamato.

The Empress was honoured with the title of Grand Empress. VII. 38.

3rd year, Spring, 1st month, 7th day. Takechi no Sukune A.D. 133. was made Prime Minister. In the beginning the Emperor was born on the same day with Takechi no Sukune, and he therefore had an extraordinary affection for him.

4th year, Spring, 2nd month, 1st day. The Emperor com- A.D. 134. manded, saying:—"Our predecessor on the throne, the Emperor Oho-tarashi-hiko, was clear-sighted and of divine valour. When he became subject to the scheme[1] and received over the plan he ruled Heaven and was in accordance with Man. He swept away the banditti, and restored right. His virtue was like a canopy, his path harmonized with development. Therefore in all the land under Universal Heaven there was none who did not recognize him as Sovereign. VII. 39. Of all things endowed with life and possessed of soul were there any which did not find their place?

We have now succeeded him in the occupation of the precious felicity. Morning and night we tremble and fear. But the people are like wriggling worms, and will not reform the savagery of their hearts. In the provinces and districts there are no Lords, in the villages there are no Chiefs.[2] Henceforward let there be established Lords in the provinces, and let there be Chiefs placed in the villages. Accordingly let men of ability of the provinces be taken and appointed Chiefs over provinces and districts, so as to form a defence for the Inner Country."[3]

5th year, Autumn, 9th month. A decree was issued to all A.D. 135. the provinces establishing Miyakko (governors) in the provinces and districts, and Inaki[4] in the villages. All were granted

---

[1] The scheme of the permutations of the five elements. "Thus water is said to overcome fire and so forth. Each dynasty is believed to be subject to the influence of the element which overcomes that prevailing with the previous dynasty, and all human affairs are referable to the same occult influence." Mayers' Manual, p. 317. This whole speech is intensely Chinese.

[2] This cannot be correct.   [3] i.e. the Gokinai.

[4] Inaki is literally rice-castle, i.e. granary. The office seems to be something like mayor. It subsequently became a mere title, and eventually a surname.

shields and spears as emblems of authority. So the mountains and rivers were made boundaries for the separation of one province and district from another, whilst the bounds of townships and villages were established by means of lanes. In this way East and West were reckoned as in a line with the sun,

VII. 40. while North and South were reckoned as athwart the sun.[1] The sunny side of the mountains was called the light-face and the shady side of the mountains the back-face.[2] In this way the people had tranquil possession of their dwellings, and the Empire was at peace.

A.D. 178. 48th year, Spring, 3rd month, 1st day. The Emperor appointed his nephew Tarashi-naka-tsu-hiko no Mikoto Prince Imperial.[3]

A.D. 190. 60th year, Summer, 6th month, 11th day. The Emperor died, aged 107.

---

[1] Meaning lanes running N. and S. and lanes running E. and W.

[2] The modern division of the provinces between Kiôto and Shimonoseki, the Sanyōdo and Sanindo, rests on this distinction.

[3] His own son had perhaps died.

BOOK VIII.

THE EMPEROR TARASHI-NAKATSU-HIKO.

(*CHIUAI*[1] *TENNŌ*.)

THE Emperor Tarashi-nakatsu-hiko was the second child of Yamato-dake no Mikoto. The Empress[2] his mother was called Futachi-iri-hime no Mikoto. She was the daughter of the Emperor Ikume-iri-hiko isachi. The Emperor's countenance was of perfect beauty, and his stature was ten feet. He was appointed Prince Imperial in the forty-eighth year of the Emperor Waka-tarashi-hiko, being at this time thirty-one years of age. The Emperor Waka-tarashi-hiko having no male offspring, appointed him as his successor. In the sixtieth year of his reign the Emperor died, and in the following year, Autumn, the 9th month, 6th day, was buried in the Tatanami misasagi in Saki, in the province of Yamato.

1st year, Spring, 1st month, 11th day. The Prince Imperial A.D. 192. assumed the Imperial Dignity.

Autumn, 9th month, 1st day. The Empress-mother was granted the honorary title of Grand Empress.

Winter, 11th month, 1st day. The Emperor commanded his Ministers, saying:—"The Prince, Our father, died before We reached the status of a youth. His divine spirit became changed into a white bird and ascended to Heaven. Our longing re- VIII. 2. gard for him knows not a day's intermission. Therefore it is Our wish to procure white birds and to keep them in the pond[3] within the precincts of the misasagi, so that, looking on these birds, we may comfort our feelings of longing." Orders were

---

[1] Chiu means the middle one of three sons ; ai, to be sad, to grieve.
[2] She was not Empress.
[3] The misasagi are surrounded with a moat.

therefore sent to the various provinces to send tribute of white birds.

Intercalary 11th month, 4th day. The province of Koshi sent tribute of four white birds. Now the messengers who were sent with the birds stayed for the night on the bank of the river Uji. Then Prince Gama-mi-wake, of Ashigami, seeing the white birds, made inquiry, saying:—"Whither are you taking these white birds?" The men of Koshi answered and said:—"The Emperor, out of his longing for the Prince, his father, intends to keep them as pets. Therefore do we bring them as tribute." Prince Gama-mi-wake spake to the men of Koshi, saying:—"These may be white birds, but when they are roasted they will become black birds." So he forcibly seized the white birds and carried them away. Hereupon the men of Koshi came and reported to the Emperor, who was indignant at the affront offered by Prince Gama-mi-wake to the late Prince, and sending troops, put him to death.

Prince Gama-mi-Wake was the younger brother of the Emperor by a different mother. The people of that time said: —"A father is Heaven, an elder brother is a Lord; how can he escape execution who is wanting in respect to Heaven, and who thwarts his Lord?"[1]

This year was the year Midzunoye Saru (9th) of the Cycle.

A.D. 193.   2nd year, Spring, 1st month, 11th day. Oki-naga-tarashi-hime was appointed Empress. Before this the Emperor had taken to him as consort Oho-nakatsu-hime, daughter of his uncle Hiko-bito Ohine. She bore to him the Imperial Prince VIII. 3. Kakosaka and the Imperial Prince Oshikuma. Next he took to him as consort Oto-hime, daughter of Oho-saka-nushi,[2] the ancestor of the Miyakko of Kukumada. She bore to him the Imperial Prince Homuya wake.

2nd month, 6th day. The Emperor made a progress to Tsunoga,[3] where he erected a temporary palace and dwelt in it. This was called the Palace of Kehi. In the same month the granary of Ahaji was established.

3rd month, 15th day. The Emperor made a tour of inspec-

---

[1] These phrases are Chinese, and therefore an anachronism in a history of this period.

[2] Great-sake-master.   [3] Tsuruga.

tion to the Southern provinces. Hereupon he left behind the Empress and the functionaries, and with two or three High officials[1] and several hundred officers in attendance, he proceeded, thus lightly equipped, as far as the land of Kiï, where he dwelt in the Palace of Tokorotsu. At this time the Kumaso rebelled and did not bring tribute. The Emperor thereupon prepared to smite the Land of Kumaso, and starting from Tokorotsu, borne over the sea, he made a progress to Anato. On the same day he sent messengers to Tsunoga and commanded the Empress, saying:—" Set out straightway from that harbour and meet me at Anato."

Summer, 6th month, 10th day. The Emperor anchored in the harbour of Toyora, while the Empress, who had set out from Tsunoga on her way there, arrived at the Strait of Nuta, and partook of food on board her ship. A great many tahi assembled beside the ship. The Empress sprinkled sake upon the tahi, which forthwith became drunk and floated to the surface. Then the fishermen, having caught numbers of these tahi, were delighted, and said:— " They are the fish given us by our wise sovereign." Therefore the fish of that place, when the sixth month comes, are in the habit of floating belly upwards as if they were drunk. This was the origin of it.

VIII. 4.

Autumn, 7th month, 5th day. The Empress anchored in the harbour of Toyora. On this day the Empress found in the sea a Nyoi[2] pearl.

9th month. The Emperor erected a Palace in Anato, and dwelt in it. It was called the Palace of Toyora in Anato.

8th year, Spring, 1st month, 4th day. The Emperor proceeded to Tsukushi. At this time Kuma-wani,[3] the ancestor of the Agata-nushi of Oka, hearing of the Emperor's arrival, pulled up beforehand a 500-branched Sakaki tree, which he set

---

[1] Daibu.

[2] The Nyoi (如 竟) is a sort of sceptre seen in the hands of Buddhist idols. It contains the Mani, one of the Sapta ratna, a fabulous pearl which is ever bright and luminous, and therefore a symbol of Buddha and of his doctrines.

A Buddhist term is of course an anachronism in this narrative.

[3] Bear (i.e. enormous), sea-monster, a fit name for a personage of a legendary narrative. See p. 61, note 3.

up on the bows of a nine-fathom ship. On the upper branches he hung a white-copper mirror, on the middle branches he hung a ten-span sword, and on the lower branches he hung Yasaka jewels. With these he went out to meet him at the Bay of VIII. 5. Saha in Suwo, and presented to him a fish-salt-place.[1] In doing so, he addressed the Emperor, saying :—" Let the Great Ferry from Anato to Mukatsuno be its Eastern Gate and the Great Ferry of Nagoya[2] be its Western Gate. Let the Islands of Motori and Abe and none else be the august baskets : let the Island of Shiba be divided and made the august pans : let the Sea of Sakami be the salt-place." He then acted as the Emperor's pilot. Going round Cape Yamaga, he entered the Bay of Oka.

But in entering the harbour, the ship was unable to go forward. So he inquired of Kuma-wani, saying :—" We have heard that thou, Kuma-wani, hast come to us with an honest heart. Why does the ship not proceed ? " Kuma-wani addressed the Emperor, saying :—" It is not the fault of thy servant that the august ship is unable to advance. At the entrance to this bay there are two Deities, one male and the other female. The male Deity is called Oho-kura-nushi,[3] the female Deity is called Tsubura-hime. It must be owing to the wish of these Deities." The Emperor accordingly prayed to them, and caused them to be sacrificed to, appointing his steersman Iga-hiko, a man of Uda in the province of Yamato, as priest.[4] So the ship was enabled to proceed. The Empress entered in a different ship by the Sea of Kuki. As the tide was out, she VIII. 6. was unable to go on. Then Kuma-wani went back and met the Empress by way of Kuki. Thereupon he saw that the august ship made no progress, and he was afraid. He hastily made a fish-pond and a bird-pond, into which he collected all the fishes and birds. When the Empress saw these fishes and birds sporting, her anger was gradually appeased, and with the flowing tide she straightway anchored in the harbour of Oka.

---

[1] A salt-pan.

[2] Near Karatsu. It was from Nagoya that Hideyoshi's expedition sailed for Corea. By the salt-place is evidently meant the whole northern coast of Kiushiu. Salt is still made here, though the chief seat of this manufacture is now the shores of the Inland Sea. See Wileman in " T.A S.J." XVII. 1.

[3] Great-magazine-lord.   [4] Hafuri.

Moreover, Itote, the ancestor of the Agata-nushi of Ito[1] in Tsukushi, hearing of the Emperor's coming, pulled up sakaki trees of 500 branches, which he set up in the bow and stern of his ship. On the upper branches he hung Yasaka jewels, on the middle branches white-copper mirrors, and on the lower branches ten-span swords, and coming to meet the Emperor at Hikejima in Anato, presented them to him. In doing so, he addressed the Emperor, saying :—" As to these things which thy servant dares to offer, mayst thou govern the universe with subtlety tortuous as the curvings of the Yasaka jewels ;[2] may thy glance survey mountain, stream and sea-plain bright as the mirror of white copper ; mayst thou, wielding this ten-span sword, maintain peace in the Empire." Thereupon the Emperor commended Itote, and called him Isoshi. Wherefore the men of that time called the native place of Itote the Land of Iso. The present name Ito is a corruption of this.

22nd day. The Emperor arrived in the district of Naka. VIII. 7. Here he dwelt in the palace of Kashihi.

Autumn, 9th month, 5th day. The Emperor addressed his Ministers, and consulted with them as to attacking the Kumaso. At this time a certain God inspired the Empress and instructed her, saying :—" Why should the Emperor be troubled because the Kumaso do not yield submission ? It is a land wanting in backbone. Is it worth while raising an army to attack it ? There is a better land than this, a land of treasure, which may be compared to the aspect of a beautiful woman—the land of Mukatsu,[3] dazzling to the eyes. In that land there are gold and silver and bright colours in plenty. It is called the Land of Silla of the coverlets of paper-mulberry.[4] If thou worshippest me aright, that land will assuredly yield submission freely, and the edge of thy sword shall not at all be stained with blood.

---

[1] This place is mentioned by a Chinese traveller to Japan in the third century of our era. " There are " (he says) " hereditary kings in Ito, who all owe allegiance to the Queen country."

[2] No doubt Maga-tama are meant.   [3] Opposite.

[4] Taku-fusuma in Japanese. This is a pillow-word, prefixed to Silla, not in the least because coverlets of cloth woven from the inner bark of the paper-mulberry were in use in that country, but because Silla (in Japanese Shiraki) suggests Shira, white, and textiles of paper-mulberry were white. By " bright colours " is probably meant dyed textile goods.

Afterwards the Kumaso will surrender.	In worshipping me,
let these things be given as offerings, namely, the Emperor's
august ship and the water-fields¹ called Ohota,² presented to
him by Homutachi, the Atahe of Anato."	When the Emperor
heard the words of the God, his mind was filled with doubt,
and straightway ascending a high hill, he looked away into the
distance.	But far and wide there was the ocean, and he saw
no land.	Hereupon the Emperor answered the God, and
said :—" We have looked all around, and there is sea, and no
land.	Can there be a country in the Great Void ? ³	Who is
the God who cheats Us with vain illusions ?	Moreover, all
the Emperors Our ancestors have worshipped the Gods of
Heaven and Earth without exception, and none has been
omitted."	Then the God again spake by the mouth of the
Empress, saying :—" I see this country lie outstretched like a
reflection from Heaven in the water.	Why sayest thou that
VIII. 8. there is no country, and dost disparage my words ?	But as
thou, O King ! hast spoken thus, and hast utterly refused to
believe me, thou shalt not possess this land.	The child with
which the Empress has just become pregnant, he shall
obtain it."

The Emperor, however, was still incredulous, and persisted
in attacking the Kumaso.	But he retreated without having
gained a victory.

A.D. 2CC.	9th year, Spring, 2nd month, 5th day.	The Emperor took
suddenly ill, and died on the following day, at the age of 52.

One version says :—" The Emperor having gone in
person to smite the Kumaso, was hit by an enemy's arrow,
and slain."

Thereupon the Empress and the Prime Minister Takechi no
Sukune suppressed the mourning for the Emperor, and did not
allow it to be known to the Empire.

Accordingly the Empress commanded the Prime Minister,
the Nakatomi⁴ Ikatsu no Muraji, Oho-miwa no Ohotomo-

---

¹ i.e., rice lands.						² Great fields.

³ The sky.	Corea is visible from the Japanese island of Tsushima, and
must have been well known to the Japanese at this time.	There has already
been frequent mention of it in the " Nihongi " itself.

⁴ Probably here used in its original signification of Middle Minister.

nushi no Kimi, Mononobe no Ikuhi no Muraji, and Ohotomo
no Takemotsu no Muraji, saying :—" The Empire is still VIII. 9.
ignorant of the Emperor's decease. If the people were to
know of it, there would be negligence." So she instructed the
four high officials to cause the functionaries to keep watch
within the Palace while the body of the Emperor was secretly
taken up and entrusted to Takechi no Sukune. He removed
it by sea to Anato, and buried it temporarily in the Palace
of Toyora, giving it a fireless temporary burial.[1]

22nd day. The Prime Minister, Takechi no Sukune, returned from Anato, and made his report to the Empress. This
year, owing to the expedition against Silla, it was impossible
to bury the Emperor.[2]

---

[1] The commentators say that for the sake of secrecy there were no lights used.

[2] An army of labourers was needed to build one of the enormous tumuli which were the fashion at this time.

BOOK IX.

OKINAGA-TARASHI-HIME NO MIKOTO.

(*JINGŌ*[1] *KŌGU*.)

OKINAGA-TARASHI-HIME NO MIKOTO was the great-grandchild of the Emperor Waka-Yamato-neko-hiko Ohohihi[2] and the daughter of Prince Okinaga[3] no Sukune. Her mother's name was Katsuraki no Taka-nuka-hime. She was made Empress in the second year of the Emperor Naka-tsu-hiko. Whilst still young, she was intelligent and shrewd, and her countenance was of such blooming beauty that the Prince her father wondered at it.

In his 9th year, Spring, the 2nd month, the Emperor Naka-tsu-hiko died in the palace of Kashihi in Tsukushi. At this time the Empress was grieved that the Emperor would not follow the Divine instructions, and had consequently died

IX. 2. a premature death. She thought she would find out what God had sent the curse, so that she might possess herself of the land of treasures. She therefore commanded her Ministers and functionaries to purge offences[4] and to rectify transgres-

---

[1] Divine merit or success.   [2] Kaikwa Tennō.

[3] Name of a place in Ohomi. This is hardly consistent with the state-ment at the end of this reign that Oki-naga (long life) was a posthumous name given her, apparently owing to the great age to which she attained.

[4] The ceremony of purification (harahi) is referred to.

Motowori observes on the parallel passage of the "Kojiki" that tsumi, offence, includes kegare, pollutions, ashiki waza, ill-deeds, and wazawahi, calamities. The offences for which the ceremony of purification was required are enumerated in the "Kojiki" as flaying alive, flaying backwards, breaking down the divisions between rice-fields, filling up irrigating channels, com-mitting nuisances, incest, and bestiality. The Oho-harahi, or Great Purifica-tion Ritual, gives a similar but more detailed description. See Ch. K., p. 230.

sions, also to construct a Palace of worship [1] in the village of Wayamada.

3rd month, 1st day. The Empress, having selected a lucky day,[2] entered the Palace of worship, and discharged in person the office of priest.[3] She commanded Takechi no Sukune to play on the lute,[4] and the Nakatomi, Igatsu no Omi, was designated as Saniha.[5] Then placing one thousand pieces of cloth, high pieces of cloth, on the top and bottom of the lute, she prayed saying:—"Who is the God who on a former day instructed the Emperor? I pray that I may know his name." After seven days and seven nights there came an answer, saying:—"I am the Deity who dwells in the Shrine of split-bell Isuzu in the district of hundred-transmit Watarahi in the province of divine-wind Ise,[6] and my name is Tsuki-sakaki idzu no mi-tama ama-zakaru Muka-tsu hime [7] no Mikoto.

Again she inquired:—"Other than this Deity, are there any IX. 3. Deities present?" The answer was:—"I am the Deity who comes forth on the ears of the flag-like Eulalia,[8] and my dwelling is in the district of Aha in Ada-fushi in Oda." She inquired:—"Are there others?" There was an answer, saying:—"There is the Deity who rules in Heaven, who rules in the Void, the gem-casket-entering-prince, the awful Koto-shiro-nushi." [9]

---

[1] Lit. religious abstinence. See above, p. 176.

[2] "Lucky day" is probably a Chinese trait. [3] Kannushi.

[4] The Japanese or Adzuma koto, described as an instrument five or six feet long, with six strings.

[5] Saniha is explained as the official who examines the utterances prompted by the Deity. The literal meaning is "pure court," from the place in which he stood during the ceremony. See Ch. K., p. 229.

[6] The epithets split-bell, hundred-transmit and divine-wind are makura-kotoba or pillow-words, which have no meaning to us. Split-bell is put before Isuzu because suzu means bell (Fr. grêlot). Wataru, "to cross over," suggests the phrase momo-tsutahe (hundred-transmit). See Ch. K., p. 247.

[7] The awful spirit of the planted Cleyera, the lady of sky-distant Mukatsu. Mukatsu, as appears from p. 221, is Corea. The Deity who dwells at Ise is the Sun-Goddess. But she chooses (apparently) to represent herself as a Corean Deity. Sakaki (Cleyera Japonica) is the sacred tree of Shintō.

[8] A tall grass, like pampas grass, hence the epithet flag-like.

[9] Koto-shiro-nushi, thing-know-master. Thing-know is a Chinese idiom for "to rule," and it is the same word which is rendered rule just above.

She inquired:—"Are there others?" There was an answer, saying:—"It is not known whether there are others or not." Hereupon the Saniha[1] said:—"There is no answer now, but they will speak again afterwards." So there was an answer, saying :—"There are the Gods who have settled to the bottom of the water of the Little Strait of Tachibana[2] in the Land of Hiuga, and who are produced and dwell there like fresh water plants. Their names are Uha-tsutsu no wo, Naka-tsutsu no wo, and Soko-tsutsu no wo.[3]

She inquired :—"Are there others?" There was an answer, saying:—"Whether there are or not is unknown." And nothing more was ever said as to the existence of other Gods.

Now that the Divine words[4] had been obtained, the Gods were worshipped in accordance with their instructions. Thereafter, Kamo no Wake, the ancestor of the Kibi no Omi, was sent to attack the Kumaso. Before many days had elapsed they freely submitted.

IX 4. Moreover, there was in the village of Notorita a man named Hashiro Kuma-washi.[5] He was a fellow of powerful frame, and had wings on his body, so that he could fly, and with them soar aloft. Therefore he would not obey the Imperial commands, but habitually plundered the people.

17th day. The Empress desired to attack Kuma-washi. So from the Palace of Kashihi she returned to the Palace of Matsunowo. At this time a whirlwind suddenly arose, and her august hat was blown off by the wind. Therefore the men of the time called that place Mikasa.[6]

20th day. She arrived at the Moor of Sosoki, where she took up arms and smote Hashiro Kuma-washi, and destroyed him. Then she addressed her courtiers, saying:—"My mind is at peace now that we have taken Kuma-washi." Therefore the name of that place was called Yasu.[7]

25th day. Going on from thence, she arrived at the district of Yamato,[8] where she put to death a Tsuchi-gumo named

---

[1] See above, p. 225.

[2] Little Strait is in the original Wodo : the Bungo Channel.

[3] See Ch. K., p. 41, also above, p. 27.

[4] The term "divine words" probably means the proper names and titles of the Deities.

[5] Feather-white bear-eagle.　　　[6] August hat.　　　[7] Peaceful.

[8] In Chikugo.

Tabura-tsu-hime. Now Tabura-tsu-hime's elder brother Natsuha had raised an army and advanced against the Empress, but on hearing that his younger sister had been already put to death, he took to flight.

Summer, 4th month, 3rd day. Proceeding northwards, she arrived at the district of Matsura in the Land of Hizen, and partook of food on the bank of the river Wogawa,[1] in the village of Tamashima. Here the Empress bent a needle and made of it a hook. She took grains of rice and used them as bait. Pulling out the threads of her garment, she made of them a line. Then mounting upon a stone in the middle of the river, and casting the hook, she prayed, saying:—" We are proceeding westward, where we desire to gain possession of the Land of Treasure. If we are to succeed, let the fish of the river bite the hook." Accordingly, raising up her fishing-rod, she caught a trout. Then the Empress said:—" It is a strange thing." Wherefore the men of the day called that place the Land of Medzura. The present name Matsura[2] is a corruption of this. For this reason, whenever the 1st decade of the 4th month comes round, the women of that land take hooks, which they cast into the river and catch trout—a custom which has not ceased unto this day. The men may angle for fish, but they cannot catch any.

This having been done, the Empress knew that there was virtue in the teaching of the Gods, and she made sacrifice anew to the Gods of Heaven and Earth. As it was her purpose in person to chastise the West, she set apart a sacred rice-field, and tilled it. Then, in order to divert water from the Naka-gaha with which to irrigate it, she dug a channel as far as the Hill of Todoroki. But a great rock stood in the way, and she was unable to pierce a channel through it. Then the Empress sent for Takechi no Sukune, and offering a sword and a mirror made him pray to the Gods of Heaven and Earth, and ask them to allow the channel to be completed. Straightway there came thunder and lightning, and stamped that rock asunder, so that the water passed through. Therefore the men of the time called that channel the Channel of Sakuta.[3]

IX. 5.

[1] Little river.
[2] Medzurashiki means "strange." Matsura is really Matsu-ura, fir-bay.
[3] Sundered field.

The Empress returned to the Bay of Kashihi, and loosing her hair, looked over the sea, saying :—" I, having received the instructions of the Gods of Heaven and Earth, and trusting in the Spirits of the Imperial ancestors, floating across the deep blue sea, intend in person to chastise the West. Therefore do I now lave my head in the water of the sea. If I am to be successful, let my hair part spontaneously into two." Accordingly she entered the sea and bathed, and her hair parted of its own accord. The Empress bound it up parted into bunches.[1]

IX. 6.

Then she addressed her ministers, saying :—" To make war and move troops is a matter of the greatest concern to a country. Peace and danger, success and failure must depend on it. If I now entrusted to you, my ministers, the duties of the expedition we are about to undertake, the blame, in case of ill-success, would rest with you. This would be very grievous to me. Therefore, although I am a woman, and a feeble woman too, I will for a while borrow the outward appearance of a man, and force myself to adopt manly counsels. Above, I shall receive support from the Spirits of the Gods of Heaven and Earth, while below I shall avail myself of the assistance of you, my ministers. Brandishing our weapons, we shall cross the towering billows : preparing an array of ships, we shall take possession of the Land of Treasure. If the enterprise succeeds, all of you, my ministers, will have the credit, while if it is unsuccessful, I alone shall be to blame. Such have been my intentions, do ye deliberate together regarding them." The ministers all said :— " The object of the measure which the Empress has devised for the Empire is to tranquillize the ancestral shrines and the Gods of the Earth and Grain, and also to protect her servants from blame. With heads bowed to the ground we receive thy commands." [2]

Autumn, 9th month, 10th day. The various provinces were ordered to collect ships and to practise the use of weapons. But an army could not be assembled. The Empress said :— " This is surely the will of a God." So she erected the Shrine of Oho-miwa, and offered there a sword and a spear. Then the troops assembled freely. Hereupon a fisherman of Ahe, by

[1] In manly fashion.
[2] This speech is copied from a Chinese book.

name Womaro, was sent out into the Western Sea, to spy if
there was any land there. He came back and said :—" There
is no land to be seen." Again a fisherman of Shika, named
Nagusa, was sent to look. After several days he returned, and
said :—" To the north-west, there is a mountain girt with
clouds and extending crosswise. This is perhaps a country."
Hereupon a lucky day was fixed upon by divination. There
was yet an interval before they should set out. Then the
Empress in person, grasping her battle-axe, commanded the
three divisions of her army, saying :—" If the drums are
beaten out of time, and the signal-flags are waved confusedly,
order cannot be preserved among the troops : if greedy of
wealth, and eager for much, you cherish self and have regard
for your own interests, you will surely be taken prisoners
by the enemy. Despise not the enemy, though his numbers
may be few ; shrink not from him, though his numbers may be
many. Spare not the violent, slay not the submissive. There
will surely be rewards for those who ultimately conquer in
battle, and of course punishments for those who turn their
backs and flee."

After this a God gave instructions, saying :—" A gentle spirit
will attach itself to the Empress's person, and keep watch
over her life : a rough spirit will form the vanguard, and be a
guide to the squadron." So when she had received the divine
instructions she did worship, and for this purpose appointed
Otarimi,[1] Yosami no Ahiko to be the Director of the ceremonies
in honour of the God.

The time had now come for the Empress's delivery. So she
took a stone which she inserted in her loins, and prayed, saying :—" Let my delivery be in this land on the day that I
return after our enterprise is at an end." That stone is now
on the road-side in the district of Ito.[2]

After this the rough spirit was told to act as vanguard of the
forces, and the gentle spirit requested to act as guardian of the
Royal vessel.

---

[1] Otarimi is the na, or personal name ; Yosami the uji, or name of the
House ; Ahiko is the Kabane, or title.

[2] Tradition pointed out *two* white egg-shaped stones a little over a foot
long as those used on this occasion. They were afterwards stolen.

Winter, 10th month, 3rd day. Sail was set from the harbour of Wani.[1] Then the Wind-God made a breeze to spring up, and the Sea-God[2] uplifted the billows. The great fishes of the ocean, every one, came to the surface and encompassed the ships. Presently a great wind blew from a favourable quarter on the ships under sail, and following the waves, without the labour of the oar or helm, they arrived at Silla. The tide-wave following the ships reached far up into the interior of the country. Hereupon the King of Silla feared and trembled, and knew not what to do, so he assembled all his people and said to them :—"Since the State of Silla was founded, it has never yet been heard that the water of the sea has encroached upon the land. Is it possible that the term of existence granted to it by Heaven has expired, and that our country is to become a part of the ocean?" Scarce had he spoken when a warlike fleet overspread the sea. Their banners were resplendent in the sunlight. The drums and fifes raised up their voices, and the mountains and rivers all thrilled to the sound. The King of Silla beholding this from afar felt that his country was about to be destroyed by this extraordinary force, and was terrified out of his senses. But presently coming to himself, he said :— "I have heard that in the East there is a divine country named Nippon, and also that there is there a wise sovereign called the Tennō. This divine force must belong to that country. How could we resist them by force of arms?" So he took a white flag, and of his own accord rendered submission, tying his hands behind his back with a white rope. He sealed up the maps and registers, and going down before the Royal vessel bowed his head to the ground, and said :—"Henceforward, as long as Heaven and Earth endure, we will obediently act as thy forage-providers. Not allowing the helms of our ships to become dry, every spring and every autumn we will send tribute of horse-combs and whips. And, without thinking the sea-distance a trouble, we will pay annual dues of male and female slaves." He confirmed this by repeated oaths, saying :— "When the sun no longer rises in the East, but comes forth

IX. 9.

IX. 10.

---

[1] In Tsushima.

[2] The words used here for Wind-God and Sea-God are purely Chinese. "Æolus" and "Neptune" would be just as appropriate in a Saga.

in the West; when the River Arinare [1] turns its course backward, and when the river pebbles ascend and become stars—
if before this we fail to pay homage every spring and every
autumn, or neglect to send tribute of combs and whips, may
the Gods of Heaven and Earth both together punish us."
Then someone said :—" Let us put to death the King of
Silla." Hereupon the Empress said :—" When I first received
the Divine instructions, promising to bestow on me the Land
of Gold and Silver, I gave orders to the three divisions of the
army, saying :—' Slay not the submissive.' Now that we have
taken the Land of Treasure, and its people have freely offered
submission, it would be unlucky to slay them." So she loosed
the cords with which he was bound, and made him her forage-
provider.

Ultimately she proceeded to the interior of that country,
placed seals on the magazines of precious treasure, and took
possession of the books of maps and registers.[2] The spear on
which the Empress leant [3] was planted at the gate of the King
of Silla as a memorial to after ages. Therefore that spear
even now remains planted at the King of Silla's gate.

Now Phasa Mikeun,[4] King of Silla, gave as a hostage Mi-
cheul-kwi-chi Pha-chin Kan-ki,[5] and with gold and silver,
bright colours, figured gauzes and silks, he loaded eighty vessels,
which he made to follow after the Imperial forces. This was
the origin of the King of Silla always sending eighty ships of
tribute.

Hereupon the kings of the two countries of Koryö and Pèkché [6]

---

[1] Supposed to be the Am-nok-kang.

[2] The Cadastral records.   [3] As a staff.

[4] The traditional kana rendering is Hasa Mukin. Phasa was the 6th King
of Silla. He reigned from A.D. 80 to A.D. 112. Mikeun or Mukin is not
clear. The last syllable corresponds with the last syllable of ni-să-keun
(尼 師 今), an old Silla word for king, mentioned in the Introduction to
the " Tongkam."

[5] The traditional kana has Mi-shi-ko-chi Ha-tori Kamu-ki. Pha-chin
was the fourth official rank in Silla (see " Tongkam," I. 31), and Kanki is said
by the Shiki to be a title. A Silla Prince named Misăheun (in Japanese
Mishikin) was sent as hostage to Japan A.D. 402. It is clear from what
follows (A.D. 205) that this is the same person.

[6] The original name of this country is Kokuryö. It did not become
officially known as Koryö until A.D. 936, but the contracted form was in use

R

IX. 12. hearing that Silla had rendered up its maps and registers,[1] and made submission, secretly caused the warlike power (of the Empress) to be spied out. Finding then that they could not be victorious, they came of themselves without the camp, and bowing their heads to the ground, and sighing, said :—" Henceforth for ever, these lands shall be styled thy western frontier provinces, and will not cease to offer tribute." Accordingly interior Governments were instituted. This is what is termed the three Han.[2]

The Empress returned from Silla.

12th month, 14th day. She gave birth to the Emperor Homuda in Tsukushi. Therefore the men of that time called the place where he was born Umi.[3]

long before, and there are examples of it in Chinese literature as early as A.D. 500 (Parker, " Race Struggles in Corea," " T.A.S.J.," XVIII., Pt. II.). The capital was Phyöngyang, at least at one time.

The Japanese name for this kingdom was Koma, a word of doubtful derivation. I think it possible that it means bear (in Corean kom), and that the Koma of Corea and the Kuma of Japan were the same race—like the Saxons of Germany and the Saxons of England. Parker, in the article just referred to (p. 216), suggests that Koma was really a part of Pèkché, and not Koryö. The town of Koma or Kuma was certainly in Pèkché territory, and was for a while the capital. But I cannot think that the Japanese could have been mistaken on this point. They were far too well acquainted with Corean matters, and with them Koryö and Koma are the same thing. It is probable nevertheless that Koma or Kumanari was at some time the seat of the race of that name, as Kumamoto in Japan was of the Japanese Kuma. It is now Ung-chhön (bear-river), near the mouth of the R. Nak-tong, and a convenient port for crossing over to Japan.

Pèkché, known to the Japanese as Kudara, was the S.-W. kingdom of Corea.

[1] i.e. the territory described in them.

[2] Corea at one time was divided into three kingdoms, called Ma-han, Sin-han, and Pyön-han, corresponding respectively to Pèkché, Silla, and Koryö. But there is some doubt on the subject.

The three Han are rendered in the kana gloss mitsu no Kara-kuni. But although Kara is sometimes used loosely for all Corea, and even to include China, I doubt much whether there ever was such a phrase as the three Karas. It looks like a mere literal translation of Samhan.

For an estimate of the historical value of this narrative of the conquest of Corea, I would refer the reader to my paper on Early Japanese History in the " T.A.S.J.," XVI. Pt. I.

[3] Birth.

One version says:—"When the Emperor Tarashi- IX. 13. nakatsu-hiko dwelt in the palace of Kashihi in Tsukushi, there were Deities who spake by the mouth of Uchi-saru-taka, Kuni-saru-taka, and Matsu-ya-tane, ancestors of the Agata-nushi of Saha, and admonished the Emperor, saying:—' If the august descendant wishes to gain the Land of Treasure, we will presently bestow it on him.' So on a later day, a lute was brought and given to the Empress. And the Empress played upon the lute, in accordance with the word of the Gods. Hereupon the Gods spake by the mouth of the Empress, and admonished the Emperor, saying:—'The land which the august descendant wishes for is, as it were, a stag's horn, and not a real country. But if the august descendant now makes due offering to us of the ship in which he sails, and of the water-field [1] called Ohota given him as tribute by Homutate, the Atahe of Anato, we will bestow on the august descendant a dazzling land, a land of plenteous treasures, fair to look upon as a beautiful woman.' Then the Emperor answered the Gods, saying:—' Gods though ye may be, why these deceiving words ? Where is there any country ? Moreover, when the ship in which We sail has been offered to you Deities, in what ship shall We sail ? Nor do I know what Gods ye are. I pray you, let me know your names.' Then the Gods gave their names, saying:—' Uha-tsutsu no wo, Naka-tsutsu no wo, Soko-tsutsu no wo.' Such were the names of the three Gods given by them. And again one said:—' I am Mukahitsu no wo, Kiki-so-ofu-itsuno mitama, Hayasa-nobori no Mikoto.' Then the Emperor spake to the Empress, and said:—' What ill-sounding things they say ! Is it a woman ? What is meant by Hayasa-nobori ?' [2] Then the Gods addressed the Emperor, saying:—' O King, since IX. 14. thou art thus unbelieving, thou shalt not possess that country. But the child which is now in the Empress's womb, he will doubtless take possession of it.' On that night the Emperor took suddenly ill, and died. Afterwards the Empress performed worship in accordance with the

---

[1] Rice-field.   [2] Speed-ascend.

directions of the Gods.[1]   Then the Empress, clad in male
attire, went on the expedition against Silla, and the Gods
guided her.   Accordingly the wave which followed the
ship reached far into the interior of the Land of Silla.
Hereupon the Silla Prince Urusohorichiu[2] came to meet
the Empress, and kneeling down, took hold of the Royal
vessel.   Bowing his head to the ground, he said :—' Henceforward thy servant will act as an interior Government for
the child of the Gods who dwells in Japan, and will not
cease to furnish tribute.' "

One version says :—" She took prisoner the Prince of
Silla, and going to the sea-side, plucked out his knee-caps,[3]
and causing him to crawl on the rocks, suddenly slew him,
and buried him in the sand.   Accordingly she stationed
there one man as Governor of Silla, and departed.   Afterwards, the wife of the Prince of Silla, not knowing where
the body of her husband was buried, all by herself conceived the thought of deluding the Governor.   So,
enticing him, she said :—' If thou wilt let me know the
place where the Prince's body is buried, I will surely
reward thee liberally, and will become thy wife.'   Hereupon the Governor believed these deluding words, and
secretly made known to her the place where the body was
buried.   Then the Prince's wife and the people of the
country, having consulted together, slew the Governor,
and having disinterred the Prince's body, buried it in
another place.   Then they took the Governor's body, and
buried it in the earth under the Prince's tomb, and taking
up the coffin, deposited it on the top of the Governor's
body, saying :—' This is as it ought necessarily to be,
according to the order of things exalted and things base.'
Hereupon the Empress,[4] when she heard of this, was

---

[1] i.e. offering the ship and lands.

[2] This transliteration follows the traditional Japanese pronunciation.   The
Corèan would be U-ryu-cho-pu-ri-chi-u.   It may be suspected that the final
u 于 is a mistake for 干 kan, a frequent element of Corean titles, perhaps
= khan, kami ?   See Parker's " Race Struggles in Corea," p. 220.

[3] A Chinese punishment.

[4] The original has Tennō, a word which, strictly speaking, is either
masculine or feminine, but which is not usually applied to this Empress.

mightily incensed, and raised a large army, with which it was her intent utterly to destroy Silla. So, with war- IX. 15. ships filling the sea, she proceeded thither. At this time the people of Silla were all afraid, and knew not what to do. Having assembled, they consulted together, and slew the Prince's wife by way of apology for their crime." [1] Hereupon the three Gods who accompanied the expedition, viz. Uha-tsutsu no wo, Naka-tsutsu no wo, and Soko-tsutsu no wo, admonished the Empress, saying :—" Let our rough spirits be worshipped at the village of Yamada in Anato." Now

---

[1] The "Tongkam," Vol. III. p. 21, has the following under the date A.D. 249, Summer, 4th month :—"The Was invaded Silla, and killed Uro. Before this the Was had sent Kalyako as Ambassador to Silla. The King made Uro entertain him. Uro said, jesting :—" Sooner or later we shall make your King our salt-slave, and your Queen our cook-wench." When the King of Wa heard this, he sent his General Uto-chiu to invade Silla. The King went out and dwelt at Yuchhon. Uro said :—" To-day's attack is owing to the words of thy servant. I pray thee let me deal with it." So he went eventually to the Wa army, and said :—" My words on a former day were a jest, and nothing more. Who would have thought that war should be waged, and that things should come to this extremity?" The men of Wa took him, and made a pile of firewood, on which they burnt him to death, and then went away. Afterwards an Ambassador came from Wa. Uro's wife begged leave from the King to entertain him on her own score. Accordingly she made the Ambassador drunk, seized him, and burnt him. The Was, enraged at this, besieged Keumsyöng,* but had to retire unsuccessful."

Notwithstanding the difference of date—A.D. 200 and A.D. 249—and other discrepancies, I believe these two narratives relate to the same events. The Prince Urusohorichiu of the Japanese account is the Uro of the Corean history. The word which I have translated Prince is 王, which might also be rendered King. But there is no King of this name in Corean history, and, as appears from a Corean authority quoted in the "Ishōnihonden," XIV. 11, Syök Uro was the son of King Nahè of Silla. The "Tongkam" relates several other events of his life, among others his appointment as Sö-pul-han (or Sö-pul-ya), whence probably the sohori of the name given him in the Japanese narrative.

Kalyako is no doubt the same person as the Katsuraki no Sotsu-hiko mentioned below as having been sent on a mission to Silla. Kal is written 葛, which is katsura in Japanese.

In "Early Japanese History" I have given reasons for thinking that, for this period, Corean history is much more in accordance with facts than that of Japan.

---

* The Silla capital.

Homutate, the ancestor of the Atahe of Anato, and Tamomi no Sukune, ancestor of the Muraji of Tsumori, represented to the Empress, saying :—" Surely thou wilt set apart unto the Gods the lands where they desire to dwell." So Homutate was appointed master of the worship of the rough spirits, and a shrine was erected in the village of Yamada in Anato.

Now in Spring, the second month of the year following the expedition against Silla, the Empress removed with her ministers and functionaries to the palace of Toyora in Anato, where she took up the Emperor's remains, and proceeded towards the capital by the sea-route. Now Prince Kakosaka and Prince Oshikuma, hearing of the Emperor's decease, as well as of the Empress's expedition to the West, and of the recent birth of an Imperial Prince, plotted secretly, saying :— " The Empress has now a child, and all the ministers obey her. They will certainly consult together and establish an infant sovereign. But shall we, the elders, obey our younger brother ? " So, pretending that it was in order to build a misasagi for the Emperor, they went to Harima, and raised a misasagi at Akashi.[1] Accordingly they joined boats together in a string across to the island of Ahaji, and so transported the stones of that island to build it. Now they made every man take a weapon, and so they awaited the Empress. Hereupon Kurami-wake, the ancestor of the Kimi of Inugami, and Isachi no Sukune, ancestor of the Kishi,[2] together joined them-

IX. 16.

----

[1] Two or three miles to the east of Maiko, on the bluff above the village of West Tarumi, there is a very large double mound, which local tradition has associated with the name of Chiuai Tennō. It is surrounded by the usual circles of clay cylinders, known in the neighbourhood as " Chiuai no sen-tsubo," i.e. " the thousand jars of Chiuai."

There is a smaller mound of circular shape close to the other, also surrounded by a circle of clay cylinders. This is no doubt the tomb of a wife, son, or minister of the personage buried in the main tumulus. The " Nihongi " tradition does not account for it.

The stones were to build the megalithic chamber.

[2] Kishi (吉 師) is obviously the same as the Silla fourteenth official grade kilsă (吉 士). See " Tongkam," I. 31. Ason, so frequently met with in later times, is also a Corean official grade. Has sukune anything to do with the Silla word for king, isăkeun ?

The " Kojiki " has " Kishi of Naniha " in this passage, no doubt rghtly. Ch. K., p. 235.

selves unto Prince Kakosaka, who made them his generals, and directed them to raise troops from the Eastern Land. Then Prince Kakosaka and Prince Oshikuma went forth together to the moor of Toga, and made a "hunt-prayer,"[1] saying:—"If our project is to be successful, then surely let us take some good game." The two Princes sat each in his shelter, when a wild-boar[2] sprang out suddenly, and climbing on to the shelter, bit Prince Kakosaka and killed him. The soldiers every one shuddered with fear. Then Prince Oshikuma addressed Kurami-wake, saying:—"This is a very ominous thing. We ought not to await the enemy here." So he withdrew his troops, and retreating again, encamped at Sumiyoshi.[3] At this time, the Empress heard that Prince Oshikuma had raised an army, and was awaiting her. She commanded Takechi no Sukune to take in his bosom the Imperial Prince, and going out across by way of the south-sea provinces,[4] to anchor in the harbour of Kiï, while the Empress's ship made straight for Naniha. At this time the Empress's ship swerved towards the midst of the sea, and was unable to proceed. She returned again to the harbour of Muko,[5] where she made divination as to this.

Hereupon Ama-terasu no Oho-kami admonished her, saying: IX. 17. —"My rough spirit may not approach the Imperial residence. Let him dwell in the land of Hirota in Mikokoro." So Ha-yama-hime, daughter of Yamashiro-neko, was appointed to worship him. Moreover, Waka-hiru-me no Mikoto admonished the Empress, saying:—"I wish to dwell in the land of Nagawo in Ikuta."[6] So Una-gami no Isachi was appointed to worship her. Again, Koto-shiro-nushi no Mikoto admonished her, saying:—"Worship me in the land of Nakata in Mi-kokoro."[7] So Naga-hime, younger sister of Ha-yama-hime, was appointed to worship him. Again the three Gods, Uha-tsutsu no wo, Naka-tsutsu no wo, and Soko-tsutsu no wo, admonished her, saying:—"Let our gentle spirits dwell at Nagawo[8] in Nuna-

---

[1] Ukehi-gari, a kind of divination.
[2] Lit. a red pig, so called from its flesh being red. The domestic pig is the white pig.
[3] Near Kōbe.　　[4] Now called Shikoku.　　[5] Now Hiōgo.
[6] Just behind the foreign settlement of Kōbe.
[7] Mikokoro here and above may mean "after my august heart."
[8] Sumiyoshi, near Kōbe.

kura in Ohotsu, so that they may look upon the ships passing back and forward." Hereupon these Gods were enshrined in IX. 18. accordance with their instructions, and the Empress was enabled to cross the sea in peace.

Prince Oshikuma, again withdrawing his troops, retreated as far as Uji, where he encamped. The Empress proceeded southwards to the land of Kiï, and met the Prince Imperial at Hitaka. Having consulted with her Ministers, she at length desired to attack Prince Oshikuma, and removed to the Palace of Shinu. It so happened that at this time the day was dark like night. Many days passed in this manner, and the men of that time said :—" This is the Eternal Night." The Empress inquired of Toyomimi, the ancestor of the Atahe of Ki, saying : —" Wherefore is this omen ? " Then there was an old man who said:—" I have heard by tradition that this kind of omen is called Atsunahi no tsumi."[1] She inquired :—" What does it mean ? " He answered and said :—" The priests'[2] of the two shrines have been buried together." Therefore she made strict investigation in the village. There was a man who said:—" The priest of Shinu and the priest of Amano were good friends. The priest of Shinu fell ill, and died. The priest of Amano wept and wailed, saying :—' We have been friends together since our birth. Why in our death should there not be the same grave for both ? ' So he lay down beside the corpse and died of himself, so that they were buried together. This is perhaps the reason." So they opened the tomb, and on examination found that it was true. Therefore they again changed their coffins and interred them separately, upon which the sunlight shone forth, and there was a difference between day and night.

3rd month, 5th day. The Empress commanded Takechi no Sukune and Take-furu-kuma, ancestor of the Omi of Wani, to lead an army of several tens of thousands of men to attack IX. 19. Prince Oshikuma. Hereupon, Takechi no Sukune and his colleague, having taken picked men, went out by way of Yamashiro as far as Uji, where they encamped north of the river. Prince Oshikuma came out from his camp, and offered

---

[1] The calamity of there being no sun.　　　　[2] Hafuri.

battle. Now there was a man called Kuma [1] no Kori, who formed the vanguard of Prince Oshikuma's army.

One version says :—" Ancestor of the Obito of Katsurano no ki." Another says :—" The remote ancestor of the Kishi of Tako."

Accordingly, in order to encourage his men, he sang with a loud voice, saying :—

> Beyond the river
> Is the rough pine-clad plain—
> To that pine-clad plain
> Let us cross over,
> With bows of *tsuki*,
> And store of sounding arrows.
> My dear fellow !
> My dear fellows !
> My cousin too !
> My cousins !
> Come ! let us join battle
> With Uchi no Aso ! [2]
> (Within a tile
> Is there any sand ?) [3]
> Come ! let us join battle !

IX. 20.

Then Takechi no Sukune, giving command to the three divisions of the army, made them all bind up their hair mallet-wise. Accordingly he made an order, saying :—" Let every one of you have spare bow-strings concealed in your top-knots, and gird on wooden swords." Having done so, in accordance with the commands of the Empress, he deluded Prince Oshikuma, saying :—" I am not greedy to possess the Empire. Only, while cherishing the infant Prince, we will obey my Lord the Prince. Why should I contend with thee in battle ?

---

[1] The reader will have noticed how frequently Kuma, bear, occurs in proper names. It is, I think, the race Kuma (in Corean, Koma) to which they should be referred.

[2] Aso is the same as Ason or 'Asomi, probably derived from Ason (阿 飡), the 6th Silla official rank. This is the first mention of this title. The reference is to Takechi (Take-uchi) no Sukune. Uchi has a pillow-word (tamaki haru) prefixed, which is quite untranslatable. Cf. Ch. K., p. 283.

[3] These two lines are, of course, utterly irrelevant. They are brought in for the sake of a play of words, with which it is not worth while troubling the reader.

I pray thee let us both cut our bow-strings, fling away our weapons, and be in harmony together. Then mayest thou, my Lord the Prince, mount to the Heavenly office, and sit a peace, making high thy pillow, and wielding at thy will the ten thousand appliances." [1]

So he openly gave orders to his army that they should all cut their bow-strings, and ungirding their swords, fling them into the river-water. Prince Oshikuma believed these deluding words, and ordered all his troops to ungird their weapons and fling them into the water of the river, and also to cut their bow-strings. Upon this, Takechi no Sukune commanded the three divisions of his army to produce their spare bow-strings, and to string their bows again, and, girt with their real swords, to advance across the river. Prince Oshikuma, seeing that he had been deceived, spake to Kurami-wake and Isachi no Sukune, saying :—" We have been deceived, and have now no spare weapons. How shall we be able to fight ? " So he withdrew his forces and gradually retreated. Then Takechi no Sukune sent forth his choice troops and pursued him, and having come up to him just at Afusaka, put him to the rout. Therefore that place was called Afusaka.[2] The army took to flight, and ran as far as Kurusu in Sasanami. Many were slain. Hereupon the blood overflowed into Kurusu. Therefore in horror of this, until this day, the fruit of Kurusu[3] is not offered to the Imperial Palace. Prince Oshikuma, not knowing whither to betake himself in his flight, called to him Isachi no Sukune and made a song, saying :—

IX. 21.

> Come ! my child,
> Isachi Sukune !
> Rather than receive a severe wound
> From the mallet [4]
> OfUchi no Aso,
> Like unto the grebe
> Let us make a plunge !

---

[1] i.e. all the machinery of Government.
[2] Pronounced Ôsaka, i.e. the hill of meeting. The pass on the road from Kiôto to Ôtsu. A railway tunnel now goes under it.
[3] Kurusu means chestnut-village.
[4] Kabu-tsuchi. See p. 123.

So they sank together in the crossing-place of Seta, and died. Then Takechi no Sukune made a song, saying :—

> The birds that dived,
> At the ferry of Seta,
> By the sea of Afumi.[1]
> Since with my eyes I cannot see them,
> Can they be still alive?

Hereupon they searched for their dead bodies, and were unable to find them. But several days after, they came out on the river-bank at Uji.[2] Then Takechi no Sukune again made a song, saying :—

> In the sea of Afumi,
> At the ferry of Seta,
> The birds that dived—
> Passing Tanakami,[3]
> Have been caught at Uji.

Winter, 10th month, 3rd day. The ministers honoured the Empress with the title of Grand Empress. This year was the year Midzunoto I (60th) of the Cycle. It was reckoned the first year of her administration of the Government.

2nd year, Winter, 11th month, 8th day. The Emperor was buried in the misasagi of Nagano, in the province of Kahachi. IX. 22. A.D. 202.

3rd year, Spring, 1st month, 3rd day. The Imperial Prince Homuda-wake was appointed Prince Imperial. Accordingly, the capital was made at Ihare. It was called the Palace of Wakazakura. A.D. 203.

5th year, Spring, 3rd month, 7th day. The King of Silla sent O-nyé-să-pöl, Mo-ma-ri Cheul-chi and Pu-ra-mo-chi with tribute. It was their desire to get back Mi-cheul Hö-chi pöl-han, who had formerly come as a hostage. With this object they tampered with Hö-chi pöl-han and caused him to use deceit, telling him to make petition and say :—" The envoys O-nyé-să-pol, Mo-ma-ri Cheul-chi, and the other have informed me that my king, on account of my long failure to return, has wholly confiscated my wife and family and made A.D. 205.

---

[1] Now called Lake Biwa, in the province of Afumi or Ômi.

[2] Uji is some miles further down the river issuing from Lake Biwa than Seta. Seta is just where it leaves the lake.

[3] The name of the upper part of the Uji River.

them slaves. I pray thee, let me return for a while to my own country and learn whether this be true or false." The Emperor forthwith gave him leave to go, and accordingly sent him away, accompanied by Katsuraki no Sotsuhiko. They reached Tsushima together, and stayed for the night at the harbour of Sabi no umi. Then the Silla envoys Mo-ma-ri Cheul-chi and the others secretly provided a separate ship and sailors, on board of which they put Mi-cheul Han-ki and made him escape to Silla. They also made a straw figure which they put in Mi-cheul Hö-chi's berth, and making it appear like a sick man, they informed Sotsuhiko, saying :—" Mi-cheul Hö-chi has taken suddenly ill, and is on the point of death." Sotsuhiko sent men to nurse him, and so discovered the deception. Having seized the three Silla envoys, he placed them in a cage which he burnt with fire and so killed them. Then he proceeded to Silla, where he touched at the harbour of Tatara. He took the Castle of Chhora, and returned. The captives taken on this occasion were the first ancestors of the Han[1] people of the four villages of Kuhabara, Sabi, Takamiya, and Oshinomi.[2]

IX. 23.

IX. 24.

---

[1] The Chinese character is 漢, i.e. the Chinese Han dynasty. The interlinear kana has ayabito, which also means Chinese. Possibly they were descendants of Chinese emigrants to Corea.

[2] Under the date A.D. 418, Autumn, the "Tongkam" (Vol. IV. 18) has the following :—

"Pak Ché-syang of Silla went to Wa and died there. The king's younger brother Misǎheun came from Wa. Before this Pok-ho (another brother of the King, who had been sent as hostage to Kokuryö) had returned. The King addressed Ché-syang, saying :—' My love for my two younger brothers is like my left and right arms. Now I have got only one arm. What does it avail ?' Ché-syang said :—' Though my abilities are those of a broken down horse, I have devoted myself to my country's service. What reason could I have for declining? Kokuryö, however, is a great country, and the king also is wise. Thy servant was able to make him understand with one word. But in dealing with the Was it will be meet to use stratagem to deceive them, and not by mouth and tongue to reason with them. I will pretend that I have committed a crime and absconded. After I have gone I pray thee arrest thy servant's family.' So he swore upon his life not to see again his wife and children, and went to Nyul-pho. The cable was already loosed when his wife came after him, lamenting loudly. Ché-syang said :— ' I have already taken my life in my hands, and am leaving for a certain death.'

At length he went to the Wa country, where he gave out that he was a

13th year, Spring, 2nd month, 8th day.   Takechi no Sukune A.D. 213.

rebel. The Lord of Wa doubted this. Before this time men of Pèkché had gone to the Wa country, and made a false report, saying :—' Silla and Kokuryö are about to plot together to attack Wa.' The Lord at length sent troops to guard the frontier. And when Kokuryö, having invaded Silla, slew those guards also, the Lord of Wa believed that the story told by the Pèkché men was true. But when he heard that the King of Silla had imprisoned the family of Misăheun and Ché-syang, he thought that Ché-syang was really a rebel. Hereupon he sent forth an army in order to attack Silla, and made Ché-syang and Misăheun guides. Coming to an island in the sea, all the generals consulted secretly how they should destroy Silla and return with Ché-syang and Misăheun's wives and children. Ché-syang, knowing this, sailed with Misăheun every day in a boat, under the pretence of making pleasure excursions. The Was had no suspicion. Ché-syang advised Misăheun to return secretly to his country. Misăheun said :—' How could I have the heart to abandon thee, my lord, and return alone?' Ché-syang said :—' Supposing that I succeed in saving my Prince's life, and thus gratify the feelings of the Great King, it will be enough, Why should I be so fond of living?' Misăheun wept, and taking his leave, made his escape back to his country. Ché-syang alone slept in the boat. He got up towards evening and waited until Misăheun was far on his way. The Was, when they found that Misăheun had disappeared, bound Ché-syang, and pursued Misăheun, but mist and darkness coming on, they could not overtake him. The Lord of Wa was enraged. He flung Ché-syang into prison, and questioned him, saying :—' Why didst thou secretly send away Misăheun?' Ché-syang said :—' As a subject of Kélin (Silla), I simply wished to carry out the desires of my Lord.' The Lord of Wa was wroth, and said :—' As thou hast now become a vassal of mine, if thou callest thyself a vassal of Kélin, thou shalt surely be subjected to the five punishments. But if thou callest thyself a vassal of the Wa country, I will certainly reward thee liberally.' Ché-syang said :—' I had rather be a puppy-dog of Kélin, than a vassal of the Wa country. I had rather be flogged in Kélin than have dignities and revenues in the Wa country.' The Lord of Wa was wroth. He flayed Ché-syang's feet, cut sedge, and made him walk on it (perhaps on the stubble left after the sedge was cut). Then he asked him, saying :—' Of what country art thou the vassal?' He said :— ' The vassal of Kélin.' He also made him stand on hot iron, and asked him :—' Of what country art thou the vassal?' He said :—' The vassal of Kélin.' The Lord of Wa, seeing that he could not bend him, put him to death by burning.

The King, hearing of this at the island of Mokto, was much grieved, and conferred on Ché-syang the posthumous title of Great Ason. He also bestowed rewards on his family, and made Misăheun marry his second daughter; and afterwards Ché-syang's wife, taking with her her three daughters, went up to a mountain whence she had a view of the Wa country, was commanded to go with the Prince Imperial and worship the Great God of Kebi in Tsunoga.¹

17th day. The Prince Imperial returned from Tsunoga. On this day the Grand Empress gave a banquet to the Prince Imperial in the Great Hall. The Grand Empress raising her cup wished long life to the Prince Imperial. Accordingly she made a song, saying :—

> This august liquor
> Is not my august liquor :
> This prince of liquors ²
> He that dwells in the Eternal land
> Firm as a rock—
> The august God Sukuna,
> With words of plenteous blessing,
> Blessing all around—
> With words of divine blessing
> Blessing again and again—
> Hath sent as an offering to thee.
>   Drink of it deeply.
>   Sa! Sa!³

and having wailed bitterly, she died. She was made the Goddess-mother of this mountain, and there is now a shrine there."

This, no doubt, relates to the same events as the above passage in the "Nihongi." Ché-syang is Mo-ma-ri and Misă-heun is Mi-cheul-Hö-chi.

The Corean names present much difficulty. I have given the Corean pronunciation of the Chinese characters with which they are written, but there is much room for doubt whether the Japanese pronunciation would not sometimes be better. The text cannot be relied on.

The interlinear kana gives as the names of the three envoys, Ureshi-hotsu, Momari Shichi, and Furamochi, and of the hostage, Mishi Kochi hotsu-kan. Here shichi is probably for 舍 知 (sya-chi), the 13th official rank in Silla.

A Chinese authority quoted by Parker, in "Race Struggles in Corea," gives one or two examples of Kilin (Kélin or Silla), words which show that 1000 years ago the language was the same as modern Corean. But I cannot recognize anything of the modern language in the Corean names of the "Nihongi." Later, all proper names in Corea are of Chinese derivation. Many of the Corean words in the "Nihongi" are names of offices, all of which are replaced in modern Corean by words of Chinese derivation.

¹ Now Tsuruga in Echizen. See Ch. K., p. 237.

² In the original "Kushi no Kami." The interpretation given above is Motowori's. This line might also mean "the wondrous deity" or the "God of liquor or sake."

³ An interjection of encouragement or incitement.

Takechi no Sukune, on behalf of the Prince Imperial, made an answering song, saying :—

> The man who brewed [1]
> This august liquor,
> Setting up on the mortar
> His drum,
> Singing all the while,
> He must have brewed it.
> This august liquor
> Is exquisitely more and more delightful.
> Sa ! Sa !

39th year. This year was the year Tsuchinoto Hitsuji A.D. 239. (56th) of the Cycle.

The History of Wei says :—" In the reign of the Emperor Ming Ti, in the third year of the period King-ch'u (A.D. 239) the Queen of Wa sent the high officer Nan-teu-mi and others to the province, where they begged permission to proceed to the Emperor and offer tribute. The T'ai-sheu,[2] Tăng-hia, sent an officer to escort them to the capital."

40th year.   A.D. 240.

The History of Wei says :—" In the first year of Chêng-Shih, Kien Chung-kiao, Wéi T'i-hi and others proceeded to the Wa country charged with an Imperial rescript and a seal and ribbon." [3]

---

[1] The Japanese word for brew is kamu, which also means to chew. Was chewing ever a part of the process of making strong drink in Japan as it is in some of the South Sea islands at the present time? The last line of this poem is of very doubtful interpretation.

[2] T'ai-sheu means governor. Thé-pang (in Chinese Tai-fang) was at one time a district of the Chinese province of Lolang in Corea. A map of China under the Tsin dynasty, however, makes Thé-pang a separate district further to the north. But the Governor of Thé-pang mentioned in the Wei history under the name of 劉 夏 and the Governor of Lolang called by the "Tong-kam" 劉 茂 are probably the same person.

Another authority makes Thé-pang identical with Namwön in Chöllato.

[3] These officials, as we learn from other sources, were sent by the Chinese authorities of Sakpang in Corea, not far from the present Treaty Port of Wönsan. See "Early Japanese History," p. 58; "Ishōnihonden," I. 11; "Tongkam," III. 17.

43rd year.

The Ruler [1] of Wa again sent high officers as envoys with tribute, named I Shing-ché, Yih-Ye-yoh,[2] and others —eight persons in all.

46th year, Spring, 3rd month, 1st day. Shima no Sukune was sent to the Land of Thak-syun.[3] Hereupon Malkeum Kanki,[4] King of Thak-syun, informed Shima no Sukune, saying:—" In the course of the year Kinoye Ne,[5] three men of Pèkché named Kutyö, Mi-chyu-nyu, and Moko [6] came to my country and said:—' The King of Pèkché, hearing that in the Eastern quarter there is an honourable country, has sent thy servants to this honourable country's court. Therefore we beg of thee a passage so that we may go to that Land. If thou wilt be good enough to instruct thy servants and cause us to pass along the roads, our King will certainly show profound kindness to my Lord the King.' [7] I then said to Kutyö and his fellows:—' I have always heard that there is an honourable country in the East, but I have had no communication with it, and do not know the way. There is nothing but far seas and towering billows, so that in a large ship, one can hardly communicate. Even if there were a regular crossing-place, how could you arrive there?' Hereupon Kutyö and the others said:—' Well, then, for the present we cannot communicate. Our best plan will be to go back again, and prepare a ship with which to communicate later.' They also said:—' If envoys should come from the honourable country, thou oughtest surely to inform our country.' Thus they went back. Hereupon

---

[1] 王.

[2] It is doubtful whether these six syllables represent the names of one, two, or three men. I cannot guess what Japanese names are meant. The " Ishōnihonden " gives some of the characters differently.

The " Shukai " edition rejects these extracts from Chinese History. They were doubtless added at a later date.

[3] The Chinese characters are 卓 淳, of which the traditional kana rendering is Toku-shiu. The " Shukai " editor says it was part of Imna (or Mimana). Its destruction by Silla is recorded below—5th year of Kimmei Tennō.

[4] The Japanese traditional rendering is Makin Kănki.

[5] A.D. 244.

[6] The Japanese kana gloss has Kutei, Mitsuru, and Mako.

[7] This is quite inconsistent with the story of Pèkché offering homage to the Empress in the early part of her reign.

Shima no Sukune sent one of his followers named Nihaya, and a Thak-syun man named Kwa-ko to the Land of Pèkché to make friendly inquiries of the King's health.

King Syo-ko [1] of Pèkché was profoundly pleased, and received them cordially. He presented to Nihaya a roll each of five kinds of dyed silk, a horn-bow [2] and arrows, together with forty bars of iron. [3] Thereafter he opened his treasure-house, and pointing to his various rare objects, said :—" In my country there is great store of these rare treasures. I have wished to pay tribute of them to the honourable country, but not knowing the way I was unable to carry out my intention. I shall now entrust them to envoys, who will visit your country in order to offer them." Nihaya took charge of this message, and on his return informed Shima no Sukune, who thereupon came back from Thak-syun.

47th year, Summer, 4th month. The King of Pèkché sent Kutyö, Mi-chu-nyu and Ma-ko with tribute. Now a tribute envoy from Silla came along with Kutyö. Hereupon the Grand Empress and the Prince Imperial Homuda wake no Mikoto were greatly delighted and said :—" People from the countries wished for [4] by our late Sovereign have now come to Court. Alas ! that they cannot meet the Emperor ! " There was not one of all the ministers who did not shed tears. But when the articles of tribute of the two countries were examined, the Silla tribute was of rare objects in very great number, while the Pèkché tribute articles were few and mean, and of no value. So inquiry was made of Kutyö and the others, saying :—" How is it that the Pèkché tribute is inferior to that of Silla ? " They answered, and said ;—" We lost our way and arrived at Sabi. [5]

IX. 27.

A.D. 247.

---

[1] There are two kings of this name in Corean history. The first died A.D. 214. This is the second, who reigned from A.D. 346 to A.D. 375. The Japanese chronology is, as usual, at fault.

[2] The Corean bow is to this day the Tatar bow described in Tylor's Anthropology as "formed of several pieces of wood or horn united with glue or sinews. Shorter than the long-bow, it gets its spring by being bent outside to string it." The Japanese bow is a variety of the ordinary long-bow.

[3] Iron is plentiful in Corea at the present day, and its quality is much esteemed.

[4] On the contrary, Chiuai Tennō would have nothing to do with them.

[5] A Sabi in Tsushima is mentioned above. But this may be a place in Corea, in which case it should be read Sapi.

Here thy servants were captured by men of Silla and confined in a gaol. After three months had passed, they wished to kill us. Then Kutyö and the rest looked up towards Heaven, and pronounced a curse. The men of Silla, fearing this curse, refrained from killing us, but robbed us of our tribute. Then they gave us the tribute of Silla in exchange for our tribute, and made it the tribute of thy servants' country, and they spake to thy servants, saying :—' Be careful what ye say, or else, as soon as we return, we will kill you.' Therefore we, Kutyö and the rest, were afraid, and made no objection. For this reason we have hardly been able to reach the Heavenly Court." Then the Grand Empress and Homuda wake no Mikoto charged the Silla envoys with this deed, and accordingly prayed to the Gods of Heaven, saying :—" Whom is it meet that we send to Pèkché to examine this matter whether it be true or false; whom is it meet that we send to Silla to investigate this charge ? " Therewith the Gods of Heaven admonished them, saying :—" Let Takechi no Sukune prepare a plan, and let Chikuma Nagahiko be the envoy. Then it will be as you desire."

IX. 28.   Chikuma Nagahiko's title (姓) is unknown. One account says :—" Chikuma Nagahiko was a man of the province of Musashi, the first ancestor of the present Obito of Tsukimoto of the Nukada Be."

The Pèkché record [1] says :—" Shimananaga hiko was perhaps this man."

Hereupon Chikuma Nagahiko was sent to Silla to call that country to an account for meddling with the Pèkché tribute.

A.D. 249.   49th year, Spring, 3rd month. Areda wake and Kaga wake were made generals. Along with Kutyö and the others they prepared a force with which they crossed over and came to Thak-syun. They were accordingly about to invade Silla, when some one said :—" Your troops are too few. You cannot defeat Silla." They respectfully sent back again Sya-pèk Kè-ro

---

[1] This Pèkché record is frequently quoted from. From the circumstance that the character 貴, honourable, is used by the author or authors before the word country in speaking of Japan, it may be inferred that it was compiled by Pèkché Coreans from their own records for the information of the Japanese. I have not much doubt that it was the work of some of the Corean scholars who visited Japan in numbers during the seventh century.

to ask for reinforcements. Mong-na Keun-chă and Sya-sya
Nokwé [1]
  These two men's surname is unknown. But Mongna
  Keunchă was a Pèkché general.
were forthwith ordered to take command of choice troops
which were sent along with Sya-pèk Kè-ro. They all assembled
at Thak-syun, invaded Silla, and conquered it. Seven provinces
were accordingly subdued, viz. Pi-chă-pun, South Kara, Tok-
kuk, Ara, Tara, Thak-syun, and Kara.[2] Then they moved
their forces, and turning westward, arrived at Ko-hyé-chin,
where they slaughtered the southern savages of Chim-mi-ta-nyé
and granted their country to Pèkché. Hereupon their King,
Syoko,[3] together with Prince Kusyu, came to meet them with IX. 29.
more troops. Then four villages, viz. Pi-ri, Phi-chung, Pho-
mi-ki, and Pan-ko, spontaneously surrendered. Thereupon
the Kings of Pèkché, father and son, met Areda wake, Mong-na
Keunchă, and the rest at the village of Wi-niu [*now called
Tsurusugi*,[4] and at an interview offered their congratulations
and dismissed . them with cordial courtesy. But Chikuma
Nagahiko remained in the Land of Pèkché with the King of
Pèkché, where they ascended Mount Phi-ki and made a solemn
declaration. Afterwards they ascended Mount[5] Ko-sya, where
they sat together upon a rock, and the King of Pèkché made a
solemn declaration, saying:—" If I spread grass for us to sit
upon, it might be burnt with fire ; and if I took wood for a
seat, it might be washed away by water. Therefore, sitting on
a rock, I make this solemn declaration of alliance to show that
it will remain undecayed to distant ages. From this time

---

[1] In Japanese Mokura Konshi and Sasa Toki.

[2] These places, in so far as they can be identified, did not belong to Silla,
but to Imna. The identification of Corean names of places presents great
difficulties, owing to the Corean mania for giving new names. The " Chôsen
Zenzu furoku," a little book published by the Japanese War Office, gives as
many as eight aliases for some towns. Nearly all have several.

[3] Reigned 346 to 375, when he was succeeded by Kusyu. The " Nihongi "
names are nearly correct.

[4] Japanese pronunciation.

[5] Mountain is in the interlinear kana mure, no doubt the modern Corean
moi. Similarly, nare, river, which occurs in Kuma-nare, is in modern Corean
năi, pronounced nè.

forward, therefore, for a thousand autumns and for ten thousand years, without pause and without limit, we shall bear the regular title of ' The Western Frontier Province,' and every spring and every autumn will attend your Court with tribute." So he took with him Chikuma Nagahiko to his capital, where he treated him with the most cordial courtesy. He also made Kutyö and the others escort him home.

A.D. 250. 50th year, Spring, 2nd month. Areda wake and his companions returned.

Summer, 5th month. Chikuma Nagahiko, Kutyö and the rest arrived from Pèkché. Thereupon the Grand Empress was delighted, and inquired of Kutyö, saying :—" The various Han [1] countries west of the sea have been already granted to thy country. Wherefore dost thou come again repeatedly ? " Kutyö and the others said to the Empress :—" The vast

IX. 30. blessings of the Celestial Court reached afar to our mean village, and our king capered with delight. Out of the fulness of his heart he has sent a return mission in token of his great sincerity. Though it come to the ten thousandth year, in what year shall we fail to attend thy Court ? " The Grand Empress gave command, saying :—" Good are thy words. These are Our intentions. We grant in addition the Castle of Tasya to serve as a station in going and returning."

A.D. 251. 51st year, Spring, 3rd month. The King of Pèkché again sent Kutyö to the Court with tribute. Hereupon the Grand Empress addressed the Prince Imperial and Takechi no Sukune, saying :—" We owe it to Heaven and not to man that we have a friendly country like Corea. Therefore it brings constantly, without missing a year, tribute of trinkets and rarities such as there have never been before. We, seeing this true affection, are always rejoiced at it, and so long as we live will heartily bestow on it Our favour."

That same year she despatched Chikuma Nagahiko to the Land of Pèkché in company with Kutyö and the others. Accordingly, in the most gracious manner, she said :—" We, in accordance with the divine testimony, having for the first time laid open a road, subdued the lands west of the sea and granted them to Pèkché, would now again draw closer the bonds of friendship and make lasting our loving bounty."

[1] Corean.

At this time the Kings of Pèkché, father and son, both together knocked their foreheads on the ground and made representation, saying : — " The immense bounty of the honourable country is more weighty than Heaven and Earth. What day, what hour shall we presume to forget it ? The sage sovereign IX. 31. dwells above, illustrious as the sun and moon ; thy servants now dwell below, solid as a mountain or hill, and will always be thy western frontier land, never to the last showing double hearts."

52nd year, Autumn, 9th month, 10th day. Kutyö and the A.D. 252. others came along with Chikuma Nagahiko and presented a seven-branched [1] sword and a seven-little-one [2]-mirror, with various other objects of great value. They addressed the Empress, saying :—"West of thy servants' country there is a river-source which issues from Mount Chölsan [3] in Kong-na. It is distant seven days' journey. It need not be approached, but one should drink of this water, and so having gotten the iron of this mountain, wait upon the sage Court for all ages." Moreover, he [4] addressed his grandson, Prince Chhim-nyu, [5] saying :—" The honourable country east of the sea with which we are now in communication has been opened to us by Heaven. Therefore does it bestow on us Celestial bounty, and dividing off the land west of the sea, has granted it to us. Consequently the foundation of our land is confirmed for ever. Thou shouldst cultivate well its friendship, and having collected our national products, wait on it with tribute without ceasing. Henceforth, grudging not even our lives, let us continue to send yearly tribute."

55th year. Syoko, King of Pèkché, died. [6]   A.D. 255. IX. 32.

56th year. Kusyu, son of the King of Pèkché, was set up as A.D. 256. king. [7]

---

[1] The traditional kana rendering is nana-saya, i.e. a " seven-sheathed sword," which is nonsense. Seven-branched is not much better.

[2] It is not clear what is meant by nanatsuko (七 子), perhaps with seven projections round the rim. See above, p. 44.

[3] Iron mountain. All this about iron is merely symbolical of constancy.

[4] The King of Pèkché.   [5] Came to the throne A.D. 384.

[6] The " Tongkam " places his death in A.D. 375.

[7] The traditional kana rendering of 王 is Kokishi, a word I do not recognize as Corean. But nearly all Corean words relating to official matters have become obsolete, being replaced by Chinese terms.

62nd year. Silla did not attend the Court. The same year
Sotsuhiko was sent to chastise Silla.

The Pèkché record says:—"The year Midzunoye Mŭma.[1]
Silla did not wait upon the honourable country. The
honourable country sent Sachihiko to attack it. The men
of Silla dressed up two beautiful women whom they sent
to meet Sachihiko at the port and inveigle him. Sachihiko
accepted them, and turning aside, attacked the land of
Kara. Kwi-pon [2] Kanki, King of Kara, and his sons, Pèk-
ku-chi, A-syu-chi, Ik-sya-ri, I-ra-ma-chyu, and I-mun-chi,
fled to Pèkché, taking with them their subjects. Pèkché
received them cordially, and Kwi-chön-chi, younger sister
of the King of Kara, went to Great Wa and addressed the
Empress, saying :—'Your majesty sent Sachihiko to attack
Silla. But he has accepted beautiful women of Silla, and
abandoned the in̄ vasion. On the contrary he has destroyed
our country. My brothers and our people have all been
driven into exile. Unable to bear my grief, I have come
hither to make this representation.' The Empress was
greatly enraged, and forthwith sent Mongna Keunchă in
command of an army to bring them together in Kara and
to restore the temples of the Earth and of Grain."

One account says :—" Sachihiko, when he learnt that
the Empress was wroth with him, did not dare to return
openly, but hid himself. He had a younger sister who
was in the service of the Imperial Palace. Hiko secretly
sent a messenger to inquire of her whether or no the
Empress's wrath had abated. She, pretending a dream,
said to the Empress:—'To-night, in a dream, I saw
Sachihiko.' The Empress was greatly enraged, and
said :—'How should Hiko dare to come ? ' The Empress's [3] words were reported to Sachihiko, who seeing
that he would not be pardoned, went into a cave of
a rock and died."

---

[1] 19th year of the Cycle, corresponding to A.D. 382.

[2] I Si-Pheum was the name of the King of Kara at this time, according to
the " Tongkam."

[3] The word for Empress is Tennô, which may also mean Emperor, and
indeed this suits the narrative better.

64th year.[1] Kusyu, King of Pèkché, died, and his son A.D. 264.
Chhim-nyu was set up as king.

65th year. King Chhim-nyu of Pèkché died.[2] His son A.D. 265.
Ahwa was a child, and his father's younger brother, Sinsă, by
usurpation was set up and made king.[3]

66th year.   A.D. 266.

This year was the second year of the period T'ai She of
the Emperor Wu Ti of the Tsin Dynasty. K'i Kü-chu of
Tsin says:—" In the 10th month of the 2nd year of the
period T'ai-she of Wu Ti, the Queen of Wa sent interpreters with tribute."

69th year, Summer, 4th month, 17th day. The Grand A.D. 269.
Empress died in the Palace of Waka-zakura at the age of 100.

Winter, 10th month, 15th day. She was buried in the
misasagi of Tatanami in Saki. On this day, by way of
posthumous honour to the Grand Empress, she was called
Okinaga Tarashi-hime no Mikoto.

This year was the year Tsuchinoto Ushi (26th) of the Cycle.

---

[1] The "Tongkam" has A.D. 384.

[2] This is mentioned almost in the same words by the " Tongkam " under
date A.D. 385—just two cycles later.

[3] The narrative from p. 246 down to this point contains a solid
nucleus of fact. There can be no doubt that Japan at an early period
formed an alliance with Pèkché and laid the foundation of a controlling
power over the territory known as Imna or Mimana which lasted for
several centuries. But the Japanese chronology cannot be right. See
"Early Japanese History," p. 62.

BOOK X.

THE EMPEROR HOMUDA.

(ŌJIN¹ TENNŌ.)

THE Emperor Homuda² was the 4th child of the Emperor Tarashi Nakatsu-hiko. His mother's name was Okinaga Tarashi-hime no Mikoto. The Emperor was born at Kata in Tsukushi in the 12th month, Winter, of the year Kanoye Tatsu,³ being the year in which the Empress smote Silla. From a child he was intelligent, penetrating, and far-sighted. In his bearing and conduct there were amazing indications of sageness. In the third year of the Grand Empress's administration of the Government, he was raised to the rank of Prince Imperial. Before this time, when the Emperor was in the womb, the Gods of Heaven and Earth granted to him the three Han.⁴ When he was born there was flesh growing on his arm in shape like an elbow-pad.⁵ As to this resemblance, the Empress judged that it was the elbow-pad worn as a manly accoutrement. Therefore he was styled by this name, and called the Emperor Homuda.

In the earliest antiquity, the tomo was commonly called Homuda.

One account says:—" In the beginning, when the Emperor was made Heir to the Throne, he went to the

---

¹ Responding to the Gods.
² The " Kojiki " calls him Homuda wake. Homuda or Honda is the name of a place.
³ 17th of the Cycle.   ⁴ Corea.
⁵ The *tomo* or leather shield worn on the fore-arm by archers as a protection against the recoil of the bow-string.

Land of Koshi, and did worship to the Great God of Tsu-tsuhi in Tsunoga. At this time the Great God and the Heir to the Throne exchanged names. Accordingly the Great God was called the God Isasa-wake and the Heir to the Throne Homuda wake no Mikoto.[1]

In the 69th year of her administration of the Government, Summer, the 4th month, the Grand Empress died.

1st year, Spring, 1st month, 1st day. The Prince Imperial assumed the Dignity. This year was the year Kanoye Tora (27th) of the Cycle. X. 2.
A.D. 270

2nd year, Spring, 3rd month, 3rd day. Nakatsuhime was appointed Empress. She gave birth to the Imperial Princess Arata, to the Emperor Oho-sazaki, and to the Imperial Prince Netori. Before this the Emperor had taken to him as concubine the Empress's younger sister, Takaki Iribime, who bore to him the Imperial Prince Nukada no Oho-naka-hiko, the Imperial Prince Oho-yama-mori, the Imperial Prince Iza no mawaka, the Imperial Princess Oho-hara, and the Imperial Princess Komida. Another concubine, a younger sister of the Empress, named Otohime, bore to him the Imperial Princess Ahe, the Imperial Princess Ahaji no Mihara, and the Imperial Princess Ki no Uno. The next concubine, daughter of Hifure no Omi, the ancestor of the Wani no Omi, by name Miya-nushi-yaka-hime, bore the Imperial Prince Uji no Waka-iratsuko, the Imperial Princess Yata, and the Imperial Princess Medori. The next concubine, named Oname-hime, the younger sister of Yaka-bime, bore the Imperial Prince Uji no waka-iratsu-me. The next concubine, named Oto-hime, daughter of Kaha-mata Nakatsu hiko, bore the Imperial Prince Wakanoke Futa-mata. The next concubine, named Mago-hime, younger sister of Osabi, Muraji of the Sakurawi-da Be, bore the Imperial Prince Hayabusa wake. The next concubine, named Naga-hime, of Idzumi in Hiuga, bore the Imperial Princes Oho-haye and Wo-haye. A.D. 271.X. 3.

In all the sons and daughters of this Emperor were together twenty Princes and Princesses.[2] The Imperial Prince Netori was the first ancestor of the Kimi of Ohota. The Imperial Prince

---

[1] There is a Semitic practice of men adopting Gods' names.
[2] Cf. Ch. K., p. 243, which makes 26 children, and differs in some details.

Oho-yama-mori was the first ancestor of the two families of the Kimi of Hiji-kata and the Kimi of Haibara. The Imperial Prince Iza no mawaka was the first ancestor of the Wake of Fukagaha.

A.D. 272. 3rd year, 10th month, 3rd day. The Eastern Yemishi all attended the Court with tribute. They were employed to make the Mŭma-zaka road.

11th month. The fishermen of several places clamoured noisily, and would not obey the Imperial command. So Oho-hama no Sukune, ancestor of the Muraji of Adzumi, was sent to subdue this clamour. He was accordingly made controller of the fishermen. This was the origin of the proverbial saying of the people of that time, viz. Sawa-ama or "clamorous fishermen."

This year King Sinsă of Pèkché was disrespectful to the Celestial Court. Therefore Ki no Tsuno no Sùkune, Hata no X. 4. Yashiro no Sukune, Ishikaha no Sukune and Tsuku no Sukune were sent to call him to an account for his rudeness. Hereupon the people of Pèkché slew Sinsă by way of apology. Ki no Tsuno no Sukune and the others accordingly established Ahwa as king, and returned (to Japan).[1]

A.D. 274. 5th year, Autumn, 8th month, 13th day. The various provinces were directed to establish Be of fishermen and Be of mountain wardens.[2]

Winter, 10th month. The province of Idzu was charged with the duty of constructing a ship 10 rods[3] in length. As soon as it was completed, it was launched on the sea for a trial. It floated lightly, and was as swift as a racer. Therefore that ship was called *Karano*.

[*It is a mistake to make the ship called Karano because it was*

---

[1] The "Tongkam," under date A.D. 392, has the following :—" 10th month. The king of Pèkché went to hunt on Ku-wön (dog-moor). Ten days elapsed without his returning. 11th month. King Sinsă of Pèkché died in his travelling palace on Dog-moor. Ahwa, son of King Chhim-nyu, came to the throne." Note that the Corean and Japanese chronologies differ by exactly 120 years, or two cycles. But the two stories are apparently irreconcilable. See below, XI. 26.

[2] Gamekeepers or huntsmen, whose business it was to supply the Imperial table.

[3] Of ten feet.

light and swift. Perhaps this is a corruption by men of later times of Karuno.[1]]

6th year, Spring, 2nd month. The Emperor made a progress A.D. 275 to the province of Afumi. When he arrived near the Moor X. 5. of Uji, he made a song, saying :—

> When I look upon the moor of Kadzu
> In Chiba,
> Both the hundred thousand fold abundant
> House-places are visible,
> And the land's acme is visible.[2]

7th year, Autumn, 9th month. Men of Koryö, men of A.D. 276. Pèkché, men of Imna, and men of Silla[3] all together attended the Court. Orders were then given to Takechi no Sukune to take these various men of Han and make them dig a pond. Therefore the pond was given a name, and was called the pond of the men of Han.[4]

8th year, Spring, 3rd month. Men of Pèkché attended A.D. 277. Court.

The Pèkché record says :—" King Ahwa came to the throne and was disrespectful[5] to the honourable country. Therefore we were despoiled of Chhim-mi-ta-ryö, Hyön-nam, Chi-chhim, Kong-na, and Eastern Han. Herewith Prince Chik-chi[6] was sent to the Celestial Court in order to restore the friendship of former kings.

9th year, Summer, 4th month. Takechi no Sukune was A.D. 278. sent to Tsukushi to inspect the people. Now Umashi no Sukune, Takechi no Sukune's younger brother, setting aside his elder brother, slandered him to the Emperor, (saying that) Takechi no Sukune had always designs upon the Empire. " I now hear," said he, " that while he is in Tsukushi, he is secretly

---

[1] *Kara* means withered, and *no*, moor, or the latter may be put phonetically for *no* the genitive particle. Karu means light. The " Shukai " editor rejects this note.

[2] From Ch. K., p. 245, q.v.

[3] The traditional kana rendering has Koma, Kudara, Mimana and Shiraki.

[4] Or " men of Kara." Compare Ch. K., p. 252.

[5] See above, p. 256, where it is said that it was King Sinsă who was dis-respectful.

[6] The " Tongkam " calls him Työnchi, and places this event in 397.

plotting to that end, saying (to himself), 'Alone I will cut off Tsukushi, and will invite the three Han to come and do homage to me, so that finally I may possess the Empire.'"

Hereupon the Emperor straightway sent messengers to slay Takechi no Sukune. Now Takechi no Sukune cried out, saying:—"I have not two hearts, but serve my prince with loyalty. What a calamity is this that I should die without a crime!"

X. 6.

Now there was a man named Maneko, ancestor of the Atahe of Iki, who in appearance strongly resembled Takechi no Sukune. All by himself he grudged that Takechi no Sukune's innocent life should be vainly thrown away. So he spoke to Takechi no Sukune and said:—"Now the Great Minister[1] serves his Prince with loyalty, and has not had a black heart. All the Empire knows this. I pray thee leave this place secretly, and, proceeding to the Court, personally unfold thine innocence. After this it will not be too late to die. Moreover the people of this time are always saying that thy slave resembles the Great Minister in appearance. Therefore I will now die in the place of the Great Minister, and so make clear the Great Minister's redness of heart."[2] So he threw himself on his sword, and slew himself. Then Takechi no Sukune, alone, grieving greatly for him, secretly left Tsukushi, and embarking on the sea, went round by way of the Southern Ocean. Anchoring in the harbour of Ki, he hardly succeeded in making his way to the Court, where he explained his innocence. The Emperor forthwith questioned Takechi no Sukune along with Umashi no Sukune, upon which these two men were each obstinate, and wrangled with one another, so that it was impossible to ascertain the right and the wrong. The Emperor then gave orders to ask of the Gods of Heaven and Earth the ordeal by boiling water. Hereupon Takechi no Sukune and Umashi no Sukune went out together to the bank of the Shiki river, and underwent the ordeal of boiling water. Takechi no Sukune was victorious. Taking his cross-sword, he threw down Umashi no Sukune, and was at length about to slay him, when the Emperor ordered him to let him go. So he gave him to the ancestor of the Atahe of Kii.

---

[1] i.e. you.　　　　　　[2] Sincerity.

11th year, Winter, 10th month. The Tsurugi, Kakaki, and Mumaya-zaka ponds were made.

This year there was a man who made representation to the Emperor, saying :—" There is in the land of Hiuga a maiden whose name is Kami-naga-hime.[1] She is the daughter of Ushi-morowi, the Kimi of Muragata. She is distinguished for beauty over all the Land." The Emperor was pleased, and wished in his heart to obtain her.

13th year, Spring, 3rd month. The Emperor sent a special messenger to summon Kami-naga-hime.

Autumn, 9th month. Kami-naga-hime arrived from Hiuga, and was straightway settled at the village of Kuhadzu. Now the Imperial Prince, Oho-sazaki no Mikoto, when he saw Kami-naga-hime, was struck with the beauty of her form, and had a constant love for her. Hereupon the Emperor became aware of Oho-sazaki no Mikoto's passion for Kami-naga-hime, and wished to unite her to him. Therewith the Emperor, on the day that he gave a banquet in the hinder palace,[2] sent for Kami-naga-hime for the first time, and so gave her the upper seat in the banqueting-room. Then he brought in Oho-sazaki no Mikoto, and pointing to Kami-naga-hime, made a song, saying :—

> Come ! my son !
> On the moor, garlic to gather,
> Garlic to gather
> On the way as I went,
> Pleasing of perfume
> Was the orange in flower.
> Its branches beneath
> Men had all plundered,
> Its branches above
> Birds perching had withered.
> [Of three chestnuts][3]
> Midmost, its branches
> Held in their hiding
> A blushing maiden.
> Come ! and for thee, my son,
> Let her burst into blossom.

X 8.

Hereupon Oho-sazaki no Mikoto, being favoured with this

---

[1] The long-haired lady. [2] i.e. the women's apartments.
[3] This is a mere makura-kotoba of little or no meaning.

poetry, forthwith understood that he was receiving Kami-naga-
hime as a gift; and, greatly delighted, made a song in reply,
saying :—

> In the pond of Yosami
> Where the water collects,
> The marsh-rope coils
> Were growing, but I knew not of them :
> In the river-fork stream,
> The water-caltrops shells
> Were pricking me, but I knew not of them.
> Oh, my heart !
> How very ridiculous thou wert ! [1]

Oho-sazaki no Mikoto, after the consummation of his union
with Kami-naga-hime, was very attentive to her, and when he
was alone with her, made a song, saying :—

> The maid of Kohada
> Of the further province !
> As of a God
> Though I had heard of her,
> We are folded in each other's arms.

Again he made a song, saying :—

> The maid of Kohada
> Of the further province—
> Oh ! how I love her
> As she lies
> Unresisting !

X. 9.

One account says :—" Ushi, the Kimi of Morogata in
Hiuga, was in the service of the Court. But having
become old in years, he was unable to serve, and so,
having ceased his service, he retired to his own land.
Thereupon he offered the Emperor his own daughter,
Kami-naga-hime. When she first arrived at Harima, the
Emperor had made a progress to the island of Ahaji, and
was hunting there. Hereupon the Emperor, looking
towards the west, saw several tens of stags swimming

---

[1] In the "Kojiki" this poem is attributed to the Emperor. See Ch. K.,
p. 249. The marsh-rope is the Brasenia peltata, according to Chamberlain.
The general meaning of the poem seems to be : " What a fool I was to be
in such despair as to be unconscious of bodily suffering, while happiness was
all the while near me ! "

towards him over the sea. Presently they entered the harbour of Kako in Harima. The Emperor addressed his courtiers, saying :—' What stags are these which come in numbers swimming over the great sea ? ' Then the courtiers all looked at them and wondered. So a messenger was sent to make examination. The messenger, when he came there, saw that they were all men, only they had for clothing deer-skins with the horns attached. He inquired of them, saying :—' What men are ye ? ' They replied, saying :—' Ushi, the Kimi of Morogata, being old in years, has ceased his service, but he cannot forget the Court. Therefore he offers his own daughter, Kami-naga-hime.' The Emperor was delighted, and sending for her, made her follow the Imperial ship. · For this reason, the men of that time called the place where they reached the shore the harbour of Kako.[1] It was perhaps at this time that the practice began of using the word kako as a general name for sailors."

14th year, Spring, 2nd month. The King of Pèkché sent as A.D. 283. tribute a seamstress named Maketsu.[2] She was the first ancestress of the present seamstresses of Kume.[3] This year the Lord of Yutsuki[4] came from Pèkché and offered his allegiance. X. 10. Accordingly he addressed the Emperor, saying :—" Thy servant was coming to offer allegiance with one hundred and twenty districts of the people of his own land, when the men of Silla prevented them, and they were all forced to remain in the land of Kara." Hereupon Katsuraki no Sotsuhiko was sent to bring the men of Yutsuki from Kara. Now three years passed, and Sotsuhiko did not come.

15th year, Autumn, 8th month, 6th day. The King of A.D. 284. Pèkché sent A-chik-ki with two quiet horses as tribute. So they were fed in stables on the acclivity of Karu. Accordingly A-chik-ki was appointed to have charge of their foddering.

[1] Kako is written with characters which mean deer-little-one.
[2] I have here followed the traditional kana pronunciation. The Corean pronunciation of the Chinese characters would be Chin-mo-chin. Another reading makes two women.
[3] In Yamato.
[4] Yutsuki is the traditional rendering of the characters 弓 月. This in Corean would be Kung-wöl.

Therefore the place where the horses were kept was named Mumaya-saka.[1] Moreover, A-chik-ki was able to read the classics, and so the Heir Apparent, Uji no Waka-iratsuko,[2] made him his teacher. Hereupon the Emperor inquired of A-chik-ki, saying :—" Are there other learned men superior to thee ? " He answered and said :—" There is Wang-in,[3] who is superior." Then Areda wake, ancestor of the Kimi of Kōdzuke, and Kamu nagi wake were sent to Pèkché to summon Wang-in. This A-chik-ki was the first ancestor of the A-chik-ki (or Atogi) no Fumi-bito.[4]

16th year, Spring, 2nd month. Wang-in[5] arrived, and straightway the Heir Apparent, Uji no Waka-iratsuko, took him

X. 11.

A.D. 285.

---

[1] Stable-hill.

[2] But he was not the heir. Oho-sazaki was heir. See Ch. K., pp. 254 and 257.

[3] The traditional reading is Wani, which is also found in the " Kojiki."

[4] Scribes.

[5] There are clear indications that the Chinese language and character were not wholly unknown in Japan from a time which may be roughly put as coinciding with the Christian epoch. But this knowledge was probably confined to a few interpreters. There were no schools, and no official records. The arrival of Wangin was therefore a most important event in Japanese history. It was the beginning of a training in Chinese ideas which has exercised a profound influence on the whole current of Japanese thought and civilization up to our own day.

The date given for it in the " Nihongi," however, cannot be correct. As I have endeavoured to show in a paper on " Early Japanese History " contributed to the Transactions of the Asiatic Society of Japan, Wangin's arrival must be placed 120 years later, i.e. in 405 instead of in 285. Whether the whole chronology of this period requires to be altered accordingly, as I am disposed to believe, or only the dates of those events which relate to Corea, is a question which has not yet received an adequate answer. It is curious that the " Kiujiki " omits all mention of them.

Corea preceded Japan by only a very short time in the establishment of schools of Chinese learning and in the institution of official records. Kokuryö established a High School in 372, and Pèkché appointed a Professor of Chinese two years later. Before this time, says the " Tongkam," Pèkché had no written records. See " Writing, Printing, and Alphabet in Corea," " J.R.A.S.," 1895.

Á-chik-ki is the Corean pronunciation of the characters 阿 直 岐. The traditional rendering in kana is Achiki or Atogi. The " Kojiki " calls him Achi-Kishi, where Kishi is written 吉 師, the name of a Corean rank of no great eminence.

as teacher, and learnt various books from him. There was none
which he did not thoroughly understand. Therefore the man
called Wang-in was the first ancestor of the Fumi no Obito.[1]
In this year King Ahwa of Pĕkché died. The Emperor then
sent for Prince Työn-chi,[2] and addressed him, saying :—" Do
thou return to thy country and succeed to the (royal) Dignity."
Accordingly he further granted to him the territory of Eastern
Han, and so dismissed him.[3]
    Eastern Han comprises Kam-na-syöng, Ko-nan-syöng,
and I-rim-syöng.[4]
    8th month. Kidzu no Sukune of Hegurï and Tada no
Sukune of Ikuba were sent to Kara. Choice troops were
granted them, and the Emperor commanded them, saying :—
" The long delay in Sotsuhiko's return must be owing to his X. 12.
being detained by the opposition of the men of Silla. Do you
go speedily, assail Silla, and open a way for him." Hereupon

<hr/>

[1] Fumi no obito, chiefs of writing.
[2] Prince Työn-chi. The " Nihongi" has 直 支 here and below (25th year),
which would be in Corean Chik-chi. But 直 is a mistake for 膔, the former
character having slipped in from the name of the horse-keeper mentioned
above.
[3] The following are the notices in the " Tongkam " relating to Prince
Työnchi's being sent to Japan :—
  " Reign of Ahwa, 6th year, Summer, 5th month. Pĕkché made friends A.D. 397
with Wa. Työnchi, the Heir Apparent, was sent as a hostage."
  " Reign of Ahwa, 14th year, Autumn, 9th month. King Ahwa of Pĕkché A.D. 405.
died. The Heir Apparent Työnchi had not returned from Wa, whither he
had gone as a hostage. Työnchi's next younger brother, Hunhê, administered
the Government in expectation of the Heir Apparent's return. The youngest
brother, Syöl-lyé, slew Hunhè, and set himself up as King. When Työnchi
heard of the King's death, he wept bitterly, and asked permission to return.
The Lord of Wa gave Työnchi one hundred soldiers as an escort. When
he arrived at the frontier, a man of Hansyöng [1] named Hè-chhung came to
meet him, and said :—'The Great King (Ahwa) having left this world,
Syöl-lyé slew his elder brother and set up himself as King. I pray that the
Heir Apparent will promptly take measures for this.' Työnchi, guarded by
the Wa soldiers, repaired to an island in the sea, and made provision there
while the people of the land killed Syöl-lyé, and going to meet (Työnchi),
established him as King." " Tongkam," III. 14.
[4] Syöng means a walled city.

<hr/>

[1] The present capital of Söul.

T

Kidzu no Sukune and his colleague moved forward their choice troops and arrived at the Silla frontier. The King of Silla was afraid, and confessed his guilt, so they brought away with them the people of Kungwöl[1] and Sotsuhiko.

A.D. 288. 19th year, Winter, 10th month, 1st day. The Emperor made a progress to the Palace of Yoshino.[2] At this time the Kuzu[3] came to his Court, and presenting to the Emperor newly-brewed sake, made a song, saying:—

> At Kashinofu
> A cross-mortar[4] we made :
> In that cross-mortar
> The great august sake that we have brewed
> Sweetly
> Do thou partake of it
> Oh! our father![5]

When the song was finished, they drummed on their mouths and looked up laughing. At the present time, on the day that the Kuzu[6] present their country's produce to the Emperor, when their song is finished they drum on their mouths and look up laughing. This custom is probably a relic of antiquity. Now the Kuzu are very plain and honest in character. They commonly gather wild berries for food, and they also boil frogs, X. 13. which they reckon a great dainty, calling them kebi. Their country lies to the south-east of the capital, on the other side of a mountain. There they dwell by the River Yoshino (amid) steep cliffs and deep ravines. The roads are narrow, with deep hollows. Therefore, although the distance from the capital is not great, their visits to Court had been rare. However, from this time forward they came frequently, bringing the produce of their country to present to the Emperor. This produce consists of such things as chestnuts, mushrooms, and trout.

A.D. 289. 20th year, Autumn, 9th month. Achi no Omi, ancestor of

---

[1] Or Yutsuki.　　　　　[2] In the south of Yamato.
[3] Local chieftains.
[4] It is not clear what a cross-mortar was. *Vide* Ch. K., p. 251.
[5] The word translated father is *chi*, which is also used more generally as a term of respect. Perhaps " Lord " might be better here.
[6] Seventeen was their number in later times, according to the Yengi Shiki.

the Atahe of the Aya[1] of Yamato, and his son Tsuga no Omi X. 14
immigrated to Japan, bringing with them a company of their
people of seventeen districts.

22nd year, Spring, 3rd month, 5th day. The Emperor made A.D. 291.
a progress to Naniha, where he dwelt in the Palace of Oho-
sumi.

10th day. He ascended a lofty tower and had a distant
prospect. Now he was attended by his concubine Yehime,
who, looking towards the west, lamented loudly. Hereupon
the Emperor inquired of Yehime, saying:—"Why dost thou
lament so bitterly?" She answered and said:—"Of late thy
handmaiden has been thinking fondly of her father and mother,
and so, looking towards the west, unawares she made lament. I
pray thee let me return for a while that I may see my parents."
Hereupon the Emperor loved Yehime's tender thought for the
warmth and coolness[2] of her parents, and addressing her,
said:—"Many years have passed since thou hast seen thy
parents. It is clearly right that thou shouldst wish to return

---

[1] Aya is the traditional Japanese rendering of 漢, i.e. Han, the name of a
Chinese dynasty. No satisfactory explanation of the reason why this
character should be read aya has been given. As a mere guess, I would
suggest that Hada or hata for 秦 (Ts'in), Kure for Wu 吳 and Aya for Han
may have been names given from the textile products with which these three
Chinese dynasties, or the emigrants, may have been associated; Hada or
Hata meaning loom or cloth generally, Kure, dyed stuffs (for Kurenawi, pink
or scarlet), and Aya, figured stuffs. There were numerous weavers among the
Corean (or Chinese) emigrants to Japan. See below, A.D. 306. For Kure,
another derivation is that which makes it mean "distant," a sense in which
it occurs more than once in the "Manyōshiu," and in a poem in the
"Nihongi," Reign of Saimei, year 4.

This family was called the Aya of Yamato to distinguish it from another
family of the same name in Kahachi. These two families were also known
respectively as the Higashi no Aya, or Eastern Aya, and the Nishi no
Aya, or Western Aya.

Motoöri ("Kojikiden," XXXIII. 39) shows that, like other events relating
to Corea in this part of the "Nihongi," this immigration must be dated 120
years later.

The Yamato Aya claimed descent from the Emperor Ling-ti of the Later
Han dynasty, who reigned A.D. 168 to 190. We are told that on the fall of
that dynasty in 221, Prince Achi fled to Corea, whence he subsequently
emigrated to Japan; but how much of this is true it is impossible to say.
Cf. Ch. K., p. 253.

[2] i.e. thoughtfulness for her parents' comfort.

and visit them." So he granted her permission, and summoning eighty fishermen of Mihara in Ahaji and making sailors of them, sent her to Kibi.

Summer, 4th month. Yehime set sail from Ohotsu[1] and departed.

X. 15. The Emperor, standing on the high tower, looked towards Yehime's ship and made a song, saying :—

> Thou Island of Ahaji
> With thy double ranges ;[2]
> Thou Island of Adzuki
> With thy double ranges—
> Ye good islands
> *   *   *   *[3]
> Ye have seen face to face
> My spouse of Kibi.

Autumn, 9th month, 6th day. The Emperor hunted in the Island of Ahaji. This island lies beyond the sea to the west of Naniha. There is a confusion of peaks and cliffs; hills and valleys succeed to one another. Fragrant herbs grow luxuriantly ; it is washed by the long billows. Moreover, great deer, wild ducks, and wild geese are abundant in that island. Therefore the Emperor made frequent excursions thither.[4] Now the Emperor, going round by way of Ahaji, made a progress to Kibi and went on an excursion to the Island of Adzuki.

11th day. He again removed his dwelling to the Palace of
X. 16. Ashimori in Hata. Then Mitomo wake presented himself and entertained the Emperor, employing his brother, children and grandchildren as stewards. Hereupon the Emperor, observing the reverential fear with which Mitomo wake waited on him, was pleased, and accordingly, having divided the province of Kibi, granted it in fee to his children ; that is to say, dividing off the district of Kahashima, he granted it to the eldest son, Inehaya wake. He was the first ancestor of the Omi of Shimo-

---

[1] Ohotsu is literally " great port." Perhaps Ohosaka is meant.

[2] Showing a double row of mountain peaks.

[3] The sixth line of the original is unintelligible.

[4] Riding in his carriage, says the original, a Chinese expression which is not meant to be taken literally.

tsu-michi.[1] Next he took the district of Kamu-tsu-michi and granted it to the middle son, Nakatsuhiko.[2] He was the first ancestor of the Omi of Kamu-tsu-michi and of the Omi of Kaya. Next he took the district of Mino and granted it to Otohiko.[3] He was the first ancestor of the Omi of Mino. Afterwards he took the district of Hakuke and granted it to Ahiru wake, the younger brother of Mitomo wake. He was the first ancestor of the Omi of Kasa. Accordingly he took the district of Sono X. 17. and granted it to his elder brother, Urakori wake. He was the first ancestor of the Atahe of Sono. And taking the district of Hatori-be,[4] he granted it to Yehime. Wherefore his descendants dwell to this day in the Land of Kibi. This is the reason of it.[5]

25th year. King Työn-chi of Pèkché died.[6] Accordingly A.D. 294. his son Ku-ni-sin became King. The King was a child. Therefore Mong-man-chi of Yamato[7] took the administration of the State. He had an intrigue with the King's mother, and his conduct was in many ways improper. The Emperor hearing this, sent for him.

The Pèkché record says :—" Mong-man-chi was the son of Mong-na Keunchă,[8] born to him of a Silla woman

---

[1] Shimo-tsu-michi means the lower road, i.e. the part of the province furthest from the capital. Kamu-tsu-michi, on the other hand, is the higher road—the part nearest the capital.

[2] Middle prince. [3] Younger prince. [4] Weavers.

[5] If we take a broad view of Japanese History we shall recognize in it a constant oscillation between two forms of government. At one time there is a strong central authority with local governors removable at pleasure or at short intervals. By degrees the latter offices become hereditary and more independent of the throne, so that eventually a sort of feudal system is the result. Then the pendulum swings back again, and under a strong ruler the old centralized government is restored, while the local nobles, deprived of effective authority, retain their titles only.

Notwithstanding the numerous imperfections of the record, it is clear that in Ojin's reign the feudal system prevailed. Towards the end of the seventh century, again, we find a much more centralized form of government. The Revolution of 1868 is a remarkable example of a rapid change from a feudal system to a strong central government. The converse process is always far more gradual.

[6] The " Tongkam " gives A.D. 420 as the year of Työn-chi's death. The usual difference of 120 years is therefore not exactly realized in this case.

[7] Or Great Wa. 大 倭.

[8] See above, p. 249. This does not look like a Japanese name.

when he invaded that country. The great services of his father gave him absolute authority in Imna. He came into our country and went back and forward to the honourable country,[1] accepting the control of the Celestial Court. He seized the administration of our country, and his power was supreme in that day. The Emperor, hearing of his violence, recalled him."

A.D. 297. 28th year, Autumn, 9th month. The King of Koryö sent an envoy to the Court with tribute. He presented an address, in which it was said :—" The King of Koryö instructs the Land of

X. 18 Nippon." Now the Heir Apparent, Uji no Waka-iratsuko, read this address and was enraged. He reproached the Koryö envoy with the rudeness of the address and tore it up.[2]

A.D. 300. 31st year, Autumn, 8th month. The Emperor commanded his ministers,[3] saying :—" The Government ship named *Karano* was sent as tribute by the Land of Idzu. It is rotten, and unfit for use. It has, however, been in Government use for a long time, and its services should not be forgotten. Shall we not keep the name of that ship from being lost, and hand it down to after ages?" The ministers, on receiving this command, made the functionaries take the timber of that ship and use it as firewood for roasting salt. Herewith they got five hundred baskets of salt, which were freely given away to the various provinces, and the latter were accordingly caused to build ships. Upon this, all the provinces at the same time sent up ships as tribute, to the number of five hundred, which all assembled in the harbour of Muko. At this time the Silla

---

[1] Japan.

[2] If this story were true, it would have to be dated 120 years later. But even then Koryö was still Kokuryö. The name Koryö did not come into official use till A.D. 918, though as a literary designation examples of it may be found as early as A.D. 500. Koryö, however, is out of place in an ostensible quotation from a formal official document of this period, and shows that this story is untrue or much garbled.

The term Nippon for Japan is also an anachronism. It was not officially notified to Corea until A.D. 670, though there are examples of its use earlier in the same century.

Waka-iratsuko did not become Heir Apparent until A.D. 309 (of the " Nihongi " chronology), and as he is there alluded to as being of tender years, he must have been at this time a somewhat precocious prince.

[3] See above, p. 257.

tribute-envoys were stopping along with them at Muko.[1] Hereupon, of a sudden, fire broke out in the Silla lodgings. It presently spread to the fleet of ships, so that many of them were burnt. In consequence of this, the Silla men were called to an account. The King of Silla, when he heard of it, was afraid, and, greatly alarmed, sent tribute of skilful workmen. They were the first ancestors of the Wina[2] Be. In the beginning, when the ship *Karano* was burnt as firewood for making salt, some was left over from the burning. It was thought strange that it did not burn, and it was accordingly presented to the Emperor. The Emperor wondered at it, and had it made into a koto, which had a ringing note, and could be heard afar off. Then the Emperor made a song, saying :—

> (The ship) *Karano*　　　　　　　　　　　X. 19. ·
> Was burnt for salt :
> Of the remainder
> A koto was made.
> When it is played on,
> (One hears) the saya-saya [3]
> Of the summer trees
> Brushing against, as they stand,
> The rocks of the mid-harbour—
> The harbour of Yura.

37th year, Spring, 2nd month, 1st day. Achi no Omi and A.D. 306. Tsuga no Omi[4] were sent to Wu,[5] to procure seamstresses. Now Achi no Omi and his companions crossed over to the Land of Koryö, and endeavoured to reach Wu. But on arriving at Koryö they knew not the road at all, and begged

---

Hiôgo, or some place in the vicinity, is meant.

[2] A place in Settsu.

[3] Saya-saya is an onomatopoetic word for rustling, equivalent to the French frou-frou.

Yura is in Ahaji. Cf. Ch. K., 285.

[4] They were Coreans. See above, p. 264.

[5] Wu 吳, called by the Japanese Go or Kure, was a Chinese dynasty, the last sovereign of which was deposed A.D. 280, long before the despatch of these envoys. We learn, however, from a note to the " Shukai " edition that this appellation was applied (perhaps popularly) to all the six dynasties established at Nanking or the neighbourhood from Wu to Chên inclusive, i.e. from A.D. 229 to 589. To this day a draper's shop is called in Japan a Go-fuku-ya, or " house for Go-clothing."

Koryö to give them persons who knew the road. The King of Koryö sent with them as guides two men called Kureha and Kureshi.[1] In this way they were enabled to reach Wu. The King[2] of Wu thereupon gave them four women as workwomen, namely Ye-hime, Oto-hime, Kure-hatori and Ana-hatori.[3]

A.D. 308.

39th year, Spring, 2nd month. The King of Pèkché sent his younger sister, the Lady Sin-chă-to,[4] to wait upon (the Emperor as his concubine). Now the Lady Sin-chă-to came over, bringing in her train seven women.

X. 20.
A.D. 309.

40th year, Spring, 1st month, 8th day. The Emperor summoned to him Oho-yama-mori no Mikoto[5] and Oho-sazaki no Mikoto, and inquired of them, saying :—" Do ye love your children?" They answered and said ·—"We love them exceedingly." Again he inquired :—" Which are most dear—the elder ones or the younger?" Oho-yama-mori no Mikoto answered and said :—"There is none like the elder." On this the Emperor showed displeasure. Then Oho-sazaki no Mikoto, who had previously observed the Emperor's expression of face, answered and said :—" The older has experienced many colds and heats, and has already become a man, so that there is no reason for anxiety about him. But in the case of a young child one knows not whether he will reach manhood or not, and for that reason he is very pitiable." The Emperor was greatly pleased and said :—" Thy words are truly in accordance with my feelings." At this time it was the Emperor's constant

---

[1] The Chinese characters given in the text seem to be only Japanese phonetic renderings of the names, and I have therefore not given them their Corean sounds, which would be Ku-nyé-pha and Ku-nyé-chi. But they do not look like real names. They appear to be made up of Kure, the name of the dynasty, or rather of the country ruled by it, and a termination.

[2] Some local authority must be intended.

[3] These names mean respectively "elder lady," "younger lady," "Kure weaver," and "hole weaver." But Ana, hole, is probably a mistake for Aya, the Japanese name of the Chinese Han dynasty. Wu (or Kure) and Han (or Aya) weavers are mentioned together below, year 14 of Yuriaku's reign. See also above, p. 265.

[4] The Japanese traditional reading is Shi-se-tsu. The " Shukai " edition rejects the name Chikchi, which in the older editions follows Pèkché. It is not in the old books, and besides his death has been already recorded above.

[5] He was the son of an inferior consort.

desire to establish Uji no Waka-iratsuko as Prince Imperial, and so he wished to conciliate the minds of the two Imperial Princes. Therefore he started this inquiry. On this account he was displeased with Oho-yama-mori no Mikoto's answer.

24th day. Uji no Waka-iratsuko was established as successor (to the throne). On the same day Oho-yama-mori no Mikoto [1] was appointed to the charge of the mountains, rivers, woods, and moors, while Oho-sazaki no Mikoto was made Assistant to the Prince Imperial, and caused to administer affairs of State.

41st year, Spring, 2nd month, 15th day. The Emperor died A.D. 310 in the Palace of Toyo-Akira at the age of 110.[2]

One account says:—" He died in the Palace of Oho-kuma."

In this month Achi no Omi and his companions arrived in Tsukushi from Wu. Now the Great God of Muna-gata [3] asked for workwomen. Therefore Ane-hime was offered to the Great God of Muna-gata. She was the ancestor of the Mitsukahi [4] no Kimi, who now dwell in the Land of Tsukushi. He then took with him the three women, and proceeded to the Land of Tsu.[5] But when he reached Muko the Emperor was dead and he was too late. Accordingly he offered them to Oho-sazaki no Mikoto. The descendants of these women are the present seamstresses of Kure and the seamstresses of Kaya.[6]

---

[1] His name, Great-mountain-warden, already indicates this office. There is a distinction between the characters for Mikoto applied to the elder and younger brothers, the latter having the more honorific character no doubt because he afterwards became Emperor. See above, p. 2.

[2] The "Kojiki" says 130. He was deified at a later period under the name of Yahata or Hachiman as the God of War, and there are many shrines in his honour standing at this day.

[3] In Chikuzen.

[4] Mitsukahi means " august messenger."   [5] Settsu.

[6] Kaya is written with the characters for " Musquito-net." There is a place in Bittchiu of this name, but written with different characters.

BOOK XI.

(*NINTOKU*[2] *TENNŌ.*)

THE Emperor Oho-sazaki was the fourth child of the Emperor Homuda. His mother's name was Nakatsu-hime no Mikoto. She was a granddaughter of the Imperial Prince Ihoki-iri-hiko. The Emperor from his childhood was intelligent and sagacious, and his face was fair to look upon. When he grew to manhood he was indulgent and humane. The Emperor Homuda died in Spring, the 2nd month of the 41st year of his reign. Now the Prince Imperial offered to cede the Dignity to Oho-sazaki no Mikoto. He would not assume the Imperial Dignity, but advised with Oho-sazaki no Mikoto, saying :—" He that shall rule over the Empire and govern the myriad subjects should overspread them like Heaven, and comprehend them like Earth. If there is above a cheerful heart with which to employ the people, the people are happy and the Empire tranquil. But here am I, a younger brother, and moreover wanting in talent. How shall I presume to succeed to the Dignity and to enter upon the Celestial task ? But thou, O great Prince, art distinguished in appearance and of a far-reaching benevolence. Thou art also of ripe years and art fit to become Lord of the Empire. The late Emperor established me as his Heir. But was this for my abilities ? No, it was simply because he loved me. Moreover, there is the weighty matter of the service of the Ancestral shrines and of the Gods of the Earth and of Grain.[3] For this thy servant is wanting in ready tact and is unmeet to

---

[1] Great-wren. See below, XI. 7.   [2] Benevolence-virtue.
[3] These expressions are simply borrowed from Chinese books, and have no bearing on Japanese ancient institutions or ideas.

fill the office. Now, there is a general principle admitted by both ancient and modern times that the elder brother should be above and the younger brother below, that the wise man should be Lord and the stupid man a vassal. Let the Prince therefore unhesitatingly assume the Imperial Dignity, and I will be simply his servant and assistant." Oho-sazaki no Mikoto answered and said :—" It was the intention of the late Emperor that the Imperial Dignity should not be vacant for a single day. Therefore he made choice beforehand of an illustrious virtue and established the Prince as his duplicate. The succession he bestowed on thee and the people he granted to thee. Let us honour his preference, and publish it throughout the land. Wanting in wisdom though I am, shall I disregard the command of the late Emperor, and without consideration comply with the request of the Prince, my younger brother ? "

He firmly declined and would not receive it, and each of them wished to transfer (the sovereignty) to the other.

At this time the Imperial Prince Nukada no Oho-naka-tsu-hiko, intending to take charge of the official rice-lands and granary of Yamato, addressed Oü no Sukune, ancestor of the Omi of Idzumo, who was the officer charged with these official rice-lands, saying :—" These official rice-lands were originally Mountain-warden-land, and therefore I will now take the management of them. Thou oughtest not to hold them."

Now Oü no Sukune reported the matter to the Prince Imperial, who spake to him, saying :—" Do thou represent the matter to Oho-sazaki no Mikoto." Hereupon Oü no Sukune made representation to Oho-sazaki no Mikoto, saying :—" The Imperial Prince Oho-naka-tsu-hiko will not allow thy servant to manage the official rice-fields which were placed in his charge." Oho-sazaki no Mikoto inquired of Maro, the ancestor of the Atahe of Yamato, saying :—" It is stated that the official rice-lands of Yamato were originally Mountain-warden-land. How is this ? " He answered and said :—" Thy servant knows not. But thy servant's younger brother, Akoko, knows." It happened that at this time Akoko had been sent to the Han [1] country and had not yet returned. Hereupon Oho-sazaki no

---

[1] Corea.

Mikoto spake to Oü, saying :—" Do thou go thyself to the Han country and summon Akoko. Go quickly, travelling day and night." So he assigned to him eighty fishermen of Ahaji as sailors. Hereupon Oü proceeded to the Han country, and straightway came accompanied by Akoko. Accordingly he was asked about the Yamato official rice-lands. He replied, saying : —" I have heard by tradition that, in the time of the Emperor who reigned in the palace of Tamaki at Makimuku,[1] the official rice-fields of Yamato were settled in the charge of Oho-tarashi-hiko no Mikoto, the Prince Imperial. At that time there was an Imperial Decree to the effect that the official rice-lands of Yamato were always to be the official rice-lands of the reigning Sovereign, and could not be held by anyone who was not the reigning Sovereign, even an Emperor's child. It is therefore wrong to say that this is Mountain-warden-land."

Then Oho-sazaki no Mikoto sent Akoko to the Imperial Prince Nukada no Oho-naka-tsu-hiko, and made him acquaint him with these circumstances. The Imperial Prince Oho-naka-tsu-hiko knew not at all what to do, and Oho-sazaki no Mikoto, recognizing that he was in the wrong, forgave him and did not punish him.

XI. 4. Thereafter Prince Oho-yama-mori[2] was full of resentment that he was passed over by the late Emperor and not established as Prince Imperial. In addition he had this cause of hatred. So he plotted, saying :—" I will kill the Prince Imperial and will ultimately ascend to the Imperial Dignity." Hereupon Oho-sazaki no Mikoto, having heard beforehand of his plot, secretly advised the Prince Imperial to prepare soldiers for his protection. Then the Prince Imperial got ready troops and awaited him. The Imperial Prince Oho-yama-mori, not knowing that soldiers had been prepared, took with him only a few hundred fighting men, and starting in the middle of the night, proceeded thither. At dawn he arrived at Uji, and was about to cross the river when the Prince Imperial, having put on

---

[1] Suinin Tennō.

[2] Clearly Oho-yama-mori is the same person who is spoken of above as Nukada no Oho-naka-tsu-hiko. Either Nukada all through the above passage is a mistake, or the genealogy (p. 255) which makes two persons of them is wrong. I think the latter more likely, Oho-yama-mori being an official designation, and Nukada, etc., the name.

hempen garments, took the helm, and secretly mingled with the ferrymen. He then took the Imperial Prince Oho-yama-mori on board and ferried him over as far as the middle of the river, where he induced the ferrymen to step on the (side of the) boat and make it heel over. Hereupon the Imperial Prince Oho-yama-mori fell into the river and sank. But he rose to the surface again, and while floating down the stream made a song, saying,—

> At the ferry of Uji
>   *   *   * 1
> Among the pole-men
> Those who are nimblest
> Will come to me.

But a large number of ambushed soldiers sprang up, so that he was unable to reach the bank, and he finally sank and died. Search was caused to be made for his dead body, and it came to the surface at the ferry of Kahara. Then the Prince Imperial seeing the dead body, made a song, saying,—

> O thou Mayumi tree
> For Adzusa bows
> That growest by the ferry—
> The ferry of Uji !
>   *   *   *
> In my heart I thought
> To cut thee,
> In my heart I thought
> To take thee,
> But at the bottom,
> Of my lord I bethought me,
> But at the top,
> Of thy spouse I bethought me.
> There I thought pitifully,
> Here I thought mournfully—
> Uncut I leave thee,
>   O thou Mayumi tree
>   For Adzusa bows ! 2

XI. 5.

---

1 The asterisks represent an untranslatable pillow-word. See Ch. K, p. 255.

2 Mayumi is the Euonymus. Adzusa is the Catalpa, a tree suitable for making bows. It has no particular meaning here. There is much differ-

So he was buried at Mount Nara. Afterwards the Prince Imperial built a palace at Uji, wherein he dwelt. Moreover in consequence of his ceding the Dignity to Oho-sazaki no Mikoto, he remained for a long time without assuming the Imperial rank. Now three years passed during which the Imperial rank was vacant. Then there was a fisherman who brought a mat-basket of fresh fish, which he offered as a present at the Uji Palace. The Prince Imperial commanded the fisherman, saying :—" I am not the Emperor," and sent him away, telling him to present it at Naniha. Oho-sazaki no Mikoto also sent him away, telling him to present it at Uji. Hereupon the fisherman's mat-basket became putrid on his journeys back and forward. So he sent it away again and procured other fresh fish, which he presented, and which were declined as on the previous day. The fresh fish again became putrid. The fisherman was grieved at his frequent returning, so he flung away the fresh fish and wept. Therefore the proverbial saying, " There is a fisherman who weeps on account of his own things," which had its origin in this.

The Prince Imperial said :—" I know that the Prince, my elder brother, is not to be moved from his resolution. Why then should I prolong my life and give trouble to the Empire ? " So he died by his own hand. Then Oho-sazaki no Mikoto, hearing of the Prince Imperial's death, was greatly shocked, XI. 6. and hastening from Naniha arrived at the Palace of Uji. Now three days had passed since the Prince Imperial's death. Oho-sazaki no Mikoto beat his breast, wept aloud, and knew not what to do. He loosed out his hair, and bestriding the corpse, called upon him thrice, saying :—" Oh, my younger brother, the Imperial Prince ! " In course of time he came to life, raised himself up, and remained in a sitting posture. Hereupon Oho-sazaki no Mikoto addressed the Heir Apparent, saying :—" Oh, what grief ! Oh, what regret ! Why didst thou pass away of thine own accord ? If the dead had any

ence of opinion among native commentators as to the meaning of this poem. It would seem as if the Prince, having thrown his brother overboard, could hardly claim much credit for clemency. But probably this is a genuine ancient poem, which the author has inserted here without much regard to fitness. The asterisks represent the untranslatable pillow-word Chihay-bito, an epithet of Uji.

knowledge, what would the late Emperor think of me?" So the Prince Imperial addressed the Prince his elder brother, saying:—"It is the command of Heaven. Who may stay it? If I should go to the place where the Emperor is, I will tell him of all the Prince, my elder brother's wisdom, and also of my abdication. But the sage Prince must surely be fatigued after the long and hurried journey which he undertook on hearing of my death." So he presented to him the Imperial Princess Yata,[1] his younger sister by the same mother, saying:— "Though she is unworthy of thy nuptials, she may in some small measure serve to be entered in the number of the side Courts." So he lay down again in his coffin and died.

Hereupon Oho-sazaki no Mikoto put on plain unbleached garments and began mourning for him, and his lamentation was exceedingly pathetic. He was buried on the top of the hill of Uji.

1st year, Spring, 1st month, 3rd day. Oho-sazaki no Mikoto A.D. 313. assumed the Imperial Dignity. The Empress was honoured with the title of Grand Empress. He made his capital at Naniha. It was called the Palace of Takatsu. The Palace enclosure and buildings were not plastered, the gable rafters XI. 7. and ridgepoles, the posts and pillars were devoid of ornament; the covering of thatch was not evenly trimmed.[2] This was that he might not delay the season of agricultural operations for the sake of his own personal caprices.

Before this time, on the day that the Emperor was born, an owl entered the parturition house. The next morning the Emperor Homuda called to him the Prime Minister Takechi no Sukune, and addressed him, saying:—"What may this portend?" The Prime Minister answered and said:—"It is a lucky omen. Moreover yesterday when thy servant's wife was in labour, a wren entered the parturition house. This also is strange!" Hereupon the Emperor said:—"Now our child and the Prime Minister's child have been born on the same day.

---

[1] She was also a daughter of the late Emperor. This shows that marriages of sisters *by the father's side only* were allowed. The Prince Imperial was able to give his sister by the mother's side in marriage. He would have had no control over his sisters by the father's side only.

[2] It should be remembered that at this period every Mikado built himself a new palace in a new locality.

In the case of both there are omens. This is an indication from Heaven. Let us take the names of these birds, and each exchanging them, call our children after them as a covenant to future generations." So he took the name "wren" (sazaki) and called the Prince Imperial by it, saying:—"The Imperial Prince Oho-sazaki."[1] And he took the name "owl" (Dzuku) and called the Prime Minister's child by it, saying:—"Dzuku

XI. 8. no Sukune." He was the first ancestor of the Omi of Heguri.

This year was the year Midzunoto Tori (10th) of the Cycle.

A.D. 314. 2nd year, Spring, 3rd month, 8th day. Iha no hime no Mikoto was appointed Empress. She was the mother of the Emperor Ohi-ne[2] Iza-ho-wake, of the Imperial Prince Suminohe no Nakatsu, of the Emperor Midzu-ha-wake, and of the Emperor Wo-asa-tsu-ma-waku-go no Sukune. Another consort, Kaminaga-hime of Hiuga, bore to him the Imperial Prince Ohokusaka and the Imperial Princess Hatahi.

A.D. 316. 4th year, Spring, 2nd month, 6th day. The Emperor addressed his ministers, saying:—"We ascended a lofty tower and looked far and wide, but no smoke arose in the land. From this we gather that the people are poor, and that in the houses there are none cooking their rice. We have heard that in the reigns of the wise sovereigns of antiquity, from every one was heard the sound of songs hymning their virtue, in every house there was the ditty, 'How happy are we.' But now when we observe the people, for three years past, no voice of

XI. 9. eulogy is heard; the smoke of cooking has become rarer and rarer. By this we know that the five grains[3] do not come up, and that the people are in extreme want. Even in the Home provinces[4] there are some who are not supplied; what must it be in the provinces outside of our domain?"

3rd month, 21st day. The following decree was issued:—

---

[1] I have elsewhere suggested that the name of the Emperor Oho-sazaki was a posthumous title given him owing to the great size of the mound (sasagi) under which he is buried near Sakai. And although there is much to be said on the other side, I am not sure that this may not after all be correct. The difference in spelling between sasagi and sazaki is immaterial.

[2] Ohi-ne or Oho-ye means great-elder-brother. It is hardly a name.

[3] Hemp, millet, rice, wheat and barley, pulse.

[4] The territory round the capital ruled immediately by the Emperor. This is a Chinese phrase, not properly applicable to Japan at this period.

" From this time forward, for the space of three years, let forced labour be entirely abolished, and let the people have rest from toil." From this day forth his robes of state and shoes did not wear out, and none were made. The warm food and hot broths did not become sour or putrid, and were not renewed. He disciplined his heart and restrained his impulses so that he discharged his functions without effort.

Therefore the Palace enclosure fell to ruin and was not rebuilt; the thatch decayed, and was not repaired; the wind and rain entered by the chinks and soaked the coverlets; the starlight filtered through the decayed places and exposed the bed-mats. After this the wind and rain came in due season,[1] the five grains produced in abundance. For the space of three autumns the people had plenty, the praises of his virtue filled the land, and the smoke of cooking was also thick.   XI. 10.

7th year, Summer, 4th month, 1st day. The Emperor was A.D. 319. on his tower, and looking far and wide, saw smoke arising plentifully. On this day he addressed the Empress, saying :— " We are now prosperous. What can there be to grieve for ? " The Empress answered and said :—" What dost thou mean by prosperity ? " The Emperor said :—" It is doubtless when the smoke fills the land, and the people freely attain to wealth." The Empress went on to say :—" The Palace enclosure is crumbling down, and there are no means of repairing it ; the buildings are dilapidated so that the coverlets are exposed. Can this be called prosperity ? " The Emperor said :—" When Heaven establishes a Prince, it is for the sake of the people. The Prince must therefore make the people the foundation. For this reason the wise sovereigns of antiquity, if a single one of their subjects was cold and starving, cast the responsibility on themselves. Now the people's poverty is no other than Our poverty ; the people's prosperity is none other than Our prosperity. There is no such thing as the people's being prosperous and yet the Prince in poverty."[2]

---

[1] The notion that the virtues of the Emperor have a direct influence on the weather is, of course, Chinese.

[2] This whole episode is the composition of some one well acquainted with Chinese literature. The sentiments are throughout characteristically Chinese, and in several cases whole sentences are copied verbatim from Chinese works.

U

Autumn, 8th month, 9th day. For the Imperial Prince Ohine Izaho-wake there was established the Mibu Be,[1] and again for the Empress there was established the Katsuraki Be.[2]

9th month. The provinces, without exception, petitioned, saying:—" Three years have now elapsed since forced labour was altogether remitted. The Palace buildings have therefore become decayed, and the Treasury empty. The black-headed

XI. 11. people have now abundance, and remnants are not picked up. Therefore in the villages there are no men without wives or women without husbands, in the houses there is store of spare provisions. If at such a time there was no payment of taxes with which to repair the Palace buildings, we fear that we should incur guilt in the sight of Heaven." The Emperor, however, continued to be patient, and would not grant their petition.

A.D. 322. 10th year, Winter, 10th month. Forced labour for the building of a Palace was imposed for the first time. Hereupon the people, without superintendence, supporting the aged and leading by the hand the young, transported timber, carried baskets[3] on their backs, and worked their hardest without distinction of night or day, vying with one another in the construction. In this manner, ere long the Palace buildings were every one completed. Therefore up to the present day he is styled the Sage Emperor.

A.D. 323. 11th year, Summer, 4th month, 16th day.. The Emperor commanded his ministers, saying:—" Viewing this land, the moors and marshes extend far and wide, and the cultivated fields are few and rare. Moreover, the river waters spread out to each side, so that the lower streams flow sluggishly. Should there

---

[1] This Be is also called the Nibu Be. There are several places in Japan of this name. It was originally the group of peasants whose duty it was to provide wet nurses, etc., for infant princes. See Ch. K., p. 268, and Moto-wori in " Kojikiden," xxxv. 12.

[2] The " Kojiki" says that these two Be were instituted as " miōdai " of the Prince and the Empress, i.e. in order to perpetuate their memory, the Be in such cases taking the name of the person or of his or her residence. The last explanation might apply to the Empress, but it is not clear how the name Mibu could perpetuate the memory of this Prince.

[3] Of earth.

happen to be continuous rains, the tide from the sea flows up against them so that one may ride in boats through the villages : and the highways, too, are covered with mud. Therefore do ye our ministers examine this together, and having ascertained the source of the divergence, make a channel for them to the sea, and, staying the contrary flow (of the tide), preserve the fields and houses."

Winter, 10th month. The plain north of the Palace was excavated, and the water from the south diverted into the Western Sea. Therefore that water was called by the name Hori-ye.[1]

Moreover, in order to prevent the overflowing of the Northern river the Mamuta embankment was constructed. At this time there were two parts of the construction which gave way and could not be stopped up. Then the Emperor had a dream in which he was admonished by a God, saying :—" There is a man of Musashi named Koha-kubi[2] and a man of Kahachi named Koromo no ko,[3] the Muraji of Mamuta. Let these two men be sacrificed to the River-God, and thou wilt surely be enabled to close the gaps." So he sought for these two men, and having found them, sacrificed them to the River-God. Hereupon Koha-kubi wept and lamented, and plunging into the water, died. So that embankment was completed. Koromo no ko, however, took two whole calabashes, and standing over the water which could not be dammed, plunged the two calabashes into the mid-stream and prayed, saying :—" O thou River-God, who hast sent the curse (to remove which) I have now come hither as a sacrifice. If thou dost persist in thy desire to have me, sink these calabashes and let them not rise to the surface. Then shall I know that thou art a true God, and will enter the water of my own accord. But if thou canst not sink the calabashes, I shall, of course, know that thou art a false God, for whom, why should I spend my life in vain ? " Hereupon a whirlwind arose suddenly which drew with it the calabashes and tried to submerge them in the water. But the calabashes,

XI. 12.

---

[1] Excavated estuary, or canal. [2] Strong-neck.
[3] Garment-child. These are personal names. Such names are in the original put after titles, but I have reversed this order, in accordance with European practice.

dancing on the waves, would not sink, and floated far away over the wide waters. In this way that embankment was completed, although Koromo no ko did not die. Accordingly XI. 13. Koromo no ko's cleverness saved his life. Therefore the men of that time gave a name to these two places, calling them " Kohakubi's Gap " and " Koromo no ko's Gap."

This year men of Silla came to the Court with tribute, and were made to labour at this public work.

A.D. 324. 12th year, Autumn, 7th month, 3rd day. The Land of Koryö sent tribute of iron shields and iron targets.

8th month, 10th day. The Koryö guests were entertained at Court. On this day the ministers and functionaries were assembled and made to shoot at the iron shields and targets presented by Koryö. Nobody could pierce the targets except Tatebito no Sukune, the ancestor of the Omi of Ikuba,[1] who shot at the iron targets and pierced them. Then the guests from Koryö, when they saw this, were struck with awe by his excellent skill in archery, and, standing up together, did obeisance to the Emperor. The next day the Emperor commended Tatebito no Sukune and gave him a title, calling him Ikuba no Toda no Sukune. On the same day a title was given to Sukune no Omi, the ancestor of the Miyakko of Ohase, and he was called Sakashi-nokori[2] no Omi.

Winter, 10th month. The Great Canal was dug in the district of Kurikuma in Yamashiro for the irrigation of the rice-fields. By this means the peasants of that district had always years of abundance.

A.D. 325. 13th year, Autumn, 9th month. Now for the first time official granaries were established at Mamuta. The Usu-me[3] Be was accordingly instituted.

Winter, 10th month. The Pond of Wani[4] was made. In XI. 14. the same month the Yokono Embankment was constructed.

A.D. 326. 14th year, Winter, 11th month. A bridge was made at the Wikahi ferry. It was this place which was called Wo-bashi.[5] In this year a highway was constructed and laid down within the capital from the South Gate extending in a straight line as

---

[1] Tatebito means shield-man, and Ikuba, target.
[2] Clever-remainder. [3] Millers. [4] In Kahachi.
[5] Small-bridge.

far as the village of Tajihi. Moreover, a great canal was dug in Konku[1] by which the water of the Ishikaha River was brought to irrigate the four waste plains of Upper Suzuka and Lower Suzuka, Upper Toyora and Lower Toyora. By bringing these under cultivation there were gained more than 40,000 K'iüng[2] of rice-land. Therefore the peasants of those places enjoyed abundance, and there was no longer the plague of bad years.

16th year, Autumn, 7th month, 1st day. The Emperor, indicating Kuhada no Kugahime, a lady of the Palace, to his personal attendants, said :—" It is our desire to bestow affection on this damsel, but, harassed by the Empress's jealousy, we have not been able to become united to her. Many years have XI. 15 passed. Why should she waste her years of bloom ? " So he made a song, saying :—

> Who will nourish
> The daughter of the Omi
> That sweeps along the bottom of the water ?[3]

Then Hayamachi, the ancestor of the Miyakko of the province of Harima, advanced alone and made a song, saying :—

> I, Hayamachi of Harima,
> (Where the dreadful tides are)
> Though full of awe,
> Like rocks tumbling down,
> I will nourish her.[4]

That same day Kugahime was given to Hayamachi. On the evening of the next day Hayamachi went to Kugahime's house. Now Kugahime would not comply with his wishes, but he persisted in approaching the curtained space. Then Kugahime

---

[1] In Kahachi.

[2] A Chinese measure of land equal to 100 mo, or more than fifteen English acres. This exact number of K'iüng occurs in a Chinese book of the Han period as the extent of land reclaimed by a similar operation.

[3] The last line is a makura kotoba not in the least suitable as an epithet of Omi, a minister. But Omi is somewhat like ami, a net, for which it is satisfactory enough. The text is doubtful.

[4] This stanza is in the ordinary 31-syllable metre, and the previous one in the same, minus the first two lines. The second line is a makura kotoba.

said :—" Thy handmaiden will end her years husbandless. How can she become my Lord's wife?" Now the Emperor, when he heard this, wished to accomplish Hayamachi's desires, so he sent Kugahime along with Hayamachi to Kuhada. But Kugahime straightway became ill and died on the journey. Therefore there is to this day the tomb of Kugahime.

A.D. 329.   17th year.   Silla did not attend the Court with tribute.

Autumn, 9th month. Toda no Sukune, ancestor of the Omi of Ikuba, and Sakashi-nokori no Omi, ancestor of the Miyakko of Ohase, were sent to inquire the reason of the failure to send tribute. Hereupon the Silla people were afraid, and

XI. 16. presented 1460 pieces of tribute, fine silks, and miscellaneous objects of all kinds—in all eighty ship-loads.

A.D. 334.   22nd year, Spring, 1st month. The Emperor addressed the Empress, saying :—" I have taken to me the Imperial Princess Yata, and am about to make her my concubine." But the Empress would not allow it. Hereupon the Emperor made a song, in which he besought the Empress, saying :—

> As a means of raising up
> Dear ones :
> As a spare bowstring
> To supply a vacancy
> I would place (her) along with (thee).

The Empress made a song in reply, saying :—

> In the case of garments
> To double them is well,
> But my Lord who would set in a row
> The couches of night—
> I wonder if he is wise.

The Emperor again made a song, saying :—

> Like the shore of Narabi [1]
> Of Cape Naniha
> That projects (into the sea)
> It must have been solely to be thy comrade
> That that child came into being.

---

[1] Narabi means to be associated with, to be a companion.

The Empress made a song in reply, saying :—

> Like the summer insect,
> The insect that seeks the fire
> Wearing double garments,[1]
> That the palace precinct should be thus,
> Nay ! it is not good.[2]

The Emperor again made a song, saying :—

> Even the traveller,
> Who with unshared tears
> Toils over the little pass of Hika
> In Asatsuma[3]—
> Well for him had he a companion !

The Empress finally refused her consent. Therefore she was silent, and answered not again.

30th year, Autumn, 9th month, 11th day. The Empress made an excursion to the land of Kii. She went as far as Cape[4] Kumano, and was coming back with leaves of the mit-suna,[5] which she had gathered there. On this day the Emperor, espying the Empress's absence, wedded the Imperial Princess Yata, and placed her in the Palace. Now the Empress, when she arrived at the Naniha ferry, heard that the Emperor had become united to the Imperial Princess Yata, and was very wroth. She flung into the sea the mitsuna leaves which she had gathered, and would not land. Wherefore the men of that day called the sea where the leaves were scattered Kashiha no Watari, or the Kashiha ferry. Now the Emperor, unaware that the Empress was angry and would not land, went in person to the Great Harbour,[6] and while awaiting the Empress's ship, made a song, saying : —

---

[1] Wings ?   [2] The meaning is here somewhat doubtful.
[3] Asatsuma is the name of a mountain in Yamato. It means "morning-wife."
[4] This is properly not a cape, but only a spur of a hill.
[5] In the original mitsuna-kashiha. Kashiha is the Quercus dentata, a kind of evergreen oak, the leaves of which were used as drinking-cups. But this term was also applied to any leaves used for this purpose. Here the leaves of another tree—the mitsuna—seem to be intended. Chamberlain makes it the aralia. See Ch. K., pp. 248-273.
[6] No doubt Naniha or Osaka.

> Ye men of Naniha,
> Haul along the bell-(hung) ship,
> Soaked as to your loins,
> Haul along that ship.
> Haul along the great august ship.

Now the Empress did not anchor at the Great Harbour, but drew onwards again, and, ascending the river, went round by way of Yamashiro, in the direction of Yamato.[1] The next day the Emperor sent an attendant named Toriyama to bring the Empress back, and made a song, saying :—

> In Yamashiro
> Overtake her, Toriyama.
> Overtake her, overtake her,
> My beloved spouse—
> I wonder wilt thou overtake and join her.

The Empress would not come back, but continued her journey as far as the River of Yamashiro, where she made a song, saying :—

> Ascending the river—
> The River of Yamashiro —
> (Peak upon peak[2]—)
> As I ascend it,
> By the river bend
> There stands luxuriant
> (Less-than-a-hundred)[3]
> An eighty-leaved tree.
> Is it the Great Lord ?

So she crossed over Mount Nara, and looking on Katsuraki, she made a song, saying :—

> Going up to Miya,[4]
> As I ascend

---

[1] Ch. K., p. 276.

[2] Peak upon peak refers to yama, mountain, the first part of Yamashiro. It is a mere ornamental epithet.

[3] Less than a hundred is a makura-kotoba of eighty. The luxuriant tree, with its plentiful foliage, reminds her of the Emperor.

[4] Miya is probably short for Takamiya in the last line of the poem but one.

The River of Yamashiro
(—Peak upon peak—)
Nara I pass
Of fertile soil ;
Yamato I pass,
Shielded by its mountains ;
The land I long to see
Is Takamiya of Katsuraki,
For there is my home.[1]

Returning again to Yamashiro, she built a Palace on the
south side of the Hill of Tsutsuki, and dwelt there.

Winter, 10th month, 1st day. Kuchi no Omi, ancestor of
the Omi of Ikuba, was sent to fetch the Empress.

One version says :—" Kuchi no Omi, ancestor of the
Omi of Wani."

Now Kuchi no Omi went to the Palace of Tsutsuki, and
wished to have audience of the Empress, but she remained
silent and answered not. Then Kuchi no Omi prostrated himself before the Empress's hall, and remained there day and
night drenched by the rain and snow, and did not move.
Hereupon Kuchi no Omi's younger sister, Kuniyori-hime, who
was in the service of the Empress, and happened just then to
be in attendance upon her, saw her elder brother wet with the
rain, and shed tears and made a song, saying :—

In the Palace of Tsutsuki,
In Yamashiro,
When I see my elder brother
Delivering his message,
My eyes fill with tears.

Then the Empress addressed Kuniyori-hime, saying :—
" Why weepest thou ? " She answered and said :—" He that
lies prostrate in the courtyard and begs an audience is thy
handmaiden's elder brother. He is wet with the rain, and XI. 20.
does not flinch, but still lies prostrate in the hope of an audience of thee. This is why I weep and am sorrowful." Then
the Empress addressed her, saying:—" Tell thy elder brother
to return with all speed. I will never go back." Kuchi
accordingly returned, and made his report to the Emperor.

11th month, 7th day. The Emperor made a progress by

---

[1] Much of this poem is of doubtful interpretation. Compare Ch. K. p. 275.

river to Yamashiro. At this time there was a mulberry branch
floating down the stream.   The Emperor looked at the mulberry branch, and made a song, saying :—

> The mulberry tree [1]
>   *   *   *   *
> Which Iha [2] no hime
> Will not listen to even absently
> May not reach (the bank),
> But by the bends of the river
> It seems to go tossing on—
> Oh ! that mulberry tree !

On the next day the Imperial cortège arrived at the Palace
of Tsutsuki.   The Empress was sent for, but she refused to
appear before the Emperor.   Then the Emperor made a song,
saying :—

> Like the radishes [3] dug up
> With the wooden hoes
> Of the women of Yamashiro
> (Peak upon peak),
> { Purely, purely,
> { Clamorously, clamorously,
> Because thou hast spoken
> I have come hither
> Like the flourishing trees
> Which I look over at.

---

[1] Mulberry is ura-kuha.   In modern Japanese kuha alone means mulberry.
Ura also means heart, and as koha means hard, there seems an allusion
to the Empress's hard-heartedness.

The Emperor compares his condition to that of the mulberry branch
drifting down the stream, and finding no rest anywhere.   The metre is
irregular.

[2] Iha means rock.   It has here a makura-kotoba prefixed to it, viz.
tsuno-sahafu, creeper-clad, which is inappropriate to Iha, when taken as the
Empress's name, though suitable to it in its original meaning.

[3] Radishes are at this day a staple food of the Japanese.   When freshly
washed they look very white and clean.   The first four lines are a mere
introduction to saha-saha, i.e. purely, and the author immediately goes on
to exchange this meaning for another meaning of the same word, viz.,
.clamorously, by a play of words common in Japanese poetry.   The only
bond of connection between the first and second halves of the poem is this
double sense of saha-saha.   "The flourishing trees" represent the Emperor's brilliant suite.   The interpretation of this poem is more or less
conjectural.   Compare Ch. K., p. 279.

Again he made a song, saying:—

> Had I not had for my pillow
> Thine arm
> White as the whiteness of the roots
> Of the radishes dug up
> With the wooden hoes
> Of the women of Yamashiro
> (Peak upon peak),
> Then mightest thou say that thou knowest me not.

Then the Empress sent a message to the Emperor, saying: —" My lord has taken the Imperial Princess Yata and made her his concubine. Now I do not wish to be associated with the Princess as Consort." So she refused to enter his presence, and the Imperial carriage returned to the Palace. The Emperor hereupon resented the Empress's great indignation, but yet continued to love her.

31st year, Spring, 1st month, 15th day. Ohine-izaho-wake A.D. 343. no Mikoto was appointed Prince Imperial.

35th year, Summer, 6th month. The Empress Iha no hime A.D. 347. no Mikoto died in the Palace of Tsutsuki.

37th year, Winter, 11th month, 12th day. The Empress A.D. 349. was buried on Mount Nara.

38th year, Spring, 1st month, 6th day. The Imperial Princess A.D. 350. Yata was appointed Empress.

Autumn, 7th month. The Emperor and Empress dwelt in a high tower to escape from the heat. At this time there was heard every night from the moor of Toga the cry of deer with a musical, yet melancholy sound, so that a feeling of pity arose in them both. But when the interlune came, the cry of the deer XI. 22. was no longer heard. Hereupon the Emperor addressed the Empress, saying:—" This evening the deer does not bell. Wherefore is this?" " The next day, a Saheki Be of the district of Wina presented a basket. The Emperor caused a steward to make inquiry of him, saying:—" What is this basket?" The answer was, " A buck." He inquired—"A deer of what place?" and was told, "Of Toga moor." The Emperor considered that this basket [1] must be the deer which

---

[1] The basket is put for the contents (like the Latin sportula), and the word is used even when there may have been no basket at all.

had belled, and he accordingly addressed the Empress, saying:
—" We have been soothed in the anxious thoughts which have
of late possessed us by listening to the belling of a deer. Now
when the day or night, and the mountain or moor of the
deer which has been caught are considered, they correspond
to the deer which belled. It is true that that man was
not aware of our feelings of affection, and that it was by
chance that he came to take it. We nevertheless cannot
resist a feeling of resentment. It is therefore our wish that
the Saheki Be shall not approach the Imperial Palace."
So he made the officials remove his residence to Nuta in
Aki. He was the ancestor of the present Saheki Be of Nuta
in Aki.

There is a popular story that a long time ago there was a
man who went to Toga, and spent the night on the moor.
Now there were two deer which lay down beside him. When
it was on the point of cock-crow, the male deer addressed the
female, saying:—" This night I had a dream in which I saw
a white mist come down copiously and cover my body. What
may this portend?" The female deer answered and said :—
" If thou goest out, thou wilt certainly be shot by men and die,
and so thy body will be smeared with white salt to correspond
with the whiteness of the mist." Now the man who was
spending the night there wondered at this in his heart. Before
it was yet dawn, there came a hunter, who shot the male deer,
and killed it. Hence the proverbial saying of the men of that
day—" Even the belling male deer follows the interpretation
of a dream."

A.D. 352   40th year, Spring, 3rd month. The Emperor wished to take
to himself the Imperial Princess Medori [1] as concubine, and
made the Imperial Prince Hayabusa wake [2] his middle man.
Now the Imperial Prince Hayabusa secretly wedded her himself, and for a long time made no report of his mission. Hereupon the Emperor, not knowing that she had a husband, went
in person to the Imperial Princess Medori's chamber. At

XI. 23.

---

[1] Princess Medori was half-sister of the Emperor by a different mother, and
full sister of the Empress.

[2] Hayabusa wake was half-brother to both Princess Medori and the
Emperor by a different mother.

this time the Imperial Princess was weaving, and her women
made a song, saying :—

> The metal loom of Heaven—
> The everlasting—[1]
> The metal-loom where
> Medori is weaving
> Stuff for an august cloak
> For Hayabusa wake !

Upon this the Emperor saw that the Imperial Prince Hayabusa wake had secretly wedded her, and was angry. But out XI. 24.
of regard for what the Empress might say, and also from
respect for the principle which governs the relation of stem
and branches,[2] he was patient and did not punish him. Now
the Imperial Prince Hayabusa wake was lying down for a
little with his head pillowed on the Imperial Princess's knee.
Whereupon he addressed her, saying :—" Which is the swiftest,
the wren or the falcon ? "[3] She said, " The falcon." Then
the Imperial Prince said :—" That means that I shall be
first." The Emperor heard these words, and his wrath was
aroused again. At this time the Imperial Prince Hayabusa
wake's attendants made a song, saying :—

> The falcon
> Ascending to Heaven
> With soaring flight—
> Let him seize the wren
> On the top of the Tsuki trees.[4]

When the Emperor heard this song, he flew into a great
rage, and said :—" We were unwilling for a private cause of
hate to destroy one related to us, and we were patient. Why
should a private cause of quarrel be converted into a matter
which affects the State ? "

So he wished to kill the Imperial Prince Hayabusa wake.

---

[1] The word translated everlasting is hisakata, lit. long-hard, an epithet
involving a similar conception of the sky to our word " firmament." By
metal is probably meant " adorned with metal fittings."

[2] i.e. the head of the family and the junior members.

[3] Hayabusa means "falcon."

[4] In the original itsuki or idzuki. This the commentators explain as fifty
(i) tsuki trees. But how would "sacred (idzu) tree " do—in allusion to the
Emperor's rank ?

Now the Imperial Prince fled with the Imperial Princess Medori, intending to place her in the Shrine of Ise. Hereupon the Emperor, hearing that the Imperial Prince Hayabusa wake had run away, straightway sent Wofuna of the Honchi Be of Kibi and Aganoko, Atahe of Saheki in Harima, saying:—" Pursue them, and when you overtake them, slay them forthwith." Hereupon the Empress addressed the Emperor, saying:—" Truly the Imperial Princess Medori is liable to severe punishment. But when she is killed I hope her body may not be exposed." Accordingly he gave orders to Wofuna and his colleague not to take the Imperial Princess's leg-jewels or arm-jewels. Wofuna and his colleague pursued them as far as Uda, and closed on them at Mount Soni. Here they hid in the herbage, and escaping by only a little, fled hastily, and crossed the mountain. Then the Imperial Prince made a song, saying:—

> Even this mountain, steep
> As a ladder,
> When I cross over it
> With thee, my love,
> Seems a restful couch.

Hereupon Wofuna and the rest, seeing that they had escaped, followed after hastily, and when they came to the moor of Komoshiro in Ise, slew them. Then Wofuna and the others searched for the Imperial Princess's jewels, and took them from within her undergarments. So they buried the bodies of the Prince and Princess on the bank of the River Ihoki, and then made their report to the Emperor. The Empress caused inquiry to be made of Wofuna and the others, saying:—" Did you see the Imperial Princess's jewels?" They answered and said, "We did not see them."

That year during the month[1] of the festival of tasting the first rice on the day of the banquet, sake was given to the princesses and ladies of the inner and outer circle. Thereupon, on the hands of two women, viz., the wife of Waka-mori-yama, Kimi of the mountains of Afumi, and Ihasakihime, one of the Uneme,[2] there were entwined excellent jewels. The Empress,

---

[1] The 11th month.

[2] Probably for yone-me, i.e. rice-woman, women attendants of the palace. They were selected for their good looks.

observing that these jewels resembled those of the Imperial Princess Medori, straightway became suspicious, and commanded an official to inquire under what circumstances they had come by these jewels. They answered and said :—" They are the jewels of the wife of Aganoko, the Atahe of Saheki." So Aganoko, being interrogated, answered and said :—" On the day that the Imperial Princess was put to death I searched her and took them." So they were about to put Aganoko to death. But he offered to the Emperor all his private lands, and prayed to escape from death. Therefore his land was confiscated, and the death penalty remitted. On this account that land was called Tama-de.[1]

41st year, Spring, 3rd month. Ki no Tsuno no Sukune was sent to Pèkché. He was the first to distinguish the boundaries of provinces and districts, and to commit to writing in detail the productions of the soil in each locality. At this time Lord Chyu,[2] the grandson of the King of Pèkché, was disrespectful, and accordingly Ki no Tsuno no Sukune remonstrated with the King of Pèkché. The King of Pèkché was afraid, and binding Lord Chyu in iron chains, delivered him up in charge of Sotsuhiko. Now Lord Chyu, when he came to Japan, straightway ran away, and concealed himself in the house of Koroshi, Obito of Nishikori in Ishikaha, deceiving him by saying : — " The Empress has pardoned thy servant's offence. Therefore have I betaken myself to thee for maintenance." A long time after the Emperor ultimately forgave him his offence.[3]

43rd year, Autumn, 9th month, 1st day. Tsuchigura, Ahiko

A.D. 353.

XI. 27.

A.D. 355.

---

[1] i.e. the price of jewels.

[2] The original has 酒, i.e. sake. Chyu is the Corean pronunciation, but it is doubtful what his name really was.

[3] We are told above, p. 256, A.D. 272 of the " Nihongi " Chronology, that King Sinsă of Pĕkchè was disrespectful, and that Ki no Tsuno no Sukune and others were sent to call him to an account. At p. 257, A.D. 277, we hear of King Ahwa being disrespectful, and a Pèkché Prince being sent to Japan as a hostage in consequence. Sotsuhiko is a name which has already occurred (p. 242, A.D. 205 of the " Nihongi " Chronology) in connection with Corean matters. But, as shown above (p. 256), King Sinsă really died in 392, and was succeeded by Ahwa. I strongly suspect that we have in the present passage only another version of the same incident, and that all three versions are much antedated.

of Yosami, caught a strange bird and presented it to the
Emperor, saying :—"I am constantly spreading nets and
catching birds in them, but never before have I caught a bird
of this kind. I therefore thought it curious, and offer it to His
Majesty." The Emperor sent for Lord Chyu and, pointing to the
bird, said :—" What bird is this ? " Lord Chyu answered and
said :—" Birds of this kind are numerous in Pèkché. They can
be tamed so as to be quite obedient to man. Moreover they are
swift of flight and prey upon all kinds of birds. The common
people in Pèkché call them *Kuchi.*" So it was given to Lord
Chyu to be fed and tamed. In no long time he succeeded in
taming it. Lord Chyu accordingly fastened to its leg a soft
leather strap, and attached to its tail a small bell.[1] Then,
placing it on his forearm, he presented it to the Emperor. On
this day he went to the moor of Mozu and hunted. At this
time a large number of hen pheasants got up, and the falcon [2]
was let loose and made to catch them. It speedily caught
several tens of pheasants. In this month the Be of Taka-ama
(falcon-sweet) was first established. Therefore the men of that
time called the place where the falcon was brought up the
village of Taka-ama.

50th year, Spring, 3rd month, 5th day. A man of Kahachi
informed the Emperor, saying :—" A wild goose has laid an egg
on the Mamuta embankment." That same day a messenger was
sent to see. He said :—" It is true." The Emperor hereupon
made a song, in which he inquired of Takechi no Sukune,
saying :—

> O Aso of Uchi !
> *   *   *   * 3
> Thou, beyond all others,[4]
> A man distant of age—

---

[1] Fr. grêlot.

[2] The taka or goshawk. The hayabusa mentioned above is a smaller
bird, probably the peregrine falcon. The best hawks for hunting were
formerly imported to Japan from Corea.

[3] An untranslatable makura-kotoba comes in here.

[4] Takechi no Sukune's death is not mentioned in the " Nihongi." A later
authority says that he died in this year, having held office for 240 years, and
lived 295 (or 299) years. Another authority states that he died in the 55th
year of Nintoku Tennō, at the age of 280. Still another says that he died in

Thou, beyond all others,
A man long in the land—
Hast thou not heard
That a wild goose has laid an egg
In Akitsushima,
The land ol Yamato ? [1]

Takechi no Sukune made a song in reply, saying :—

Our great Lord
Who rules tranquilly,
Right is he, right is he
To ask me.
For in Akitsushima,
In the land of Yamato,
Never have I heard
That a wild goose has laid an egg.

53rd year.   Silla did not attend the Court with tribute.

5th month.   Takahase, ancestor of the Kimi of Ködzuke, was sent to ask the reason of the failure to send tribute.   On his way he took a white deer, and returning with it, presented it to the Emperor.   He then chose another day and started on his journey.   Shortly after, the Emperor sent in addition Takahase's younger brother Tamichi, and commanded him, saying :— " If Silla is recalcitrant, raise an army and invade that land." So he gave him chosen troops.   Silla raised an army and made opposition.   Now the Silla men offered battle daily.   But Tamichi made strong his barriers, and would not go out.   Now a Silla soldier who had been let out from the camp was taken prisoner.   So being questioned as to the condition of affairs, he answered, saying :—" There are mighty men, called the ' Hundred Thrusters,' [2] nimble and valorous, who always form the right van of the army.   Therefore if you observe this and attack the left, it will be routed."   Now Silla allowed the left to

A.D. 365.
XI. 29.

the 78th year of Nintoku Tennō's reign, which, as one account says that he was born in the 9th year of Keikō Tennō, would make him 312 years of age at his death.   It has been suggested that there were several persons of this name who succeeded each other as hereditary prime ministers.   But the simpler explanation is that the chronology at this period is wildly inaccurate, as there is plenty of other evidence to show.

[1]   See Ch. K., p. 283.   Wild geese do not nest in Japan.

[2]   It may be only one man of this name.

X

be vacant, and filled up the numbers of the right. Hereupon Tamichi, drawing up his picked cavalry,[1] attacked their left,

XI. 30. upon which the Silla troops were defeated. Accordingly letting go his men, he bore down on the enemy and slew several hundreds of them. So he took prisoners the people of four villages, with whom he returned to Japan.[2]

A.D. 367.   55th year. The Yemishi rebelled. Tamichi was sent to attack them. He was worsted by the Yemishi, and slain at the Harbour of Ishimi.[3] Now one of his followers obtained Tamichi's armlet and gave it to his wife, who embraced the armlet and strangled herself. When the men of that time heard of this they shed tears. After this the Yemishi again made an incursion and carried off some of the people. Accordingly they dug up Tamichi's tomb, upon which a great serpent started up with glaring eyes, and came out of the tomb. It bit the Yemishi, who were everyone affected by the serpent's poison, so that many of them died, and only one or two escaped. Therefore the men of that time said : "Although dead, Tamichi at last had his revenge. How can it be said that the dead have no knowledge ? "

A.D. 370.   58th year, Summer, 5th month. By the road which passes to the south of the grove of firs at Arehaka,[4] there suddenly sprang up two kunugi[5] trees, which joined over the road so that the ends of their branches met.

Winter, 10th month. The Land of Wu and the Land of Koryö together attended the Court with tribute.[6]

A.D. 372.   60th year, Winter, 10th month. The guardians of the

---

[1] I do not regard this as any proof that the Japanese had cavalry at this time. The author is, I think, only using a Chinese phrase which suggested itself to his memory.

[2] The "Tongkam" mentions descents by Japanese in 440 in which a number of Coreans were carried off.

[3] In Kadzusa. This is the traditional kana for 伊 寺. How the last character came to be read *Shimi* is not clear.

[4] Arehaka means ruined tumulus. The well-known temple of Tennōji at Osaka now stands here.

[5] Quercus serrata, Hepburn.

[6] It is not to be supposed that China or even Koryö ever sent "tribute" to Japan. Presents were no doubt exchanged, which both sides very likely represented to their subjects as "tribute."

Shiratori misasagi[1] were told off as labourers on the public works. Now the Emperor approached the place of the works. Hereupon Meki, one of the guardians of the misasagi, became suddenly changed into a white deer, and ran away. Upon this the Emperor commanded, saying :—" This misasagi has always been empty, and therefore I meant to abolish its guardians and for the first time to employ them as labourers. But now that I see this portent, I am filled with profound awe. Let not the guardians of the misasagi be disturbed." So he gave them to the Hashi no Muraji.[2]

XI. 31.

62nd year, Summer, 5th month. The Governor[3] of the province of Tōtomi presented a memorial, saying :—" There is a great tree which has floated down the Ohowigaha until it was stopped in a bend of the river. It is ten girths[4] in size. It has one stem which divides into two at the extremity." Now Akoko, Atahe of Yamato, was sent to make a boat of it. He conveyed it by way of the Southern Sea, and brought it to the Harbour of Naniha, where it was enrolled among the number of the Imperial vessels.

A.D. 374.

This year the Imperial Prince Nukada no Ohonakatsu hiko hunted in Tsuke. Now the Imperial Prince, looking down over the moor from a mountain-top, espied something in shape like a hut. So he sent a messenger to look at it. The messenger returned and said :—" It is a muro." Accordingly he sent for Ohoyama-nushi, the Inaki of Tsuke, and inquired of him, saying :—" That thing which is on the moor—what kind of muro is it ? " He informed him, saying :—" It is an ice-muro." The Imperial Prince said :—" How is the ice stored ? Moreover, for what is it used ? " He said :—" The ground is excavated to a depth of over ten feet. The top is then covered with a roof of thatch. A thick layer of reed grass is then spread, upon which the ice is laid. The months of summer have passed and yet it has not melted. As to its use—when the hot months

XI. 32.

---

[1] The tomb, or rather cenotaph, of Yamato dake.
[2] Who were charged with matters connected with the misasagi. Se above, p. 181.
[3] Provincial governors 國 司 are now mentioned for the first time.
[4] The character rendered "girth" is 圍, which is a measure of half a cubit according to some, of three feet by others. However, a ten-girth tree is merely a loose expression for a large tree.

come it is placed in water or sake and thus used." The Imperial Prince straightway brought some of that ice, and presented it to the Palace. The Emperor was delighted with it, and from that time forward it became the rule always to store up ice from the last month of winter until the second month of spring when the ice melts.

A.D. 377.   65th year. In the province of Hida there was a man called Sukuna, who was so formed that on one trunk he had two faces. The faces were turned away from each other. The crowns met, and there was no nape of the neck. Each had hands and feet. There were knees, but no popliteal spaces or heels.

XI. 33.   He was strong and nimble. He carried swords on his right and on his left side, and used bow and arrow with all four hands at once. On this account he was disobedient to the Imperial command, and took a pleasure in plundering the people. Hereupon the Emperor sent Naniha-neko Take-furu-kuma, ancestor of the Omi of Wani, who put him to death.

A.D. 379.   67th year, Winter, 10th month, 5th day. The Emperor made a progress to the plain of Ishitsu in Kahachi, where he fixed upon a site for a misasagi.

18th day. The building of the misasagi was commenced. On this day there was a deer which suddenly got up in the moor and ran in among the labourers, where it lay down and died. Now, its sudden death appearing strange, they looked to see where it was hurt, upon which a shrike came out of its ear and flew away. Accordingly they looked into its ear, and found that the skin was all bitten off. So this was the reason why they called that place the plain of Mozu no mimi.[1]

This year, at a fork of the River Kahashima, in the central division of the Province of Kibi, there was a great water-snake which harassed the people. Now when travellers were passing that place on their journey, they were surely affected by its poison, so that many died. Hereupon Agata-mori,[2] the ances-

---

[1] Shrike-ear. This plain lies inland from Sakai, near Osaka. The misasagi is still intact, and is, perhaps, the largest of its kind in Japan. Richiu Tennō and Hanzei Tennō are buried one on each side of Nintoku.

[2] District-warden.

tor of the Omi of Kasa, a man of fierce temper and of great bodily strength, stood over the pool of the river-fork and flung into the water three whole calabashes, saying :—" Thou art XI. 34. continually belching up poison and therewithal plaguing travellers. I will kill thee, thou water-snake. If thou canst sink these calabashes, then will I take myself away, but if thou canst not sink them, then will I cut up thy body." Now the water-snake changed itself into a deer and tried to draw down the calabashes, but the calabashes would not sink. So with upraised sword he entered the water and slew the water-snake. He further sought out the water-snake's fellows. Now the tribe of all the water-snakes filled a cave in the bottom of the pool. He slew them every one, and the water of the river became changed to blood. Therefore that water was called " The pool of Agata-mori." [1]

At this time pestilential vapours arose more and more, and there were one or two cases of rebellion. Hereupon [2] the Emperor, rising early in the morning and going to bed (late) at night, lightened the taxes, reduced the imposts, and so was generous to the people. He dispensed virtue and practised kindness, therewithal encouraging the indigent. He showed sympathy for the dead, and inquired after the sick, providing for the orphan and the widow. In this way the decrees of his Government were diffused into wide operation, and the Empire was at peace, so that for over twenty years nothing untoward happened.

87th year, Spring, 1st month, 16th day. The Emperor A.D. 399. died.

---

[1] The traditional kana rendering of the Chinese character translated "water-snake" is midzuchi. Midzu is water, and chi a honorific term meaning "elder." Midzuchi means indifferently water-snake or water-god, the two ideas being intimately associated in the Japanese mind. Dennys, in his " Folk Lore of China," quotes from the *North China Herald* as follows :—" The River-God is in every case (where the waters of inundations were abated by them) a small water-snake, which popular fancy has converted into a deity." The poisonous breath of serpents is an article of popular faith in many countries.

[2] From " Hereupon " down to " operation " is taken almost verbatim from a Chinese book.

Winter, 10th month, 7th day. He was buried in the misa-sagi on Mozu moor.[1]

---

[1] The Emperor's age is not given here. The "Kojiki" makes him eighty-three years of age at his death. Others say 110. But if we allow him to have been at least sixteen when he fell in love with Kami-naga-hime (see above, p. 259) in A.D. 282, he cannot have been less than 132 at the time of his death.

BOOK XII.

THE EMPEROR IZA-HO-WAKE.

(*RICHIU*[1] *TENNŌ.*)

THE Emperor Iza-ho-wake was the eldest son of the Emperor Ohosazaki. His mother's name was Iha no hime no Mikoto. She was the daughter of Katsuraki no Sotsuhiko. He was made Prince Imperial in Spring, the 1st month of the 31st year of the reign of the Emperor Ohosazaki. He was then fifteen years of age. The Emperor Ohosazaki died in Spring, the 1st month of the 87th year of his reign.

After the period of mourning, and in the interval before he assumed the exalted Dignity, he wished to take Kurohime,[2] the daughter of the Hata no Yashiro no Sukune, to him as concubine. The wedding presents[3] having been already given, he sent the Imperial Prince Nakatsu of Suminoye to give notice of the lucky day. Now Prince Nakatsu having assumed the elder Prince's name, by this means seduced Kurohime. On this night the Imperial Prince Nakatsu[4] came away, having forgotten his wrist-bells in Kurohime's house. On the following night, the Heir to the Throne, not knowing that the Imperial Prince Nakatsu had himself seduced her, went there. He entered the chamber, drew aside the curtain, and sat down upon the jewel-couch. Then there was a sound of bells at the head of the couch. The Heir wondering at this, inquired of

---

[1] That is, " He who treads in the middle" (the right path).
[2] Black lady.　　　　　　　　[3] Probably a trait of Chinese manners.
[4] Nakatsu means " of the middle," tsu in this and similar words being the genitive particle.

Kurohime, saying :—" What bells are these ? " She answered
and said :—" Are they not the bells which thou didst bring last
night ? Wherefore dost thou ask thy handmaiden any more
about them ? " The Heir naturally concluded that the Imperial Prince Nakatsu had assumed his name and by this
means seduced Kurohime, so he retired in silence.

Now the Imperial Prince Nakatsu, fearing that trouble would
come of this, was about to kill the Heir to the Throne, and
secretly raising a force, surrounded his Palace. Then Heguri
no Tsuka no Sukune, Mononobe no Ohomahe no Sukune, and
Achi no Omi, the ancestor of the Aya no Atahe, these three
men, gave information to the Heir, but he would not believe
them.

> One version says :—" The Heir was drunk and would
> not get up."

Therefore the three men assisted the Heir, and making him
mount on horseback, caused him to escape.

> One account says :—" Ohomahe no Sukune took the
> Heir to the Throne in his arms and mounted him on a
> horse."

The Imperial Prince Nakatsu, not knowing that he was absent,
set fire to his Palace. The fire lasted all night without being
extinguished. When the Heir arrived at the Hanifu Hill in
the Province of Kahachi he became sober, and looking back to
Naniha, he saw the blaze of fire. He was greatly alarmed, and
fled hastily by way of Ohosaka in the direction of Yamato.
When he got as far as Mount Asuka, he met a girl at the
entrance of the mountain, of whom he inquired, saying :—
" Are there any men on this mountain ? " She answered and
said :—" This mountain is full of many armed men. Thou
hadst better go round and cross over by the Tagima road."
Hereupon the Heir thought to himself:—" By listening to the
words of this girl I have been enabled to escape calamity." So
he made a song, saying :—

> At Ohosaka,
> The girl that I met—
> When I asked her the way,
> She said not, "right on,"
> She said, " Tagima way."

So he turned aside again, and having raised the troops of that district, made them follow him, and crossed over by way of Mount Tatsuta. At this time several tens of armed men came in pursuit of him. The Heir, looking at them from a distance, said :—" Who are those men who are coming ? And why is their pace so hurried ? Can they be an enemy ?" Accordingly they hid themselves on the mountain, and waited. When they approached, one man was sent to inquire of them, saying:—" What men are ye, and whither go ye ?" They answered and said :—" We are fishermen of Nojima in Ahaji. XII. 4. Hamako, the Muraji of Adzumi,[1] on behalf of the Imperial Prince Nakatsu [One account says Sato-tomo, Muraji of Adzumi], has sent us in pursuit of the Heir to the Throne." Hereupon he brought out the troops which were in ambush, and surrounding them, captured[2] them every one. At this time Akoko, the Atahe of Yamato, who from the first had loved Prince Nakatsu, and was privy to his conspiracy, secretly assembled choice troops to the number of several hundred at Kurusu in Kakibami, and on behalf of Prince Nakatsu withstood the Heir. Now the Heir, not knowing that he was beset with troops, went out for several ri from the mountain. He was stopped by a large force of armed men, and was unable to advance. So he sent a messenger and inquired of them, saying :—" What men are ye ?" They answered and said :— " Akoko, Atahe of Yamato." And in their turn they questioned the messenger, saying :—" Who has sent thee ?" He said :— " The Prince Imperial has sent me." Then Akoko, fearing lest there might be a numerous army there, said to the messenger :—" Information has reached me that something unusual has happened to the Prince Imperial, and in order to assist him I am waiting upon him with this force that I have prepared." The Heir, however, doubted his intentions, and tried to kill him. Whereupon Akoko was afraid, and offering as a present his own younger sister Hinohime,[3] through her begged that his capital offence might be pardoned. He was pardoned

---

[1] See above, p. 256, where his ancestor was made prefect of the fishermen.

[2] As usual, " captured " stands for " slew."

[3] The Princess of the Sun.

accordingly. It was prolably at this time that the custom began of the Atahe of Yamato sending tribute of ladies of the Palace.[1]

The Heir took up his abode in the shrine of Furu no Iso no Kami. Hereupon the Imperial Prince Midzuha wake, discovering the absence of the Heir, sought him out and followed him. The Heir, however, suspected the intentions of the Prince, his younger brother, and would not send for him. Then the Imperial Prince Midzuha wake sent a message to the Heir, saying:—" Thy servant has not a black heart. Only, distressed at the absence of the Heir, he has come hither." Hereupon the Heir sent a message to the Prince, his younger brother, saying:—" I have escaped hither alone in fear of the rebellion of Prince Nakatsu. Why should I not suspect thee? So long as the Imperial Prince Nakatsu lives his sole endeavour will still be to do me a mischief, and I wish sooner or later to get rid of him. Therefore, if thou hast really not a black heart, return again to Naniha, and kill the Imperial Prince Nakatsu. After that I will see thee." The Imperial Prince Midzuha wake represented to the Heir, saying :—" Is not the Great Man's[2] anxiety excessive? At present the Imperial Prince Nakatsu's unprincipled conduct is detested by the officials and the people alike. His own household, moreover, are against him, and think him a brigand. He stands alone, and there is nobody whom he can consult. I knew of his rebellion, but I had not received the commands of the Heir, and was therefore merely indignant at it. Now that I have received an order, why should I make any difficulty about killing the Imperial Prince Nakatsu? All that I fear is that when I have killed him thou mayest still suspect thy servant.[3] I pray that a trusty person may be selected, and I desire that he should make clear my loyalty." Accordingly the Heir joined to him Dzuku no Sukune and so despatched him. Hereupon the Imperial Prince Midzuha wake made lament, saying :—" The Heir and the Imperial Prince Nakatsu are both my elder brothers : which shall I obey? Which shall I oppose? If, however, I destroy the unprincipled and adhere to the righteous, who can suspect

---

[1] Uneme. [2] A Chinese honorific for " you."
[3] Ch. K., p. 289.

me ?" So he went to Naniha and observed the state of things with the Imperial Prince Nakatsu. The Imperial Prince Nakatsu, thinking that the Heir had fled away and disappeared, had made no preparation. Now he had a Hayato [1] named Sashihire. Prince Midzuha wake sent for Sashihire secretly and tampered with him, saying :—" If thou wilt kill the Imperial Prince for me, then will I surely reward thee liberally." So he took off his coat and trousers of brocade and gave them to him. Sashihire, relying on his words of allurement, all by himself took his spear, and watching the time when the Imperial Prince Nakatsu went into the privy, stabbed him to death, and entered the service of Prince Midzuha wake. Hereupon Dsuku no Tsukune made representation to the Imperial Prince Midzuha wake, saying :—" Sashihire has killed his own lord for the sake of another, and although for us he has done a great service, yet towards his own lord his conduct has been heartless in the extreme. Shall he be allowed to live ?" So he killed Sashihire.

That same day the Prince proceeded towards Yamato, and at midnight arrived at Iso no Kami, and made his report. Hereupon the Heir summoned to him the Prince his younger brother, and was liberal of his favour to him, granting him the Mura-ahase official granaries. On this day Hamako, Muraji of Adzumi, was arrested.

1st year, 2nd month, 1st day. The Prince Imperial assumed the Dignity in the Palace of Waka-zakura at Ihare.

Summer, 4th month, 17th day. The Emperor summoned before him Hamako, Muraji of Adzumi, and commanded him, saying :—" Thou didst plot rebellion with the Imperial Prince Nakatsu in order to overturn the State, and thy offence is deserving of death. I will, however, exercise great bounty, and remitting the penalty of death, sentence thee to be branded." [2] The same day he was branded near the eye.

XII. 6.

A.D. 400.

---

[1] See above, p. 100. In this passage it seems used as a general name for retainer. Chamberlain renders it " man-at-arms " in the corresponding passage of the " Kojiki."

[2] Literally " inked." The branding consisted in tattooing a mark on the face or other part of the person. Until quite recently criminals were branded on the arm with ink, each prison having its own special mark. Branding was originally one of the " five punishments " of China.

Accordingly the men of that time spoke of the "Adzumi eye." The fishermen of Nojima who had been Hamako's followers were also pardoned their offence, and employed as labourers at the official granaries of Komoshiro in Yamato.

Autumn, 7th month, 4th day. Kurohime, daughter of Hata no Sukune, was appointed Imperial concubine. She was the mother of the Imperial Prince Oshiha of Ichinobe in Ihazaka, of the Imperial Prince Mima, and of the Imperial Princess Awomi.

XII. 7.

One account says:—"The Imperial Princess Ihi-toyo." His next concubine, the Imperial Princess Hatahi, was the mother of the Imperial Princess Nakashi.

This year was the year Kanoye Ne (37th) of the Cycle.

A.D. 401

2nd year, Spring, 1st month, 4th day. The Imperial Prince Midzuha wake was appointed Heir [1] to the Throne.

Winter, 10th month. The capital was established at Ihare. At this time Heguri no Dsuku no Sukune, Soga no Manchi no Sukune, Mononobe no Ikofutsu no Ohomuraji, and Tsubura no Oho-omi together administered the affairs of the country.

11th month. The Ihare pond was made.

A.D. 402.

3rd year, Winter, 11th month, 6th day. The Emperor launched the two-forked boat [2] on the pond of Ichishi at Ihare, and went on board with the Imperial concubine, each separately, and feasted. [3] The Lord Steward [4] Areshi set sake before the Emperor. At this time a cherry flower fell into the Emperor's cup. The Emperor wondered at this, and sending for Mononobe no Nagamake no Muraji, commanded him, saying:—"This flower has come out of season. Whence does it come? Do thou thyself seek." Hereupon Nagamake no Muraji went himself and sought for the flowers. He found them on Mount Wakikamunomuro and presented them to the Emperor. The Emperor was delighted to get such a rare thing, and so made them the name of the Palace. Therefore

XII. 8.

---

[1] Note that the brother was made heir, though there were children.

[2] See above, p. 297.

[3] i.e. one in one fork of the boat, the other in the other.

[4] Kashihade no Omi. The context shows that this is here an official designation, and not a mere title, much less a surname.

it was called the Palace of Ihare no Wakazakura.[1] This was the origin of the name.

In this month the original title of "Nagamake no Muraji" was altered to "Wakazakura Be no Miyakko," and the Lord Steward, Areshi, was styled Wakazakura Be no Omi.

4th year,[2] Autumn, 8th month, 8th day. Local Recorders A.D. 403. were appointed for the first time in the various provinces, who noted down statements, and communicated the writings of the four quarters.

Winter, 10th month. The Iso no kami conduit was excavated.

5th year, Spring, 3rd month, 1st day. The three Deities[3] A.D. 404. who dwell in Tsukushi appeared within the palace and said :— "Why are we robbed of our people? We will now disgrace thee." Hereupon the Emperor prayed, but his prayer was not answered.

Autumn, 9th month, 18th day. The Emperor went a-hunting to the Island of Ahaji. On this day the Kahachi Horse-keepers' Be were in attendance on the Emperor, and held XII. 9. the bit. Before this the Horse-keepers' Be had been branded[4] on the face, and none of their wounds had yet healed. Now the God Izanagi, who dwells in the island, spoke by the mouth of a hafuri, saying :—"I cannot endure the stench of blood." Accordingly divination was made, and the answer was, "The God dislikes the smell of the branding of the Horse-keepers' Be." Therefore from that time forward the branding of the Horse-keepers' Be was utterly discontinued.

19th day. There was a sound as of a blast of wind which cried aloud in the Great Void, saying:—"O thou Prince, inheritor of The Sword!"[5] Again there was a voice which

---

[1] i.e. young cherry. This cannot be correct. See above, 3rd year of Jingō Kōgu, whose capital was also at Ihare, and was called Wakazakura.

[2] We have not yet got down to times of accurate chronology. Wani's arrival was in 405, and it is not likely that recorders were appointed till a good many years later. Examples of these "statements" occur frequently below. Most of them fall under the description of folk-lore.

[3] Probably the three children of the Sun-Goddess mentioned at p. 37.

[4] The branding here is not a criminal punishment, but only a distinctive mark.

[5] The sword was one of the Regalia.

said :—" Thy younger sister ¹ of bird-frequented Hata has gone to be buried at Hasa. [Another version is :—" Sanakita no Komotsu ² no Mikoto has gone to be buried at Hasa."] Suddenly a messenger arrived in haste, who said :—" The Imperial concubine is dead." The Emperor was greatly shocked, and straightway ordering his carriage,³ returned.

22nd day. The Emperor arrived from Ahaji.

Winter, 10th month, 11th day. The Imperial concubine was buried. After this the Emperor, vexed with himself that he had not appeased the divine curse, and had so caused the death of the Imperial concubine, again sought to ascertain where the fault lay. Some one said :—" The Kimi of the Cart-keepers ⁴ went to the Land of Tsukushi, where he held a review of all the Cart-keepers' Be, and he took along with them the men allotted to the service of the Deities. This must surely be the offence." The Emperor straightway summoned to him the Kimi of the Cart-keepers and questioned him. The facts having been ascertained, the Emperor enumerated his offences, saying :— " Thou, although only Kimi of the Cart-keepers, hast arbitrarily appropriated the subjects of the Son of Heaven.⁵ This is one offence. Thou didst wrongfully take them, comprising them in the Cart-keepers' Be after they had been allotted to the service of the Gods of Heaven and Earth. This is a second offence." So he imposed on him the expiation of evil and the expiation of good,⁶ and sent him away to Cape Nagasa, there to perform the rites of expiation. After he had done so, the Emperor commanded him, saying :—" Henceforward thou mayest not have charge of the Cart-keepers' Be of Tsukushi." So he confiscated them all, and allotted them anew, giving them to the three Deities.

A.D. 405   6th year, Spring, 1st month, 6th day. The Imperial Princess Hatahi of Kusaka was appointed Empress.⁷

XII. 10.

---

¹ Kurohime, the Imperial concubine, is meant.
² Apparently another name for Princess Hata.
³ The word carriage is not to be taken too literally. The kana interlinea‑ gloss has Ohon mŭma ni tatematsurite, which means " mounted his horse."
⁴ Kuruma-mochi.   ⁵ The Emperor.
⁶ i.e. a fine of the articles required in the ceremony of purgation or expiation. See above, p. 48.
⁷ She was the Emperor's half-sister.

9th day. A Treasury was instituted and a Treasury[1] Be established.

2nd month, 1st day. The Emperor sent for Futohime no Iratsume and Takatsuru no Iratsume, daughters of Prince Funashi wake, and having bestowed them in the Empress's palace,[2] made them both his concubines.[3] Upon this the two XII. II. concubines lamented continually, saying :—"Alas! Whither has the Prince, our elder brother, gone?" The Emperor heard their lamentation, and inquired of them, saying :—"Why do ye lament?" They answered and said :—"Thy handmaidens' elder brother, Prince Washizumi, is strong and nimble. Alone he has taken a running leap over an eight-fathom house, and gone away. Many days have passed that we have not spoken to him face to face. Therefore do we lament." The Emperor was pleased to hear of his great strength, and sent for him. But he would not come. Again messenger after messenger was sent to summon him, but still he would not come, and continued to reside in the village of Suminoye. After this the Emperor ceased to demand his presence. He was the first ancestor of the two houses of the Miyakko of Sanuki and the Wake of Ashikuhi in Aha.

3rd month, 15th day. The Emperor's precious body became ill at ease, and, the elements of water and earth being inharmonious, he died in the Palace of Waka-zakura, at the age of seventy.[4]

[1] The Treasury means the office, the Be the staff. The "Kogo-jui" says :— "Until the reign of the latter Ihare no Waka-zakura (i.e. Richiu Tennō) the three Han failed not to send tribute for many generations. Beside the Sacred Treasury, there was erected an Inner Treasury, where the official property was classified and deposited. Achi no Omi and Wang-in (or Wani), the learned men of Pèkché, were made to record the ingoings and outcomings. A Treasury Be was first established." If we allow for the error of two cycles, this year, A.D. 405, is the very year in which Wang-in arrived. But the "Nihongi" chronology cannot yet be depended on.

The "Shoku-in-rei" says :—"The Interior Treasury Department has one Chief, who has control of gold and silver, jewels, precious utensils, brocade and satin, sarsnet, rugs and mattresses, and the rare objects sent as tribute by the various barbarians."

[2] Women's apartments.

[3] The character used implies a subordinate rank.

[4] Other calculations make him sixty-four, seventy-seven, eighty-five, and eighty-seven. It is obvious that none of them can be relied on.

Winter, 10th month, 4th day. The Emperor was buried in
the misasagi on the Plain of Mozu no Mimi.

THE EMPEROR MIDZUHAWAKE.[1]

(*HANZEI TENNŌ*[2]

OR

XII. 12.   *HANSHŌ TENNŪ*.)

The Emperor Midzuhawake was a younger brother by the
same mother of the Emperor Izaho-wake. He was appointed
Prince Imperial in the second year of the Emperor Izaho-
wake. The Emperor was born in the Palace of Ahaji. At his
birth his teeth were like one bone,[3] and his appearance was
beautiful. Now there was a well called Midzu no wi (the
beautiful well) from which water was drawn to wash the Heir[4]
to the Throne. A tajihi[5] flower had fallen into this well and
it was accordingly made the name of the Heir to the
Throne. The tajihi flower is what is now the itadori flower.
Therefore he was styled the Emperor Tajihi[6] no Midzuhawake.

The Emperor Izaho-wake died in Spring, the 3rd month of
the 6th year of his reign.

A.D 406.   1st year, Spring, 1st month, 2nd day. The Heir Apparent
assumed the Imperial Dignity.

---

[1] Midzu ha means beautiful teeth.

[2] This is explained to mean " the Emperor who turned matters into the
right path," han meaning turn, and sei or shō " right."

[3] In the Bamboo Books (" Legge's Chinese Classics "), p. 143, there is
mention of an ancient Chinese king whose teeth were one piece of bone.
The " Kojiki " says (Ch. K., p. 292) :—" The length of his august teeth was
one inch, and their breadth two lines, and the upper and lower [row] corre-
sponded exactly, like jewels strung [together]."

[4] He was not Heir at this time.

[5] The Polygonum Cuspidatum. Hepburn.

[6] The " Seishi roku " states that in consequence of this incident Tajihi Be
were established in all the provinces to be the villages for the hot baths of
the Imperial Princes.

Autumn, 8th month, 6th day. Tsuno hime, daughter of Kogoto, ancestor of the Omi of Ohoyake, was appointed XII. 13. Imperial concubine.[1] She was the mother of the Imperial Princess Kahihime, and of the Imperial Princess Tsubura. Moreover, he took to him the Imperial concubine's younger sister Otohime, who bore to him the Imperial Princess Takara and the Imperial Prince Takabe.

Winter, 10th month. The capital was established at Tajihi[2] in Kahachi. It was called the Palace of Shibagaki.

At this time the rain and wind were seasonable, and the five kinds of grain reached maturity ; the people enjoyed abundance, and the Empire was at peace.

This year was the year Hinoye Mŭma (43rd) of the Cycle.

6th[3] year, Spring, 1st month, 29th day. The Emperor died[4] A.D. 410. in the chief sleeping-chamber.

---

[1] The word for concubine here is 夫 人. We have now had three ranks of concubines mentioned, showing that Chinese customs were coming in. In the older reigns the only distinction made is that of the Empress and other consorts.

[2] This is hardly consistent with the story of the tajihi flower on the previous page.

[3] The original reading is 6th. The " Shukai" editor would correct it into 5th from the " Kiujiki." It signifies extremely little which reading we take, as no reliance can yet be placed on any of the dates given.

[4] The age of this Emperor is not stated here. The " Kojiki " says sixty.

BOOK XIII.

THE EMPEROR WO-ASA-TSUMA WAKUGO NO SUKUNE.[1]

(*INGIŌ[2] TENNŌ.*)

THE Emperor Wo-Asa-tsuma wakugo no Sukune was a younger brother by the same mother of the Emperor Midzuha wake. From infancy to puberty,[3] the Emperor was kind and unassuming. When he attained to manhood, he became very ill and lost the free use of his limbs.

The Emperor Midzuha wake died in Spring, the 1st month of the 5th year of his reign. Hereupon the Ministers held counsel, saying :—" There are at the present time the Imperial Princes Wo-Asa-tsuma wakugo no Sukune and Oho-Kusaka, children of the Emperor Oho-sazaki. The Imperial Prince Wo-Asa-tsuma wakugo no Sukune, however, is the elder, and of an affectionate, dutiful disposition." So they chose a lucky day, and kneeling down, offered him the Imperial signet. The Imperial Prince Wo-Asa-tsuma wakugo no Sukune declined it, saying :—" I am an unlucky man, long afflicted with a grievous disease, which I cannot shake off. I am unable to walk. Of myself, without informing the Emperor, I have secretly treated

XIII. 2. my disease by self-mutilation,[4] in the hope of getting rid of it, but still I am not healed. Therefore the former Emperor chid me, saying :—' What greater extreme of unfilialness can there be than this conduct of thine, in wantonly mutilating thy body

---

[1] Wo, male ; Asa-tsuma (morning-wife) is the name of a place ; wakugo, young child ; Sukune, name of dignity.

[2] Ingiō is from the "Shooking," the Canon of Yaou, § 1, where Legge translates "sincerely courteous."

[3] The words translated infancy and puberty are in the original descriptive of the mode of dressing the hair at these periods of life in China.

[4] The precise meaning is doubtful.

because thou sufferest from disease ? However long thou mayst live, thou must never succeed to the throne.' Moreover, the two Emperors, my elder brothers, despised me and thought me a fool, as is known to all the Ministers. Now the Empire is a great organization : the Imperial Dignity is a vast institution : and to be the father and mother of the people is the office of a sage. How can such a charge be given to a fool ? Make another choice of some wise Prince, and let him be established as Emperor. I, the unworthy one, may not presume to fill the office." The Ministers bowed down twice, and said : —" The Imperial Dignity should not be long vacant ; the command of Heaven should not be modestly refused. We, thy servants, fear that if thou, the Great Prince, dost delay the time, and in opposition to the general desire dost refuse to rectify the name and dignity, the nation's hopes will be disappointed. We pray therefore that the Great Prince, notwithstanding his sufferings, will yet assume the Imperial Dignity." The Imperial Prince Wo-Asa-tsuma wakugo no Sukune said :— " It is a weighty matter to take charge of the ancestral temples and the temples of the earth and of grain.[1] I, the unworthy one, am grievously ill, and am incompetent to fill this office worthily." He continued to decline it, and would not give his consent. Hereupon all the Ministers persisted in their petition, saying :—" In the humble opinion of thy servants, thou, the XIII. 3. Great Prince, art eminently worthy to take over charge of the Temples of thy Imperial Ancestors. Even the myriad people of the Empire all deem thee fit. We pray thee, O Great Prince, to give thy consent."

1st year, Winter, 12th month. The Prince's concubine, A.D. 412. Osaka no Oho-nakatsu hime no Mikoto, was grieved at the mutterings of vexation of the Ministers, and taking in her own person water for washing the hands, came before the Imperial Prince and addressed him, saying :—" Thou, O Great Prince, having declined to assume the Dignity, it has remained vacant for years and months. The Ministers and functionaries are grieved, and know not what to do. I pray thee, O Great Prince, comply with the general wish, and, however reluctantly, assume the Imperial Dignity." The Imperial Prince, however,

---

[1] i.e. " the state."

was loath to consent, and turning his back upon her, sat
without saying a word. Hereupon Oho-nakatsu hime no
Mikoto was afraid, and not knowing how to retire, remained
in attendance on the Prince for four or five half-hours. It was
then the 12th month, and the wind was blowing fierce and
chill. The water in the basin which Oho-nakatsu hime had
brought overflowed and became frozen on her arm. Unable to
endure the cold, she was almost dying. The Imperial Prince
looked round, and was shocked. He helped her to her feet,
and said to her :—" The succession to the Dignity is so weighty
a matter that I could not abruptly assume it. Therefore I have
not complied up to the present. Now, however, the request of
the Ministers is manifestly just. Why should I persist in my
refusal?" Hereupon Oho-nakatsu hime looked up delighted,
and told all the Ministers, saying :—" The Imperial Prince is
about to give ear to the request of the Ministers. Now is the
time to offer him the Imperial signet." Thereupon the
XIII. 4. Ministers were much rejoiced, and on that same day delivered
up to him the Imperial signet with repeated obeisances. The
Imperial Prince said :—" Ye Ministers have, on behalf of the
Empire, made a joint request of unworthy me. How can I
presume to persist in refusing it?" So he assumed the
Imperial Dignity.

This year was the year Midzunoye Ne (49th) of the Cycle.

A.D. 413.   2nd year, Spring, 2nd month, 14th day. Osaka no Oho-
nakatsu hime was appointed Empress. On this day there was
established on behalf of the Empress the Osaka Be.[1]

The Empress was the mother of the Imperial Prince Kinashi
Karu, of the Imperial Princess Nagata no Oho-iratsume, of the
Imperial Prince Sakahi no Kuro-hiko, of the Emperor Anaho,
of the Imperial Princess Karu no Oho-iratsume, of the Imperial

---

[1] The " Kojiki " says that the Osaka Be was established as the Empress's
na-shiro, which Chamberlain renders by " proxy." I would prefer to call it
" name-sake." The object was to perpetuate the name of the Empress—at
least, if this account is correct. But there was an Osaka Be already in
existence. It is mentioned in the 39th year of Suinin's reign. Besides, the
Osaka Be were the executioners, a circumstance with which it is difficult to
reconcile the statement in the text. It is true, however, that the Empress's
full name was Osaka no Oho-nakatsu hime, Osaka being the name of her
residence.

Prince Yatsuri no Shiro-hiko, of the Emperor Oho-hatsuse Waka-take, of the Imperial Princess Tajima no Tachibana no Oho-iratsume, and of the Imperial Princess Sakami.

At an earlier period, when the Empress was at home with her mother, she was walking alone in the garden, when the Miyakko of the Land of Tsuke passed along the road which was beside the garden. He was on horseback, and looking over the hedge, he addressed the Empress, and said mockingly : —"What an excellent gardener thou art." He also said :— "Pray, madam, let me have one of those orchids." The Empress accordingly plucked an orchid root, and gave it to the XIII. 5. man on horseback, asking him for what purpose he wanted the orchid. The man on horseback answered and said :—"I am going to the mountain, and it is to brush away the midges." Then the Empress reflected on this within her mind, and recognized the want of respect in the words of the man on horseback. So she addressed him, saying :—" Sir,[1] I shall not forget this."

Afterwards, in the year in which the Empress attained the felicitous rank, she sought out the man on horseback who had asked her for an orchid, and having stated his former offence, wished to have him put to death. Hereupon the man who had asked for the orchid knocked his forehead on the ground, and making a deep obeisance,[2] said :—" Truly thy servant's guilt is deserving of ten thousand deaths. At that time, however, I did not know that thou wert of high rank." Hereupon the Empress remitted the penalty of death, but deprived him of his title and called him Inaki.[3]

3rd year, Spring, 1st month, 1st day. An envoy was sent to A.D. 414. Silla to procure a good physician.

Autumn, 8th month. The physician arrived from Silla, and was forthwith made to treat the Emperor's disease. No long time after, he was healed of his disease. The Emperor was

---

[1] The Chinese character translated "sir" means literally head or chief. The Japanese word intended is probably Obito or Obuto, which, I take it, is an abbreviation of Oho-bito, great man. In Chinese Tajen (in Corean Tain), i.e. great man, is used as a personal pronoun in addressing men of rank. Our own word "master" (magister, magnus) has a somewhat similar history.

[2] Kowtow in Chinese.

[3] Inaki was a lower title than Miyakko.

rejoiced, and having rewarded the physician liberally, sent him back to his own country.

4th year, Autumn, 9th month, 9th day. The Emperor made a decree, saying :—" In the most ancient times, good government consisted in the subjects having each one his proper place, and in names[1] being correct. It is now four years since We entered on the auspicious office. Superiors and inferiors dispute with one another : the hundred surnames[2] are not at peace. Some by mischance lose their proper surnames ; others purposely lay claim to high family. This is perhaps the reason why good government is not attained to. Deficient in wisdom although We are, how can We omit to rectify these irregularities ? Let the Ministers take counsel, and inform me of their determination." All the Ministers said :—" If Your Majesty, restoring that which is lost and correcting that which is perverted, will thus determine Houses and surnames, your servants will stake their lives in recommending the adoption of such a measure."

28th day. The Emperor made a decree, saying :—" The ministers, functionaries, and the Miyakko of the various provinces each and all describe themselves, some as descendants of Emperors, others attributing to their race a miraculous origin, and saying that their ancestors came down from Heaven.[3] However, since the three Powers of Nature[4] assumed distinct forms,[5] many tens of thousands of years have elapsed, so that single Houses[6] have multiplied and have formed anew ten thousand surnames of doubtful authenticity. Therefore let the people of the various Houses and surnames wash themselves and practise abstinence, and let them, each one calling the Gods to witness, plunge their hands in boiling water." The caldrons of the ordeal by boiling water were therefore placed on the " Evil Door of Words " spur of the Amagashi Hill. Every-

---

[1] Literally surnames and personal names. What is really meant is titles. There were no proper surnames at this time. See above, p. 27.

[2] The word for "hundred surnames " is 百 姓, which is also used for the nation generally, and in later times in Japan for the peasantry. Here its original meaning must be kept in view.

[3] The " Sei-shi-roku " contains numerous instances of this.

[4] Heaven, Earth, and Man. *Vide* Mayers, p. 302.

[5] Since the creation, as we would say.   [6] Uji.

body was told to go thither, saying :—" He who tells the truth will be uninjured ; he who is false will assuredly suffer harm."

This is called Kuka-tachi. Sometimes mud was put into a caldron and made to boil up. Then the arms were bared, and the boiling mud stirred with them. Sometimes an axe was heated red-hot and placed on the palm of the hand.

Hereupon every one put on straps of tree-fibre, and coming to the caldrons, plunged their hands in the boiling water, when those who were true remained naturally uninjured, and all those who were false were harmed. Therefore those who had falsified (their titles) were afraid, and slipping away beforehand, did not come forward. From this time forward the Houses and surnames were spontaneously ordered, and there was no longer any one who falsified them.[1]

5th year, 7th month, 14th day. There was an earthquake. A.D. 416. Before this time Tamada no Sukune, grandson[2] of Katsuraki no Sotsuhiko, had been commanded to superintend the temporary burial of the Emperor Midzu-ha-wake. On the evening after the earthquake, Aso, Ohari no Muraji, was sent to examine the condition of the shrine of temporary burial. Now all the men assembled, and none were absent except Tamada no Sukune, XIII. 8. who was not present. Aso reported to the Emperor, saying :— " Tamada no Sukune, the High Officer of the Shrine of temporary interment, was not to be seen at the temporary place of interment." Accordingly, Aso was sent again to Katsuraki to see Tamada no Sukune. On this day it so happened that Tamada no Sukune had gathered together men and women and was holding revel. Aso made a statement of all the circumstances to Tamada no Sukune. Tamada no Sukune was afraid that trouble might ensue, and gave Aso a horse as a present. However, he secretly waylaid Aso and killed him on the road. Therefore he ran away and concealed himself within the precinct of the tomb of Takechi no Sukune. When the Emperor heard this, he sent for Tamada no Sukune.

[1] This measure can only have been applicable to a dominant caste. The nation cannot have all been subjected to the ordeal at Amagashi. Doubtless, then as now, the bulk of the people cared little for genealogies, and indeed had none but personal names.

[2] Below, XIV. 20, he is the son of Sotsuhiko.

Tamada no Sukune was suspicious, and put on armour under his clothing and so presented himself. The border of the armour projected from within his garment. The Emperor, in order to ascertain clearly how this was, made an Uneme, named Woharida, present sake to Tamada no Sukune. Now the Uneme observing distinctly that there was armour underneath his clothing, reported this particularly to the Emperor. The Emperor got ready soldiers and was about to kill Tamada no Sukune, when he secretly ran away and hid in his house. The Emperor again despatched soldiers, who surrounded Tamada's house, took him, and put him to death.

Winter, 11th month, 11th day. The Emperor Midzu-ha-wake was buried in the Mimihara Misasagi.

A.D. 418.
XIII. 9.
7th year, Winter, 12th month, 1st day. There was a banquet in the new Palace.[1] The Emperor in person played on the lute,[2] and the Empress stood up and danced. When the dance was ended, she did not repeat the compliment. At that time it was the custom at a banquet for the dancer, when the dance was ended, to turn to the person who occupied the highest place, an say, "I offer thee a woman." Now the Emperor said to the Empress :—" Why hast thou failed to say the usual compliment ? " The Empress was afraid. She stood up again and danced, and when the dance was over, she said :—" I offer thee a woman." The Emperor forthwith inquired of the Empress, saying :—" Who is the woman whom thou offerest me ? I wish to know her name." The Empress could not help herself, and addressed the Emperor, saying :— " It is thy handmaiden's younger sister, whose name is Oto-hime."[3] Otohime's countenance was of surpassing and peerless beauty. Her brilliant colour shone out through her raiment, so that the men of that time gave her the designation of Sotohori Iratsume.[4] The Emperor's wishes had dwelt upon

---

[1] The interlinear kana has miya, palace, for 室, oftener rendered muro. But nihi-muro, new muro, is probably the word really meant.

[2] Koto.

[3] Otohime means simply "the younger lady."

[4] Clothing - pass - maiden. The "Kojiki" makes her the Emperor's daughter. Cf. Shelley's—

> "Child of Light ! thy limbs are burning,
> Through the vest which seems to hide them."

Sotohori Iratsume, and therefore it was that he insisted on the
Empress's offering her to him, while the Empress, knowing
this, was reluctant to make the compliment. Now the Emperor
was delighted, and the very next day he despatched a messenger
to summon Otohime. At this time Otohime dwelt with her
mother at Sakata in the land of Afumi. But she feared the
feelings of the Empress and therefore refused to come. Again
seven times she was sent for, and yet she obstinately refused
and did not come. Upon this the Emperor was displeased,
and again gave command to one of the Toneri, a Nakatomi
named Ikatsu [1] no Omi, saying :—" The damsel Otohime, who
was given to me by the Empress, has not come although sent
for. Do thou go thyself and bring Otohime here with thee, and
I will surely reward thee liberally." Hereupon Ikatsu no Omi,
having received the Imperial command, withdrew, and having
concealed a stock of provisions in his clothing, went to Sakata,
where he prostrated himself in Otohime's courtyard, and
said :—" By command of the Emperor, I summon thee."
Otohime answered and said :—" Far be it from me not to
fear the Emperor's command. But I am unwilling to hurt the
Empress's feelings. Thy handmaiden will not come, though XIII. 10.
it should cost her her life to refuse." Then Ikatsu no Omi
answered and said :—" As thy servant has received the
Emperor's commands, I must bring thee back with me. If I
bring thee not back, I shall surely incur punishment. Therefore it is better to die lying prostrate in this courtyard than to
return and undergo the extreme penalty." So for seven days
he lay prostrate in the courtyard, and although food and drink
were offered to him, he refused to taste them, but secretly ate
the provisions in his bosom. Hereupon Otohime said :—" By
reason of the Empress's jealousy, thy handmaiden has already
disobeyed the Emperor's commands. To be the ruin of my
Lord, who art his faithful servant, would be another crime on
my part." Accordingly she came along with Ikatsu no Omi.
When they reached Kasuga in Yamato they had food by the
well of Ichihi. Otohime herself gave sake to the Omi, and
soothed his spirit. The Omi that same day arrived at the

[1] As he was Toneri, the Ikatsu no Omi is clearly a mere title, like the no
Kami's of recent times.

capital, and having lodged Otohime at the house cf Akoko, the Atahe of Yamato, made his report to the Emperor. The Emperor was greatly rejoiced. He commended Ikatsu no Omi, and showed him liberal favour. The Empress, however, showed her vexation, and Otohime could therefore not approach the interior of the Palace. Accordingly, a separate building was erected for her at Fujihara, and she dwelt there.[1] On the night that the Empress gave birth to the Emperor Oho-hatsuse, the Emperor for the first time went to the Fujihara Palace. The Empress hearing this, was angry, and said:— "Many years have passed since I first bound up my hair and became thy companion in the hinder palace. It is too cruel of thee, O Emperor. Wherefore, just on this night when I am in childbirth and hanging between life and death, must thou go to Fujihara?" So she went out, set fire to the parturition house, and was about to kill herself. The Emperor, hearing this, was greatly shocked, and said:—" We are wrong." So with explanations he soothed the mind of the Empress.

A.D. 419.   8th year, Spring, 2nd month. The Emperor went to Fuji-
XIII. 11.   hara and secretly observed how matters were with Sotohori Iratsume. That night Sotohori Iratsume was sitting alone, thinking fondly of the Emperor. Unaware of his approach, she made a song, saying :—

> This is the night
> My husband will come.
> The little crab—
> The spider's action
> To-night is manifest.[2]

The Emperor, when he heard this song, was touched by it, and made a song, saying :—

---

[1] Hence perhaps the name Soto-wori-hime, or the Lady who lives without. as opposed to Oho-nakatsu hime, the dame of the Great Interior.

[2] It was considered that when a spider clung to one's garments, it was a sign that an intimate friend would arrive. Little crab is another name for spider. Sotohori hime was in after times looked on as the "Muse of poetry." This poem is a regular Tanka, as are the others in this passage.

> Loosening and removing
> The brocade sash
> Of small pattern,
> Not often have I slept—
> But one night only.

The next morning, the Emperor looked at the cherry flowers beside the well, and made a song, saying :—

> As one loves the cherry
> Sweet of blossom,
> Did I love another,
> Then her I should not love—
> The girl whom I love.

This came to the Empress's ear, and she was very wroth. Hereupon Sotohori Iratsume addressed the Emperor, saying :— " Thy handmaiden desires to be always near the Royal Palace, and night and day without ceasing to view the glory of Your Majesty. But the Empress, being thy handmaiden's elder sister, is, on her account, continually resentful towards Your Majesty, and is also vexed because of thy handmaiden. I pray therefore that I may be removed far from the Royal dwelling, and I wish to live at a distance. This might perhaps cause the Empress's jealousy somewhat to abate." The Emperor XIII 12. forthwith built anew a palace in Chinu in Kahachi, and made Sotohori Iratsume to dwell there. And for this reason he frequently went a-hunting to the moor of Hine.

9th year, Spring, 2nd month. The Emperor made a progress A.D. 420. to the Palace of Chinu.

Autumn, 8th month. The Emperor made a progress to Chinu.

Winter, 10th month. The Emperor made a progress to Chinu.

10th year, Spring, 1st month. The Emperor made a progress A.D. 421. to Chinu. Hereupon the Empress addressed him, saying :— " Thy handmaiden is not a whit jealous of her younger sister. Only she fears that the people may be distressed by Your Majesty's frequent progresses to Chinu. I humbly pray thee to diminish the number of thy visits." Thereafter his excursions thither were infrequent.

A.D. 422.   11th year, Spring, 3rd month, 4th day.   The Emperor made
a progress to the Palace of Chinu.   Sotohori Iratsume made a
song, saying :—

> For ever and ever,
> Oh ! that I might meet my Lord !
> As often as drift beachward
> The weeds of the shore of ocean
> (Where whales are caught).

Then the Emperor spake to Sotohori Iratsume, saying :—
" No other person must hear this song.   For if the Empress
heard it, she would surely be greatly wroth."   Therefore the
men of that time gave a name to the shore-weed and called it
Na-nori-ahi-mo.[1]

XIII. 13.   Before this time, when Sotohori Iratsume dwelt in the Palace
of Fujihara, the Emperor commanded Ohotomo Muruya no
Muraji, saying :—" Of late we have gotten a beautiful woman,
the younger sister of the Empress by the same mother.[2]   In
Our heart we dearly love her, and it is Our desire that her
name should be handed down to after ages.   How can this be
done ? "   In accordance with the Imperial command, Muruya
no Muraji proposed a plan for the Emperor's approval.   Consequently the Miyakko of the various provinces were charged to
establish Fujihara Be on behalf of Sotohori hime.

A.D. 425.   14th year, Autumn, 9th month, 12th day.   The Emperor
hunted in the island of Ahaji.   Now the deer, monkeys, and
wild boar, like dust-clouds, confusedly, filled the mountains and
valleys.   They sprang up like flames of fire, they were dispersed
like flies.   And yet all day long not a single beast was caught.
Herewith the hunt was suspended, and divination was made
anew.   Then the God of the Island[3] gave an oracular utterance,

---

[1] Na-nori-ahi means " mutually to tell one's name," and mo is the general
word for seaweed.   There is a seaweed so called, but what this circumstance
has to do with the story is not clear.

[2] The traditional kana has haha-hara-kara.   As hara-kara by its derivation means " of the same womb," it is needless to prefix haha, mother.   But
this shows that when these kana glosses were written, hara-kara had come
to mean simply brother or sister, as it does at present.

[3] Izanagi.

saying :—" It was by my intent that no beast was caught. In the bottom of the sea of Akashi there is a pearl. If this pearl is sacrificed to me, ye shall be able to catch all the beasts." Hereupon they proceeded to assemble the fishermen of the various places, and made them search the bottom of the sea of Akashi. When they dived into the sea, however, they were unable to reach the bottom. But there was one fisherman named XIII. 14. Wosashi, a fisher of Naga-zato in the province of Aha, who excelled all the fishers. He tied a rope to his loins, and went down to the bottom of the sea. After some time he came forth, and said :—" In the bottom of the sea there is a great sea-ear,[1] and this place is shining." Everybody said :—" Probably the pearl which the God of the Island has asked for is in this sea-ear's belly." Again he went in and searched for it. Hereupon Wosashi came to the surface with the great sea-ear in his arms, but his breath had ceased, and he died on the surface of the waves. Afterwards a rope was let down and the bottom of the sea was measured. The depth was found to be sixty fathoms. When the sea-ear was split open, a true pearl was found in its belly, in size like a peach. This was offered to the God of the Island, and a hunt being made, they caught many beasts. But they grieved that Wosashi had met his death by entering the sea, and made a tomb, in which they reverently interred him. That tomb exists at the present day.

23rd year, Spring, 3rd month, 7th day. The Imperial Prince A.D. 434. Kinashi Karu was made Heir to the Throne. He was fair to look upon, and those who saw him spontaneously loved him. His sister by the same mother,[2] the Imperial Princess Karu no Oho-iratsume, was also beautiful. The Heir Apparent's thoughts were constantly bent on becoming united to the

---

[1] The ahabi or Haliotis tuberculata.

[2] The prominence given to brotherhood and sisterhood by the same mother in the " Nihongi," as in Homer, has not, it appears to me, the significance attributed to it by McLennan's theory, which would trace back such terms to a time when the mother was the only parent as to whom there could be no doubt. It seems to me that the father's parentage is here taken for granted, the phrase really meaning brother or sister by the mother's side *as well as* by the father's, and that such phrases are merely indications of polygamous customs, not necessarily of promiscuity or polyandry.

Imperial Princess Oho-iratsume, but he dreaded the guilt,[1] and was silent. But his passion had become so violent that he was well-nigh on the point of death. Hereupon he thought to himself, " I will not die for nothing. It may be a crime, but how can I endure ? " At last he became secretly united to her, and so his desperate passion became somewhat abated. Accordingly he made a song, saying :—

> On the foot-dragging mountain,
> Rice-fields are made ;
> So high is the mountain,
> The water-pipes are run beneath—
> Like them the hidden tears
> That I wept for my spouse,
> The unshared tears
> That I wept for my spouse,
> But to-day, this very day,
> Freely our bodies touch.[2]

XIII. 15.

24th year, Summer, 6th month. The soup for the Emperor's meal froze, and became ice. The Emperor wondered, and had divination made in order to learn the meaning of it. The diviner said :—" There is domestic disorder,[3] perhaps the illicit intercourse of near relations with one another." Then some one said :—" The Heir Apparent, Kinashi Karu, has seduced his younger sister by the same mother, the Imperial Princess Karu no Iratsume." So examination was made, and it was found that these words were true. The Heir Apparent being the successor to the Throne, it was impossible to punish him,

---

[1] See Ch. K., Introd., p. xxxviii. I do not feel sure that Chamberlain is right in attributing to Chinese influence the stigma attached to unions of brothers and sisters of the full blood. See a paper on " The Family and Relationships in Ancient Japan," in the " Transactions of the Japan Society," 1892-93.

[2] A somewhat different version of this poem is given in the " Kojiki." See Ch. K., p. 296. I have adopted one or two of Motowori's emendations. See " Kojikiden," xxxix. 23. " Foot-dragging " is a makura-kotoba or conventional epithet of mountain, used because in ascending a mountain we drag one foot painfully after the other. At least, that is the common interpretation. The metre is somewhat irregular naga-uta.

[3] i.e. incest.

so the Imperial Princess Karu no Iratsume was banished to Iyo.[1] At this time the Heir Apparent made a song, saying :—

> I, the Great Lord,
> To an island am banished :
> Remaining behind in the ship,
> I will certainly come back again.   XIII. 16.
> Let my bed be respected—
> (In words indeed
> I shall call it my bed)
> Let my spouse be respected.[2]

Again he made a song, saying :—

> The maiden of Karu
> (The Heaven-soaring),
> If she wept violently,
> Men would know of it—
> Like the doves of Mount Hasa,
> She weeps with a suppressed weeping.[3]

42nd year, Spring, 1st month, 14th day. The Emperor died.   A.D. 453. His years were many.[4]

[1] The " Kojiki " makes the Prince to be banished. and Motowori thinks with some reason that this must be the true version of the story. For one thing (he says), women have always been more lightly punished in Japan than men for the same offence, and the particular character of the fault in this case makes such a discrimination all the more reasonable. Moreover, it is hardly possible to construe the poem which follows otherwise than as composed by Prince Karu when about to be banished. An ancient note to the " Nihongi " (see below) speaks of the Prince as having died by his own hand in Iyo.

[2] The word for bed is tatami, now applied to the thick mats used to cover the floor of a Japanese house. At this time the tatami only covered the sleeping-place. There was a superstition forbidding people to meddle with the bed of an absent person, as to do so would bring down calamity on him. The word translated " respect " is yume, taboo, religious abstinence. The third line of this poem is literally " a ship-remainder," by which is understood " one who remains behind in a ship after the other passengers have landed." There are, however, other explanations. See Ch. K., p. 300.

[3] The metre of this poem is irregular. " Heaven soaring " is a conventional epithet applied to Karu, which is the name of a place, because Kari means " a wild goose "—hardly a sufficient reason to our Western minds.

[4] Seventy-eight, says the " Kojiki." Another authority says eighty. But his mother, the Empress Iha no hime, died A.D. 347, and she had ceased to cohabit with her husband A.D. 342 (see above, p. 285), so that he would be at least 110 at the time of his death.

Now the King of Silla, when he heard that the Emperor had died, was shocked and grieved, and sent up eighty tribute ships with eighty musicians of all kinds. They anchored at Tsushima, and made great wail. When they arrived in Tsukushi they again made great wail. Anchoring in the harbour of Naniha, they all put on plain white garments, and bringing all the articles of tribute, and stringing their musical instruments of all kinds, they proceeded from Naniha to the capital.[1] Sometimes they wept and wailed, sometimes they sang and danced, until at length they assembled at the Shrine of temporary interment.

Winter, 10th month, 10th day. The Emperor was buried in the misasagi of Naga-no no hara in Kahachi.

11th month. The Silla messengers of condolence, when the funeral ceremonies were concluded, returned home.

Now the men of Silla had always loved Mount Miminashi and Mount Unebi, which are hard by the capital city. Accordingly, when they arrived at the Kotobiki Hill, they looked back, and said:—"Uneme haya! Mimi haya!" This was simply because they were unpractised in the common speech, and therefore corrupted Mount Unebi, calling it Uneme, and corrupted Mount Miminashi, calling it Mimi. Now the Yamato no Muma-kahi[2] Be, who were in attendance on the men of Silla, heard these words, and conceived a suspicion that the Silla men had had intercourse with the Uneme. So they made them go back, and gave information to the Imperial Prince Ohohatsuse. The Imperial Prince straightway threw the Silla messengers every one into prison, and put them to an examination. Then the Silla messengers made a statement, saying:— "We have done the Uneme no harm. Our words were simply expressive of our love for the two mountains close to the capital." Upon this it was recognized that the charge was groundless, and they were all released. But the people of Silla resented it greatly, and further reduced the kinds of articles sent as tribute and the number of ships.

---

[1] Anaho in Yamato.　　　　[2] Horse-keepers.

Misasagi of Ingiō Tennō.

THE EMPEROR ANAHO.

(ANKŌ[1] TENNŌ.)

The Emperor Anaho was the second child of the Emperor Wo-asa-tsuma waku-go no Sukune.

One account says :—" The third child."

XIII. 18. His mother's name was Osaka no Oho-nakatsu-hime no Mikoto. She was the daughter of the Imperial Prince Waka-nuke-futa-mata.[2]

The Emperor died in the 42nd year of his reign, Spring, the 1st month. In Winter, the 10th month, the funeral ceremonies were completed. At this time the Heir Apparent was guilty of a barbarous outrage in debauching a woman. The nation censured him, and the Ministers would not follow him, but all without exception gave their allegiance to the Imperial Prince Anaho. Hereupon the Heir Apparent wished to attack the Imperial Prince Anaho, and to that end secretly got ready an army. The Imperial Prince Anaho also raised a force, and prepared to give battle. It was at this time that the terms " Anaho arrow-notch " and " Karu arrow-notch "[3] began. Now the Heir Apparent, knowing that the Ministers would not follow him, and that the people were uncompliant, went away and hid in the house of the Mononobe, Ohomahe no Sukune. The Imperial Prince Anaho, hearing this, forthwith surrounded it. Ohomahe no Sukune came forth from the gate to meet him, upon which the Imperial Prince Anaho made a song, saying :—

> To Oho-mahe
> Wo-mahe [4] Sukune's
> Metal-gate's shelter,
> Thus let us repair,
> And wait till the rain stops.

---

[1] Ankō means peace.   [2] A son of Ōjin. See Ch. K., p. 242.

[3] The parallel passage of the " Kojiki " (Ch. K., p. 298) has "inside" for "notch," and an ancient note explains that in the case of Prince Karu's arrows, the "notch" or "inside" was of copper, whereas those of Prince Anaho were " like those of the present time," i.e. presumably of iron. Moto-wori thinks that the arrow-points are intended.

[4] It is a question whether Oho-mahe and Wo-mahe are one person or two brothers. The metre of this poem is imperfect Tanka.

Ohomahe no Sukune made a song in answer, saying :—

> Because the courtier's
> Garter-bell
> Has fallen off,
> The courtiers make a noise :
> Ye country-folks also beware ! (of making a noise) [1]

So he addressed the Imperial Prince, saying :—" I beseech thee, harm not the Heir Apparent. Thy servant will advise with him." Accordingly the Heir Apparent died by his own hand in the house of Ohomahe no Sukune.

One account says that he was banished to the Land of Iyo.[2]

12th month, 14th day. The Imperial Prince Anaho assumed the Imperial Dignity, and the Empress was honoured with the title of " Grand Empress." The capital was forthwith removed to Isonokami.[3] It was called the Palace of Anaho.

At this time the Imperial Prince Ohohatsuse wished to betroth to him the daughters of the Emperor Midzuhawake.[4]

[The names of these daughters are not found in any of the records.]

Hereupon the Imperial Princesses answered and said :— " Thou, my Lord, art much given to violence, and to sudden fits of anger, so that he who sees thee in the morning is slain in the evening, and he who sees thee in the evening is slain in the morning. Now, thy handmaidens' countenances are not distinguished for beauty, nor their minds for cleverness. If in manners and speech we should be no whit agreeable to the princely expectation, how shouldst thou receive us to thy intimacy ? For this reason we are unable to obey thy com-

[1] This is supposed to contain a remonstrance addressed to Prince Anaho's party for making a fuss about such a small matter as the escape of Prince Karu, which is compared to the loss of the grêlot of a courtier's garter.
[2] This is the " Kojiki " version.
[3] In Yamato.
[4] He died A.D. 411, at the age of 60, so these princesses were now (A.D. 453) not exactly young. They were his cousins by the father's side.

mands." To the last they kept out of his way, and would not give ear to him.[1]

1st year, Spring, 2nd month, 1st day. On behalf of the Imperial Prince Ohohatsuse the Emperor desired to betroth to

him the Imperial Princess Hata-hi, a younger sister of the Imperial Prince Ohokusaka,[2] and for this purpose sent Ne no Omi, ancestor of the Omi of Sakamoto, to request her of the Imperial Prince Ohokusaka, saying :—"I beseech thee let me have the Imperial Princess Hata-hi, whom I desire to espouse unto the Imperial Prince Ohohatsuse." Hereupon the Imperial Prince Ohokusaka answered and said :—"Thy servant has for some time suffered from a severe illness, which cannot be healed. He may be compared to a ship which has taken in its cargo and is waiting for the tide. Death, however, is our destiny ; and there is no sufficient reason for regret. Only I cannot die in peace because my younger sister, the Imperial Princess Hata-hi, will be left alone and unprotected. If now Your Majesty will not loathe her for her ugliness, and will allow her to complete the number of the duckweed flowers,[3] it will be a matter for the deepest gratitude. How should I decline the favour of thy commands ? In order, therefore, to show my

---

[1] This and many other stories in the "Nihongi" show that the position of women in these times was by no means one of abject dependence on their male relatives.

[2] They were children of the Emperor Nintoku, who died A.D. 399, aged 122. The "Shukai" suggests that the Prince and Princess here named were grandchildren, and not children of Nintoku, but the more obvious explanation of the difficulty is that the chronology is entirely untrustworthy.

[3] "An aquatic plant with peltate floating leaves, probably a Lemnanthemum, or marsh-flower." Williams. The allusion is to the opening stanzas of the first ode of the She-king, translated by Dr. Legge as follows :—

> K'wan, K'wan go the ospreys
> On the islet in the river.
> The modest, retiring, virtuous, young lady :—
> For our prince a good mate is she.
>
> Here long, there short, is the duckweed
> To the left, to the right, borne about by the current.
> The modest, retiring, virtuous, young lady :—
> Waking and sleeping he sought her.

sincerity, I offer thee my private treasure, called the Oshiki[1] jewel head-dress [others say 'standing head-dress,' and others, again, Ihaki (rock-tree) head-dress], which I make so bold as to present to thee by the hand of Ne no Omi, the minister whom thou didst send to me. I beg thee to accept of it, although it is an object of no value, as a token of my good faith."

Hereupon Ne no Omi, when he saw the Oshiki jewel head-dress, was struck with its beauty, and the thought occurred to him of stealing it and making it his own treasure. So he falsely represented to the Emperor, saying :—"The Imperial Prince Ohokusaka refused to obey thy orders, and spake to thy servant, saying :—'Shall he, though of the same house, have my XIII. 21. younger sister to wife?'" Having done so, he retained the jewel head-dress, and did not present it to the Emperor, but made it his own.

Hereupon the Emperor believed Ne no Omi's slanderous words, and was greatly wroth. He raised an armed force, with which he surrounded the house of the Imperial Prince Oho-kusaka and slew him.

At this time the Hikakas, Kishi of Naniha, father and sons, were all in the service of the Imperial Prince Ohokusaka, and they were all grieved that their lord should die without a crime. Accordingly the father took in his arms the Prince's head and the two sons took up each one of the Prince's legs and cried aloud, saying :—"Alas! Our Lord has died without a crime. Were we three, father and sons, who served him in life, not to follow him in death, we should be no true retainers." So they cut their throats, and died beside the Imperial corpse. The army, to a man, all wept tears. Upon this the Emperor took Nakashi hime,[2] the Imperial Prince Ohokusaka's wife, and bestowing her within the Palace, made her his concubine. Ultimately he sent for the Imperial Princess Hata-hi and gave her to the Imperial Prince Ohohatsuse to wife.

This year was the year Kinoye Mŭma (31st) of the Cycle.

2nd year, Spring, 1st month, 17th day. Nakashi hime no A.D. 455.

---

[1] Oshiki means literally " push-wood " or " push-tree." Its application here is uncertain.

[2] The " Kojiki " gives here a different name.

Mikoto was appointed Empress. The Emperor loved her exceedingly.

Before this time Nakashi hime no Mikoto bore Prince Mayuwa to the Imperial Prince Ohokusaka. On his mother's account he escaped punishment, and was always brought up within the Palace.

A.D. 456.
XIII. 22.
3rd year, Autumn, 8th month, 9th day. The Emperor was assassinated by Prince Mayuwa [a detailed account is given in the history of the Emperor Ohohatsuse's reign]. After three years he was buried in the misasagi of Fushimi at Sugahara.

BOOK XIV.

THE EMPEROR OHO-HATSUSE WAKATAKE.[1]

(*YŪ-RIAKU*[2] *TENNŌ.*)

THE Emperor Oho-hatsuse Waka-take was the fifth child[3] of the Emperor Wo-asa-tsuma Waku-go no Sukune. When the Emperor was born, a supernatural radiance filled the building.[4] When he grew to manhood, he was distinguished for sturdy strength.

In the 8th month of the 3rd year of his reign, the Emperor Anaho went to the Mountain Palace with the intention of taking the hot baths. At length he went up into a lofty tower and was enjoying the prospect. Accordingly he commanded sake to be brought and a banquet to be held. So then, whilst his mind was at ease and his pleasure at its height, in the course of conversation he turned to the Empress and addressed her, saying :—

[The daughter of the Emperor Izahowake was called the Imperial Princess Nakashi hime. She was also called the Imperial Princess Nagata no Oho-iratsume. The Imperial Prince Ohokusaka, a child of the Emperor Oho-sazaki, took to wife the Imperial Princess Nagata, who bore to him Prince Mayuwa. Afterwards the Emperor

---

[1] Hatsuse is the name of a place in Yamato. Waka-take means young brave.

[2] Yū-riaku means manly stratagem or counsel. The events related in this Book read more like genuine history, and the chronology, though it still leaves much to be desired, is not so wildly inaccurate as before.

[3] He was really the fifth son. See above, p. 315.

[4] The same thing in nearly the same words is related of one of the Later Han Emperors of China.

Anaho, giving heed to the slander of Ne no Omi, put to death the Imperial Prince Ohokusaka and appointed the Imperial Princess Nakashi hime Empress. An account of this is given in the history of the reign of Anaho Tennō.

" Our younger sister " [it seems to have been the ancient custom to address one's wife as "younger sister "], "although thou art Our friend, We fear Prince Mayuwa." Now Prince Mayuwa —who was only a boy—was playing below the tower, and heard everything that was said. Afterwards the Emperor Anaho, making a pillow of the Empress's knees, fell asleep in daylight
XIV. 2. drunkenness. Hereupon Prince Mayuwa, watching the time when he was sound asleep, stabbed and murdered him. On this day one of the Oho-toneri ran [his name and surname are wanting[1]], and said to the Emperor[2]:—"The Emperor Anaho has been murdered by Prince Mayuwa." The Emperor was greatly shocked, and straightway being suspicious of his elder brothers, put on his armour and girded himself with his sword. Taking command of his troops in person, he urgently questioned the Imperial Prince Yatsuri no Shiro-hiko. The Imperial Prince, seeing that he wished to do him a mischief, sat silent and said not a word. So the Emperor drew his sword and slew him. Next he urgently questioned the Imperial Prince Sakahi no Kurohiko. But this Imperial Prince also knew that he was about to do him a mischief, and sat silent, saying not a word.[3] The Emperor's rage became still more violent, so with the further object of killing Prince Mayuwa as well, he examined him as to the reason of his conduct. Prince Mayuwa said :—"Thy servant has never sought the Celestial Dignity. He has only revenged himself on his father's enemy." The Imperial Prince Sakahi no Kurohiko, who feared profoundly the suspicion in which he was held, communicated secretly with Prince Mayuwa, and they at last found an oppor-
XIV. 3. tunity of getting away together. They fled to the house of the Oho-omi[4] Tsubura. The Emperor sent a messenger to ask

---

[1] This note is rejected by the " Shukai " edition. It is certainly frivolous.
[2] i.e. to the Emperor Yūriaku.
[3] The " Kojiki " relates these events quite differently.
[4] Oho-omi is written with the characters read in later times Daijin, i.e. Great Minister or Prime Minister.

for them. The Oho-omi replied by a messenger, saying :— " I may possibly have heard of a vassal in time of trouble taking refuge in a Royal chamber, but I had never seen Princes conceal themselves in the house of a vassal. At this very time the Imperial Prince Sakahi no Kurohiko and Prince Mayuwa, trusting profoundly in thy servant's heart, have come to thy servant's house. How can I have the heart to send them to thee?" In consequence of this the Emperor raised a still greater army and surrounded the Oho-omi's house. The Oho-omi came out, and standing in the courtyard, tied his garters. At this time the Oho-omi's wife brought the garters, and heart-broken, alas! made a song, saying [1] :—

> The Omi child
> Cloth trousers
> Nine-fold having put on—
> Standing in the courtyard
> His garters he adjusts !

The Oho-omi, when he had finished dressing, advanced to the gate of the camp, where he knelt down and said :—" Thy servant cannot obey thy orders, even though his refusal costs him his life. There is a saying of a man of old, ' The will of even a common man cannot be taken from him.' [2] This is precisely thy servant's case. I humbly beseech the Great Prince to allow thy servant's daughter, Kara-hime, and the seven buildings [3] of Katsuraki, which I now offer thee, to be received as a ransom for their offences." The Emperor would not permit XIV. 4. it, but set fire to the houses and burnt them. Hereupon the Oho-omi with the Imperial Prince Kurohiko and Prince Mayuwa were all burnt to death together. Now Nihe no Sukune, Muraji of the Sakahi Be, took in his arms the Imperial Prince's dead body and so was burnt to death. His household [the names are wanting [4]] took up that which was burnt, but were never able to sort out the bones. They were deposited in one coffin and

---

[1] This poem seems intended to express wonder at her husband's care for his appearance at a moment when his life was at stake.

[2] " Confucian Analects," Book IX. chap. xxv. 1.

[3] Granaries, as the " Kojiki " informs us.

[4] A silly note. No wonder the " Shukai " edition rejects it.

buried together on the hill south of Tsukimoto in Imaki no Aya.[1]

Winter 10th month, 1st day. The Emperor resented the Emperor Anaho's having formerly wished to transfer the kingdom to the Imperial Prince Ichinobe no Oshiha,[2] and to commit the succession definitively to his charge. So he sent a man to the Imperial Prince Ichinobe no Oshiha, and treacherously arranged with him to go a-hunting. Inviting him to go on an excursion to the moors, he said :—Karabukuro,[3] the Kimi of the Sasaki mountain in Ohomi, tells me XIV. 5. that now on the Kaya moor in Kutawata in Ohomi, there are wild boars and deer in plenty. The horns they bear are like the twigs of withered trees, their legs are thick together like a grove of bushes, the breath which they breathe resembles the mists of morning. Along with the Imperial Prince, I wish in the first month of winter, when the sky is cloudy and the cold wind blows keenly, to go for an excursion to the moors, where we may somewhat divert our minds by running archery."[4] The Imperial Prince Ichinobe no Oshiha accordingly followed the hunt. Hereupon the Emperor Ohohatsuse drew his bow and putting his horse to a gallop, called out falsely, saying, " There is a wild boar ! " and shot the Imperial Prince Ichinobe no Oshiha dead. A man of the Imperial Prince's household named Uruwa, of the Saheki Be [another name is Nakachiko], took the dead body in his arms. In his consternation he knew not what to do, but writhed on the ground and called aloud upon his master, going to and fro. The Emperor put him to death also.

In this month the Imperial Prince Mimŭma,[5] who had formerly been pleased with Musa, a place belonging to the XIV. 6. Kimi of Miwa, and wishing to shake off his cares, went thither. While on his way he unexpectedly fell in with a force which had been sent against him.[6] He joined battle with them at the

---

[1] This means literally the new-comer Aya or Han. See below, xix. 22.

[2] The eldest son of Richiu Tennō. See p. 306. He was, no doubt, thought too young to succeed to the throne at his father's death in 405.

[3] Kara bag. There is also a name Yamato-bukuro.

[4] i.e. shooting animals with the bow and arrow while one's horse is at a gallop.

[5] The Prince of the august horses. A son of Richiu Tennō.

[6] By the Emperor.

well of Iha in Miwa, but was soon taken prisoner. When about to be executed, he pointed to the well and pronounced a curse, saying :—" This water may be drunk by the people only : royal persons alone may not drink of it."

11th month, 13th day. The Emperor ordered commissioners to erect a lofty pavilion at Asakura in Hatsuse,[1] in which he assumed the Imperial Dignity, and at last established the Palace. He appointed Matori, Heguri no Omi as Oho-omi and Muruya, Oho-tomo no Muraji and Me, Mononobe no Muraji he made Ohomuraji.[2]

1st year, Spring, 3rd month, 3rd day. The Imperial Princess A.D. 457. Kusaka no Hatahi hime was appointed Empress. [Another name for her is Tachi-bana-hime.]

In this month three concubines were appointed. The senior of these, named Kara-hime, daughter of the Oho-omi of Tsubura in Katsuraki, was the mother of the Emperor Shiraga take-hiro-kuni-oshi Waka-Yamato-neko, and of the Imperial Princess Waka-tarashi-hime. [Also called the Imperial Princess Taku-hata no Iratsume.] This Imperial Princess attended to the sacrifices of the Great Deity of Ise.[3] Next XIV. 7. there was Waka-hime, daughter of the Omi of Kibi no Kamutsumichi.[4] [One book says she was the daughter of Kibi no Kuboya no Omi.] She bore two sons. The elder was called the Imperial Prince Ihashiro, and the younger the Imperial Prince Hoshikaha no Waka-miya. Next there was Woguna Kimi, daughter of Fukame, Omi of Wani in Kasuga. She was the mother of Princess Kasuga no Oho-iratsume [also called Princess Takahashi.] Woguna Kimi was originally an Uneme. The Emperor gave one night to her and she became pregnant. Ultimately she gave birth to a girl. The Emperor had suspicions and would not bring her up. When the girl was able to walk, the Emperor was in the great hall with the Oho-muraji Me, of the Mononobe, in attendance on him. The girl

---

[1] The interlinear kana gloss has Hase.

[2] The " Shokugenshō " says :—" The Prime Minister (Oho-omi or Daijin) conducts the Government in conjunction with the Ohomuraji." Another authority says that the Oho-omi was a civil and the Ohomuraji a military officer. The titles were hereditary in these Houses. They became extinct towards the end of the sixth century.

[3] The Sun-Goddess.   [4] The upper province of Kibi, now Bizen.

crossed the courtyard. Me, the Ohomuraji, looking round, said to the Ministers :—"What a pretty girl! There is a saying of the men of old, 'Thou art like thy mother.'[1] [This ancient saying is not clear.] Whose little girl is she said to be who is walking with leisurely pace in the pure court?" The Emperor said :—"Why dost thou ask?" Me no Ohomuraji answered and said :—"When thy servant looks at this little girl walking, she appears to him strongly to resemble the Emperor." The Emperor said :—"Every one who sees her makes the same remark. Sed insolitum est, quum ei unam solum noctem dederim, eam concepisse et filiam peperisse. Quam ob rem suspiciones mihi excitatae sunt." Ohomuraji dixit :—"Sed in hac unâ nocte quoties cum eâ rem habuisti?" "Septies," in-

XIV. 8. quit Imperator. Ohomuraji loquitur :—"Si haec femina puro corpore et purâ mente recepit unam noctem quam ei dedisti, cur tam facile concipis suspiciones et nolis fidere alterius castitati? Servus tuus audivit feminas quae facile praegnantes fiant vel tactu braccarum concipere. Multo magis, quum totam noctem dederis, sine justâ ratione non debes suspiciones concipere."

The Emperor, by order to the Ohomuraji, made the little girl an Imperial Princess, and appointed her mother to be a concubine.

This year was the year Hinoto Tori (34th) of the Cycle.

A.D. 458. 2nd year, Autumn, 7th month. Iketsu hime of Pèkché,[2] in despite of the Emperor's intention to favour[3] her, had an amour with Tate of Ishikaha.

In an old book it is said :—"Tate, the ancestor of the Obito of Momoahi in Ishikaha."

The Emperor was greatly enraged, and giving his commands to the Ohomuraji Muruya, of the Ohotomo House, sent some Kume Be who stretched the four limbs of the woman on a tree. The tree was placed over a cupboard, which was set fire to, and she was burnt to death.

The "Shinsen"[4] of Pèkché says :—"In the 6th year of

---

[1] These words are in Japanese.

[2] Corea has been hardly mentioned for fifty years or so. Probably some of the events allotted to the previous period really belong to this interval.

[3] i.e. wed.   [4] i.e. new compilation, the name of a book.

the Cycle ¹ King Kèro ascended the throne. The Emperor sent Aretoku hither to ask for a nyörang. Pèkche adorned the daughter of the Lady Moni, called the Nyörang Chökké, and sent her as tribute to the Emperor." ²
Winter, 10th month, 3rd day. The Emperor made a progress to the Palace of Yoshino, and on the 6th he proceeded to Mimase. Giving orders to the wardens, he indulged in the chase. They climbed the towering peaks, they crossed the wide jungles. Before the shadows fell, out of ten, seven or XIV. 9. eight had been caught. Every time they hunted, they caught many, so that the birds and beasts were almost exhausted. At length they rested by the springs and groves, and sauntered together in the thickets and meadows. Halting his footmen, the Emperor counted the chariots and horses. Then he inquired of the Ministers, saying :—" It is a pleasure of the hunting-field to make the stewards cut up the fresh meat. Suppose that you and We cut it up ourselves ? " The Ministers were taken aback and could find no answer. Hereupon the Emperor became very wroth, and drawing his sword, slew one of the stewards named Mumakahi of Ohotsu. On this day the Imperial cortège arrived from the Yoshino Palace. The people of the province all shook with fear. In consequence the Grand Empress and the Empress, hearing of this, were full of apprehension, and sent to meet him Hi-no-hime, the Uneme of Yamato,³ to offer him sake. The Emperor, seeing the beauty of the Uneme's countenance,⁴ and the elegance of her appearance, softened his looks, and with a pleased expression, said :—
" How should I not wish to behold thy pleasing smile ? " So

¹ Corresponding to A.D. 429. The "Tongkam" places this event in A.D. 455.
² The use of the words " Emperor " and " tribute " shows that this " new compilation," like the " Pèkché record " already mentioned, was probably the work of Corean literati domiciled in Japan. Nyörang is in the Chinese 女 郎 (lady), which in modern Japanese means a harlot. The Interlinear Kana is Yehashito, which probably means "beautiful person." The nyörang were no doubt concubines of inferior rank. The word rendered lady is 夫 人, a title of the wives of officials above a certain rank. Aretoku is not like a Japanese name.
³ The Atahe of Yamato was her father.
⁴ She was of a marriageable age before the accession of Richiu Tennō in A.D. 400, and we are now at 458.

XIV. 10. hand in hand with her, he entered the hinder palace, where he addressed the Empress Dowager, saying :—"In to-day's hunt we took many birds and beasts. We wished along with the Ministers to cut up the fresh meat and to have a banquet on the moor. But having proposed this to them, not one of them gave us an answer. Therefore did We get angry." The Empress Dowager, knowing the feeling which dictated these words of the Emperor, mollified him, saying :—"The Ministers did not understand that your Majesty, in connection with the sport on the hunting-field, was establishing a Fleshers' Be, and therefore did condescend to ask their opinion, so that their silence was reasonable, and it was hard for them to reply. But even now it is not too late to offer them.[1] I will make a beginning with myself. My steward Nagano is good at making mince meat.[2] I beg permission to present him to thee." The Emperor knelt down and accepted him, saying :—"It is good." This is what the rustic means when he says :—"The nobles understand each other's hearts." The Empress Dowager saw the Emperor's gratification, and pleasure filled her bosom. She further wished to offer men, and said :—"There are my two scullions, Masakida and Takame,[3] of the Mito Be of Uda. I beg leave to add these two men to the others to form a Fleshers' Be." From this time forward Akoko no Sukune, the Miyakko of the province of Yamato, sends some of the

XIV. 11. Kotori Wake of Saho to form the Fleshers' Be. The Omi, the Muraji, the Tomo no Miyakko, and the Kuni no Miyakko also, following (the Empress's example), presented some, one after another.

In this month the Fumubito[4] Be, and the Toneri[5] Be of Kahakami, were instituted.

The Emperor, taking his heart for guide, wrongfully slew many men. The Empire censured him, and called him "The greatly wicked Emperor." The only persons who loved him

---

[1] Men to serve as fleshers.

[2] It must be remembered that the Japanese having no table-knives, all flesh is cut up small before it is served.

[3] A curious name ! It means "High Heaven." Uda is the name of a Kōri of Yamato. There is a village there called Mitobe, which means Imperial House Be. It probably was an appanage of the Empress.

[4] Scribes.   [5] Palace attendants.

were Awo Musa no Suguri [1] of the Scribes' Be and Hakatoko, Hinokuma no Tami-tsukahi. [2]

3rd year, Summer, 4th month. Kunimi, Abe no Omi [His A.D. 459. other name was Shikotohi], uttered a slander respecting the Imperial Princess Taku-hata and Takehiko, Ihoki Be no Muraji, the bath-official, saying :—" Takehiko has had illicit intercourse with the Imperial Princess." Takehiko's father, Kikoyu, hearing this rumour, was afraid lest calamity might overtake him- XIV. 12. self, and persuaded Takehiko to come with him to the River Ihoki. There, pretending to make cormorants dive into the water to catch fish, he took him unawares and slew him. When the Emperor heard this, he sent messengers to question the Imperial Princess. The Imperial Princess answered and said :— " Thy handmaiden knows nothing." Suddenly the Imperial Princess took a divine mirror and went to Isuzu no Kahakami, [3] and watching for a time when no one was passing, buried the mirror, and hanged herself. The Emperor became suspicious on account of the Imperial Princess's absence, and constantly sent persons in the dead of night to search in all directions. When they came to Kahakami, a rainbow appeared, like unto a serpent, four or five rods in length. When they dug the place from which the rainbow sprang they found the divine mirror, and no great distance off, they discovered the Imperial Princess's body. On ripping her open and making examination, there was in her belly something like water, and in the water there was a stone. Kikoyu was thus enabled to establish his son's innocence, but on the other hand he had remorse for having slain him. He revenged him by killing Kunimi, and then fled and hid in the Shrine of Isonokami.

4th year, Spring, 2nd month. The Emperor went a-hunting A.D. 460. with bow and arrows on Mount Katsuraki. Of a sudden a tall XIV. 13. man appeared, who came and stood over the vermilion valley. [4]

---

[1] Suguri is written with Chinese characters which mean " village master." It is said to be a Corean word.

[2] Tami-tsukahi means " employer of the people." It seems to be a title of a low class. It may be observed that the " Kojiki " strives to put a favourable construction on Yūriaku's conduct.

[3] Where the Ise shrines are.

[4] Fairy-land. It is perhaps here the name of a place, Tanikahi.

In face and demeanour he resembled the Emperor. The Emperor knew that he was a God, and therefore proceeded to inquire of him, saying :—" Of what place art thou Lord ? " The tall man answered and said :—" I am a God of visible men.¹ Do thou first tell thy princely name, and then in turn I will infcrm thee of mine." The Emperor answered and said :— " We are Wake-take no Mikoto." The tall man next gave his name, saying :—" Thy servant is the God Hito-koto-nushi." ² He finally joined him in the diversion of the chase. They pursued a deer, and each declined in favour of the other to let fly an arrow at him. They galloped on, bit to bit, using to one another reverent and respectful language, as if in the company of genii. Herewith the sun went down, and the hunt came to an end. The God attended on the Emperor and escorted him as far as the Water of Kume. At this time the people all said :—" An Emperor of great virtue ! "

Autumn, 8th month, 18th day. The Emperor made a progress to the Palace of Yoshino.

28th day. He made a progress to Kahakami no Ono,³ where he commanded the forest wardens to drive the wild beasts. He lay in wait hoping to shoot them himself, when a gad-fly came swiftly flying. Then a dragon-fly flew thither suddenly, bit the gad-fly, and went away with it. The Emperor was pleased at its attention, and commanded his Ministers, saying : —" Do ye on Our behalf compose an ode in praise of this XIV. 14. dragon-fly." As none of the Ministers made so bold as to compose an ode, the Emperor forthwith composed a short piece,⁴ saying :—

> These tidings some one
> Told in the Great Presence,
> How in Yamato
> On the Peak of Womura
> Four-footed game was lying :

---

¹ i.e. who has assumed mortal form.

² Lit. one-word-master. The " Kojiki " expands this into " The Deity who dispels with a word the evil, and with a word the good." See Ch. K., p. 319. The " Kiujiki " makes him a son of Susanowo.

³ The little moor of the upper stream.

⁴ 口 號. This was the name of a particular kind of Chinese poetry of four or eight lines.

The Great Lord,
When he heard this,
Stood at his throne
Entwined with jewels,
Stood at his throne
Entwined with cloth :
Waiting for the game
Whilst I [1] remained :
Waiting for the wild-boar
Whilst I was standing,
My arm in the fleshy part,
Was stung by a gad-fly :
But soon a dragon-fly
That gad-fly did bite.
Even a creeping insect
Waits upon the Great Lord.
Thy form it will bear,
O Yamato, land of the dragon-fly ! [2]

One book has, instead of " the great presence," " the great Lord."

One book has, instead of "stood at his throne," " remained in his throne."

One book has, instead of from " even a creeping insect " (inclusive) to the end, the following :—

That in this wise
It should be famous,
The Heaven-filling [3]
Land of Yamato
Was called the Land of the Dragon-fly. [4]

Therefore in honour of the Dragon-fly this place was called Akitsu no. [5]

[1] The change from the third to the first person is much less marked in the Japanese. It is not to be supposed that the Emperors actually composed these verses themselves, nor perhaps any others ascribed to them in the " Nihongi." The hand of the Court-poet is plain in the honorific epithets and forms given to him therein.

[2] The word for throne is agura. It was no doubt something of the nature of a camp-stool.

[3] Heaven-filling. See above, p. 135, note 5. The metre is irregular naga-uta.

[4] This is the " Kojiki " version.

[5] The moor of the Dragon-fly. See above, p. 134, note 8.

5th year, Spring, 2nd month. The Emperor hunted on Mount Katsuraki. Suddenly there came a supernatural bird, in size like a sparrow, with a long tail which trailed upon the ground. Now this bird chirruped, saying :—" Have a care! Have a care! " Then suddenly there appeared, issuing furiously from the herbage, a raging wild boar of which they had been in chase, and pursued the men. The huntsmen in great terror climbed up into trees. The Emperor commanded his attendants, saying :—" When a savage beast meets with man, it straightway halts. Encounter it with a shot from your bows, and then stab it." The attendants were of an effeminate nature. They climbed up trees, and changed countenance, and their five senses were masterless. The raging wild boar came straight on, and tried to bite the Emperor. But the Emperor with his bow pierced it and stayed its course. Then, raising his foot, he killed it with a kick. Hereupon, when the chase was over, he wanted to cut down the attendants. The attendants, when about to be executed, made a song, saying :—

Oh! my elder brother,
Thou alder-tree branch—
Over Ariwo,
To which I climbed up in flight,
Dreading
XIV. 16. The snorting of the wild-boar,
That was shot
By Our great Lord
Who rules peacefully ! [1]

The Empress, hearing their lament, was sorry for them, and tried to stay (the execution). The Emperor said :—" The

---

[1] This translation exactly reverses the order of the lines of the original. The " Kojiki" version (*vide* Ch. K., p. 318) varies somewhat. Ariwo I take (doubtfully) to be a proper name. The " Kojiki" says that it was the Emperor who climbed into the tree, and Motoöri takes this view. I agree with Chamberlain that this won't do. Perhaps something has been omitted in the " Kojiki" narrative. The insertion of the single word Toneri in one place would make it agree with the " Nihongi." It is not likely that a poem should have been composed to commemorate the Emperor's ascent into a tree.

The alder-tree branch is addressed as " elder brother " in gratitude for its protection.

Empress is taking part, not with the Emperor, but with the
attendants." She answered and said :—" The people all say,
' His Majesty is fond of the chase, and loves game. Is not
this wrong?' If now Your Majesty, on account of a savage
boar, puts to death your attendants, Your Majesty is, as it
were, not different from a wolf." The Emperor with the
Empress went up into their carriage and returned home.
Amid cries of "Long live the Emperor!" he said:—
"How delightful is this! Everybody has caught game, and
We have caught good words, which We have brought back
with us."[1]

Summer, 4th month. Lord Kasyuni [i.e. King Kèro] of
Pèkché, having learnt by rumour that Iketsu hime [viz. the
Nyörang Chök-ke] had been put to death by burning,[2] held
counsel, saying :—" The ancient custom of sending tribute of
women to be made Uneme is contrary to decorum, and is
injurious to our country's reputation. Henceforward it is
unmeet that women be sent as tribute." Accordingly he inti-
mated to his younger brother, Lord Kun[3] [i.e. Lord Kon-chi],
saying :—" Do thou go to Japan,[4] and serve the Emperor."
Lord Kun answered and said :—" My Lord's commands must
not be disobeyed. I pray thee give me one of thy consorts,
and then I will undertake this mission." Lord Kasyuni
accordingly took one of his consorts who was pregnant, XIV. 17.
and having given her in marriage to Lord Kun, said:—
"The month for the delivery of this pregnant consort of
mine has already arrived. If she should be delivered on
the journey, I pray thee place (the child) on board a ship,
and whatever place thou mayest have arrived at, cause it
to be at once sent back to this country." So at last he
took his leave, and went on his mission to the (Japanese)
Court.

---

[1] This passage, from "If now Your Majesty" down to "with us," is
copied, with a few trifling alterations, from a Chinese book. Motoöri dis-
misses the whole incident of the Empress's interference as a silly imitation
of Chinese models. He is doubtless right.

[2] See above, p. 338.

[3] The traditional Kana rendering of 軍 君 (War-lord) is Komukishi.

[4] Japan is 日 本, or Nippon, by which name this country was not known
till much later.

6th month, 1st day. The pregnant consort realized the words of Lord Kasyuni, and gave birth to a child in the island of Kahara in Tsukushi. So this child was given the name of Lord Shima.[1] Upon this Lord Kun straightway took a ship and sent Lord Shima to his country. He became King Mu-nyöng. The people of Pèkché call this island Chuto.[2]

Autumn, 7th month. Lord Kun entered the capital. After this he had five children.

The Pèkché Shinsen says:—" In the year Kanoto ushi (A.D. 461[3]) King Kèro sent his younger brother, Lord Konchi, to Great Wa, to wait upon the Emperor and to confirm the friendship of former sovereigns."

A.D 462. 6th year, Spring, 2nd month, 4th day. The Emperor made an excursion to the small moor of Hatsuse. There, viewing the aspect of the hills and moors, in an outburst of feeling, he made a song, saying :—

> The mountains of Hatsuse,
> The secluded—
> They stand out
> Excellent mountains !
> They run out
> Excellent mountains !
> The mountains of Hatsuse,
> The secluded -
> Are full of various beauties !
> Are full of various beauties ![4]

Hereupon he gave a name to the small moor, and called it Michi no Ono.[5]

---

[1] Shima is the Japanese for island. The Corean is syöm, the two words being no doubt identical. See " Early Japanese History" in " T.A.S.J.," Vol. XVI. i. p. 68.

[2] Master-island.

[3] This date is noteworthy as being the first in the " Nihongi " which is confirmed by Corean history. It is true that it occurs only in a note, which was probably added by a later hand. But the narrative of the text no doubt refers to the same event. From this time forward the " Nihongi " chronology is never grossly inaccurate, though it would be too much to say that it can yet be depended on. See " Early Japanese History " in " T.A.S.J.," XVI. i. p. 67.

[4] Metre irregular.   [5] i.e. the small moor of the road.

3rd month, 7th day. The Emperor wished to make the XIV. 18.
Empress and his concubines plant mulberry trees with their
own hands, in order to encourage the silk industry. Hereupon
he gave orders to Sukaru [This is a personal name] to make a
collection of silkworms throughout the country. Now Sukaru
made a mistake and collected babies,[1] which he presented to
the Emperor. The Emperor laughed greatly, and gave the
babies to Sukaru, saying :—" Do thou bring them up thyself."
Accordingly Sukaru brought them up hard by the Palace
enclosure. So he was granted a title, and was called Chihisako
Be[2] no Muraji.

Summer, 4th month. The Land of Wu[3] sent envoys with
tribute.

7th year, Autumn, 7th month, 3rd day. The Emperor A.D. 463.
commanded Sukaru Chihisako Be no Muraji, saying :—" It is
our desire to see the form of the Deity of Mimuro Hill. [*Some
say that the Deity of this mountain is Oho-mono-shiro-nushi no
Kami. Others say Uda no Sumi-zaka no Kami.*] Thou dost
excel in strength of body. Go thyself, seize him, and bring
him here." Sukaru answered and said :—" I will make the
attempt, and go to seize him." So he ascended the Hill of
Mimuro and caught a great serpent, which he showed the
Emperor, who had not practised (religious) abstinence. Its
thunder rolled, and its eyeballs flamed. The Emperor was
afraid, and, covering his eyes, would not look upon it, but fled
into the interior of the Palace. Then he caused it to be
let loose on the Hill, and giving it a new name, called it
Ikadzuchi.[4]

8th month. One of the Toneri named Oho-sora,[5] of the Bow- XIV. 19.

[1] The Japanese for silkworm is Kahiko. Kahi means to keep, to nurture,
and ko is " little one ; " so there was some excuse for Sukaru's mistake.

[2] Chihisako means " little child." The title and office seem merged in one
here.

[3] The Wu dynasty came to an end A.D. 280, and at this time the Sung
dynasty held rule, but, as Mr. E. H. Parker has pointed out, Wu was also a
territorial designation of that part of China about Nanking. Of course, by
tribute is meant presents. The Japanese early adopted the Chinese
arrogant way of speaking of foreign nations.

[4] Thunderbolt.

[5] Oho-sora means The Great Void (of Heaven). We have had above a
name Takama, i.e. High Heaven.

makers' Be of Kibi, went home on some urgency. Sakitsuya
Omi of Lower Kibi [In one book it says:—"The Kuni no
Miyakko, Yama, Kibi no Omi"], detained Oho-sora, and for
several months would not consent to allow him to go up to the
capital. The Emperor sent Mike no Kimi, a man of valour, to
fetch him. Oho-sora came in obedience to the summons, and
said :—" Sakitsuya took young girls to represent the Emperor's
men, and grown-up women to represent his own men. Then
he made them fight with one another, and on seeing that the
young girls were victorious, drew his sword and slew them. At
another time he took a small cock, which he called the
Emperor's cock, and pulled out its feathers and clipped its
wings. Then he took a large cock, which he called his own
cock, attached to it a bell,[1] and armed its spurs with metal.
Then he matched them together, and when the naked bird got
the better of the other, he again took out his sword and killed
it." When the Emperor heard this story, he sent thirty
soldiers of the Monono Be, who put Sakitsuya to death, with
seventy persons of his household.

This year Tasa, Omi of Upper Kibi, while on duty beside
the Palace, praised Waka-hime abundantly to his friends,
XIV. 20. saying :—" Of all the beautiful women in the Empire, there is
none to compare with my wife. How blooming! How
gentle! How graced with various charms! How radiant!
How genial! What perfection in every feature! She uses
not flower of lead :[2] she adds not oil of orchids. Through
the wide ages her equals are but few : in the present day she
stands alone and peerless." The Emperor inclined his ear,
and listening from a distance, rejoiced in his heart. So with
the object of obtaining Waka-hime for himself, and making
her one of his concubines, he appointed Tasa Governor of
Imna,[3] and promptly favoured Waka-hime. When Tasa no Omi
wedded Waka-hime, she bore to him Ye-kimi and Oto-kimi."[4]

Another book says :—" Tasa no Omi's wife, by name

---

[1] Small bells like the French grêlots were used as ornaments to the wrist
or attached to garters.
[2] White lead ceruse.
[3] Mimana or Kara in Corea, where there was a Japanese resident.
[4] Elder lord and younger lord.

Ke-hime, was the daughter of Tamado no Sukune, son of Katsuraki no Sotsuhiko. The Emperor, hearing of the serene beauty of her form, slew her husband, and wedded her himself."

After Tasa had arrived at his post, he learnt that the Emperor had married his wife, and with the object of obtaining succour, he went to Silla, which at that time did not do service to the Central Land.[1] The Emperor gave orders to Tasa no Omi's son Otokimi, and also to Akawo Kibi no Ama[2] no Atahe, saying:—" Do ye go and chastise Silla." At this time a skilled artisan of Western Aya named Kwan-in Chiri,[3] who was near the Emperor, came forward and represented to him, saying:—" There are in the Land of Han[4] many who are more skilful than thy slave. Let them be sent for and made to serve thee." The Emperor commanded his Ministers, saying:—" Then let Kwan-in Chiri be joined to Otokimi and the others, and let him get instructions from Pèkché; at the same time let an Imperial rescript be delivered directing Pèkché to offer skilled men."

Hereupon Otokimi, in execution of these commands, took with him a body of men and proceeded as far as Pèkché. When he entered that land, a God of the country,[5] assuming the form of an old woman, suddenly met him on the road. Otokimi inquired of her whether the country was far or near. The old woman answered and said:—" If thou goest on for one day more, thou wilt then arrive there." Otokimi thought to himself that the way was too far, and returned without having chastised it. He got together the Imaki[6] skilled artisans who had been given as tribute by Pèkché on a large island, and under the pretence of awaiting a fair wind, tarried there for several months. Tasa no Omi, the Governor of Imna, pleased that Otokimi had gone away without chas-

XIV. 21.

---

[1] The " Central Land " is evidently Japan. The Kana has " Mikado."

[2] Fishermen.

[3] Possibly these are the names of two men. The Western Aya were the Aya of Kahachi.

[4] Corea.   [5] This must refer to Silla.

[6] Imaki is the name of a place in Yoshino in Yamato. It means " new-comer," and the term may have been applied in the first place to this batch of emigrants to distinguish them from previous ones.

tising Silla, secretly sent a man to Pèkché, to warn Otokimi, saying :—" Is thine own head so firm that thou canst chastise others? A report has reached me that the Emperor has wedded my wife, with the result that he has had children by her. [The children are mentioned above.¹] As I now fear that calamity may reach my own person, it is well that I should XIV. 22. wait with foot uplifted. Do thou, my son, come over and betake thyself to Pèkché, and prevent it from communicating with Japan, while I will repair to and hold Imna, and will also hold no communication with Japan." Otokimi's wife Kusu-hime had profound patriotic sentiment; the sense of duty between lord and vassal was strong in her; her loyalty sur-passed the bright sun ; her principles excelled the evergreen fir. She abominated such treason, and having stealthily killed her husband, secretly buried him in the chamber. Then she remained in the large island with Akawo, Ama no Atahe, in charge of the skilled artisans presented by Pèkché. The Emperor, hearing that Otokimi was missing, sent Katashiha, Hitaka no Kishi, and Ko An-chön.² These messengers together made their report to the Emperor. They³ were accordingly ultimately settled in the village of Hirokitsu in Ato in the province of Yamato, where many of them died of disease. In consequence of this, the Emperor commanded Muruya, Ohotomo no Ohomuraji, to instruct Tsukami, Yamato no Aya⁴ XIV. 23. no Atahe to remove Ko-kwi, of the Potters' Be, Kyön-kwi, of the Saddlers' Be, In-să-ra-ka, of the Painters'⁵ Be, Chöng-an-na, of the Brocade-weavers' Be, and Myo-an-na, the Inter-preter, all belonging to the New Aya,⁶ to other residences at the following three places, viz., Upper Momohara, Lower Momohara, and Magami no Hara.

¹ As a matter of fact, they are not; the "Shukai" rejects this note. As the "Shukai" editor points out, all this cannot belong to the same year of Yūriaku's reign.

² Ko An-chön. Probably a Corean. Chön means copper cash, which were unknown in Japan at this time.

³ This must refer to the Pèkché artisans.

⁴ Otherwise called the Eastern Aya.

⁵ The first mention of the art of painting.

⁶ The Aya or Han would now appear to have three branches—the Eastern or Yamato Aya, the Western or Kahachi Aya, and the New or Imaki Aya, whose introduction is here related. They all consisted of skilled men from Corea.

A certain book says :—" Otokimi, Kibi no Omi, returned
from Pèkché, and presented a Be of Aya workmen, a Be
of tailors, and a Be of fleshers."

8th year, Spring, 2nd month. Awo, Musa no Suguri, and A.D. 464.
Haka-toko, Hinokuma no Tami-tsukahi, were sent to the
Country of Wu.

From the accession of the Emperor up to this year eight
years had now passed, during which the Land of Silla was refractory and given to vain talk, and did not send presents. Therefore they feared the intentions of the Central Land,[1] and
cemented friendship with Koryö. Consequently the King of
Koryö sent one hundred picked soldiers to guard Silla. After
a while, one of these Koryö soldiers returned to his own
country on furlough. Now he took with him a Silla man as XIV. 24.
groom. Turning to him, he addressed him, saying :—" Thy
country will be conquered by my country ere long." [One
book says :—Thy country will in the end become our territory,
and that ere long.] When the groom heard this, he pretended
a pain in his belly, and retiring, remained behind. At length
he made his escape to his own country, and told what
had been said. Hereupon the King of Silla knew that Koryö's
guard was mere pretence, and sent messengers to run and tell
the people to kill the cocks kept in their houses. The people
knew his meaning, and killed all the men of Koryö[2] resident in
the country. Only one Koryö man was left, who seized an
opportunity to effect his escape and flee to his own country,
when he told the whole story. The king of Koryö accordingly raised an army and encamped by the city of Chhyuk-
chong-nyu. [*One book says the city of Tokushiki.*] At length
they made music, with song and dance. Hereupon the King
of Silla, hearing in the night the Koryö army singing and
dancing on all sides, became aware that the enemy had occupied the whole land of Silla. So he sent a man to the King of
Imna, saying :—" The King of Koryö has attacked our country.
At this present time, like the fringes sewn on a flag,[3] the condi-

---

[1] Japan.
[2] Kokuryö, the proper name of this country, resembles the onomatopoetic
word for the crowing of a cock : English, cock-a-doodle-doo ; French,
kokeriko ; Japanese, Bekkakō.
[3] Which are always wobbling about.

tion of the land is more precarious than that of a pile of eggs.
XIV. 25. The thread of life is short, and may not at all be reckoned. I
humbly beg that the Japanese Authorities [1] will assist me with
war generals."

Accordingly the King of Imna persuaded Ikaruga, Kashihade
no Omi, Wonashi, Kibi no Omi, and Akameko, Naniha no
Kishi to go to the assistance of Silla. Kashihade no Omi and
the others halted before they reached the camp, and before the
Koryö generals had fought with Kashihade no Omi and the
others, they were all afraid. So Kashihade no Omi and his
colleagues did their best to keep the troops in good heart, and
urged them to get ready the means of attack. Then suddenly
they advanced and took the offensive. For more than ten
days they and the Koryö men kept watch on one another.
When night came on they pierced a steep place, and made a
hollow way, along which they passed all the baggage wagons
and prepared an ambush. At dawn the Koryö men thought
to themselves :—" Kashihade no Omi and the others are stealing away." So they came in pursuit with their whole army.
Then the troops in ambush, both horse and foot, were let go,
and taking them from both sides, put them to a great rout. It
was from this that the enmity between the two countries sprang.
[By the two countries are meant Silla and Koryö.]

Kashihade no Omi and his colleagues spake to Silla, saying:
—" Thou with the utmost weakness wert pitted against the
utmost strength, and had it not been for the assistance of the
Government [2] troops thou wouldst assuredly have been taken at
a disadvantage and thy territory annexed. By this campaign
be warned never in future to be disobedient to the Celestial
Court." [3]

---

[1] In the original 日 本 府. The "Shukai" editor alters this to 官 府 or
official authorities, for no better reason than that the latter term is the one
used in Kimmei's reign. 日 本 occurs frequently after this time, no doubt
being employed retrospectively. Probably the actual word used by the King
of Silla was Wă.

[2] i.e. Japanese.

[3] It is difficult to say how much truth there is in this Corean episode. The
"Tongkam" lends no corroboration. On the contrary the only notices of
Japan which it contains about this time relate to Japanese descents on the
Silla Coast. One is recorded in 459, one in 463, and one in 476. No un-
usual enmity between Silla and Koryö at this time is mentioned in the

9th year, Spring, 2nd month, 1st day. Katabu,[1] Ofushi Kahachi no Atahe, and an Uneme were sent to sacrifice to the Deity of Munagata.[2] Katabu and the Uneme, having arrived at the altar-place,[3] were about to perform the rites, when Katabu debauched the Uneme. When the Emperor heard this, he said :—" When we sacrifice to the Gods and invoke from them blessings, should we not be watchful over our conduct ? " So he sent Naniha no Hidaka no Kishi to put him to death. But Katabu straightway took to flight, and was not to be found. The Emperor again sent Toyoho, Yuge [4] no Muraji, who searched the districts of that province far and wide, and at length caught and slew him at Awi [5] no hara, in the district of Mishima.

3rd month. The Emperor desired to chastise Silla in person, but a God warned him, saying :—" Go not." For this reason the Emperor did not carry out his intention of going, but gave orders to Ki no Woyumi no Sukune, Soga no Karako no Sukune, Ohotomo no Katari [6] no Muraji, and Wokahi no Sukune, saying : —" Silla occupies the Western Land : age after age he has done us homage : he did not neglect visits of ceremony : his payment of tribute was duly discharged. But since We have come to rule the Empire, he has betaken himself beyond Tsushima, and concealed his traces outside of Chamna. He prevents Koryö from sending tribute, he devours the walled cities of Pèkché. Nay, more—his missions of ceremony to this court have been neglected and his tribute remains unpaid. With the savage

" Tongkam." Nor does this narrative square very well with what is related below, xiv. 26, 27. I am inclined, nevertheless, to believe that it has a solid foundation of fact, only that the dates must be wrong.

From " having pierced " to " great rout " is copied mutatis mutandis from a Chinese history of the Wei period, reign of Wu Ti, and Kashihade no Omi's speech to the King of Silla is extracted from the same source.

[1] This curious name means " fragrance-giver."

[2] In Yamato.

[3] The Kana rendering is Kamu-niha (divine courtyard), which is not exactly an altar, but a plot of ground set apart for the worship of the Gods. See above, p. 81, note 9.

[4] Bow-makers.

Awi is indigo, the Polygonum tinctorium.

[6] The Katari were reciters attached to the Court. Unfortunately we know very little about them, or what the subjects of their recitations were.

heart of the wolf he flies away when satiated, and sticks fast when starving. I appoint you four ministers to be generals. Take a royal army and chastise him. Let the punishment of Heaven be reverently executed."

Hereupon Ki no Woyumi no Sukune laid a complaint before the Emperor through Ohotomo no Muruya no Ohomuraji, saying :—" Thy servant, although feeble and incompetent, will respectfully obey the Emperor's orders. But now thy servant's wife has departed this life, and there is nobody to take care of thy servant. Do Thou, my Lord, I beseech Thee, represent this matter fully to the Emperor." Hereupon Ohotomo no Muruya no Ohomuraji represented it fully. When the Emperor heard this complaint, he uttered a sigh of pity. He took an Uneme from the hither province of Kibi, Ohomi [1] by name, and giving her to Ki no Woyumi no Sukune, attached her to his person to take care of him. So at length he sent him off with a shove to his axle.

Ki no Woyumi no Sukune and the rest accordingly entered Silla, butchering as they went the districts along their way. The King of Silla heard by night on all sides the drums of the Government army, and becoming aware that they had completely conquered the land of Tok,[2] fled in confusion with several hundred cavalry. Thereby ensued a great defeat. Woyumi no Sukune pursued and slew the enemy's general in the midst of his army. The whole land of Tok was reduced to order, but there was a remainder which would not submit. Ki no Woyumi no Sukune again withdrew his troops, and having effected a junction with Ohotomo no Katari no Muraji and the others, they again, with a great display of forces, fought with the remaining band. This evening Ohotomo no Katari no Muraji and Ki no Okazaki no Kume no Muraji were both slain while fighting with all their might. Tsumaro, a follower of Katari no Muraji, of the same surname,[3] afterwards came amongst the army and asked for his master. He went along the ranks and sought for him, making inquiry, and saying :—" Where is my master, Lord Ohotomo ? " Then some one informed him, saying :—

XIV. 28.

---

[1] Great sea.

[2] See above, p. 249, where it would seem that Tok was a part of Kara.

[3] Or title.

"Thy masters [1] have, indeed, been slain by the enemy," and pointed out to him the place where the dead bodies were. Tsumaro hearing this, leaped and exclaimed, saying:—"My master has fallen. What avails it that I alone should remain unhurt?" Accordingly he too went against the enemy, and in the same hour perished. Soon after, the rest of the band retired of their own accord, and the Government army also followed their example, and fell back. The general-in-chief, Ki no Woyumi no Sukune, fell ill and died.

Summer, 5th month. Ki no Ohiha no Sukune, when he heard that his father was dead, forthwith proceeded to Silla, and taking from Wokahi no Sukune his command of horse, foot and ships, with the various lesser offices, exercised absolute authority. Hereupon Wokahi no Sukune had a profound resentment towards Ohiha no Sukune and made a false report to Karako no Sukune, saying:—"Ohiha no Sukune has told thy servant, saying:—' Ere long I will take the command of Karako no Sukune from him too.' I pray thee be well on thy guard." In consequence of this there was a coolness between Karako no Sukune and Ohiha no Sukune. Upon this the King of Pèkché, hearing that there was a coolness between the commanders arising out of trifling causes, sent a man to Karako no Sukune and the others, saying:—" I wish to view the frontier of the land. I pray you be so kind as to come and join me." Herewith Karako no Sukune and the rest went on with bridle-bits in a line until they came to a river, when Ohiha no Sukune let his horse drink from the river. Then Karako no Sukune shot at Ohiha no Sukune from behind, and hit the hinder part of his saddle frame. Ohiha no Sukune looked round startled, and shot Karako no Sukune down into the mid stream, so that he died. So the three Omi, having from before this time been rivals with one another, fell out by the way, and returned back without having reached the Palace of the King of Silla.

Hereupon the Uneme, Ohomi, following the dead body of Woyumi no Sukune, arrived in Japan. She at length complained to Ohotomo no Muruya no Ohomuraji, saying:— "Thy handmaiden knows not where to bury him. I beseech thee let a good place be selected by divination." The Oho-

XIV. 29.

_____
[1] *Sic* in original.

muraji accordingly reported to the Emperor, who gave command to the Ohomuraji, saying :—" The Commander-in-chief, Ki no Woyumi no Sukune, tossing his head like a dragon, and glaring like a tiger, surveying with extensive view the eight cords,¹ overwhelmed the rebellious, and dashed against the four seas.² So his body was worn out by ten thousand ri,³ and his life succumbed in the three Han. To show Our compassion, let there be appointed officials to conduct his funeral. Thou, my Lord Ohotomo, art of the same province and a near neighbour of the Lords of Ki, so that thy connection with him is of old standing." Hereupon the Ohomuraji, having received the Emperor's commands, sent Wotori Hanishi⁴ no Muraji to construct a tumulus at the village of Tamuwa, and bury him there. Upon this Ohomi, unable to contain herself for pleasure, sent to the Ohomuraji six Corean slaves named Muro, Te-maro, Oto-maro, Mi-kura, Wogura and Hari.⁵ They are the Yake-bito⁶ Be of the village of Kashimada in hither Kibi. Wokahi no Sukune came specially in attendance on Ki no Woyumi no Sukune's corpse. He remained, however, himself in the Land of Tsuno⁷ and sent Yamato-ko no Muraji [it is not clear what was the surname of this Muraji⁸] with a present of an eight-hand mirror to Ohotomo no Ohomuraji to make a petition, saying :— " Thy servant cannot bear to serve the Celestial Court along with my Lord of Ki.⁹ Therefore I beg permission to remain and reside in the Land of Tsuno." Upon this the Ohomuraji laid the matter before the Emperor on his behalf, and he was

XIV. 30

¹ The eight cords, or measuring tapes, i.e. the eight quarters of the universe.

² The four seas are not put for Japan, but for the universe. All this bombast is copied from a Chinese book.

³ i.e. by distant campaigning.

⁴ The Hanishi were the clay-workers whose office it was to make the clay images which were set up round the tombs of the Emperors. His appointment was therefore an appropriate one. But although the office and the title sometimes coincided, as in this case, they had often nothing to do with each other. A few pages back we had a Katari no Muraji (Chief of the Reciters) and a Kashihade no Omi (Lord Steward) in command of troops in Corea.

⁵ These names are Japanese.   ⁶ Domestics.   ⁷ In Suwō.

⁸ This is a stupid note which the " Shukai " very properly rejects. In " Nihongi " language Yamato-ko no Muraji *is* the surname.

⁹ i.e. Ki no Ohiha no Sukune.

allowed to remain and dwell in the Land of Tsuno. This was the beginning of the Tsuno no Omi first dwelling in the land of Tsuno, and being called Tsuno no Omi.

Autumn, 7th month, 1st day. The province of Kahachi re- XIV. 31. ported :—" The daughter of a man of the district of Asukabe named Hiakŭson, Tanabe no Fubito, was wife to a man named Kariu, Fumi no Obito, of the district of Furuchi. Hiakŭson.

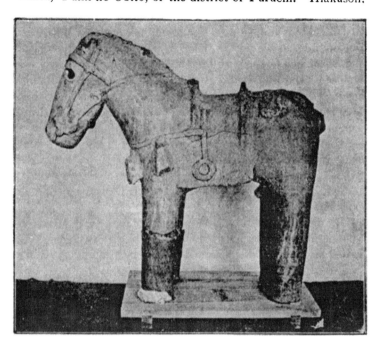

Clay Horse.

hearing that his daughter had given birth to a child, paid a visit of congratulation to his son-in-law's house. He came home by moonlight, and was passing at the foot of the Homuda[2] misasagi at Ichihiko hill, when he fell in with a horseman mounted on a red courser, which dashed along like the flight of

---

[1] Both Hiakŭson and Kariu are Chinese words. This story is apparently a report by one of the recorders whose appointment is mentioned above, p. 307.

[2] Ōjin Tennō.

a dragon, with splendid high springing action, darting off like a wild goose.[1] His strange form was of lofty mould; his remarkable aspect was of extreme distinction. Hiakŭson approached and looked at him. In his heart he wished to possess him, so he whipped up the piebald horse which he rode and brought him alongside of the other, head by head and bit by bit. But

XIV. 32. the red horse shot ahead, spurning the earth, and, galloping on, speedily vanished in the distance. Hereupon the piebald horse lagged behind, and, slow of foot, could not overtake the other. But the rider of the courser, knowing Hiakŭson's wish, stopped and exchanged horses with him, upon which they took leave of each other and separated. Hiakŭson, greatly rejoiced at obtaining such a steed, hastened home and placed him in the stable, where he took off his saddle, foddered him, and went to sleep. The next morning the red courser had become changed into a horse of clay. Hiakŭson, wondering at this in his heart, went back, and, making search at the Homuda misasagi, found the piebald horse standing among the clay horses. So he took it, and left in its stead the clay horse which he had received in exchange.[2]

A.D. 466. 10th year, Autumn, 9th month, 4th day. Awo, Musa no Sukuri, and the others arrived in Tsukushi with two geese presented by Wu. These geese were bitten by Minuma no Kimi's dog and died.

Another book says :—" These geese were bitten by a dog
XIV. 33. belonging to Nimaro, Tsukushi no Mine no Agata nushi, and died."

Hereupon Minuma no Kimi, unable to contain himself for fear and sorrow, presented to the Emperor ten large wild geese with bird-keepers, and begged that his offence might thus be compounded for. The Emperor granted his petition.

Winter, 10th month, 7th day. The bird-keepers presented by Minuma no Kimi were settled in two places, viz. the villages of Karu and Ihare.

---

[1] As usual, this *purpureus pannus* is copied from a Chinese author.

[2] The clay horses here referred to were of the kind described at p. 181 as having been substituted for the living horses previously sacrificed at the tomb. Some of these have been preserved, and specimens may be seen in the Museum at Uyeno, Tōkiō. The illustration represents one of these.

11th year, Summer, 5th month, 1st day. It was reported A.D. 467.
from the district of Kurimoto in the province of Ohomi that
white cormorants dwelt on the shore at Tanagami. Orders
were therefore given to establish toneri [1] of Kahase.

Autumn, 7th month. There was a refugee from Pèkché
who gave his name as Kwisin. It was also stated that Kwisin
was a man of the Land of Wu. The Ihare no Kure [2] no Kotobiki and the Sakate no Yakata-maro are his descendants.

Winter, 10th month. A bird of the Bird-department was
bitten by a dog belonging to a man of Uda and died. The
Emperor was angry, and, branding him on the face, made him
one of the Bird-keepers' Be. Hereupon some office coolies from
the provinces of Shinano and Musashi, who were on night duty
at the Palace, talked to one another, saying:—"Ah! In our
country we pile up birds as high as a small tumulus and eat of
them morning and evening, but still some are left. Now, for XIV. 34.
the sake of one bird, the Emperor has branded a man on the
face. He is a very unjust and wicked master." The Emperor,
hearing this, ordered them to gather and make a heap (of birds),
and as the office coolies were unable to complete it on the spot,
he commanded that they should be enlisted in the Bird-keepers'
Be.[3]

12th year, Summer, 4th month, 4th day. Awo, Musa no A.D. 468.
Sukuri, and Haka-toko Hinokuma no Tamitsukahi went on a
mission to Wu.

Autumn, 10th month, 10th day. The Emperor commanded
the carpenter Mita of Tsuke ["Mita of Winabe," [4] says one
book—probably erroneously] to commence the erection of a
lofty edifice. Hereupon Mita ascended this high building, and
ran about nimbly on all sides as if he were flying. An Uneme
of Ise looked up to the top of this high edifice and marvelled
at his nimble movements, so that she fell down on her face in
the courtyard, and upset a dish of meat which she was serving

---

[1] No doubt to take charge of the cormorants. Kahase, which means
river-reach, may or may not be a proper name.

[2] Kure is the same as Wu, a part of China. Kotobiki means lute-player.
It came to be a proper name.

[3] From which it would seem that the office coolies were of higher rank
than the Bird-keepers.

[4] Winabe is the name of a place in Settsu. Tsuke is in Yamato.

to the Emperor. The Emperor forthwith suspected that Mita had debauched this Uneme, and conceiving to himself the thought of executing him, charged the Mononobe with this duty. At this time Hada no Sake[1] no Kimi was in attendance. He wished by the voice of his lute to make the Emperor understand, so placing his lute crosswise, and playing upon it, he said :—

> Be there for five hundred years
> Prosperity
> To the maid of Ise
> Of Ise
> (Of the divine wind),
> And until it is spent
> Let me attend
> With faithful service
> On the Great Lord.
> Let my life, too,
> Be as long,
> Said the carpenter,
> The poor carpenter ![2]

Hereupon the Emperor understood the voice of the lute, and pardoned the offence.

13th year, Spring, 3rd month. Hadane no Mikoto, great-great-grandson of Saho-hiko,[3] secretly seduced the Uneme Yamanobe no Koshimako. When this came to the Emperor's ears, he gave Hadane no Mikoto in charge to Mononobe no Me no Ohomuraji, and made him call him to account for it. Hadane no Mikoto purged his offence by the payment of eight horses and eight swords, and then made a song, saying :—

> For the sake of Koshimako,
> Of Yamanobe,

---

[1] Sake is 酒 rice-beer. This person was, perhaps, a descendant of the Corean Prince Chhyu mentioned above, A.D. 353, and whose name is written with the same character. The word Hada, however, points to a Chinese ancestry. Hada is the Japanese traditional rendering of the character for T'sin, the Chinese dynasty of that name.

[2] Some commentators explain part of this poem differently. The metre is irregular.

[3] It is not clear why so remote a descendant of a Mikado should be called Mikoto.

Some one boasts that
The eight horses
Are not even to be grudged.

Me no Ohomuraji, hearing this, reported it to the Emperor,
who made Hadane no Mikoto lay out his treasures on the
ground at Tachibana moto [1] of Ichinobe in Yega. He ultimately
took the village of Nagano in Yega, and gave it to Mononobe
no Me no Ohomuraji.

Autumn, 8th month. There was a man of Miwikuma in the XIV. 36.
province of Harima called Ayashi no Womaro, who was strong
of body and stout of heart, and did wanton outrage, committing
robberies on the highways, and preventing traffic. He intercepted the boats of merchants and plundered them every
one. He had also disobeyed the laws of the country by
neglecting to pay his taxes.

Hereupon the Emperor sent Ohoki, Kasuga no Wono no
Omi, in command of one hundred soldiers who feared not
death. They all together took torches, and having surrounded
his house, set fire to it. Now from the midst of the flames
there came forth furiously a white dog, which pursued Ohoki
no Omi. This dog was as big as a horse. But the complexion of
Ohoki no Omi's spirit did not change.[2] He drew his sword and
slew it, whereupon it became changed into Ayashi no Womaro.

Autumn, 9th month. The carpenter, Mane, of the Wina
Be, planed timber with an axe,[3] using a stone as ruler. All
day long he planed, and never spoiled the edge by mistake. XIV. 37.
The Emperor visited the place, and, wondering, asked of him,
saying:—"Dost thou never make a mistake and strike the
stone?" Mane answered and said:—"I never make a mistake!" Then the Emperor called together the Uneme, and
made them strip off their clothing and wrestle in open view
with only their waistcloths on. Hereupon Mane ceased for a
while, and looked up at them, and then went on with his planing.
But unawares he made a slip of the hand, and spoilt the edge

---

[1] Tachibana moto means "orange-stem, or orange-bottom," and possibly
is to be taken here in this sense, and not as the name of a place.

[2] Here is the magician (world-wide) who can change himself into a beast,
but on being wounded or killed is obliged to assume his natural form.

[3] The plane was apparently unknown.

of his tool.   The Emperor accordingly rebuked him, saying :—
"Where does this fellow come from that, without respect to us,
he gives such heedless answers with unchastened heart ? "   So
he handed him over to the Mononobe to be executed on the
moor.

Now amongst his comrades there was a carpenter who
lamented for Mane, and made a song, saying :-

> The much to be regretted
> Carpenter of Winabe—
> The ink-cord he applied,—
> When he is no more,
> Who will apply it ?
> Alas ! that ink-cord ! [1]

When the Emperor heard this song, his feelings changed to
remorse, and he said with a sigh of regret :—" How many men
I have destroyed ! "   So he mounted a messenger of mercy on
a black horse of Kahi, and made him gallop to the place of
execution to stop it and pardon him.   The cords with which
he was tied were unbound, and he, too, made a song,
saying :—

> As the night [2]
> Black was the horse of Kahi—
> Had they but saddled him,
> My life were lost—
> Ah ! that horse of Kahi !

XIV. 38.

Instead of "My life were lost," one book has, "He
would not have arrived (in time)."

A.D. 470.   14th year, Spring, 1st month, 13th day.   Awo, Musa no
Sukuri, and the others, in company with envoys from the Land

---

[1] The ink-cord is a contrivance for ruling lines on wood, used to this day
by Japanese carpenters.   A cord is passed through a pot of ink and then
drawn taut, and let go so as to strike the wood.   A chalked line is sometimes used in the same way in this country.   See illustration in "Transactions of Japan Society," Vol. II. p. 217.   The metre of this poem is
irregular, being a tanka with an additional line of seven syllables between
the second and third.

[2] This is one of many explanations of the conventional epithet nubatama,
applied to dark or black things.

of Wu, and bringing with them skilled workmen presented by Wu, viz. Aya weavers and Kure [1] weavers, as well as the seamstresses Ane-hime and Oto-hime, anchored in the harbour of Suminoye. In this month the Shihatsu highway was carried through as a road for the guests from Wu. It was called the Kure-saka. [2]

3rd month. The Emperor commanded the Omi and Muraji to go to receive the envoys from Wu. The men of Wu were accordingly settled on the moor of Hinokuma, which was therefore called Kure-hara. [3] The seamstress Ane-hime was presented to the God of Oho-Miwa, and Oto-hime was appointed to the Be of Aya seamstresses. The Aya weavers, the Kure weavers and the seamstresses—these were the founders of the Asuka Seamstresses' Be and of the Ise Seamstresses' Be.

Summer, 4th month, 1st day. The Emperor, wishing to make a feast for the men of Wu, asked the ministers, one after another, saying :—" Who will be the best man to keep them company at table ? " The ministers all said :—" Ne no Omi will be the proper person." The Emperor accordingly gave command to Ne no Omi, and appointed him to keep them company in eating. Ultimately the men of Wu were entertained at Taka-nukuhara in Iso no Kami. [4] Now a Toneri was sent secretly XIV. 39. to observe the ornamentation. The Toneri reported to the Emperor, saying :—" The jewel head-dress worn by Ne no Omi is very noble, and extremely lovely." Moreover, everybody said, " He also wore it before when he went to receive the men of Wu." Hereupon the Emperor, wishing to see it himself, gave orders to the Omi and Muraji, and made them present themselves before the hall in the dress which they wore at the banquet. The Empress looked up to Heaven and, with sobs and tears, lamented bitterly. The Emperor inquired of her, saying :—" Why weepest thou ? " The Empress, leaving the

---

[1] For Aya and Kure the Chinese characters are 漢 and 吳, i.e. Han and Wu, the Chinese dynasties so called. But in this connection the Japanese render these names by Aya and Kure.

The " Shukai " editor has a note here to the effect that Han is Chang-an and Loh-yang, formerly capitals of Han ; Wu is Chien-kang (Chien-yeh ?), the Wu capital, near the present Nanking.

[2] Wu acclivity.   [3] The plain of Wu. It is in Yamato.
[4] Yamato.

couch, answered him, saying:—"This jewel head-dress was presented on behalf of thy handmaiden by her elder brother, Prince Oho-kusaka, when, in obedience to the orders of the Emperor Anaho, he offered her to Your Majesty.[1] Therefore I conceived suspicion of Ne no Omi, and unawares shed tears and wept for grief." When the Emperor heard this he was astonished, and was very wroth. He pressed it sharply home to Ne no Omi, who replied, saying:—"I have deserved to die! I have deserved to die! Truly it is thy servant's fault." The Emperor commanded, saying:—"From this time forward let Ne no Omi, his children, his descendants, and his eighty connections have no concern with the order of Ministers of State." He was about to put Ne no Omi to death, but he ran away and hid himself. Arriving at Hine, he made a rice-castle, in which he stood on the defensive, but was ultimately slain by the Government forces. The Emperor ordered the officials to divide his descendants into two parts, one of which was constituted common people of the Oho-kusaka Be, and was allotted in fief to the Empress; the other part was given to the Chinu no Agata-nushi, and made sack-bearers. So having sought out a descendant of Hikaka, Naniha no Kishi,[2] a title was granted to him, and he was made Oho-kusaka Be no Kishi.

XIV. 40.

After matters had become quiet, Wone[3] no Omi [Wone no Omi was the son of Ne no Omi], when lying down at night, said to some one:—"The Emperor's castle is not strong; my father's castle is strong." These words came to the Emperor's ears. He sent a man to see Ne no Omi's house. It was really as had been said. Therefore he seized him and put him to death. Ne no Omi's descendants were made Sakamoto no Omi. From this they had their beginning.

A.D. 471.

15th year. The Hada House[4] was dispersed. The Omi and Muraji each enforced their services at pleasure, and would not allow the Hada no Miyakko to control them. Consequently Sake, Hada no Miyakko, made a great grievance of

---

[1] See above, p. 330.   [2] See above, p. 331.   [3] Wo means little.
[4] Hada. Several families of this name are mentioned in the "Seishiroku." They were believed to be descended from She Hwang-Ti, the celebrated Chinese Emperor of the T'sin dynasty, who reigned B.C. 221 to 209.

this, and took office with the Emperor. The Emperor loved and favoured him, and commanded that the Hada House should be assembled and given to Lord Sake of Hada. So this Lord, attended by excellent Be workmen of 180[1] kinds, XIV. 41. presented as industrial taxes fine silks, which were piled up so as to fill the Court. Therefore he was granted a title, viz. Udzu-masa. [Some say Udzumori masa, the appearance of all being piled up so as to fill.[2]]

16th year, Autumn, 7th month. The Emperor ordered those A.D. 472. provinces and districts which were suitable for mulberry trees to plant mulberry trees. He again dispersed to other places the Hada House, and made them bring tribute of industrial taxes.

Winter, 10th month. The Emperor ordered the Aya Be to be brought together, and established their Tomo no Miyakko, granting him the title of Atahe.

One book says:—"Granted the Aya no Omi the title of Atahe."

17th year, Spring, 3rd month, 2nd day. The Hanishi[3] no A.D. 473. Muraji were made to present pure vessels suitable for serving the Emperor's morning and evening meals. Hereupon Ake, the ancestor[4] of the Hanishi no Muraji, presented to the Emperor a Be of his private subjects of the village of Kusasa in the province of Settsu, of the villages of Uchi and Fushimi in the province of Yamashiro, of the village of Fuji-kata in the XIV. 42. province of Ise, and also from Tamba, Tajima and Inaba, and named them the Nihe[5] no Hanishi Be.

18th year, Autumn, 8th month, 10th day. The Mononobe A.D. 474. Ushiro no Sukune and the Mononobe Me no Muraji were sent to smite Ise no Asahi no Iratsuko. Asahi no Iratsuko, hearing of the approach of the Government troops, opposed them in battle at Awohaka[6] in Iga. Priding himself on his skill in archery, he addressed the Government army, saying:—"Who

---

[1] 180 is, of course, a fancy number.

[2] This is an attempt to connect this name with *tsumoru*, to be piled up.

[3] Potters.

[4] Ancestor here cannot mean founder of the House.

[5] Nihe means food; these potters were for the supply of the Emperor's table utensils.

[6] Green tumulus.

is a match for the hand of Asahi no Iratsuko? The arrow
which he lets fly will pierce two thicknesses of armour." The
Government troops were all afraid, and Ushiro no Sukune did
not dare to advance to the combat. They awaited each other
for two days and one night. Hereupon the Mononobe Me no
Muraji armed himself with his sword, and making Oho-wono-
te,[1] of the Mononobe of Kiku in Tsukushi, take his shield and
call out in the midst of the army, advanced along with him.
Asahi no Iratsuko saw them from afar off, and shot an arrow
through Oho-wono-te's shield and two-fold armour which at
the same time entered the flesh of his body to the depth of
XIV. 43. an inch. Oho-wono-te screened with his shield the Mononobe,
Me no Muraji, and Me no Muraji caught Asahi no Iratsuko
and slew him. Accordingly Ushiro no Sukune, beside himself
with shame, for seven days did not make his report to the
Emperor. But the Emperor inquired of his Ministers in
attendance, saying :—" Why does not Ushiro no Sukune make
his report?" Now there was a man named Sanuki no Ta-
mushi Wake who came forward and addressed the Emperor,
saying :—" Ushiro no Sukune is a coward. For the space of
two days and one night he was unable to seize Asahi no
Iratsuko. Then the Mononobe, Me no Muraji, taking with
him Oho-wono-te, a Mononobe of. Kiku in Tsukushi, caught
and slew Asahi no Iratsuko." When the Emperor heard
this he was angry, and promptly taking away from Ushiro
no Sukune his Be of Wina,[2] gave it to the Mononobe Me no
Muraji.

A.D. 475. 19th year, Spring, 3rd month, 13th day. By Imperial
command, the Anaho Be was established.[3]

A.D. 476. 20th year,[4] Winter. The "King of Koryö raised a great
army and utterly smote Pèkché. There was but a small
remnant left, which assembled and occupied Chhang-ha.[5]
Their victuals became exhausted, and deep was hereupon the

---

[1] Great-axe-hand.

[2] The village of Wina-Be, in Ise, with its inhabitants.

[3] In memory of the Emperor Anaho.

[4] The "Tongkam" date is 475. We have now arrived at pretty exact
chronology.

[5] 倉 下. The traditional Kana renders this Hesu-oto—perhaps an
attempt to reproduce the native Corean name.

weeping and lamentation. Upon this the Koryö generals addressed their King, saying:—"There is something extraordinary in the temper of Pèkché. Whenever thy servants observe them, they seem unaware of their own ruin. It is to be feared that they will again spread forth and revive. We pray that they may be at length got rid of." The King said:—"No! I, the unworthy one, have heard that the Land XIV. 44. of Pèkché is under the jurisdiction of the Country of Japan, and that this connection is of old standing. It is also known to all the neighbouring countries that their King repairs to Japan and serves the Emperor." Ultimately it (the proposal to exterminate the Pèkché people) was abandoned.

The Pèkché record says:—"King Kèro, year Kinoto U (475), Winter. A large army from Koryö came and besieged the great castle for seven days and seven nights. The Royal castle surrendered, and at length they destroyed Wi-nyé. The King, Queen, and Princes all fell into the hands of the enemy."

21st year, Spring, 3rd month. The Emperor, hearing that XIV. 45. Pèkché had been conquered by Koryö, gave Kuma-nari to A.D. 477. King Munchu, and so lent aid to his country. The men of that day all said:—"The Land of Pèkché, though their race was destroyed, assembled and lamented at Chhang-ha. They with true hearts appealed to the Emperor, who restored their country."

King Munchu was King Kèro's younger brother by the mother's side. An ancient Japanese record says:—"The statement that Kumanari was given to King Mata[1] is probably an error. Kumanari is a separate village of the district of Lower Takori[2] in Imna."

.

[1] 末 多. The Coreans call him 牟 大, i.e. Mu-tè. He was Munchu's successor. The Traditional Kana has Arushi for 下, lower. The Corean for Lower is arè.

The syllable ko in this name is probably an error, as below (reign of Keidai), Upper Tari and Lower Tari are mentioned as districts. National vanity is a powerful stimulus to the mythopœic faculty, and the above narrative must be taken with a few grains of salt. But it is no doubt true in the main. The "Tongkam," which gives a short account of the war, says that Silla sent an army of 10,000 men to the assistance of Pèkché. Under the year 475 it records the removal of the Pèkché capital to Ung-

22nd year, Spring, 1st month. Prince Shiraga was made Heir Apparent.

Autumn, 7th month. A man of Tsutsukaha in the district of Yosa in the province of Tamba, the child of Urashima of Midzunoye, went fishing in a boat. At length he caught a large tortoise,[1] which straightway became changed into a woman. Hereupon Urashima's child fell in love with her, and made her his wife. They went down together into the sea and reached Hōrai San,[2] where they saw the genii. The story is in another Book.[3]

23rd year, Summer, 4th month. King Munkeun[4] of Pèkché died.

chin. Now Ung-chin or Ung-chhön (熊 津 or 熊 川) was a town in Kyöng-syang-do, near the present Keumhè, and the meaning is Bear-port or Bear-river, evidently, therefore, the same with the Kuma-nari of the text. Kuma is for koma, the Corean word for bear, and nari is a dialectical or ancient form of năi (pronounced nè), river. It occurs above in the name of the river which the King of Silla swears by at p. 231. Ung-chin or Kuma-nari was in the Imna territory, the capital of which was Keumhè, then controlled by Japan, and it is not at all improbable that it should be ceded to Pèkché on this occasion.

The "Tongkam" mentions a Japanese descent on the eastern coast of Silla in 476. They were driven off with a loss of 200 men.

[1] Or turtle.

[2] "Mount Hōrai is the P'êng-Lai-Shan of the Chinese, one of the Three Isles of the Genii, which were believed to lie in the Eastern Sea, opposite to the coast of China. This happy group was the paradise of the Genii, who there maintained a sempiternal vigour by quaffing the waters of the fountain of life which flowed for them in a perpetual stream. The pine, the plum, the peach-tree, and the sacred fungus grow for ever upon its rocky shores ; and the ancient crane builds its nest upon the giant limbs of its never-dying pine." Catalogue of Japanese paintings in the British Museum, Anderson, p. 224. See also Dickins' "Taketori-Monogatari," in the "R.A.S. Transactions." The "Manyōshiu," an ancient collection of Japanese poems, contains a beautiful version of this legend, which has been rendered into English verse by Mr. B. H. Chamberlain, in his "Classical Poetry of the Japanese," and of which a prose version may be found in my grammar of the Japanese written language. The Chinese and Japanese legendary lore associated with Hōrai San is of boundless extent.

The Interlinear Kana renders Hōrai San by Tokoyo no Kuni, or Eternal Land, which is quite inadequate.

[3] The "Shukai" editor rejects this as an unauthorized addition.

[4] There is no Pèkché king of this name. King Sam-Keun (三 斤), who died in this year (the month differs), is doubtless meant. The first

The Emperor summoned within the Palace Prince Mata
(Mutè), the second of Prince Konchi's five sons, who was young
in years, but intelligent. He himself stroked the Prince's face
and head, and made a gracious decree, appointing him to reign
over that country. He also gave him weapons, and at the
same time furnished him with 500 soldiers of the Land of
Tsukushi to escort him to his country. He became King
Tong-syöng.[1]
This year, tribute was sent from Pèkché in excess of the
regular amount.
Tsukushi no Achi no Omi and Umakahi no Omi, in command of a naval force, attacked Koryö.
Autumn, 7th month. The Emperor took to his sick-bed,
and was ill at ease. By an Imperial decree he committed
rewards and punishments, together with financial matters, great
and small alike, to the charge of the Prince Imperial.
8th month, 7th day. The Emperor's disease became more
and more grave. He took leave of all the functionaries. He
pressed all their hands with sobs and lamentations, and died
in the Great Hall, having left command to Ohotomo no XIV. 48
Muruya no Ohomuraji and Yamato-Aya no Tsuka no Atahe,
saying :—"At the present time, the world is one household :
smoke and fire are 10,000 ri distant :[2] the people are well-
ordered : the four barbarians are submissive. This is by the
will of Heaven, which desires to bestow peace throughout

character 文 came in somehow from the name of the preceding King
(文 州) Munchu. The following is from the " Tongkam," IV. 32, under
the date A.D. 477. " Summer, 4th month. The King of Pèkché appointed
his eldest son Samkeun to be Heir Apparent. Hèku of Pèkché killed his
Prince Munchu. The Heir Apparent Samkeun came to the throne. His
age was thirteen. The military administration of the country was placed
in entire charge of Hèku. Before this Hèku exercised authority in an
arbitrary way, and corrupted the laws, cherishing feelings of disloyalty to
his Prince. The King (Munchu) was unable to control him. Hereupon
the King went hunting and stayed abroad for the night, and Hèku sent a
robber who murdered him." Hèku was put to death in the following year.
In 479 we have the following :—" Winter, 11th month. King Samkeun
of Pèkché died, and was succeeded by Mutè, son of King Munchu's younger
brother Kônchi.
[1] East Castle, probably in allusion to the Eastern situation of Ungchin.
[2] War is far off.

the land. Therefore with careful mind inciting myself, I have been every day watchful for that day, for the sake of the people. The Omi, the Muraji and the Tomo no Miyakko daily attend the court : the Governors of provinces and of districts in due season assemble in court. How shall they not with their whole hearts diligently observe the Imperial decrees? In principle our relation is that of Prince and vassal, but in feeling it is also that of father and child. It was my hope that by the help of the wisdom of the Omi and Muraji the hearts of the people both in the capital and elsewhere might be rejoiced, and I desired long to preserve peace throughout the Empire. But unexpectedly disease has come upon me. It has rooted itself deeper and deeper, and has greatly increased. This is the common lot of humanity, and is not worth wasting words over.

XIV. 49

But in the capital and in the country the clothing and caps have not yet attained to freshness and neatness : civilization and Government still remain short of perfection. When I begin to reflect on this, I am simply lost in chagrin. But it is now many years since I could be described as in the vigour of youth. My strength of body and of mind have together become worn out. What I now do is of course not for my own benefit, but solely from a desire to facilitate the nourishment of the people. Therefore is it that I do this. What one of the descendants of mankind is absent from my thought? For the sake of the Empire, private feelings should be severed. At the present time [1] Prince Hoshikaha cherishes treason in his heart. His conduct is wanting in friendliness towards (his brethren).[2] It has been said by a man of old :—' There is no one who knows the minister so well as his Lord : there is no one who knows the child so well as his father.' Even supposing that Hoshikaha should make up his mind to unite (with his brethren) in ruling the State, certain disgrace would come universally upon the Omi and Muraji, and a cruel poison overflow the nation. Now a bad descendant is to be dreaded for the people's sake : a good

XIV. 50.

[1] See p. 337.

[2] " His brethren " is not in the original, but there is an allusion to the Shooking (Legge, Vol. III. Pt. II. p. 535), where the complete phrase is found.

descendant is sufficient to sustain the burden of the Great Task.[1] Although this is a matter concerning Our House, in principle it does not admit of concealment. The Ohomuraji and the officials of the Home Department are widespread and pervade the whole country: the Prince Imperial, who is in the position of becoming my successor, is known to the world for his benevolence and filial piety. His conduct is such that he is a sufficient person to carry out Our ideas. If along with him ye administer the Empire, even although Our eyes are closed, what room is there for repining?"[2]

In one book it is said:—"It is known to all the world that Prince Hoshikaha is of an evil disposition and of a violent heart. If unfortunately after Our death he should attempt to harm the Prince Imperial, ye and the officials of the Home Department are very numerous. Strive your utmost to render each other mutual aid, and let there be no contemptuousness."

At this time Oshiro, Kibi no Omi, General of the expedition against Silla, arrived at the province of Kibi, and passed by his house. Afterwards 500 Yemishi under his command, hearing of the Emperor's death, spoke to one another, saying :—"The Emperor who controls our country is dead. The opportunity should not be lost." So assembling themselves into a band, they invaded the neighbouring districts. Hereupon Oshiro came from his house, and meeting the Yemishi at Port Saba,[3] fought with them, and shot at the Yemishi. But some skipped and others lay down, thereby succeeding in avoiding the arrows. In the end he was unable to shoot them. Therewith Oshiro twanged his empty bow by the sea-shore, and of the skippers and skulkers two companies were shot to death.[4] Two cases of arrows were all used up. So he called to boatmen and asked them for arrows. But they were afraid, and of their own accord retired. Then

XIV. 51.

---

[1] The sovereignty.

[2] This speech is copied, with some unimportant changes, from a passage in a Chinese History of the Sui dynasty, where it is assigned to the Emperor Kaotsu, who died A.D. 604, i.e. 125 years *after* the death of Yūriaku.

[3] In Suwō.

[4] Chinese legend mentions archers so skilful that they could shoot birds and beasts without any arrows whatever.

Oshiro set up his bow, and taking it by the end, made a song,
saying :—

> On the way he met them,
> The Boy of Oshiro !
> It is in Heaven only that
> Unheard of he will be,
> For on Earth at least
> He will be heard of.

Having finished this song, he slew many men with his own
hand and pursued them on as far as Port Uragake in the Land
of Tamba, where they were all massacred.

XIV. 52.

One book says :—" He pursued them as far as Uragake,
and then sent men who slew them all."

BOOK XV.

THE EMPEROR SHIRAGA [1] -TAKE-HIRO-KUNI-OSHI-WAKA-YAMATO-
NEKO.

(SEINEI[2] TENNŌ.)

THE Emperor Shiraga-take-hiro-kuni-oshi-waka-Yamato-neko
was the third child of the Emperor Ohohatsuse-waka-take.
His mother's name was Katsuraki no Kara-hime. The
Emperor's hair was white [3] from his birth. When he grew up
to manhood, he loved the people. The Emperor Ohohatsuse
had a special admiration for him amongst all his children, and
in the 22nd year of his reign appointed him Prince Imperial.
The Emperor Ohohatsuse died in the 8th month of the 23rd
year of his reign. Then Kibi no Waka-hime secretly addressed
the Imperial Prince, the younger son Hoshikaha, saying :—
" If thou dost desire to ascend to the Imperial rank, do thou
first of all take the office of the Treasury." The eldest son,
the Imperial Prince Ihaki, hearing this advice of the Lady his
mother to her younger son, said :—" Although the Prince
Imperial is my younger brother, why should he be betrayed ?
This thing should not be done." But Prince Hoshikaha
would not give ear. He rashly followed the advice of the
Lady his mother. Finally he took possession of the Treasury,
and locked the outer door, therewith making provision against XV. 2.

---

[1] Shiraga means white hair. The " Kojiki " gives his name as Shiraga
no oho-Yamato-neko.

[2] Seinei, pure and tranquil.

[3] The same thing is related of the Chinese philosopher Laotze and other
Chinese worthies.

disaster.   He exercised arbitrary authority, and squandered
the official property.   Hereupon Ohotomo no Muruya no Ohomuraji spake to Yamato no Aya no Tsuka no Atahe, saying :—
" The time has now come when the dying injunctions of the
Emperor Ohohatsuse are to be fulfilled.   It is meet that we
should comply with them and do service to the Prince
Imperial."   So they raised an armed force and besieged the
Treasury.   They blockaded it from without, and setting fire
to it, roasted to death the Imperial Prince Hoshikaha.   At
this time Kibi no Waka-hime, the Imperial Prince Ihaki, Ani-
kimi,[1] his elder brother by a different father, and Ki no Okazaki
no Kume[2] were roasted to death along with him.   Then
Wone, the Agata-nushi of Mino in Kahachi, in trepidation
and alarm, burst away from the fire and made his escape.   He
embraced the legs of Ayahiko, Kishi of Kusakabe, and through
him begged his life of the Ohomuraji, Ohotomo no Muruya,
saying :—" Thy slave Wone, the Agata-nushi, was the faithful
servant of the Imperial Prince Hoshikaha, but yet he was not
rebellious towards the Prince Imperial.   He prays that a
generous mercy be accorded him, and a human life spared.
Accordingly Ayahiko represented this fully to Ohotomo, the
Ohomuraji, on his behalf, and he was not entered in the rank
of those who were executed.   Wone thereupon made representation to the Ohomuraji through Ayahiko, saying :—" My
Lord Ohotomo the Ohomuraji, owing to thy great mercy
bestowed on me, my life, which was in imminent danger, has
been continued and lengthened so that I can see the light of
day."   So he hastened to present to the Ohomuraji ten chō of
XV. 3. rice-land at Ohowido in the village of Kume in Naniha.   He
also presented rice-land to Ayahiko as a return for the favour
shown him.

In this month, the Omi of the upper province of Kibi,
hearing of the disturbances at the Court, wished to aid their
uterine brother, the Imperial Prince Hoshikaha, and came
floating over the sea with a fleet of forty war vessels.   When
they arrived they heard of the roasting to death, and went
away again without landing.   The Emperor straightway sent

---

[1] Or Ye-kimi.   This name means elder Lord.
[2] Probably for Kume no Muraji.

messengers to call the Omi [1] of Upper Kibi to an account, and to deprive them of the mountain Be of which they had control.

Winter, 10th month, 4th day. The Ohomuraji, Ohotomo no Muruya, attended by the Omi and Muraji, delivered to the Prince Imperial the Seal.

1st year, Spring, 1st month, 15th day. The Emperor, by A.D. 480 command to the officials, prepared an arena at Mikakuri in Ihare, and there assumed the Imperial Dignity. He at length established his Palace, and honoured Katsuraki no Kara-hime with the title of Grand Consort.[2] The Ohomuraji, Ohotomo no Muruya, was made Ohomuraji, and the Oho-omi of Matori in Heguri was made Oho-omi, so that both were continued in their former positions. The Omi, Muraji, and Tomo no Miyakko each took the rank belonging to their several offices.

Winter, 10th month, 9th day. The Emperor Ohohatsuse was buried in the misasagi on the Takawashi plain in Tajihi. At this time the Hayato lamented night and day beside the misasagi, and refused the food which was offered them. Seven days passed, and then they died. The officials constructed a mound to the north of the tumulus, where they were buried with due ceremony. This was the year Kanoye Saru (57th) of XV. 4. the Cycle.

2nd year, Spring, 2nd month. The Emperor, vexed that he A.D. 481. had no children, sent the Ohomuraji, Ohotomo no Muruya, to the provinces, and established the Be of Shiraga no Toneri,[3] the Be of Shiraga no Kashihade,[4] and the Be of Shiraga no Yugehi,[5] in the hope of leaving a trace which might be seen of posterity.

Winter, 11th month. For the purpose of the offerings of the feast of first-fruits, Wodate, of the Be of Kume of Iyo, ancestor of the Yamabe no Muraji and Governor of Harima, was sent thither. In the new muro of Hosome, Miyakko

---

[1] No doubt the Yamamori Be or Mountain wardens mentioned in the reign of Ōjin

[2] Kara-hime, not having been Empress, could not be appointed Grand Empress like other Imperial relicts.

[3] Attendants.   [4] Stewards.

[5] Lit. quiver-bearers, or archers, a part of the Imperial Guard. The " Kojiki " mentions only a Shiraga Be.

of the Oshinomi Be and Obito of the granary of Shijimi in the district of Akashi, he saw Ohoke and Woke, sons of the Imperial Prince Oshiha of Ichinobe. He took them together reverently to his bosom, recognized them as his lords, and attended to their nurture with extreme care. From his own private income he arranged for the construction of a palace of brushwood, in which he lodged them temporarily, and

XV. 5. mounting a swift steed, hastened to inform the Emperor. The Emperor was astonished, and after exclaiming for a good while, he said with emotion :—" Admirable! Delightful! Heaven in its bountiful love has bestowed on us two children." In this month he sent Wodate with a token of authority, and some of the Toneri in attendance on him, to Akashi to meet them (and escort them back).

The story [1] is given in the history of the Emperor Woke.

A.D. 482. 3rd year, 1st month, 1st day. Wodate and his companions arrived in the province of Settsu, escorting Ohoke and Woke. Then Omi and Muraji were sent, with emblems of authority and a royal green-canopied carriage,[2] to meet them and bring them into the Palace.

Summer, 4th month, 7th day. Prince Ohoke was appointed Prince Imperial, and Prince Woke was made an Imperial Prince.

Autumn, 7th month. Regina (princess) Ihitoyo primum coivit cum marito in Palatio Tsunuzashi. Dixit alicui :—" Nunc aliquantum cognovi viam feminarum. Quid habet mirum in se? Non sum cupida unquam rursus coëundi cum viro." [It is not clear that she had a husband at this time.]

9th month, 2nd day. The Omi and Muraji were sent on circuit to inspect the manners and customs.

Winter, 10th month, 4th day. An edict was made prohibiting dogs, horses, and playthings from being offered to the Emperor.[3]

XV. 6. 11th month, 18th day. The Omi and Muraji were feasted in the Great Court, and received presents of floss-silk. They

---

[1] See below, XV. 8, also Ch. K., p. 328.

[2] This is purely Chinese. Motowori says that no such vehicles were ever known in Japan.

[3] These same words are found in a History of the Chinese Sui Dynasty, under the year 581 A.D.

were all allowed to take as much as they pleased themselves, and they went forth exerting their utmost strength.

In this month, the various outlying provinces beyond the sea all sent envoys with tribute.

4th year, Spring, 1st month, 7th day. The envoys of the A.D. 483. various outlying provinces beyond the sea were feasted in the Audience Hall, and received presents of various values.

Summer, Intercalary 5th month. There was a national drinking festival, which lasted five days.[1]

Autumn, 8th month, 7th day. The Emperor personally held an inspection[2] of prisoners. On this day the Yemishi and Hayato together rendered homage.

9th month, 1st day. The Emperor was present in the Hall of Archery. He invited the functionaries and the envoys from beyond the sea to join in the shooting. Each received presents varying in value.

5th year, 1st month, 16th day. The Emperor died in the A.D. 484. Palace. His years were many.[3]

Winter, 11th month, 9th day. He was buried in the misasagi on the Sakato plain in Kahachi.

THE EMPEROR WOKE. XV. 7.

(*KENZŌ*[4] *TENNŌ.*)

The Emperor Woke (otherwise called Kume no Wakako) was the grandchild of the Emperor Ohoye[5] no Izaho-wake and son of the Imperial Prince Ichinobe no Oshiha. His mother's name was Hayehime.

---

[1] The History of the Chinese Emperor Ming Ti (58—75 A.D.) has mention of a great drinking festival lasting five days.

[2] Williams says that 錄 in this phrase means "to release." No doubt the object was to release such as were deserving of pardon.

[3] His age is reckoned variously by other authorities at thirty-nine and forty-one.

[4] Illustrious ancestry.

[5] His name is not given elsewhere with the prefix Ohoye, which means "great elder brother."

In the 'Genealogy' it is said:—"The Imperial Prince Oshiha of Ichinobe took to wife Hayehime, daughter of Ari no Omi, and at length had by her three sons and two daughters. The first was named Winatsu hime, the second Prince Ohoke, also called Shima no Wakako, also called Ohoshi no Mikoto, the third was named Prince Woke, also called Kume no Wakako, the fourth was named Princess Ihitoyo, also called Princess Oshinomibe, and the fifth Prince Tachibana. In one book Princess Ihitoyo is ranked above Prince Ohoke. Ari no Omi was the son of Hada no Sukune."

The Emperor, having lived for a long time on the borders, was thoroughly acquainted with the miseries of the people, and whenever he saw them oppressed, he felt as if his own four members were plunged in a ditch. He dispensed virtuous influence, he bestowed blessings ; the regulations of government were everywhere enforced ; charity was shown to the poor, and the husbandless were supported. The Empire rendered him cordial allegiance.

In the 10th month of the 3rd year of the Emperor Anaho, the Emperor's father,[1] the Imperial Prince Ichinobe no Oshiha was slain, together with the Toneri, Saheki be no Nakachiko, by the Emperor Ohohatsuse on the moor of Kaya.[2] They were accordingly buried in the same grave. Thereupon the Emperor[3] and Prince Ohoke, hearing that their father had been shot to death, were afraid, and both escaped and hid themselves. The Toneri, Omi, Kusakabe no Muraji ;Omi is the personal name of Kusakabe no Muraji], with his son Adahiko, secretly served the Emperor and Prince Woke, so that they avoided disaster by fleeing to the district of Yosa in the province of Tamba. Omi at length changed his name and called himself Tatoku, but being still afraid of being put to death, he fled from this place to a cave in Mount Shijimi in the province of Harima. There he strangled himself. The Emperor, being still ignorant whither Omi had gone, urged his elder brother, Prince Ohoke, to turn his steps towards the district of Akashi in the province of Harima. There they both changed their names to Tamba

XV. 8.

---

[1] i.e. Emperor Woke's father.   [2] See above, p. 336.

[3] Woke is meant.

no Waraha,[1] and entered the service of the Obito of the Shijimi granaries.

The Obito of the Shijimi granaries was Hosome Oshinomi Be no Miyakko.

Adahiko at this time did not leave them, but remained constant to his duty as their vassal.

In Winter, the 11th month of the 2nd year of the reign of the Emperor Shiraga, the Governor of the province of Harima, Wodate Iyo no Kumebe, ancestor of the Yamabe no Muraji, went to the district of Akashi to make arrangements in person for the offerings of the festival of first-fruits.

One writing says:—" Went on a circuit to the kohori and agata [2] to collect the land tax."

It so happened that he arrived just when the Obito of the XV. 9. granaries of Shijimi was holding a house-warming for a new muro and was extending the day by adding to it the night. Hereupon the Emperor spake to his elder brother, Prince Ohoke, saying:—" Many years have passed since we fled hither to escape ruin. It belongs to this very evening to reveal our names and to disclose our high rank." Prince Ohoke exclaimed with pity:—" To make such an announcement ourselves would be fatal. Which of us could keep safe his person and avoid danger?" The Emperor said:—" We, the grandsons of the Emperor Izahowake, are a man's drudges, and feed his horses and kine. What better can we do than make known our names and be slain?" At length he and Prince Ohoke fell into each other's arms and wept, being unable to contain their emotion. Prince Ohoke said:—" In that case who else but thou, my younger brother, is capable of making a heroic effort, and is therefore fit to make this disclosure?" The Emperor refused firmly, saying:—" Thy servant has no ability. How can he make so bold as to display virtuous action?" Prince Ohoke said:—" There are here none to excel my younger brother in ability and wisdom." And in this way they mutually held back each in favour of the other for two or three times. It was ultimately arranged, with the Emperor's consent, that he should make the announcement. Together they XV. 10. went to the outside of the muro and sat down in the lowest

---

[1] The boys of Tamba.   [2] Districts.

place. The Obito of the granary ordered them to sit beside the cooking-place and hold lights to right and left. When the night had become profound, and the revel was at its height, and every one had danced in turn, the Obito of the granary addressed Wodate, saying :—" Thy servant observes that these light-holders honour others, and abase themselves; they put others before, and themselves behind. By their respectfulness they show their observance of just principles ; by their retiring behaviour they illustrate courtesy. They are worthy of the name of gentlemen." Upon this Wodate played on the lute and gave orders to the light-holders, saying :—" Get up and dance." Then the elder and younger brothers declined in each other's favour for a good while and did not get up. Wodate urged them, saying :—" Wherefore all this delay ? Get up quickly and dance." Prince Ohoke got up and danced. When he had done, the Emperor stood up in his turn, and having adjusted his dress and girdle, proposed a health for the Muro, saying :—

The Dolichos roots[1] of the new muro which he has upbuilt ;
The pillars which he has upbuilt—
These are[2] the calm of the august heart of the master of the house :
The ridge-poles which he has raised aloft—
These are the grove[3] of the august heart of the master of the house :
The rafters which he has set—
These are the perfect order of the august heart of the master of the house :
The laths which he has placed—
These are the fairness of the august heart of the master of the house :

---

[1] The Dolichos roots present a difficulty. They are better known for yielding a starchy food like arrowroot than as material for house-building. The stems are mentioned below. Another objection is that their introduction here spoils the symmetry of the composition, which though not exactly poetry, is something closely verging on it. I would prefer to omit the words " Katsura ne tsuki-tatsuru " of the original, so that the first two lines would become only one, viz.—

" The pillars of the new muro which he has upbuilt."

[2] i.e. represent.

[3] Grove. The commentators say this means shigeki, thick, which in Japanese is a metaphor for cordial, hearty, kind.

The Dolichos cords which he has tied—[1]
These are the endurance of the august life of the master of the house :
The reed-leaves it is thatched with—
These are the superabundance of the august wealth of the master of the XV. II.
    house :

> On all sides [2] (of it) there are fields of fresh culture :
> With the ten-span rice-ears,
> Of these fresh fields,
> In a shallow pan
> We have brewed sake.
> With gusto let us drink it,
> O my boys !
> Whenever we dance
> Uplifting the horns of a buck [3]
> Of these secluded hills
> (Weary to the foot)
> Sweet sake from Yega market-town
> Not buying with a price,
> To the clear ring of hand-palms
> Ye will revel,[4]
> Oh ! my immortal ones ! [5]

When he had ended proposing this health, he sang to the
accompaniment of music, saying :—

*   *   *   *[6]

The willow that grows by the river—

---

[1] i.e. tied the laths (of sedge) to the uprights of the walls, which were then
plastered with a mixture of mud and straw. The firmness with which they
were tied represents the endurance of the master's life.

[2] In this passage, as in the well-known poem attributed to Susa no wo, I
have ventured to render idzumo as equal to idzukumo, on all sides, although
without native authority.

[3] Animal dances, in which the performer represented a deer, wild boar,
butterfly, bird, etc., were common in ancient Japan. The Shishi mai, or
lion-dance, danced by two boys, one of whom wears a grotesque mask supposed to represent a lion, and the other supports the body, made of cotton
stuff, may still be seen in the streets.

[4] The word for " revel " is uchi-age, which means literally to strike up.
But the uchi (strike) must also be taken with " hand-palms " in the sense
of " clapping."

[5] A way of saying, " May you live for ever ! " In this passage the author
had in mind a speech in Japanese, the original language of which, although
mainly expressed by Chinese ideographs, can be conjectured with some
degree of certainty.

[6] The first line of this poem contains the single word Ina-mushiro, " sleep-

> When the water has gone,
>   It raises up (its stem that was) bent down,
>   And its roots perish not.

Wodate addressed him, saying :—" Capital ! Pray let us hear something more."

The Emperor at length made a special dance,
    This is what was anciently called a Tatsutsu (stand out) dance. The manner of it was that it was danced while standing up and sitting down.
and striking an attitude, said :—

> Of Yamato,
>   Soso chihara
>   Asachihara[1]
>   The younger Prince am I.

Hereupon Wodate thought this profoundly strange, and asked him to say more. The Emperor, striking an attitude, said :—

> The sacred cedar[2]
>   Of Furu in Isonokami—[3]
>   Its stem is severed,
>   Its branches are stripped off.
>   Of him who in the Palace of Ichinobe
>   Governed all under Heaven,[4]
>   The myriad Heavens,
>   The myriad lands—
>   Of Oshiha no Mikoto
>   The august children are we.[5]

---

ing-mat" (a rice straw mat), a conventional epithet or makura-kotoba of kaha, skin, perhaps because the Japanese used skins for sleeping on at one time. It has, properly speaking, nothing to do with kaha, river, but the unexpected conjunction is witty—from a Japanese point of view. The allusion to the position of the two Princes is plain.

[1] Chihara, or as it may be read Ashihara, means reed plain, a poetical term for Japan. *So so* is interpreted as an onomatope representing the rustling of reeds. *Asa* is shallow, and asachihara is said to be a plain on which the reeds grow short. The speech (or poem) is a (no doubt with intention) mysteriously worded announcement of Woke's rank as an Imperial Prince.

[2] The sugi or Cryptomeria Japonica.
[3] In Yamato.   [4] He never reigned. See above, p. 336.
[5] There is hardly any metre here. This passage is just on the border line between poetry and prose.

Wodate was greatly astonished. He left his seat, and, vexed with himself,[1] made repeated obeisance to them. He under- took to provide for them, and brought his people to prostrate themselves reverently. Then he levied all the inhabitants of that district, and in a few days built a palace, in which the Princes were temporarily lodged. Going up to the capital, he asked that some one should be sent to meet the two Princes. The Emperor Shiraga was rejoiced to hear this, and exclaimed, saying :—" We have no children ; we must make them our successors." Along with the Oho-omi and the Ohomuraji, he settled on a plan within the forbidden precinct.[2] So Kumebe no Wodate, the Governor of Harima, was sent with emblems of authority, and accompanied by personal attendants of the Emperor, to go to meet them at Akashi. In Spring, the 1st month of the third year of the Emperor Shiraga, the Emperor,[3] with Prince Ohoke, arrived at the province of Settsu, where Omi and Muraji were sent with emblems of authority xv. 13. and a Royal green-canopied carriage to meet them and bring them into the Palace. In Summer, the 4th month, Prince Ohoke was appointed Prince Imperial, and the Emperor was raised to the rank of Imperial Prince.

In Spring, the 1st month of the 5th year of his reign, the Emperor Shiraga died. In this month the Prince Imperial Ohoke and the Emperor ceded to each other the Dignity, and for a long time did not occupy it. Therefore the Emperor's elder sister,[1] the Imperial Princess Awo of Ihi-toyo, held a Court and carried on the Government in the Palace of Tsunuzashi in Oshinomi, styling herself Oshinomi no Ihitoyo no Awo no Mikoto. A poet of that day made a song, saying : —

> In Yamato
> What I long to see
> Is the Tsunuzashi Palace
> In this Takaki[3]
> Of Oshinomi.

Winter, 11th month. Ihitoyo, Awo no Mikoto died. She was buried in the misasagi on the Hill of Haniguchi in Katsuraki.

---

[1] For the neglect shown to the Princes.
[2] A Chinese term for the Palace.   [3] Viz. Woke.
   The " Kojiki " makes her his maternal aunt.
   Takaki means high castle, but is here the name of a place.

12th month. There was a great assembly of the officials, at which the Prince Imperial Ohoke took the Imperial Seal, and placing it on the seat occupied by the Emperor, did him repeated obeisance. He then took his place among the Ministers, and said :—" This rank of Emperor should be occupied by a man possessed of merit. The disclosure of our rank, and our being sent for by the late Emperor, is all a result of the policy of my younger brother. I resign the Empire in his favour." The Emperor, on the other hand, resigned it on the grounds that as a younger brother he might not presume to assume the Dignity, and also because he was aware that the Emperor Shiraga had appointed his elder brother Prince Imperial with the previous purpose of transmitting it to him.

XV. 14. For these two reasons he firmly declined, saying :—" When the sun and moon appear, is it not impossible that a candle should not give way before their radiance ? When a seasonable rain falls, is it not superfluous trouble to go on watering from a pond ? [1] The conduct which should be esteemed by him who is in the position of a younger brother is to serve his elder brother by devising methods of averting from him disaster, to illustrate virtue, and to unravel complications without putting himself forward. For if he puts himself forward, he will be wanting in the reverence which is due from a younger brother. Woke cannot bear to put himself forward.[2] It is an immutable law that the elder brother should be affectionate and the younger brother reverent. So I have heard from our elders. How can I of myself alone make light of it ? " The Prince Imperial Ohoke said :—" The Emperor Shiraga, by reason of my being the elder brother, at first assigned to me all the affairs of the Empire. But I am ashamed to accept it. Now the great Prince's conduct is established in beneficial retirement,[3] so that those who hear him utter sighs of admiration.

---

[1] From " When " to " pond " is taken from a Chinese book.

[2] From " The conduct " to " forward " is imitated from a passage in the ' Liki.''

[3] He probably makes allusion to the Yih-king, Diagram xxxiii. Sect. 6, which is thus translated by Legge : " The sixth line, undivided, shows its subject retiring in a noble way. It will be advantageous in every respect." This means, perhaps, that his modest behaviour proves that his reign will be beneficial to the people.

He has displayed the qualities of an Imperial scion, so that all who see him let fall tears. The pitiable gentry will rejoice to bear the gladness of sustaining the Heavens: the wretched black-haired people will be delighted to enjoy the happiness of treading the earth. Therewith the four corners of the earth will be made solid, so as to flourish perpetually to ten thousand ages. His meritorious work will approach that of creation; XV. 15 his honest policy will illuminate the age. How pre-eminent! How recondite! Words fail me to describe. How shall I, albeit his elder, put myself forward before him? If, having no merit, I should accept the throne, self-reproach would surely be the result. I have heard that the office of Emperor ought not to remain long vacant, and that the will of Heaven should not be evaded out of humility. Let the Great Prince make the Temples of the Earth and of Grain his thought, and let him make the people his heart." As he uttered these words, his earnest emotion led him to shed tears. Upon this the Emperor saw that if he persisted in his refusal to come forward, he would be [1] acting contrary to his elder brother's wishes, and gave his consent. But he would not take his place on the Imperial throne. The world was rejoiced to see how well they sincerely yielded in each other's favour, and said:—
" Excellent! With such good feeling between elder and younger brother, the Empire will tend to virtue: with such love between relations, the people will stimulate benevolence."

1st year, Spring, 1st month, 1st day. The Oho-omi and the A.D. 485. Ohomuraji made a representation to the Emperor, saying:—
" The Prince Imperial Ohoke, out of the abundance of his XV. 16. wisdom, has delivered over the Empire. Your Majesty, in his rightful governance, ought to accept the vast inheritance, and thus becoming the Lord of the Temple of Heaven, to continue the infinite line of his ancestors, so as, above, to correspond to the mind of Heaven, and, below, to satisfy the hopes of the people. To refuse to enter upon the Dignity would be to cause the destruction of the hopes of all the Gold and Silver [2] frontier lands, and of all the functionaries both far and near. It belongs

---

[1] The " Nihongi" introduces a 不 (not) here. The " Kiujiki " reading seems preferable, and I have followed it in the translation.

[2] Corea is called the gold and silver country at p. 221

to you by the will of Heaven, and has been ceded to you by the Prince Imperial. Your wisdom is abundant, and your good fortune conspicuous. While young you were diligent, humble, respectful, affectionate and docile. May it please you to comply with the command of your elder brother, and take over the conduct of the great undertaking." The Emperor made an order, saying :—" Be it so." Accordingly he summoned the Ministers of State and the functionaries to the Yatsuri Palace in Hither Asuka, and there assumed the Imperial Dignity, and the functionaries entered upon office, to the great delight of all.

XV. 17.
One book says the Emperor Woke had two palaces, one at Wono, the other at Ikeno. Another book says that he made his palace at Mikakuri.

In this month, Princess Wono of Naniha was appointed Empress, and a general amnesty was made.

Princess Wono of Naniha was the daughter of Prince Wakugo of Oka, grandson of Prince Ihaki, who was the great-grandson of the Emperor Wo-asatsuma-wakugo no Sukune.

2nd month, 5th day. The Emperor spoke, saying :—" The late Prince, having met with much misfortune, lost his life on a desert moor. We were then a child, and fled away and concealed Ourselves. Then, by a piece of undeserved good fortune, We were sought out and sent for, and were raised up to continue the Great Work. We have searched for his honoured bones far and wide, but there is no one who can tell where they are." Having finished speaking, the Emperor and the Prince Imperial Ohoke burst into tears of passionate emotion, which they could not control.

In this month the Emperor summoned together the old people, and in person made inquiry of them one after another. Now there was one old woman who came forward and said :—" Okime knows where the honoured bones were buried, and begs permission to point out the place to the Emperor."

Okime was the old woman's name. It is stated below that the younger sister of Yamato-bukuro no Sukune, ancestor of the Kimi of Mount Sasaki in the province of Ohomi, was called Okime.

Thereupon the Emperor and the Prince Imperial Ohoke,

taking with them the old woman, made a progress to the moor
of Kaya in Kutawata in the province of Ohomi, where they dug
them up, and found that it was really as the old woman had
said.	Looking down into the grave, they made lament, and
their words showed deep and passionate feeling.	From
antiquity until now never was there anything so cruel.	The XV. 18.
body of Nakachiko [1] lay across the honoured bones, and were
mixed with them so that it was impossible to distinguish them
from one another.	Then there appeared the nurse of the
Imperial Prince Ihazaka, who made representation to the
Emperor, saying:—" The upper teeth of Nakachiko had fallen
out, so that by this they can be distinguished."	But although
they were able, in accordance with the nurse's words, to distinguish the skulls, they never succeeded in separating the
bones of the four members.	Accordingly a pair of misasagi
were erected on the moor of Kaya resembling each other, so
that they seemed but one.	The funeral rites also were alike.
The Emperor ordered the old woman, Okime, to live in the
neighbourhood of the palace, where he treated her with respect
and showed her kindness, not allowing her to be in want.

In this month he made an order, saying:—" Old woman!
thou art desolate and infirm, and walking is not convenient for
thee.	Let there be a rope stretched across to support thee
when thou goest out and comest in.	And let there be a bell
attached to the end of the rope, so that there may be no need
for any one to announce thee.	When thou comest, ring this
bell, and we shall know that thou art coming."	Herewith the
old woman, in obedience to the Imperial order, rang the bell
before she came forward.	The Emperor, hearing from afar the
sound of the bell, made a song, saying :—

> Past Wosone,
> In Asajihara,
> The far-extending { moor !
> { bell
> There the bell tinkles !
> Okime must be coming ! [2]

---

[1] See above, XIV. 5.

[2] The point of this poem is not to be expressed in English. It rests on
the similarity of the first syllable of nute, bell, with nu, a moor, which must
be read twice in different senses.	The first half of the poem takes nu in the
latter sense.	With the latter half it is only the first syllable of *nute*.

3rd month, 1st day of the Serpent [1] (the 2nd). The Emperor went to the Park, and there held revel by the winding streams.

Summer, 4th month, 11th day. The Emperor made an order, saying :—" The means by which a sovereign encourages the people is no other than the granting of office : that by which a country is exalted is naught else but the granting of rewards for merit. Now the former Governor of Harima, Kumebe no Wodate [his other name was Ihadate], sought Us out, came to meet Us, and raised Us up. His merit is manifold. Let him not hesitate to express his wishes." Wodate thanked the Emperor, saying :—" The mountain office [2] has always been my desire." He was appointed to the mountain office, and a new title was granted him, viz. the House of the Yamabe no Muraji. [3] Kibi no Omi was associated with him, and the Yamamori Be were made their serfs. The Emperor praised his good qualities, made conspicuous his deserts, showed gratitude for his services, requited his kindness, and treated him with the utmost affection. His prosperity was unequalled.

5th month. Karabukuro no Sukune, Kimi of Mount Sasaki, who was implicated in the assassination of the Imperial Prince Oshiha, when about to be executed, bowed down his head to the ground, and his words expressed extreme sorrow. The Emperor could not bear to put him to death, so he added him to the misasagi guardians, making him at the same time mountain-warden, [4] and erasing his name from the census registers. He was then handed over to the jurisdiction of the Yamabe no Muraji. [5]

---

[1] This unusual way of designating the day of the month suggests that a different document is here quoted from.

[2] i.e., Warden of the Mountains, or, as we should say, " Woods and Forests." It included the charge of game.

[3] Muraji of the Mountain Be.   [4] Game-keeper

[5] The erasure of his name from the register was on account of his being attached to the service of the misasagi ; the mountain wardenship placed him under the jurisdiction of the Yamabe no Muraji.

May not these guardians of the Imperial tombs have been among the ancestors of the Eta or Hinin, a pariah caste (abolished by the revolution of 1868), who lived in villages by themselves, and did not intermarry with or have any social intercourse with other Japanese ? They followed the occupations of leather-dressers, shoemakers, buriers of dead animals,

But Yamato-bukuro no Sukune, by reason of the good services of his younger sister, Okime, was granted his original
title, namely, the House of the Kimi of Mount Sasaki.

6th month. The Emperor visited the Hall of Avoidance XV. 20.
of the heat, and had music there. The Ministers were assembled, and a banquet was prepared for them.

This year was the year Kinoto Ushi (2nd) of the Cycle.

2nd year, Spring, 3rd month, 1st day of the Serpent (2nd). A.D. 486.
The Emperor went to the Park, where he held revel by the
winding streams. At this time he assembled in great numbers
the Ministers, the High Officials, the Omi, the Muraji, the
Kuni no Miyakko, and the Tomo no Miyakko, and made revel.
The Ministers uttered reiterated cries of "Long live the
Emperor." [1]

Autumn, 8th month, 1st day. The Emperor addressed the
Prince Imperial Ohoke, saying:—"Our father the late
Prince was, for no crime, slain with an arrow shot by the
Emperor Oho-hatsuse, and his bones cast away on a moor.
Even until now, I have been unable to get hold of him, and
my bosom is filled with indignation. I lie down to weep, and
as I walk abroad I cry aloud. It is my desire to wash away
the disgrace cast on us by our enemy. Now, I have heard
that no one should live under the same Heaven as his father's
enemy, that no one should lay aside arms against the enemy
of his brother, that no one should dwell in the same country
with the enemy of his comrade. Even the son of a common
man, rather than serve with the enemy of his parents, sleeps
on a coarse mat, and making a pillow of his buckler, refuses
office. He will not dwell in the same country as his enemy, but
whenever he meets him, in market or in Court, will not lay
aside his weapon until he has encountered him in combat.
Much more I who, two years ago, was raised to the rank of XV. 21.
Son of Heaven! It is my desire to demolish his misasagi,

---

executioners, and watchmen of cemeteries. The name Hinin (not-man)
accords well with the circumstance mentioned here of their names being
erased from the census registers. They were supposed to belong to the
service of the dead, and no longer to be reckoned with the living.

Most of the misasagi had from one to five guardians' houses allotted to
them.

[1] Ban-zai or Man-zai, lit. 10,000 years. This term is still in use.

to crush his bones, and fling them broadcast. Would it not be a filial act to take revenge in this way?" The Prince Imperial Ohoke could hardly answer for sighing and sobbing. He remonstrated with the Emperor, saying :—" It is not well to do so. The Emperor Oho-hatsuse presided over the Empire as the rightful director of the myriad machinery of Government. Court and country looked up to him with joy. He was an Emperor, whereas the late Prince our father, although an Emperor's son, met with obstacles in his career, and never rose to the Imperial Dignity. Looking on the matter in this light, there is the difference of exalted and base. And if thou hadst the heart to demolish the misasagi, who would recognize as Lord and do service to the Soul of Heaven? This is one reason why the tomb should not be destroyed. Moreover, had it not been for the warm affection and special favour bestowed on the Emperor and Ohoke by the Emperor Shiraga, wouldst thou ever have attained to the precious Dignity? But the Emperor Oho-hatsuse was the father of the Emperor Shiraga. Ohoke has heard that it has been said by all the ancient sages, 'Without words there can be no response; without virtue there is no requital.'[1] If there is cause for gratitude, and no return is made, this is profoundly prejudicial to good morals. Your Majesty feasts the Country, and his virtuous conduct is felt far and wide over the Empire. But if he pulls down the misasagi, and shows himself in an opposite light to Court and Country, Ohoke fears that it will become impossible to govern the land and to bring up the people as his children. This is a second reason why it should not be destroyed." The Emperor said, " It is well," and countermanded the work.[2]

XV. 22.

---

[1] Virtue is in Chinese active, not merely the negation of vice.

[2] The " Kojiki " tells a somewhat different story. *Vide* Ch. K., p. 336. This misasagi (which I have visited) is at the present day a round single mound, encircled by a moat, but there are sufficient remains of the second mound and of the original moat to show that it was once a double-topped misasagi of the ordinary type. See above, p. 136. A large quantity of earth must have been removed in order thus to deprive this tomb of its distinctive character as an Imperial tumulus, and to give it the appearance of the tomb of a mere subject. It appears as if both the " Nihongi " and " Kojiki " regarded the demolition of a misasagi as an impious action, and tried to minimize it.

9th month. Okime, being decrepit from old age, asked leave to return to her home, saying:—" My vigour has decayed. I am old, infirm, and emaciated. Even with the help of the rope I am unable to walk. I pray thee let me return to my native place,[1] so that there I may spend my last days." When the Emperor heard this he was moved with pity. He gave her a present of a thousand pieces, and grieving in anticipation at the divergence of their paths, he repeatedly lamented that they could no longer meet. So he gave her a song, saying :—

> Oh ! Okime !
> Okime of Afumi !
> From to-morrow,
> Hidden by the deep mountains,
> Thou wilt no more be seen !

Winter, 10th month, 6th day. The Emperor entertained his Ministers. At this time the Empire was at peace ; the people were not subjected to forced labour, the crops reached maturity, and the peasantry were prosperous. A measure of rice was sold for one piece of silver,[2] and horses and kine covered the moors.

3rd year, Spring, 2nd month, 1st day. Kotoshiro Ahe no A.D. 487. Omi, acting by Imperial command, went on a mission to Imna. Hereupon the Moon-God, by the mouth of a certain man, XV. 23. addressed him, saying:—" My ancestor Taka-mimusubi had the merit in conjunction (with other Deities) of creating Heaven and Earth. Let him be worshipped by dedicating to him people and land. I am the Moon-God, and I shall be pleased if an offering is made according to his desire." Koto-shiro accordingly returned to the capital, and reported these

---

[1] Lit., The Mulberry and Euphorbia trees. There is an allusion to a verse in the " Chinese Book of Odes " (Legge, Vol. IV. p. 337) :—

> " Even the mulberry trees and the tsze (of one's home)
> Must be regarded with reverence."

[2] This is the first mention of coin in the " Nihongi." It is impossible to say what the measure of rice was, or what the value of the coin. Indeed, I take the whole passage to be a flight of the author's fancy, stimulated by his recollections of Chinese literature. It contains several phrases borrowed from Chinese works. See Index—Currency.

D d

things fully to the Emperor. The Utaarasu rice-fields were dedicated to the God, and Oshimi no Sukune, the ancestor of the Agatanushi of Yuki, was appointed to attend upon his shrine.

3rd month, 1st day of the Serpent (8th). The Emperor went to the Park, where he held revel by the winding streams.

Summer, 4th month, 5th day. The Sun-Goddess, by the mouth of a certain man, addressed Kotoshiro, Ahe no Omi, saying :—" Let the Ihare rice-fields be dedicated to my ancestor Taka-mimusubi." Kotoshiro accordingly reported the matter to the Emperor, and in compliance with the Goddess's request, fourteen chō [1] of rice-land were dedicated to him. The Atahe of Shimo no agata in Tsushima was appointed to attend upon his shrine.

13th day. The Saki-kusa Be [2] was established.

25th day. The Emperor died in the palace of Yatsuri.

In this year, Ki no Ohiha no Sukune, bestriding and making a base of Imna, held communication with Koryö. In order to rule the three Han on the west, he established a government, and styled himself a Deity. By means of a plan laid by Cha-ro-na-kwi and Tha-kap-syo of Imna he slew Mak-ni-kè, the heir to the throne of Pèkché, at Irin.[3] [This is a place in Koryö.] He built the castle of Tè-san,[4] and then stood on the defensive as regards the Eastern province, cutting off the harbour by which supplies were transported, and causing the army to suffer from famine. The King of Pèkché was greatly enraged, and despatched General Ko-ni-kè and an officer of the military store department, named Mak-ko-kè, in command of troops to Tè-san, to lay siege to it. Upon this, Ohiha no Sukune moved forward his army, and attacked them

---

[1] See below, XXV. 18.

[2] Saki-kusa is literally the herb of happiness. It is also called man-nen-gusa, or the " herb of 10,000 years." It was said to grow in the Court of the Temple to the sovereign's ancestors. The " Seishiroku " says :—" In the reign of the Emperor Kenzō, the officials were summoned to a banquet. At this time, a herb of three stems was growing in the courtyard of the palace. One of these was plucked up and presented to the Emperor, who thereupon conferred on the donor the title of Saki Be no Miyakko."

[3] Irin is called in Ōjin's reign, year 16, a place in Imna.

[4] The Kana rendering is Shitoromo or Shitoromure.

with continually growing valour. All that opposed him were put to the rout. But he was but one against a hundred. Suddenly his weapons ran short, and his power became exhausted. He saw that he could not bring matters to a conclusion, and returned from Imna. Consequently the Land of Pèkché slew Cha-ro-na-kwi, Tha-kap-syo, and their people— more than three hundred men.[1]

THE EMPEROR OHOKE.[2]   XV. 25.

(*NINKEN*[3] *TENNŌ*.)

The Emperor Ohoke's personal name was Ohoshi.[4]

Otherwise Ohosu. This is the only instance of an Emperor's personal name[5] or designation being stated. It is taken from an old manuscript.

His designation was Shima no Iratsuko.[6] He was the elder brother by the same mother of the Emperor Woke. In his childhood he was intelligent, of quick parts and great attainments. When he grew to man's estate, he was kind, indulgent and gentle.

At the death of the Emperor Anaho, he took refuge in the

---

[1] The "Tongkam" does not mention this affair, but there is no reason to doubt that the "Nihongi" narrative is substantially true.

The "Kojiki" practically ends here. Nominally, it is carried down to the death of Suiko in A.D. 628, but all after this is mere genealogy.

[2] Also read Oke. Ohoke is the "Kojiki" reading.

[3] Benevolent-talented.

[4] Big-leg or big-foot. The name is written above, XV. 7, with characters which mean big-stone.

[5] Or taboo name. In China the use of the personal name is not thought respectful except by a chief or parent. Instead of it the designation (字) is used. The latter was assumed at the age of fifteen (or twenty), when the ceremony of capping took place. In writing the personal names of the Emperors of the reigning dynasty, the Chinese are careful to alter one or two strokes of the character.

[6] Shima no Wakako, above, XV. 7.

district of Yosa in the province of Tamba. In the first year of the reign of the Emperor Shiraga, Winter, 11th month, Wodate, Yamabe no Muraji, Governor of Harima, went to the Capital and requested permission to go to fetch him. The Emperor Shiraga accordingly caused Wodate, provided with symbols of authority, and accompanied by his own personal attendants, to proceed to Akashi, and respectfully to go to meet him. Ultimately, in the third year of his reign, Summer, the 4th month, the Emperor Ohoke was appointed Prince Imperial.[1] In his fifth year, the Emperor Shiraga died, and the Emperor abdicated the Empire in favour of the Emperor Woke, becoming Prince Imperial as before. In the third year of his reign, Summer, the 4th month, the Emperor Woke died.

A.D. 488. 1st year, Spring, 1st month, 5th day. The Prince Imperial assumed the Imperial rank in the Palace of Hirotaka in Isonokami.

One book says :—" There were two palaces of the Emperor Ohoke, the first at Kahamura,[2] the second at Takano in Shijimi. The pillars of the Hall remain undecayed until this day."

XV. 26. 2nd month, 2nd day. His former consort, the Imperial Princess Kasuga no Oho-iratsume,[3] was appointed Empress.

The Princess Kasuga no Oho-iratsume was the daughter of the Emperor Oho-hatsuse by Woguna Kimi, daughter of Fukame, Wani no Omi.

She at length bore to him one son and six daughters. The first was called the Imperial Princess Takahashi no Oho-iratsume ; the second was called the Imperial Princess Asatsuma ; the third was called the Imperial Princess Tashiraga ; the fourth was called the Imperial Princess Kusuhi ; the fifth was called the Imperial Princess Tachibana ; the sixth was called the Emperor Wo-hatsuse no Waka-sazaki. When he came to possess the Empire, he made his capital at Namiki in Hatsuse. The seventh was called the Imperial Princess Mawaka.[4]

---

[1] This is a curious way of putting it, but the original is so.
[2] This is the temporary palace built by Wodate. See above, XV. 5.
[3] See above, XIV. 7, for an account of her birth.
[4] The " Kojiki " makes Mawaka a Prince.

One book has a different arrangement, the Imperial Princess Kusuhi taking the third place and the Imperial Princess Tashiraga the fourth.

Next there was Nuka-kimi no Iratsume, daughter of Hiuri, Wani no Omi, who bore one daughter who was made the Imperial Princess Kasuga no Yamada.

One book says :—" Ohonuka no Iratsume, daughter of Hifure, Wani no Omi, bore one daughter who was made the Imperial Princess Yamada no Oho-iratsume, also called the Imperial Princess Akami." Notwithstanding the trifling difference of the documents, the facts are the same.

Winter, 10th month, 3rd day. The Emperor Woke was buried in the misasagi on the hill of Ihatsuki at Kataoka.

This year was the year Tsuchinoye Tatsu (5th) of the Cycle.

2nd year, Autumn, 9th month. The Empress Naniha no A.D. 489. Wono, fearful on account of her long-standing want of respect (for the Emperor), died by her own hand. XV. 27.

One authority says :—" In the time of the Emperor Woke, the Prince Imperial Ohoke was present at a banquet. He took up a melon to eat, but there was no knife. The Emperor Woke himself took a knife and commanded his wife Wono to carry it and present it to the Prince Imperial. She came before him, and, in a standing position, laid the knife on the melon tray. Moreover, on the same day, she poured out sake, and, in a standing position, gave it to the Prince Imperial to drink. In consequence of this disrespect, she feared to be put to death, and died by her own hand."

3rd year, Spring, 2nd month, 1st day. The Isonokami Be A.D. 490. of palace attendants [1] was established.

4th year, Summer, 5th month. Kashima Ikuba no Omi and A.D. 491. Hohe no Kimi, being guilty of crimes, were both thrown into prison, where they died.

5th year, Spring, 2nd month, 5th day. General search was A.D. 492 made in the provinces and districts for the dispersed Saheki Be, and a descendant of Nakachiko of the Saheki Be was made Saheki no Miyakko.

[1] Toneri.

Nakachiko of the Saheki Be is mentioned in the history of the reign of Woke Tennō.

6th year, Autumn, 9th month, 4th .ay. Hitaka no Kishi was sent to Corea to fetch skilled artizans. This autumn, after Hitaka no Kishi was despatched, there was a woman dwelling at Mitsu[1] in Naniha who made lament, saying :—

> Woes me, my youthful[2] spouse !
> For to me he is an elder brother,
> And to my mother too an elder brother.

The sound of her lament was exceeding pathetic, even to the rending of men's bowels.[3] A man of the village of Hishiki, named Kaso, hearing it, came in front of her, and said :— "Why is thy lamentation so exceedingly sorrowful?" The woman answered and said :—"Think of the autumn garlic's ever clustering growth."[4] Kaso said :—"Thou art right. Now I understand what thou hast said." But a companion of his, not comprehending her meaning, inquired, saying :—"By what dost thou understand?" He answered and said :— "Funame of the Naniha Jewellers' Be was wedded to Karama no Hataye[5] and bore to him Nakume,[6] who was wedded to a man of Sumuchi named Yamaki and bore to him Akitame. Karama no Hataye and his daughter Nakume having both died, Yamaki, the man of Sumuchi, had illicit intercourse with Funame[7] of the Jewellers' Be, and had by her a son named Araki, who took to wife Akitame. Upon this Araki set out for Koryö in the suite of Hitaka no Kishi. Therefore his wife Akitame, restless and full of longing, has lost her wits and become distraught, and the sound of her lamentation is very touching, even to the rending of men's bowels."

Funame of the Jewellers' Be and Karama no Hataye became husband and wife, and had a daughter named

---

[1] The august harbour.　　　　　[2] Literally young herb or grass.

[3] Cf. the Biblical expression "bowels of compassion."

[4] By the clusters of the garlic bulbs in autumn she indicates the some-what complicated family relations described below.

[5] Kara-fisher's-field.　　　　　[6] The (professional) weeping woman.

[7] His wife's mother. This union was regarded as incestuous.

Nakume. Yamaki, a man of Sumuchi, married Nakume, and had a daughter named Akitame. Yamaki's wife's father Karama no Hataye and the latter's child Nakume having both died, Yamaki, the man of Sumuchi, had an amour with his wife's mother, Funame of the Jewellers' Be, the fruit of which was Araki. Araki took to wife Akitame. One book says:—" Funame of the Jewellers' Be bore Nakume to her first husband Karama no Hataye ; again to her second husband Yamaki, a man of Sumuchi, she bore Araki, so that Nakume and Araki were sister and brother by a different father. Consequently Nakume's daughter Akitame called Araki [1] her mother's elder brother. Nakume having married Yamaki, bore Akitame. More- over, Yamaki having had illicit intercourse with Funame had by her Araki, so that Akitame and Araki were sister and brother by a different mother. Consequently Akitame called Araki her elder brother. In ancient times women called their brothers se [2] (elder brother), without distinction of age ; while men called their sisters imo (younger sister). Hence the expression, ' To my mother an elder brother, to me an elder brother.' " [3]

In this year Hitaka no Kishi returned from Koryö, and delivered to the Emperor the artizans Sunyuki and Nonyuki.[·] They were the ancestors of the Koryö tanners of the village of Nukada in the district of Yamabe in the province of Yamato.

7th year, Spring, 1st month, 3rd day. Wo-hatsuse Waka- sazaki no Mikoto was appointed Prince Imperial. A.D. 494. XV. 30.

8th year, Winter, 10th month. The people said :—"At this A.D. 495. time there is peace throughout the land; the officials fill their offices worthily. Everywhere within the seas there is a move- ment towards good feeling; the subjects pursue peacefully their avocations." This year the five grains were produced in abundance, the silkworm and wheat afforded a rich harvest.

---

[1] In the speech above quoted.
[2] Se and imo also mean respectively husband and wife.
[3] This note is from the "Shiki" or "Scholiast."
· Possibly the Japanese reading of the characters is preferable, viz. Suruki, Toruki.

Far and near there was purity and calm, and the population multiplied.

A.D. 498. 11th year, Autumn, 8th month, 8th day. The Emperor died in the Chief Bedchamber.

Winter, 10th month, 5th day. He was buried in the misa-sagi at the foot of the Hanifu acclivity.

BOOK XVI.

THE EMPEROR WOHATSUSE WAKA-SAZAKI.[1]

(*MURETSU*[2] *TENNŌ*.)

THE Emperor Wohatsuse waka-sazaki was the eldest son of the Emperor Ohoke. His mother was called the Empress Kasuga no Iratsume. He was made Prince Imperial in the seventh year of the Emperor Ohoke. When he grew to manhood, he was fond of criminal law, and was well versed in the statutes. He would remain in Court until the sun went down, so that hidden wrong was surely penetrated. In deciding cases he attained to the facts.[3] But he worked much evil, and accomplished no good thing. He never omitted to witness in person cruel punishments of all kinds, and the people of the whole land were all in terror of him.

In the 11th year, the 8th month of his reign, the Emperor Ohoke died. The Minister of State Heguri no Matori no Omi usurped the government of the country and tried to reign over Japan. Pretending that it was for the Emperor's eldest son, he built a palace, and ultimately dwelt in it himself. On all occasions he was arrogant, and was utterly devoid of loyal principle. Now the eldest son wished to betroth to himself Kagehime, the daughter of Mononobe no Arakahi no Ohomuraji, and sent a middleman to Kagehime's house to arrange for their union. But Kagehime had already formed an illicit connection with XVI. 2. Shibi, son of Matori, the Minister of State. Fearing, however, to offer opposition to the eldest son's proposal, she answered

---

[1] Wo, little ; hatsuse, name of place ; waka-sazaki, young-wren.

[2] Muretsu, martial ardour.

[3] This description from "When" down to "facts" is taken from the history of the Chinese Emperor Mingti of the Later Han Dynasty.

him, saying:—"Thy handmaiden wishes to wait upon thee on the street of Tsubaki-ichi." Accordingly the eldest son, in order to go to the place of assignation, sent one of his personal attendants to the house of the Oho-omi Heguri to ask for official horses, saying that he did so by his command. The Oho-omi mocked him, pretending that he would send them, and said:—"For whom (else) are official horses kept? Of course his orders shall be obeyed." But for a long time he did not send them. The eldest son cherished resentment at this, but controlled himself, and did not let it appear on his countenance. Ultimately he went to the place of assignation, and taking a place among the song-makers,[1] took hold of Kagehime's sleeve, and was loitering about unconcernedly, when suddenly Shibi no Omi came, and pushing away the eldest son from Kagehime, got between them. Hereupon the eldest son let go Kagehime's sleeve, and turning round, confronted Shibi no Omi, and addressing him straight in the face, made a song, saying:—

XVI. 3.
> Of the briny current,[2]
> The breakers as I view,
> By the fin of the Tunny
> That comes sporting
> I see my spouse standing.

[One book has "harbour" instead of "briny current."]
Shibi no Omi answered with a song, saying:—

> Dost thou tell me, O Prince! to yield to thee
> The eight-fold bamboo fence[3]
> Of the Omi's child?

---

[1] In Japanese uta-gaki, i.e. poetry-hedge. The utagaki seems to have been a sort of poetical tournament. The "Kojiki" (Ch. K., p. 330) gives a different and not very intelligible account of this war of verses. That work places it at the beginning of an earlier reign, and makes the Emperor Woke the hero. The whole story is no doubt the work of some romancist. It would be a mere waste of time to try to sift out what grains of truth it may contain. It indicates, however, very different and much more unrestricted social relations between the sexes than that which prevailed in China and other Eastern countries. Of this there is abundant other evidence.

[2] Shibi means tunny-fish. This suggests the introduction of the "briny current" of the first line.

[3] The fence in this and the following verses is the enclosure of the bridal chamber. See above, pp. 13, 54.

The eldest son made a song, saying :—

> My great sword
> Hung at my girdle I will stand ;
> Though I may not draw it,
> Yet in the last resort
> I am resolved to be united to her.

Shibi no Omi answered with a song, saying :—

> The great Lord's
> Eight-fold retiring-fence
> He may try to build,
> Still for want of strict care,[1]
> The retiring-fence is not built.

The eldest son made a song, saying :—

> The eight-fold fastening fence
> Of the Omi's child
> Should an earthquake come, shaking,
> Reverberating below,
> 'Twill be a ruined fastening fence.

[A various version of the first line is " eight-fold Kara fence."]

The eldest son gave Kagehime a song, saying :—

> If Kagehime, who comes and stays
> At the head of the lute,[2]
> Were a jewel,
> She would be a white sea-ear[3] pearl—
> The pearl that I love.

Shibi no Omi answered on behalf of Kagehime, and made a song, saying :—

> The great Lord's
> Girdle of Japanese loom

XVI. 4.

---

[1] " For want of strict care " is in the original Ama-shimi. This word contains an allusion to the Omi's name Shibi. Mi and bi are often interchanged in Japanese.

[2] i.e. on my right hand.

[3] The sea-ear is in Japanese ahabi, which may be intended to suggest ahazu, " not to become united to."

Hangs down in a bow.[1]
Whosoever it may be—
There is no one (but me) whose love she requites.

The eldest son then for the first time saw that Shibi had already possessed Kagehime, and became conscious of all the disrespect shown him by the father and the son. He blazed out into a great rage, and forthwith, on that same night, proceeded to the house of Ohotomo no Kanamura no Muraji, where he levied troops and concerted his plans. Ohotomo no Muraji waylaid Shibi no Omi with a force of several thousand men. He slew him at Mount Nara.

One book says:—"Shibi was spending the night in Kagehime's house, and that same night he was slain."

At this time Kagehime followed on to the place where he had been slain, and seeing that he had already been put to death, was shocked, so that she did not know what she was doing, and tears of sorrow filled her eyes. At length she made a song, saying:—

Passing Furu
In Iso no Kami,
Passing Takahashi
In Komo-makura,
Passing Oho-yake
Where things are in plenty
Passing Kasuga
Of the spring-day,
Passing Wosaho
The spouse-retiring,
In a precious casket,
Placing boiled rice,
In a precious vase,
Placing water also,
She lets fall tears as she goes.
Alas! for Kagehime.[2]

[1] The sole reason why the second and third lines are introduced is to bring in tare, "to hang down." The same word is repeated in the fourth line with the meaning "who," thus producing a word-play, of which Japanese poets are fond.

[2] This poem contains a succession of plays on words, some of which are very obscure, and all are lost in an English version. Komo-makura means a matting pillow, i.e. a roll of matting used as a pillow. Makura is frequently followed by takaku, high, in the phrase makura takaku suru, "to make high

Hereupon Kagehime, when the funeral was over, and she was about to return home, said, with an utterance choked by grief:—"Alas! to-day I have lost my beloved husband." So she burst into tears of sorrow, and in a state of distraction made a song, saying :—

> Like a deer
> That, drenched with water, hides
> In the valley of Nara,—
> (Of fertile soil)—
> Is the young lord of Shibi—
> (The water-besprinkled[1]) :—
> Make him not thy prey. Oh! thou wild boar!

Winter, 11th month, 11th day. Ohotomo no Kanamura no Muraji spake to the eldest son, saying:—"The rebel Matori ought to be slain. I pray thee let me attack him." The eldest son said:—"We are about to have civil war in the Empire, and without a rare warrior, we shall be unable to accomplish anything. When I consider this well, I find that thou art the man."[2] So he laid his plans in concert with him. XVI. 6.

Hereupon Ohotomo no Ohomuraji,[3] in personal command of the troops, led them to besiege the house of the Oho-omi, and setting fire to it, burnt it. His style of command was like the scattering of clouds.

Matori no Oho-omi, resenting the failure of his enterprise, and feeling that his life was doomed, that his designs had reached a limit, and that his hopes had vanished, cursed the salt (sea) far and wide, and at length was put to death along with his people. When he uttered the curse, the only place which he forgot was the sea-brine of Tsunoga, and this he did

one's pillow." This is probably why makura is here associated with Taka-hashi. Oho-yake means great storehouse. Hence the epithet attached to it. "Of the spring-day" is a regular makura-kotoba or pillow-word of Kasuga, because kasuga is like kasumeru, to be hazy, and the weather is hazy in spring. Wosaho contains wo, male, which accounts for the epithet "spouse-retiring" in the next line. The commentators have much more to say about these verses. The metre is irregular.

[1] This line has reference to the meaning of Shibi, viz. tunny-fish.
[2] This speech is adapted from a Chinese author.
[3] He was not Ohomuraji till afterwards. See below.

not curse. Therefore the Emperor eats salt from Tsunoga, and avoids eating the salt of other seas."[1]

12th month. Ohotomo no Kanamura no Muraji having completely suppressed the insurrection, and restored the Government to the eldest son, asked permission to offer him the August Title, saying:—" Now there are no sons left of the Emperor Ohoke but Your Majesty, nor is there any second person to whom the people can give allegiance. Moreover, relying on the support of Supreme Heaven,[2] thou hast cleared away the wicked bands. By thy wise counsels and thy manly determination thou hast made the Celestial authority and the Celestial revenues to flourish. Japan must have a ruler, and who is there but thee to rule over Japan? I humbly pray

XVI. 7. Your Majesty reverently to respond to the Divine Spirit of Earth by giving development to the luminous commands, casting a lustre on Japan, and widely taking over charge of the silver region."[3]

Hereupon the eldest son commanded the functionaries to prepare a sacred terrace at Namiki[4] in Hatsuse, where he ascended to the Imperial Dignity, and at length established his capital. On this day, Ohotomo no Kanamura no Muraji was made Ohomuraji.

A.D. 499. 1st year, Spring, 3rd month, 2nd day. Kasuga no Iratsume was appointed Empress. [It is not clear who her father was.]

This year was the year Tsuchinoto U (16th) of the Cycle.

A.D. 500. 2nd year, Autumn, 9th month. The Emperor ripped up the belly of a pregnant woman and inspected the pregnant womb.[5]

A.D. 501. 3rd year, Winter, 10th month. He plucked out men's nails. and made them dig up yams.[6]

11th month. He commanded Ohotomo no Muruya[7] no

---

[1] Compare above, p. 337, where the water of a well was cursed.

[2] Motoöri objects to this phrase as Chinese.   Viz. Corea.

[4] Namiki means a row of trees, an avenue lined with trees.

[5] This is a charge made against Show, King of Shang, in the "Shoo-king." See Legge's "Chinese Classics," Vol. III. p. 285.

[6] Dioscorea Japonica.

[7] There is something wrong here. Ohotomo no Muruya was Prime Minister (see p. 322) in the 7th year of Ingiō Tennō (A.D. 418). Muruya is no doubt a slip for Kanamura.

Ohomuraji to make a levy of labourers of the province of Shinano, in order to build a castle in the village of Minomata. It was called Kinouhe.

In this month, Wi-ta-nang [1] of Pèkché died and was buried on the top of the hill of Takada.

4th year, Summer, 4th month. He pulled out the hair of A.D. 502. men's heads, made them climb to the tops of trees, and then XVI. 8. cut down the trees, so that the men who had climbed were killed by the fall. This he took a delight in.

In this year, King Malta [2] of Pékchè, for his lawless oppression of his subjects, was at length deposed by the people of that country and King Shima raised to the throne. He was made King Munyöng.

The Pèkché " Shinsen " says :—" King Malta lawlessly oppressed the subjects, and the people united to remove him. Munyöng was set up. His sobriquet was King Shima. He was the son of Prince Konchi, and therefore the elder brother of King Malta by a different mother. When Konchi went to Wa, he arrived at an island in Tsukushi where King Shima was born to him. He was sent back from the island, and did not reach the capital (of Japan). Owing to his having been born on an island, he received the name of Shima. There is now in the sea of Kawara [3] an island called Nirim Shima [4] which is the King's birthplace. Therefore the Pèkché people call this island Nirim Shima. Considering that King Shima was King Kèro's son, and King Malta King Konchi's son, the expression ' elder brother by a different mother ' is not clear." [5]

---

[1] This is the Corean pronunciation of the characters given, but very likely these are not the proper characters for his name, and are only a phonetic Japanese rendering of the sound. The traditional Kana rendering is Otara.

[2] Or Mata if the Japanese pronunciation is taken. His real name was Mutè.

[3] The traditional Kana pronunciation.

[4] The traditional Kana has sema, for the Corean syöm, island. Nirim means Lord.

[5] The " Tongkam " (Vol. V. 4) account of these events is as follows :— " Autumn, 8th month (A.D. 501). Pèkché built the Castle of Karim (in Chöllado), which was occupied by a garrison under a military officer named Chak Ka.

Winter, 11th month. Chak Ka of Pèkché slew his Lord Mutè. Before

A.D. 503. 5th year, Summer, 6th month. The Emperor made men lie down on their faces in the sluice of a dam and caused them to be washed away : with a three-bladed lance he stabbed them. In this he took delight.

A.D. 504. 6th year, Autumn, 9th month, 1st day. The Emperor made a decree, saying :—"As a measure for transmitting a kingdom, a son is raised up to honour.[1] But we have no successor :
XVI. 9. wherewithal shall we hand down our name to posterity? In accordance, therefore, with old Imperial precedents, we establish the Wohatsuse Toneri and make them assume the designation of this reign, so that it may not be forgotten for ten thousand years."

Winter, 10th month. The Land of Pèkché sent Lord Mana with tribute. The Emperor, considering that for many years Pèkché had not sent tribute, detained him, and would not let him go.

A.D. 505. 7th year, Spring, 2nd month. He made men climb up trees and then shot them down with a bow, upon which he laughed.

Summer, 4th month. The King of Pèkché sent Lord Shika with tribute, and a separate memorial, saying :—" Mana, the previous tribute-messenger, was no relation of the Sovereigns of Pèkché. Therefore I humbly send Shika to wait upon the Court." He eventually had a son named Lord Pöp-să. He was the ancestor of the Kimi of Yamato.

A.D. 506. 8th year, Spring, 3rd month. Nudas feminas super latas

this when the King appointed Chak Ka commandant of the garrison of Karim, he did not wish to go, and declined on the score of ill-health. The King would not listen to his excuse, and he therefore hated the King. Upon this the King went a-hunting on the plain east of Săchhă. Again he hunted in the plain north of Ung-chhön. Again he hunted in the plain west of Săchhă. Being prevented from returning by a great fall of snow, he stayed for the night at the village of Mapho, where Chak Ka sent a man to assassinate him. A month later he was buried and received the name of Tong-syöng. His son Shima, otherwise called Yöryung, came to the throne.

Spring, 1st month (A.D. 502). Chak Ka of Pèkché was executed. He had taken position in the castle of Karim and rebelled. The King proceeded with an army to the city of Utu and ordered an attack upon him. Chak Ka came out and surrendered. He was put to death and his body flung into the River Pèk-Kang."

[1] Is made Prince Imperial.

tabulas imposuit et, equis adhibitis, fecit ut coirent cum eis. Tum, examinatione habitâ, quarum pudenda madida erant, eas interfecit, quarum autem madida non erant, eas fecit servas publicas. These things he took a pleasure in.

At this time he dug a pond and made a park which he filled XVI. 10. with birds and beasts. Here he was fond of hunting, and of racing dogs and trying horses. He went out and in at all times, taking no care to avoid storms and torrents of rain. Being warmly clad himself, he forgot that the people were starving from cold; eating dainty food, he forgot that the Empire was famishing. He gave great encouragement to dwarfs and performers, making them execute riotous music. He prepared strange diversions, and gave licence to lewd voices. Night and day he constantly indulged to excess in sake in the company of the women of the Palace. His cushions were of brocade, and many of his garments were of damask and fine white silk.

Winter, 12th month, 8th day. The Emperor died in the Palace of Namiki.

COSIMO is a specialty publisher of books and publications that inspire, inform, and engage readers. Our mission is to offer unique books to niche audiences around the world.

COSIMO BOOKS publishes books and publications for innovative authors, nonprofit organizations, and businesses. COSIMO BOOKS specializes in bringing books back into print, publishing new books quickly and effectively, and making these publications available to readers around the world.

COSIMO CLASSICS offers a collection of distinctive titles by the great authors and thinkers throughout the ages. At COSIMO CLASSICS timeless works find new life as affordable books, covering a variety of subjects including: Business, Economics, History, Personal Development, Philosophy, Religion & Spirituality, and much more!

COSIMO REPORTS publishes public reports that affect your world, from global trends to the economy, and from health to geopolitics.

FOR MORE INFORMATION CONTACT US AT
INFO@COSIMOBOOKS.COM

✳ if you are a book lover interested in our current catalog of books

✳ if you represent a bookstore, book club, or anyone else interested in special discounts for bulk purchases

✳ if you are an author who wants to get published

✳ if you represent an organization or business seeking to publish books and other publications for your members, donors, or customers.

COSIMO BOOKS ARE ALWAYS
AVAILABLE AT ONLINE BOOKSTORES

VISIT COSIMOBOOKS.COM
BE INSPIRED, BE INFORMED

Lightning Source UK Ltd.
Milton Keynes UK
18 June 2010

155802UK00001B/37/P